NEWS NOW

Visual Storytelling in the Digital Age

NEWS NOW

Visual Storytelling in the Digital Age

THE CRONKITE TEAM

Susan C. Green
Arizona State University

Mark J. Lodato
Arizona State University

Carol B. Schwalbe
University of Arizona

B. William Silcock, Ph. D.
Arizona State University

LONDON AND NEW YORK

First published 2012 by Pearson Education, Inc.

Published 2016 by Routledge
2 Park Square, Milton Park, Abingdon, Oxon OX14 4RN
711 Third Avenue, New York, NY 10017, USA

Routledge is an imprint of the Taylor & Francis Group, an informa business

Credits and acknowledgments borrowed from other sources and reproduced, with permission, in this textbook appear on the appropriate page within text or on pages 289–290.

ISBN: 9780205695911 (pbk)

Cover Designer: Nancy Sacks

Library of Congress Cataloging-in-Publication Data

News now : visual storytelling in the digital age/Susan C. Green . . . [et al.].
p. cm.
ISBN-13: 978-0-205-69591-1
ISBN-10: 0-205-69591-4
1. Broadcast journalism. 2. Online journalism. I. Green, Susan C.
PN4784.B75N495 2011
070.1'9—dc23

2011028757

Please visit the companion website at www.routledge.com/9780205695911

Dedication

For Walter and his students

Susan C. Green

The only way I was able to complete this project was through the love of my partner, Robin Phillips. She read all my work, held my hand through every painful edit and encouraged me to keep going even when this "quick" project turned into a three-year journey! I also want to thank my parents. My mother, Iris Green, taught me the value of working hard, and my father, Ray Green, introduced me to Walter Cronkite each night. They both taught me that knowledge is everything. Thank you both!

Mark J. Lodato

Long nights, lost weekends and a "summer project" that lasted three years. There's no doubt that this effort is dedicated to my wife, Valery, and children Tyler and Sydney, who, despite it all, recognized the importance of this project and never waivered in their love and support. Finally, thanks to my parents for providing me with a lifetime of encouragement, a strong moral compass and respect for the power of education.

Carol B. Schwalbe

My husband, Cecil, kept me going during long days hunched over the keyboard. He lifted my spirits with silly jokes and my energy level with Hershey Kisses. Our cats, Cocoa and Blue, kept me company for hours on end, curled up alongside my computer. To my parents I will be forever indebted for instilling the value of hard work, the love of language and the expectation of doing your best. For our family, an exemplar of those values was Walter Cronkite, whom we welcomed into our living room every evening.

B. William Silcock

My 91-year-old mother, Ruth Nordstrom Silcock, inspires me to be a wordsmith. My father, Burton William Silcock, taught me curiosity and conversation. They planted the roots of my journalism. Its branches include three sisters who love to share books–Gloria, Merilee and Penny–and three social media savvy children-Nick, Jane and John. Wise pruning by friends Dale, Ken and Jason, and most important the daily nourishment and inspiration of my bride, Angela (forever my executive producer), means our book will bear fruit for students and professionals for years to come.

Contents in Brief

Contents

PART ONE
CONTENT

PART TWO
REPORTING

PART THREE
PRODUCTION

PART FOUR
VALUES

Foreword

Walk through the newsrooms and classrooms of the Cronkite School as I have, and it's unlikely that you'll find students worried about the future of the news industry. Instead, you'll discover young women and men excited about the opportunities ahead. And that's reassuring, because in this changing world the need for quality journalism has never been more critical, and that means we need quality journalists.

This book builds on the bedrock of journalism principles practiced by Walter Cronkite and carved into the reporting platforms of each student who graduates from "his" school. Organized into four main themes—content, reporting, production and values—this book is ideal for college broadcast reporting and producing courses or as a valuable newsroom resource for traditional journalists transitioning into the digital era of social media journalism.

The book's 14 chapters engage readers in a visual way that won't be confused with the outdated broadcast textbooks of previous generations. Whether it's how to use social media as a reporting tool, turn a television news package into a sharp online piece or produce a great newscast, News Now provides the answer in a format that's engaging, even to a generation of students with shorter attention spans. You might just find yourself choosing to keep this book instead of selling it back at the end of the semester.

I have been both impressed and heartened to see the combination of new technology and editorial excellence in the work of Cronkite students. Recent graduates are working in our newsrooms and at other traditional outlets, such as CNN, USA Today and Business Week. Others are Fulbright Scholars studying overseas. Some have taken a more entrepreneurial route and started their own websites. Now the Cronkite Team has taken the forward-thinking approach that produced these success stories and put it on paper. Turn the pages, and discover your own path.

Steve Capus, president, NBC News

Preface

News Now: Visual Storytelling in the Digital Age sets a new precedent for broadcast news textbooks with a visually stimulating style that encourages students to immerse themselves in the basic principles of broadcast journalism:

> "Less important is the medium by which a story is disseminated. More important is getting the story right and considering how it can be used across multiple platforms, including television, radio and online."

With this textbook, journalism students are expertly guided down the various avenues of broadcasting as they uncover what it means to *get the story right.*

Too often, broadcast news textbooks focus narrowly on television, radio or online theory and practice. Reaching beyond broadcast news fundamentals, this textbook is designed to get students thinking about and participating in the world of new media as well as the social environment. Today's young journalists are expected to produce across all platforms with an awareness of the broader social and media contexts.

Preparing students for a mobile, interactive and highly competitive workplace

This book provides students with the *why* and the *how* for success in a career in journalism. Students learn not only *why* they need to be prepared for all aspects of media reporting but also *how* to be prepared. With reporting and writing techniques at its core, this book equips students to think through every element of the story: What audio best tells each part of the story? Which picture or video captures the moment? Which images or words might stereotype or offend? Which choices might cross ethical or legal boundaries? By using this modern, comprehensive approach to visual newsgathering, students will develop the essential skills needed to answer these questions without hesitation on the job. They will also develop an understanding of the importance of working across multiple platforms in an inclusive, legal and ethical fashion. This awareness and cross training can produce the most versatile young journalists of today's generation.

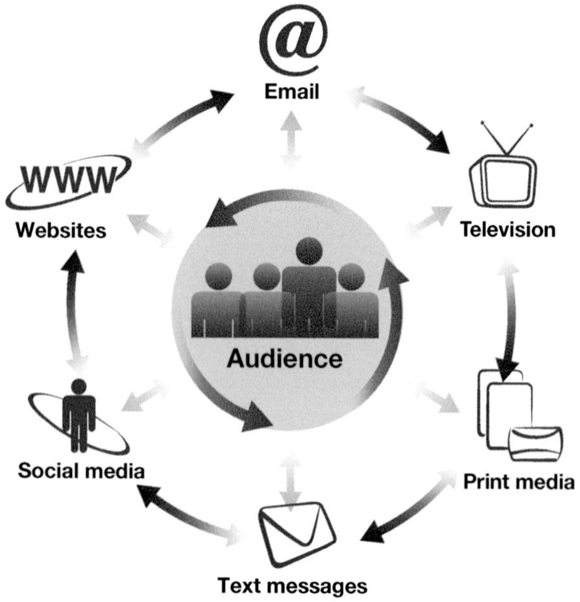

FIGURE **1.6** **The Flow of Information**

Today's audiences receive information from many different sources simultaneously. They also use tools and networks to share large amounts of information.

Practical and engaging features offer a hands-on experience and enhance student learning

Visual storytelling

News Now exposes the next generation of journalists to all facets of visual storytelling. This textbook provides students with the visual toolset every aspiring journalist needs in order to be competitive in the work force, including the ability to identify strong visual elements, the skills to write for broadcast and online media outlets, and the know-how to conceptualize creative new approaches to storytelling through social media.

HOW INVESTIGATIONS BEGIN

An investigative story may be based on a tip, an event or a document. But getting from tip to solid story can be a long process. First, you must translate that good tip into a theory that will serve as the basis of your investigation.

TIP		THEORY
A new style of highway median barrier fails, causing a deadly accident.		New median barriers do not work properly and put lives at risk.
An anonymous caller claims local police are sleeping on the job on the graveyard shift.		Police are sleeping on the job when they should be patrolling the streets.
A local union claims an airline is failing to approve overtime for maintenance workers.		Lack of timely maintenance is causing delays or other problems for travelers or, at worst, safety problems.

The textbook demonstrates these principles with **a dynamic, colorful design.** Reflecting the highly visual approach of today's broadcast media, the design of *News Now* helps students quickly find the information they need—and presents that information with the clarity and visual flair of today's best multimedia journalism. When providing examples or instructions and explaining techniques, this book gives students a **visual walk-through** to help them learn, visualize and arrange every element of the process or story. A substantial art program, numerous video stills and examples of stellar photojournalism demonstrate the importance of imagery to the telling of a coherent and captivating story.

Side by Side explorations provide students with diverse opportunities to review complementary and opposing elements (images, text, opinions) to develop a deeper understanding of the material and encourage critical thinking about how elements can be used—or misused—in the service of journalism. By understanding what does and does not work and why, students develop the ability to make informed decisions.

SIDE BY SIDE

Let's say the police are called out to do a sweep in a neighborhood. One reporter might put together a story that shows a lot of police cars and police arresting people. The story might also show drugs or guns. The message: This is a dangerous place, so police are shutting it down.

But another reporter might produce a story showing how the neighborhood block watch worked together to make this a safe place for families to live and play. Told from a mother's point of view, the sweep is a good thing. Finally, her neighborhood is becoming safe enough for her kids to play outside.

Broadcasting Basics

The book includes **Checklists, Time Savers, Rules of Thumb,** and **Pitfalls** features offering quick, practical tips for applying a larger concept or strategy. A timeline placed at the back of the book overviews the history of broadcast and online journalism.

A REPORTER'S TRAVEL BAG

Must-Haves

- Media credentials
- Business cards
- Smart phone
- Pens
- Pencil (works better than pen in bad weather)
- Paper (white—for camera white balance)
- IFB (earpiece)
- Passport
- USB drive
- Energy bars
- Spare change

For the Extra Pockets

- Small flashlight
- Binoculars
- Gaffers tape
- Swiss army knife or similar multipurpose tool
- Hand sanitizer
- Batteries
- Audio recorder
- Sewing kit and safety pins

Checklists distill key sections into easy-to-remember lists.

RULE OF THUMB

You are more likely to run into copyright problems if you copy the most memorable part of the work.

Rules of Thumb offer practical, field-tested advice.

PITFALLS

Five Common Mistakes

There are five key mistakes most people make when they shoot video.

1. Not using headphones
2. Missing sequences
3. Lack of organization
4. Forgetting to tell the story
5. Failing to be a caring human being

Using real-life stories to caution young journalists about common problem situations, **Pitfalls** offer additional context and support for making difficult decisions in the newsroom and on the beat.

TIMESAVER

Here are some helpful tips to keep you organized:

- Create story file folders for each working idea.
- Track when and how you contacted sources.
- Keep copies of emails and other correspondence.
- Take notes during phone conversations.
- Finish your workday by reviewing accomplishments and next-day tasks.

Time Savers provide shortcut strategies aimed at saving students valuable time.

The end of the book features **A Brief History of Broadcast and Online Journalism,** a timeline that situates key developments in the history of broadcast journalism within a larger social, cultural and political context. Understanding the history and story behind the evolution of broadcasting allows students to see how new technologies and ideas have shaped and will continue to influence the way they produce the news.

1900–1919

RADIO	**1901** Using a kite as an antenna, Italian inventor Guglielmo Marconi transmits the first radio signal across the Atlantic Ocean.	**1906** American Lee De Forest invents the vacuum tube that amplifies radio signals. **1906** Canadian Reginald Fessenden makes the first public broadcast of voice and music.	**1912** Russian-born radio operator David Sarnoff relays breaking news of the "Titanic" sinking.	**1920** KDKA, the first commercial radio station, goes on air in Pittsburgh to broadcast the election of President Warren Harding.
DIGITAL	**1900** Eastman Kodak introduces the Brownie camera. It's cheap and easy to use.	**1905** German inventor Alfred Korn sends the first photos by telegraph.	**1910** Thomas Alva Edison demos the first talking pictures.	**1914** Germany's Leica launches the first 35 mm camera.
LEGAL / BUSINESS		**1912** Radio Act requires that broadcasters need a license and that the U.S. government regulates the airwaves.		
WORLD NEWS	**1901** President William McKinley is assassinated. Theodore Roosevelt takes his place.	**1909** Adm. William Peary reaches the North Pole.	**1914** World War I erupts in Eastern Europe.	**1917** Lenin's Communist government crushes opponents during the Russian Revolution.
POP CULTURE	**1901** Actress Marlene Dietrich is born in Germany. **1903** Boston Americans beat Pittsburgh Pirates in first World Series. **1903** Orville and Wilbur Wright's airplane makes the first powered flight.	**1905** Columbia Phonograph Company makes the first two-sided disc. **1907** "Mutt and Jeff" is the first daily comic strip.	**1915** Albert Einstein postulates the general theory of relativity.	**1918** World flu epidemic kills 22 million people. **1919** Members of the Chicago White Sox throw the World Series to the Cincinnati Reds in the "Black Sox" Scandal.

Real-world applications

In addition to the basics of who, what, where, when, why and how, this book also teaches the core skills of reporting, interviewing, capturing media, writing and producing with real-world examples written by industry professionals. In addition to many special contributions from practitioners with specific areas of expertise, there are a variety of features that give students the opportunity to explore core skills through a range of lenses, including diversity, ethics, legal issues and different audiences in order to develop a practical, multidimensional understanding of broadcast journalism.

In **Voices From the Newsroom,** professional profiles showcase the experiences, stories and advice of an extraordinary array of journalists from various media in newsrooms around the country and around the world. These successful journalists provide students with a detailed look at the many opportunities available to them and the potential for their future career paths. They also provide expertise

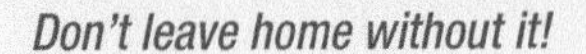

VOICES from the Newsroom

Don't leave home without it!

What are the little things experienced reporters never leave home without?

Nichole Szemerei, reporter,
WCIA-TV (ABC), Champaign, Ill.

Earmuffs and gloves! The weather can always change drastically. There's nothing worse than trying to do your job when you're frozen solid. Be prepared for the unknown. And spare change. A toll road can be the quickest way to a breaking story.

Zahed Arab, reporter
KLAS-TV (CBS), Las Vegas

Snacks. You never know where you'll be sent and how long you'll be away if breaking news happens.

Linda So, reporter
WMAR-TV (ABC), Baltimore

Sewing kit and safety pin. I have had one too many wardrobe malfunctions, and these really come in handy when you've lost a button that must be in place.

Manny Fantis, executive producer of Digital Content
WUSA-TV (CBS), Washington, D.C.

I'm going old school . . . a Swiss army knife (or a Leatherman) and gaffers tape. When you're by yourself, you are also your own engineer, especially if you're in a bureau. You need to be prepared to repair.

Diana Alvear, correspondent
ABC News One, Chicago

IFB (earpiece). One with a small end and one with a larger end. I never know when I'll have to go live. You'd be surprised at how many sat trucks/photogs do not have a spare one. And Shout Wipes for the inevitable stain on my clothes.

and insight into a variety of newsroom situations, providing students with a firsthand perspective of what it's like to work in a newsroom, including the daily challenges.

What Would You Do? features present students with practical or ethical situations they might encounter while working a story and ask them to think through how they would respond based on what they have learned in each chapter. For example, in Chapter 13, Diversity, students are asked to determine whether or not to include pictures of three African-American teens who are suspects in a vandalism case. These *real* scenarios allow students to develop ethical awareness and prepare for similar situations they might encounter during their careers.

Let's say you are covering a story about a synagogue that has been attacked by vandals. There is spray paint graffiti on the walls, and windows have been broken. The three people arrested in the case are juveniles. The police say they are connected to a series of attacks on several businesses in the area. The three teens also are African-American. Do you use the pictures of the teens charged in the case? If you don't use the pictures, do you say the teens are African-American?

Career guidance that matters

News Now also offers students **career guidance that matters.** Chapter 14, Producing Your Career, provides expert strategies and advice from authors who have launched the careers of hundreds of successful professional broadcast journalists. A checklist presents students with step-by-step guidelines they need to follow in order to secure a successful internship in the field.

❶ **Joe Smith** 555-881-1391
JoeSmith@gmail.com

❷ **Media Experience**

- KAET-TV (PBS) **NewsWatch**—Multimedia Journalist, Anchor — Jan. 2010-Present
  - Reporter and anchor in an award-winning newsroom that produces multiple live newscasts each week that are broadcast to more than 1.2 million people throughout Arizona.
- Mesa Channel 11—Multimedia Journalist — June 2009-Present
  - Film, edit and produce news packages and public service announcements for government television station. Run a Chyron graphic generator during live broadcasts of city council meetings and other civic events.
- Cronkite Village Television—Entertainment Show Anchor — Sept. 2007-March 2008
- The Blaze Radio Station—News Reporter — Sept. 2007-Dec. 2007

Internships

- KNXV-TV ABC 15, News Department — Aug. 2008-Dec. 2008
  - Worked with crews to interview people, including Arizona Attorney General Terry Goddard, assisted on live shots, pitched and set up stories and wrote for ABC15.com and the 10 o'clock newscast.
- KNOW99 Television — Jan. 2009-May 2009
  - **Worked as a fi**eld reporter, shooting, editing, producing and writing 18 packages for air and posting them online for Phoenix's education channel.
- KNXV-TV ABC 15, Sonoran Living — Jan. 2008-May 2008
  - Helped organize and book guests, set up props, wrote scripts, logged tapes and assisted on live shots.

❸ **Skills**

- **Profi**cient in Final Cut Pro, Avid, ENPS, Photoshop, WordPress, Dreamweaver, Sony XDCAM
- Fluent in Spanish

❹ **Education**

Bachelor of Arts, Broadcast Journalism — Class of 2011
Walter Cronkite School of Journalism and Mass Communication
Arizona State University

❺ **Awards**

- Roy W. Howard National Collegiate Reporting Competition — March 2010
  - One of nine winners nationwide selected to take a journalism study trip to Japan

❻ **References**

Sue Brown	Steve Miller	Joe Grange
Executive Producer	News Director	Managing Editor
ABC News	KNXV-TV	NewsWatch
212-456-0000	602-502-4444	480-491-1111
SueBrown@gmail.com	Stevemiller@yahoo.com	joegrange@newswatch.com

POSSIBLE INTERVIEW QUESTIONS

- Tell me about your greatest success so far.
- Tell me about your worst failure. What was the lesson you learned?
- If I talked with the people you worked with, what would they tell me about you that I probably wouldn't know from this interview?
- What are your strengths/weaknesses? (Answering this isn't as easy as you think.)
- How will you continue growing?
- Tell me about somebody who has been a role model or inspiration. Whom have you learned the most from? Who has been your best critic?

Acknowledgments

We begin with Walter Cronkite. His way with words went beyond the bass tones that anchored the CBS newscast each night. His words soothed a nation in 1963 and bounced in jubilation six years later when Neil Armstrong walked on the moon. Tear-filled words. Celebratory words. Words that challenged and criticized from a position of credibility. It is his legacy, the Cronkite legacy, that we acknowledge first and foremost in this book and that we share with tomorrow's storytelling journalists around the world.

We came together as an author team in Walter's school—the Walter Cronkite School of Journalism and Mass Communication at Arizona State University. Walter loved his school. Every fall until his health failed, he came for a visit. He spoke to students, ate lunch with the faculty and honored the finest journalists in America.

Walter taught us about the way it is, the way it was and even the way it will always be. "Old anchorman never fade away," he said, closing out his last regular broadcast. "They just keep coming back for more. I will be away on assignment for the next few years."

We would be remiss not to acknowledge our fellow faculty members, staff and leadership team, especially Dean Christopher Callahan.

We also thank the many professionals who contributed to the richness and accuracy of the text:

Nancie Dodge, faculty associate, Walter Cronkite School of Journalism and Mass Communication
Al Feinberg, NASA Public Affairs
Rick Gevers, agent, Rick Gevers and Associates
Erik Hellum, senior vice president, Townsquare Media
Tanin Hussain, research manager, KPNX-TV (NBC), Phoenix
Jim Jacoby, lecturer, Walter Cronkite School of Journalism and Mass Communication
Dr. Fran Matera, associate professor, Walter Cronkite School of Journalism and Mass Communication
John Meisner, chief operating officer, Republic Media and president/general manager, KPNX-TV (NBC), Phoenix
Eve Pruden, performance coach, Eve Pruden and Associates
Mike Walter, president, Walter Media

A *very* special thanks goes to our co-author, Carol Schwalbe, whose expert eye ensured sharper, clearer prose that merged many voices into one interconnected whole.

Behind every book is an amazing publishing team. We thank Melissa Mashburn, our acquisitions editor and Karon Bowers, editor in chief, who championed the vision for this book. Susan Messer and Meg Botteon guided us through early drafts of the manuscript, and we offer a very special thanks to Angela Mallowes, who shepherded us through the final stages to publication on the editorial side, as well as to Barbara Mack, who worked on the production side to keep things moving and on schedule.

The authors would also like to thank the following outside reviewers for helping to shape this content:

Aje-Ori Agbese, University of Texas, Pan American
Frank Barnas, Valdosta State University
Jack Breslin, Iona College
Scott Shibuya Brown, California State University, Northridge
Rich Cameron, Cerritos College
Kymberly Fox, Texas State University
Susan Hague, Delgado Community College
Ginni Jurkowski, State University of New York, Geneseo
Jacqueline Layng, University of Toledo
Bernard "Barney" McCoy, University of Nebraska-Lincoln
Marilee Morrow, Marietta University
Merrill Morris, Gainesville State College
Ray Niekamp, Texas Stat University, San Marcos
Darren Osburn, St. Charles Community College
Charles Riley, City University of New York
Joe Sampson, Miami University
Jody Santos, Assumption College
Sam Swan, University of Tennessee
Tracy Montgomery Schoenberg, editor, New Milford Patch
David Swartzlander, Doane College
Keith Sweze, University of Central Oklahoma

Authors/Contributors

The authors of *News Now* have decades of journalism and teaching experience. Three are full-time faculty members at the Cronkite School of Journalism and Mass Communication at Arizona State University. In 2010 the Cronkite School finished first in the country in the prestigious Hearst Journalism Awards and the Society of Professional Journalists Mark of Excellence Awards.

DR. B. WILLIAM SILCOCK is an associate professor of broadcast journalism at the Cronkite School and twice was selected as a Fulbright Scholar. As director of Cronkite Global Initiatives and curator of the Hubert Humphrey Fellows at Arizona State University, he lectures and trains journalists around the world. He has pioneered research on global television news culture. His work is published in *Journalism Quarterly*, the field's most prestigious research journal, and in *Journalism Studies,* the *Journal of Mass Media Ethics* and the *Journal of Broadcasting & Electronic Media*.

Silcock is also an active television news documentary producer. His work *Backstage at a Presidential Debate: The Press, the Pundits and the* People won a 2004 juried faculty Award of Excellence from the Broadcast Education Association and a Gold Award of Excellence from the Houston International Film Festival.

His first textbook, *Managing Television News: A Handbook for Ethical and Effective Television News Producing*, was published in spring 2005. A former television anchor, producer and news director, Silcock worked for eight years as the managing editor of news at KOMU-TV (NBC) in Columbia, Missouri, while a faculty member at the University of Missouri School of Journalism.

CAROL B. SCHWALBE is an associate professor and the Soldwedel Family Professor of Journalism at the University of Arizona, where she teaches editing, photojournalism and science journalism. During the eight years she taught at the Cronkite School, her students produced the award-winning Cronkite Zine **http://cronkitezine.asu.edu,** which showcases the work of Cronkite students. Her own websites have won Best of Competition and an Award of Excellence from the Broadcast Education Association, as well as several Best of the Web design competitions from the Association for Education in Journalism and Mass Communication.

Her scholarly research interests include the role of images in shaping ideas and public opinion during the early years of the Cold War, ethical concerns about publishing violent images, and the visual framing of the Iraq War on the Internet. She has written chapters for several textbooks on multimedia journalism, diversity and best practices for online companion sites for the classroom.

Schwalbe came to the Cronkite School in 2002 from *National Geographic* magazine in Washington, D.C., where she was a senior articles editor. She was also a senior articles editor for *National Geographic Traveler*, a member of the launch team for nationalgeographic.com and the senior online producer for the travel section of the National Geographic website.

MARK J. LODATO is the assistant dean and news director at the Cronkite School. As assistant dean, he supervises the television and radio curriculum, including students participating in *Cronkite NewsWatch*. The winner of many national awards, *Cronkite NewsWatch* is broadcast live four times a week across Arizona via PBS. Advanced undergraduate and graduate students cover top stories in the Phoenix area and across the state. While expanding *NewsWatch* in English and Spanish, Lodato launched partnerships with NBC, Univision, MSNBC and Fox Sports Arizona.

Before joining the Cronkite School, he worked for 16 years as a television reporter and anchor in top markets, including Washington, D.C., San Francisco and Phoenix. During his on-air career, Lodato received numerous Emmy and Associated Press awards for his live, investigative and feature reporting. He also served as news director at the University of Maryland's Philip Merrill College of Journalism.

SUSAN C. GREEN is the broadcast director of the Cronkite News Service at the Cronkite School. She came to Arizona State University in August 2006 from KNXV-TV, where she served as managing editor at the ABC affiliate. In her 21 years as a broadcast professional, Green held positions at stations in Phoenix, Washington, D.C., Los Angeles and New York City.

In her first year at ASU, Green helped launch the Cronkite News Service to provide student-produced news stories to television stations across Arizona. Her students' work has been broadcast in Phoenix, Tucson and Yuma. Green has prepared students for live talkbacks on MSNBC. She is also the faculty adviser for ABC News on Campus, one of only six bureaus in the country where students provide content for on-air as well as online.

Green also serves as assistant news director of *Cronkite NewsWatch*, the Cronkite School's award-winning, student-produced newscast. In that role, Green helped the program expand from once a week to four times a week.

Green began her career at an NBC affiliate in Phoenix, moving up from associate producer to executive producer. She has also held executive producer positions at television stations in Washington, D.C., and New York City, and she has worked as a writer and producer at KTTV in Los Angeles. She wrote and produced the Telly Award-nominated A&E documentary *The Man Who Would Be Chief* and received a Peabody Award for WABC's coverage of September 11, 2001.

ADDITIONAL CONTRIBUTORS The authors called upon other award-winning Cronkite School full-time and part-time faculty to contribute chapters or elements where they have expertise, including law, video journalism and social media.

Melanie Asp Alvarez, faculty associate and executive producer, Cronkite NewsWatch
Daniel C. Barr, faculty associate and attorney, Perkins Coie
Steve Doig, professor and Knight Chair in Journalism
Dan Gillmor, director, Knight Center for Digital Media Entrepreneurship, and Kauffman Professor of Digital Media Entrepreneurship
Jim Manley, faculty associate and president, Manley Media Productions
Jason Manning, director of Student Media, Arizona State University
Leslie-Jean Thornton, assistant professor
Gilbert Zermeño, faculty associate and investigative producer and video journalist, KPHO-TV (CBS), Phoenix

News NOW

CHAPTER OUTLINE

CHAPTER 1

"Our job is only to hold up the mirror—to tell and show the public what has happened."

—*WALTER CRONKITE*

Contributed by Jason Manning,
Director of Student Media,
Arizona State University

News Judgment

The definition of news has been debated for centuries, but most professional journalists agree on a few common elements. News is information that is important, timely, interesting and relevant to a particular audience.

News judgment—*deciding* what is **important, timely, interesting** and **relevant**—is a big part of a professional journalist's job. Reporters, editors and producers use news judgment every day to decide what to cover:

- **IMPORTANT:** Will this information have significance in the lives of my audience?
- **TIMELY:** Is this information new and recent enough to have an impact on my audience?
- **INTERESTING:** Will this information interest my audience? Is it compelling or surprising?
- **RELEVANT:** Does this information apply to a significant portion of my audience?

FIGURE **1.1** **News Meter**
Visualizing a news meter can help you determine the importance of a potential news item.

As you evaluate a potential news item, ask yourself whether it meets the four criteria above—and to what degree. Now imagine a News Meter. The far left side of the meter reads "No News," and the far right side reads "Big News." Answering *yes* to each of the questions above would move the meter's needle to the right. Answering *no* would keep the needle on the left. Keep in mind that the criteria are closely related and often overlap.

DEVELOPING GOOD NEWS JUDGMENT

You are a reporter for a local television station. You hear about a car crash on the main freeway in your city. How do you and your editor determine the potential newsworthiness of this story? As you read each fact, think about how it might affect the News Meter in Figure 1.1.

Is it important?	The crash snarls local traffic traffic for hours. The crash only causes a short, minor slowdown. The crash results in major injuries to multiple people. The crash results in minor injuries to a few people.
Is it timely?	The crash happened within the past hour. The crash happened hours ago, and you're just learning about it.
Is it relevant to your audience?	The crash knocks out power to 15 city blocks. The crash knocks out power to a few houses. The crash affects traffic patterns and commutes for a large number of people. The crash has only minor impact on traffic.
Is it interesting?	First responders to the crash made a dramatic rescue of trapped passengers. The crash was a typical fender bender with only one police car responding.
Does it meet ALL the criteria?	The crash snarled traffic for hours, knocked out power to 15 blocks, involved your city's mayor and culminated in a heroic rescue of victims by local firefighters.

The People Formerly Known as the Audience

Traditionally, professional news organizations defined, reported and disseminated news. The audience chose which news stories to read or view based on the news outlets available in a particular community. A person might read a handful of newspapers and magazines and watch a few local and national news programs on television.

These days, however, the audience is not just a passive receiver of news from a handful of sources. The use of digital technology has changed how news is produced and consumed. The audience has been empowered in ways that have altered journalism.

As you look at the top of the column to the right, think about how news consumption has changed in the past 20 years. Not only have the methods of consuming news shifted to different platforms, but the speed of news consumption and the volume of content consumed have also changed dramatically.

People can access thousands of sources for content and store hours of reading, listening or viewing material for later use. People can view, listen to and read what they want, when they want. They can also create their own content to share with audiences of their choosing.

> "When the people formerly known as the audience employ the press tools they have in their possession to inform one another, that's citizen journalism."
>
> —JAY ROSEN, NEW YORK UNIVERSITY

Professor Jay Rosen of New York University observes that the "people formerly known as the audience" now take part in defining and producing the news. This audience has turned the news into an ongoing conversation and a participatory activity. These people now have a say in what is important, timely, relevant and interesting.

20 Years Ago

* Newspaper/magazine subscriptions
* TV—cable and broadcast
* Radio
* Reader or viewer letter to newspaper or station
* Traditional mail, phone calls
* Reading/viewing news

Present

* Automated, customized feeds to computers or mobile devices
* Home satellite, digital cable, DVR, Web video
* Satellite radio, podcasts
* Commentary on the Web—social media, blogs, comments on news sites
* Text messages, email, video calls
* Reporting and spreading news

FIGURE 1.2 **Accessing/Interacting with the News**
The box on the top lists how most people accessed news content 20 years ago. The box on the bottom lists ways in which people access and interact with news content today. This list will continue to change and evolve in the coming years.

The Web Changes Everything

The set of Web-based services and applications popularly known as **Web 2.0** played a large part in this transformation of the relationship between journalists and the audience. When the World Wide Web became popular in the mid-1990s, it mostly facilitated one-way communication between those with the technical knowledge to create and publish Web pages and those who viewed those pages on computer screens. Text and graphics were the primary media formats used in this early version of the Web, which could be considered **Web 1.0**.

The upgrades in Web-based applications and services that became known as **Web 2.0** made multiway communication easy and allowed people without a high level of technical knowledge to publish and share content, including audio and video (Figure 1.3). Digital storage became affordable and widely available. Cloud computing, along with advances in mobile technology, meant that content of all kinds could be accessed from almost anywhere. Broadband Internet connections allowed for easy uploading and sharing of multimedia content.

The number of news sources—both professional and nonprofessional—grew exponentially. Web 2.0 technologies also allowed people to talk back to—and publicly talk about—traditional news organizations. Social media services created huge, interconnected networks of content consumers and producers, allowing large amounts of information to be shared with millions of people in short periods of time.

What does the future hold? What kinds of technologies and services will be known as **Web 3.0**? The answer is not entirely clear, but some clues have emerged. These have to do with technology that creates and organizes content on your behalf based on your previously known activity and preferences. Sites like Pandora and applications like iTunes Genius are examples. In both cases, new music streams are gathered, created, organized or suggested for your use based on information already available about you and/or your previous preferences and choices. Instead of seeking out this new information or content, it automatically finds you.

WEB 1.0

One-Way Communication
Viewing, Reading Content
Personal Web Pages
Visiting Websites
Computer-Based Applications

WEB 2.0

Multidirectional Communication
Creating, Sharing Content
Blogs, Social Media
Receiving Customized Feeds
Applications in the Cloud

FIGURE **1.3** **Web 1.0 Versus Web 2.0**

In its early years, the Web was primarily a passive experience. The interactivity of Web 2.0 means new challenges and opportunities for journalists.

Emerging technologies

This leap in technology has huge implications for news and journalism. Each member of the audience you serve may have access to a customized, constantly flowing news and information feed, based on thousands of individual attributes that are already known about his or her preferences, habits, location and history. As a journalist and as a news consumer, you will have to decide how to do your best work in this environment.

Current and emerging digital technologies have given news consumers much more control, a trend illustrated in Figure 1.4. News organizations now deal with an audience that can—collectively and individually—take part in the gathering and production of news. The members of the audience—the new consumers of news—can also immediately and publicly critique news organizations' performance and debate the issues brought forth in news coverage. Through social media networks, news consumers' comments and critiques can spread quickly to large numbers of people. News consumers can also carefully choose which information they receive—from a vast menu of choices. They can vote with their clicks and collectively appoint one story or topic as more important or interesting than another. They can act as independent, nonprofessional reporters by publishing and sharing original information, or they can help professional news organizations cover events by submitting their own information and content for professional journalists to use. News consumers now exercise a lot of control over the news. Many media organizations have embraced the empowerment of news consumers. Most news sites now include "share and comment" buttons that allow users to quickly post links and commentary to social media networks or to email them to friends and contacts.

If you are under 30 years of age, this comes as no surprise. You likely grew up using many of the Web applications and technologies described above. Traditional journalism organizations, however, are still adjusting to these relatively recent changes. Part of your job may be to help your news organization understand how its audience uses technology and how that technology can improve journalism.

Figure 1.5 shows where people get their news. Note that local television is still the most popular source, but it is losing ground. Viewership of local TV news dropped 25 percent between 1994 and 2008. Online news consumption, by contrast, grew 1,850 percent between 1996 and 2008. Online news consumption continues on an upward trend, largely driven by younger consumers.

2000

46% of adults use Internet

5% with broadband at home

50% own a cell phone

0% connect to Internet wirelessly

< 10% use "cloud"

= slow, stationary connections built around my computer

2010

79% of adults use the Internet

66% havo broadband at homo

85% own a cell phone

57% connect to Internet wirelessly (via smartphone, laptop or iPad)

> two-thirds use "cloud"

= fast, mobile connections built around outside servers and storage

FIGURE 1.4
The New News Audience

Consumers have changed the ways they access media—and the media are working hard to keep up with their habits.

Source: Pew Internet & American Life Project, Lee Rainie, "The Internet Is the Change Agent: Then and Now," slide 2 in presentation "New News Audience: 12 Ways consumers have changed in the digital age," Nov. 13, 2009. Accessed April 1, 2011, at: http://www.pewinternet.org/Presentations/2009/50--The-new-news-audience.aspx. Data updated January 2011.

Streams of information

News, for many people, now unfolds as a stream of information from various sources—both professional and nonprofessional. As news events happen, the first report might come in the form of a Facebook update, a tweet or a text message. These first reports might come from a professional news organization or an individual who is not a journalist. As the story unfolds, news consumers will continue to receive a stream of information made up of a mix of professional and nonprofessional reportage that is received in various formats on various devices.

As news breaks, it is immediately analyzed and commented on. Streams of information, commentary and analysis can be nearly instantaneous and can reach news consumers in almost any location.

“This is what this YouTube-Facebook-instant messaging generation does. Witness. Record. Share.”

—WASHINGTON POST REPORTER JOSE ANTONIO VARGAS writing about students who immediately recorded and posted images and messages during the mass shooting at Virginia Tech in 2007.

When the tragic mass shooting occurred at Virginia Tech on April 16, 2007, Washington Post reporters went to Facebook to find people who had witnessed the tragic events firsthand. Their efforts paid off when one of the reporters found an eyewitness who provided a dramatic account of what had happened.

The Post's series of articles was a part of a package of stories that won the 2008 Pulitzer Prize for Breaking News. The series included stories on how the Virginia Tech students themselves—most of them non-journalists—reported and shared information about the event.

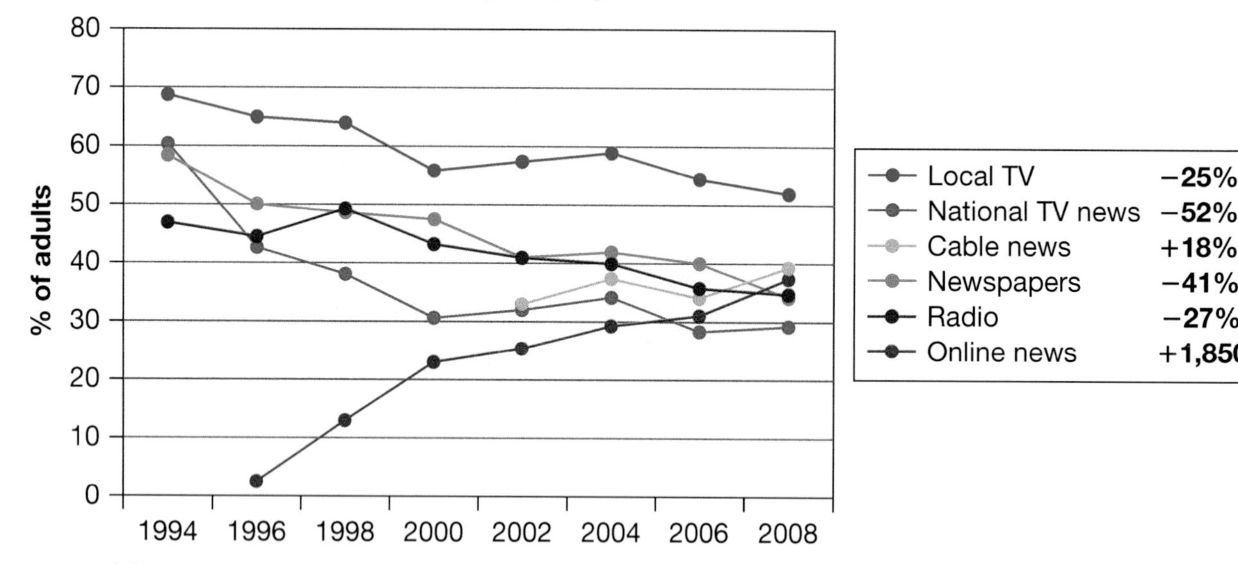

FIGURE **1.5 Customizing the News**

Technology has allowed people to customize the news to their own interests and to access news at the time and place of their choosing. News consumption has become a personal, local, social and mobile activity.

Source: Pew Internet & American Life Project, Lee Rainie, “The Internet Is the Change Agent: Then and Now,” slide 8 in presentation “New News Audience: 12 Ways consumers have changed in the digital age,” Nov. 13, 2009. Accessed April 1, 2011, at: http://www.pewinternet.org/Presentations/2009/50--The-new-news-audience.aspx.

NEWS IS PERSONAL, LOCAL, SOCIAL AND MOBILE

News is *personal*

News consumers can customize news and information to fit their interests. Through RSS, Twitter and other services, they can subscribe to individual feeds of information from particular sources or on specific topics.

If you are interested in business news, you might subscribe to RSS feeds from The Wall Street Journal or Business Week. You might also follow prominent reporters or columnists from those publications on Twitter.

News is *social*

News consumers are a social bunch, constantly sharing information and ideas. This sharing occurs through social media services like Facebook and other informal networks. News consumers use all kinds of technologies to access news, create content and communicate with others.

If a natural disaster struck your town, you might share links and headlines via Twitter or Facebook and also use those services to provide ideas and commentary *about* the news and to receive the commentary and opinions of others. Through social media or other networks, you might connect with people who are directly affected by the disaster or who witnessed it firsthand. Family and friends of the people in your town will also communicate about the disaster through their networks—from wherever they are in the world.

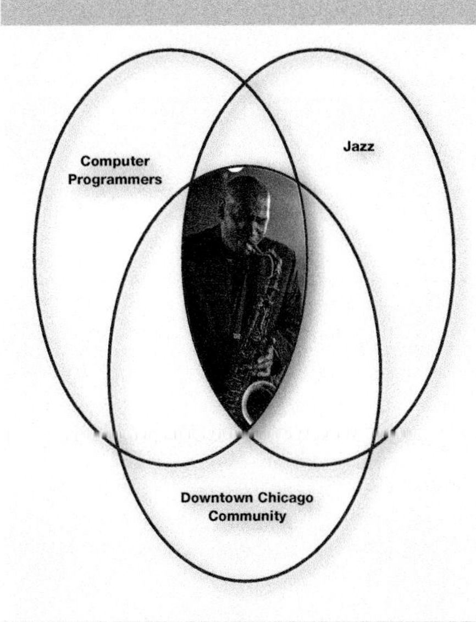

News is *local*

News consumers consider themselves part of many communities. A community can, of course, exist in a geographic location, but it can also be a group of people with shared interests. News consumers are highly attuned to news that affects their communities.

A computer programmer who lives in downtown Chicago and loves to play jazz music is a member of the geographic communities of his particular block, the downtown district and the city of Chicago. He is also a member of communities that share interest in computer programming and jazz music. He may be members of many more communities based on his history and interests.

News is *mobile*

News consumers may receive, produce or discuss news almost anywhere at any time. The proliferation of mobile devices allows for constant communication.

When U.S. Airways Flight 1549 crash-landed in the Hudson River in New York City on January 15, 2009, the first photos of the aftermath were taken from mobile phones and shared on Twitter and Facebook. Eyewitnesses called news organizations to provide live, firsthand accounts, and the passengers of the plane were calling and communicating with loved ones minutes after the incident—before they were ferried to shore.

"There's a plane in the Hudson. I'm on the ferry going to pick up the people. Crazy."

—Twitter user Janis Krums, who posted the first known image of the aftermath of U.S. Airways Flight 1549's crash landing in the Hudson River on January 15, 2009. The photo was linked to, republished and broadcast by hundreds of professional news organizations.

Understanding the Flow of Information

As a professional journalist, you should understand how multiple, simultaneous streams of information flow to your audience as well as to you, and you should use those streams to do the best journalism possible. Figure 1.6 shows how these streams of information interact and intersect. You should understand that information about a particular news topic will be available from professional and nonprofessional sources alike. This information must be verified and vetted for accuracy, and once you have done so, it can be an important and even vital part of news coverage.

In other words, you need to be a reporter *and* curator—or caretaker—of news. You must dig up original information *and* be willing to point to good information from other sources (with attribution, of course). You should become an expert on particular beats and topics so that you will have the knowledge necessary to vet vast amounts of information and make sense of it for news consumers.

You should also understand how to use technology to add your original reporting to the streams of information flowing to news consumers. It is important that you have at least a rudimentary understanding of Web and mobile technology. In addition to traditional news gathering and production skills, you should stay on top of new technologies that allow you to quickly create content in multiple formats and disseminate it to news consumers.

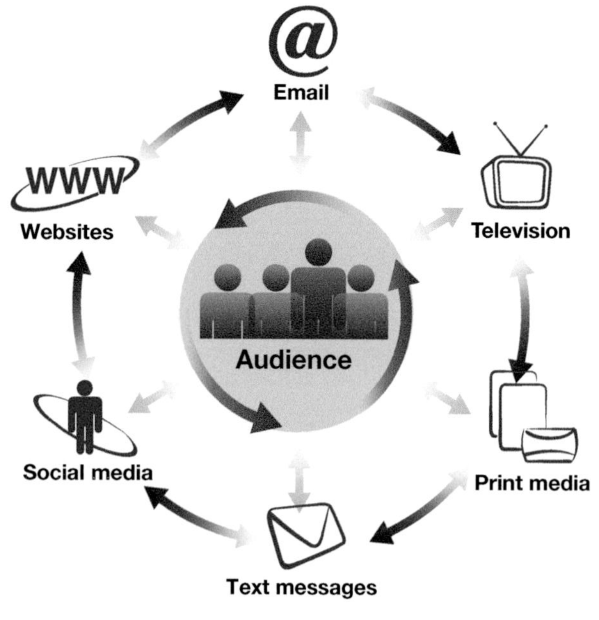

FIGURE **1.6** **The Flow of Information**

Today's audiences receive information from many different sources simultaneously. They also use tools and networks to share large amounts of information.

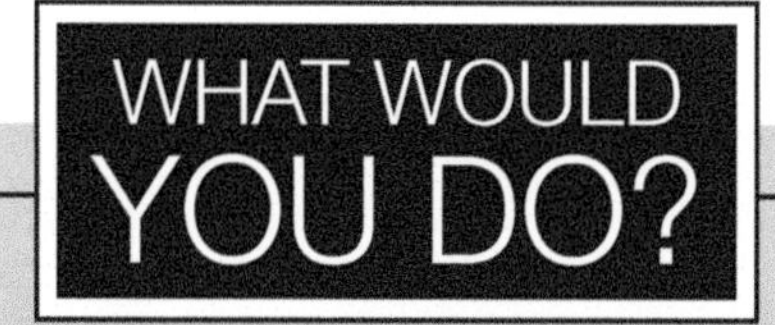

You are assigned to cover city hall. You see a tweet from a city worker whom you follow that claims the mayor has done something unethical. You will certainly contact the worker for more information. What else will you do? What other steps will you take that will help you evaluate this person's credibility and the reliability of the information you receive? What kind of questions will you ask him or her? If the initial information seems plausible, what will be your next steps?

VETTING INFORMATION

Media literacy is one of the most important skills a journalist or news consumer can develop. Being media literate means knowing that some pieces of information or sources available to us are more valuable and reliable than others. To vet information, ask yourself the following questions:

- Is the information attributed to a source, or is it anonymous? Anonymous information is much less valuable and reliable than information that can be traced to a source.
- Who or what is the source of the information? Who owns the information or is ultimately responsible for it? Can you verify, with certainty, that the purported source of the information is the true source?
- What is the record and reputation of the source of the information?
- What are the background, biases, political leanings and economic interests of the person or organization that is the source of the information?
- What are all the possible motivations of the person or organization responsible for the information?
- Is there a way to verify the truthfulness of the information? Are there other sources or records you can check? Can the original source provide support or corroborating evidence?

Evolving Stories and Topics

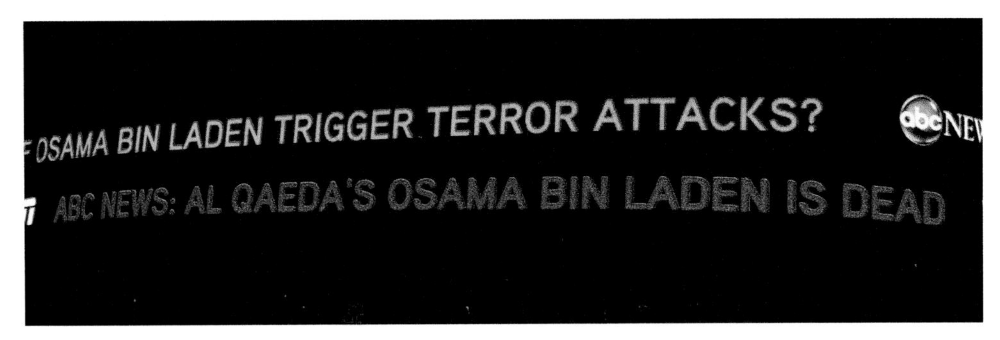

News tickers at Times Square in New York City announce the death of Osama Bin Laden on May 1, 2011.
Chevaan Daniel, Hubert H. Humphrey Fellow, Walter Cronkite School 2010–2011

The traditional story or package, scheduled to be published or broadcast at a particular time, is not always effective in a world of constant streams of information, particularly when it comes to breaking or developing news events. In most professional newsrooms, coverage is now built piece by piece as information and context become available. News consumers receive news in a series of updates—from professional and nonprofessional sources.

Traditional stories still play an important role in connecting disparate pieces of information and providing context, but unconnected, isolated stories do not provide the best coverage.

Instead, City University of New York journalism professor Jeff Jarvis argues that carefully cared-for topic pages should be the new building blocks of journalism:

> [I] want a page, a site, a thing that is created, curated, edited, and discussed. It's a blog that treats a topic as an ongoing and cumulative process of learning, digging, correcting, asking, answering. It's also a wiki that keeps a snapshot of the latest knowledge and background. It's an aggregator that provides annotated links to experts, coverage, opinion, perspective, source material. It's a discussion that doesn't just blather but that tries to accomplish something. . . . It's collaborative and distributed and open but organized.
>
> Think of it as being inside a beat reporter's head, while also sitting at a table with all the experts who inform that reporter, as everyone there can hear and answer questions asked from the rest of the room—and in front of them all are links to more and ever-better information and understanding.
>
> This is the way to cover stories and life.*

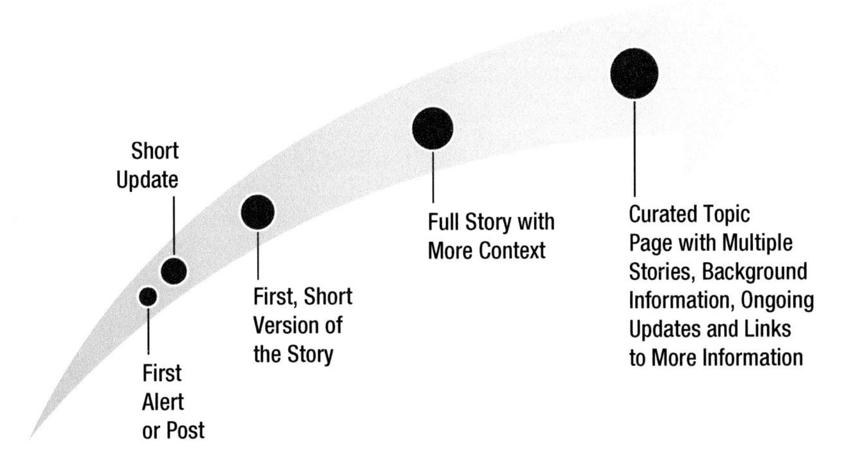

FIGURE 1.7 **Evolution of Breaking/Developing News**
News coverage now begins with a series of updates and may evolve into a curated topic page.

*From Jeff Jarvis, "The building block of journalism is no longer the article," BuzzMachine.com, found at http://www.buzzmachine.com/2008/09/30/the-building-block-of-journalism-is-no-longer-the-article/

How a Newsroom Works

Each newsroom carries its own identity, but most television newsrooms operate in much the same way. Their morning, day and night **shifts** all begin with similar responsibilities. Here is a typical day at KNXV-TV (ABC) in Phoenix:

IDEA: Before a story is approved or assigned, it starts as an idea. This idea can come from any number of sources, including viewers, readers, public agencies, companies and, of course, the news staff itself. Assignment editors track news wires and other news sources like networks, newspapers and websites.

DECISION: In television newsrooms, it's called an editorial meeting. Newspapers refer to it as a budget meeting. Here managers and other staff members consider ideas and make assignments for field crews, writers and producers.

ACTION: Once the idea has been approved and assigned, reporters typically start making calls to get information and line up interviews. Then it's time to get out the door!

SHAPING: While reporters work in the field, producers are creating rundowns that detail what stories are in each newscast, who is responsible for the content and how much time each piece will take.

IN THE NEWSROOM: Web producers are posting video and photos online to help tell the story. Reporters file Web updates from the field via laptop, mobile device or phone.

The Starting Lineup

Assignment Editor: *Collects all possible stories of the day and brings them to the morning meeting*

Newscast Producer: *Listens to ideas and begins to formulate plan for her newscast still several hours away*

Reporter: *Heads out the door to track down stories; often updates newsroom on progress*

Online Editor: *Tracks local and national news coming into the newsroom and continually updates online content*

Producer: *A producer is an off-air content creator. Producers can supervise on-air newscasts, online content and work in the field*

IN THE STUDIO: As a newscast approaches, studio production crew members prepare the set and review the rundown.

ON-AIR: Anchors have read the scripts and taken their positions on set. The director follows the rundown and instructs the studio crew, while the producer monitors the length and content of the newscast.

ON THE STREET: In the field, some reporters have written and edited their stories, called packages, and fed them electronically back to the station. Others have returned to write and edit at the station.

AFTER THE NEWSCAST: The day doesn't end with the last lines of a live report. Reporters still need to write another version of their story or continue reporting through the next newscast to the end of the shift. They will also update the online versions of their stories. Producers hand off any unused stories to the next newscast and note any problems that need to be addressed. The director and studio crew begin prepping for the next newscast, which may be only 30 minutes away.

Executive Producer: *Supervises several producers at once, approves reporters' scripts and maintains good grasp of the whole team's effort*

Videographer: *Works hand in hand with reporter in the field to ensure quality video; edits the story*

Anchor: *Writes copy, records promotions, even goes out to cover a story before finally reading scripts and sits on set*

Newscast Director: *Oversees the control room and studio floor crew, ensuring that the cameras are in the right place at the right time and that the show visually matches the producer's rundown*

Finding News to Report

How do you find news for your audience?

Major events

Some news is obvious. Accidents, crimes and natural disasters that pass the news judgment test—meaning they are important, timely, interesting and relevant—deserve your time and attention. But don't limit yourself to the latest high-profile event. Crucial news goes on under the radar. You will have to dig into your assignments and your beats to find it.

Sources

News may come from sources with whom you have developed relationships, particularly if you work on a particular beat. Get to know the major players and experts in the area you're covering. But be careful: Never let a relationship with a source keep you from doing the best job possible. Becoming overly close or friendly with sources could keep you from doing good journalism.

The audience

News can also come from members of the community whom you don't yet know. Encourage your audience to have an ongoing conversation with you about the news you cover.

All media

Many great ideas for news coverage can come from the media content you read, view, listen to and interact with on a daily basis. Maintaining a healthy "media diet" is a necessity. Consume media that keep you well informed and inspire new ideas. Even when you are not officially on duty as a journalist, you should be learning about your world, nation and local community. Seek out specialized information about particular beats you cover. Learn how to set up automated online searches and feeds that will bring you new information relevant to your beat and areas of interest.

FIND THE NEWS!

You have just been assigned the police and crime beat for your city. How will you find news to report?

First, any major crime or event involving local law enforcement is obviously news that you should cover. However, the event may have angles that aren't obvious. You will have to dig into the world of crime and law enforcement to discover what they are.

Second, you need to get to know people who can be sources: law enforcement officials, beat cops, defense attorneys, judges, criminal justice scholars and community activists. Visit them, get to know them and ask them for help in learning about what they do.

Third, ask for feedback from people in the community. How do they feel about law enforcement in your city? Do they feel safe? Do they have confidence in local police officials? Are particular crimes or problems not being covered? You need to ask.

Fourth, maintain a healthy, steady media diet built around your beat. Who are the other reporters and news organizations working on police and crime? Make sure you follow their coverage. Who in the community is blogging about crime and law enforcement issues? Who are the criminal justice experts at your local college? Can they recommend books or journals to read? Set up RSS feeds and automatic searches that capture all kinds of reporting on police and crime issues.

Rules for Digital and Social Media

Technology has provided journalists with countless ways to connect to their audience. Along with these new opportunities come the potential pitfalls. What will be the nature of your communication with your audience? Will conversations with your audience translate to solid content and coverage decisions? Which technologies will give your journalism the greatest reach and impact? What technologies does your audience use to access your content? What format does your audience find most effective?

Newsroom managers and staff will have to choose wisely where and how to spend their time and resources. Here are some points to consider:

- Which is more important—getting information quickly online or gathering more content for a later, more in-depth piece? If both are important, how does a newsroom balance these competing needs?
- Will you hold exclusive content or post it to your website immediately?
- How much context and information do you need before you break a story?
- Who will post content through social media, and how often, under daily and breaking circumstances?
- Who is authorized to make publishing decisions and to be the voice of your news organization?
- What is the overall tone of your social media identity? Some news organizations go for a casual, conversational style, while others are more formal.
- What is the newsroom's main goal in media integration? Once a mission is defined (e.g., "Attract more viewers for newscasts" or "Use as a newsgathering source" or "Reach as many news consumers as possible"), it will be easier to focus on the when, why and how of getting the job done.

Once newsroom leaders establish such rules, they should review and update them regularly as technology and circumstances change. It is up to a news organization's leadership team to determine how its content will live and breathe in these varied formats and what type of news identity it hopes to create. And it's often up to the reporters, editors and producers to ensure that this mission is fulfilled.

Measuring News Consumption

Most news organizations attempt to count *how many* people read, hear, view and use their content. They also attempt to measure *how much* content is read, heard, viewed or used—and *how often*.

Understanding these measurements can help journalists better serve their audience and know the impact of their reporting on their community. And it can help journalists understand which technologies and platforms are most effective and where to invest time and resources. News organizations also use this information to set advertising prices and to let advertisers and business partners know the potential reach of their news products. In turn, advertisers and business partners use the information to figure out which news products might be good investments.

Measuring news consumption has become more challenging as technology has transformed the way people interact with news. People can personalize and customize their news consumption in ways that are difficult to track. Satellite radio changed how news consumers interact with audio content that was previously received via broadcast radio. Digital video recorders (DVRs), streaming video, video downloads and video-on-the-Web services, such as Hulu, have changed how news consumers get video content that was previously received via broadcast or cable television. Downloads, subscriptions and video/audio stream "starts" and "stops" are increasingly important ways of measuring news consumption.

Broadcast and Web ratings companies are searching for ways to measure media consumption across multiple platforms and devices.

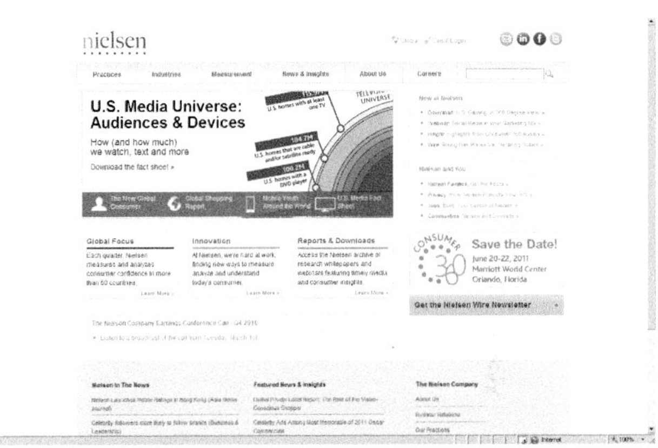

Television

For national audience measurement, Nielsen, the primary TV ratings company in the United States, uses "people meters" and "TV meters," devices that are attached to televisions and combined with special remote controls to measure how many people from a sample group watch particular programs. On a local level, a similar system is used in the largest markets. Midsize markets rely on less sophisticated meters, while the smallest areas rely on paper diaries filled out by viewers. In addition to total numbers of viewers, Nielsen gathers demographic information about viewers—age, ethnicity, location, socioeconomic level—in an attempt to figure out what type of programming appeals to certain segments of the population. Based on the information it collects, Nielsen gives "rating points" and "share points" to TV programs.

Ratings are the percent of households that tune into a particular program.

Audience Share is the percent of the television-watching audience that is tuned into a particular program or network at a given time.

Radio

Arbitron Inc. is the primary radio ratings service in the United States. It uses daily diaries filled out by listeners and electronic devices called "Personal People Meters" to track individuals' listening habits. According to Arbitron, most radio professionals and businesses use the Average Quarter-Hour Rating as the standard measurement. The following is Arbitron's explanation of its ratings system:

Average Quarter-Hour Persons (AQH Persons)

The average number of persons listening to a particular station for at least five minutes during a 15-minute period.

Average Quarter-Hour Rating (AQH Rating)

The AQH Persons estimate expressed as a percentage of the population being measured. This estimate is printed for the MSA [Metropolitan Statistical Area] and DMA [Designated Market Area]. It can also be computed for the TSA [Total Survey Area].
[AQH Persons / Population] x 100 = AQH Rating (%)

Cume Persons

The total number of different persons who tune to a radio station during the course of a daypart [The time segments that divide a radio or TV day for ad scheduling purposes.] for at least five minutes.

Cume Rating

The Cume Persons audience expressed as a percentage of all persons estimated to be in the specified demographic group.
[Cume Persons / Population] x 100 = Cume Rating (%)

Rating (AQH or Cume)

The audience expressed as a percentage of the total population.
[Listeners / Population] x 100 = Rating (%)

Share

The percentage of those listening to radio in the Metro who are listening to a particular radio station.
[AQH Persons to a Station / AQH Persons to All Stations] x 100 = Share (%)

Metro

Includes a city (or cities) whose population is specified as that of the central city together with the county (or counties) in which it is located. The Metro also includes contiguous or additional counties when the economic and social relationships between the central and additional counties meet specific criteria. Arbitron Metros generally correspond to the Metropolitan Statistical Areas (MSAs) defined by the U.S. Government's Office of Management and Budget. They are subject to exceptions dictated by historical industry usage and other marketing considerations.

Total Survey Area (TSA)

A geographic area that encompasses the Metro Survey Area and may include additional counties located outside the Metro which meet certain listening criteria to Metro-licensed stations.

Designated Market Area (DMA®)

The DMA is composed of sampling units (counties or geographically split counties) and is defined and updated annually by Nielsen Media Research, Inc., based on historical television viewing patterns. A county or split county is assigned exclusively to one DMA.

Arbitron reports radio listening estimates for the Top 50 DMAs (ranked on TV households) in the Radio Market Reports of all Standard radio markets whose Metros are located within the DMA and whose names are contained in the DMA name.

Source: Arbitron http://www.arbitron.com/radio_stations/tradeterms.htm

Web

Web measurement programs like Google Analytics are used by media organizations to internally track usage of their websites, including how many users visit their website in a particular period of time, which pages receive the most views, how much time users spend on particular pages, how users navigate through the site, how users enter the site and where users go when they leave the site. Companies like Nielsen and comScore provide public rankings and ratings of websites based on the number of people who visit them. They also provide private detailed Web traffic analysis to paying clients. The main units of web traffic measurement are page views and unique visitors. Page views are the number of times a single web page is viewed in a particular period of time. Unique visitors are the number of individual users who visited a website or webpage in a particular period of time. Various technologies have been employed to measure Web traffic. These include audience sampling as well as the use of "cookies," which are small pieces of code that websites embed in users' Web browsers to track online activity.

Depending on the goals of a particular news organization and the audience it wants to serve, loyalty—the amount of time a person spends with news content and how often he or she returns to the same source of news—may be as important, or more important, than overall numbers. When it comes to measuring news, the quality of a news consumer's experience is as important as the total number of people consuming news or the total number of programs watched or Web pages viewed.

TYPE OF MEDIA	WHAT GETS MEASURED
NEWSPAPERS 	**Circulation:** The number of newspapers distributed by a news organization on a daily, weekly or monthly basis. Circulation is usually self-reported by the news organization but is often certified by an outside auditor, such as the Audit Bureau of Circulations, an independent industry group that audits and certifies the circulation of most U.S. newspapers.
WEBSITES 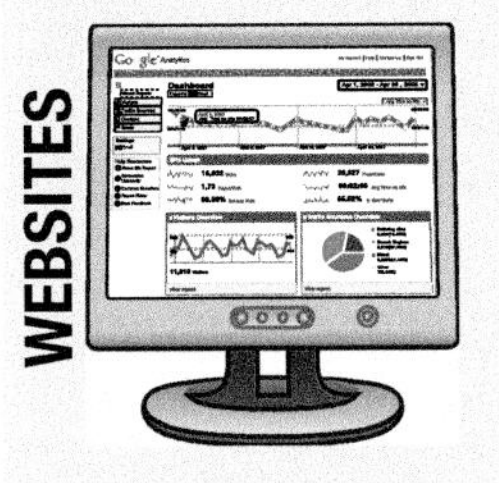	**Traffic:** The number of times a Web page is viewed in a period of time (page views) or the number of individual visitors to a Web page or website in a period of time (unique visitors). Google Analytics is used by many media companies and news producers to measure Web traffic internally. Companies like Nielsen and comScore provide public rankings and ratings of websites.
TELEVISION 	**Ratings**: The number of people or households that watch a single broadcast or showing of a particular program. The Nielsen Company provides ratings data for television audiences in the United States through sampling—tracking the viewing habits of a randomly selected group of people in order to predict the viewing habits of the larger population.
RADIO 	**Ratings:** The number of people who listen to individual broadcasts of radio programs. Arbitron, the main radio ratings company in the United States, uses daily diaries filled out by listeners and electronic devices called "Personal People Meters" to track how many people are listening to individual stations or programs.

FIGURE 1.8 **Measuring News Consumption**

Objectivity, Bias and Transparency

We will cover journalism ethics in Chapter 12, "Charting Your Ethical Course." But, so you can begin thinking about some of the ethical decisions you will face, here are a few ideas.

In the world of instant and constant analysis of news, reporters and news organizations have come under heavy scrutiny for the decisions they make and have been highly criticized for perceived biases. The traditional idea of objectivity in reporting has been criticized and re-evaluated. **Objectivity** in the journalistic sense means that the reporting seeks to give fair treatment to all important and viable arguments surrounding a particular issue. It also means that reporters take a neutral stance on issues that they cover—not favoring any particular point of view so that all can be covered fairly. The principle of objectivity in reporting has given journalists a stable and effective way to cover issues fairly and to build credibility with the audience.

Critics of the traditional notion of objectivity, however, argue that no person can be truly be objective—that one's background, upbringing and personal beliefs have an effect on the way a story is

> "Our job is not to make up anyone's mind, but to open minds—to make the agony of decision-making so intense that you can escape only by thinking."
>
> —FRED FRIENDLY, CBS NEWS PRODUCER*

reported. These critics argue that instead of pursuing an unattainable goal of objectivity, journalists should be transparent about their backgrounds, beliefs and biases—and let news consumers decide whether their work is valuable.

Others argue that objectivity is a nebulous concept that is difficult for journalists and their audience to understand. As a journalist, your approach to objectivity will most likely be defined by your personal beliefs and by your organization's rules and guidelines.

Many news organizations now include a public editor who serves as an ombudsman between the organization's editorial decisions and the audience's perceptions of objectivity and fairness. News organizations continuously struggle to find constructive and positive ways to talk to news consumers about the decisions they make. Nevertheless, anonymous or nearly anonymous comments on news organizations' websites are now widely seen as a less valuable way to interact with news consumers.

Critiques of news organizations and reporters are a permanent part of the news process. All journalists must look for ways to explain themselves and the reporting process to news consumers and should welcome appropriate constructive criticism.

WHAT WOULD YOU DO?

A commenter on your news organization's website accuses you of bias and inaccuracy in your reporting. Will you respond? Why or why not? If you do respond, how will you reach this person? How will you communicate with him or her?

*Source: globalstock / istock

THE PILLARS OF GOOD JOURNALISM

Dan Gillmor, professor
Walter Cronkite School of Journalism and Mass Communication

In this excerpt from his blog, Dan Gillmor argues that adherence to a set of core principles—the "Pillars of Good Journalism"—is better than striving to attain pure objectivity.

Thoroughness

When I was a reporter and, later, a columnist, my first goal was to learn as much as I could. After all, gathering facts and opinions is the foundation of reporting. I liked it best when I felt I had left 95 percent of what I'd learned out of the final piece. The best reporters I know always want to make one more call, check with one more source. (The last question I ask at all interviews is, "Who else should I talk with about this?")

Today, thoroughness means more than asking questions of the people in our Rolodexes (circular or virtual). It means, whenever possible, asking our readers for their input, as I did when I wrote my book (and other authors are doing on theirs). Competitive pressures tend to make this a rare request, but I'm convinced that more journalists will adopt it.

Accuracy

Get your facts straight.

Say what you *don't* know, not just what you do. (If the reader/listener/viewer does know what you don't, you've just invited him/her to fill you in.)

Fairness

This one is so difficult, in practice, as accuracy is simple. Fairness is often in the eye of the beholder. But even here I think a few principles may universally apply.

Fairness means, among other things, listening to different viewpoints and incorporating them into the journalism. It does not mean parroting lies or distortions to achieve that lazy equivalence that leads some journalists to get opposing quotes when the facts overwhelmingly support one side.

Fairness is also about letting people respond when they believe you are wrong. Again, this is much easier online than in a print publication, much less a broadcast.

Ultimately, fairness emerges from a state of mind. We should be aware of what drives us, and always willing to listen to those who disagree. The first rule of having a conversation is to listen—and I know I learn more from people who think I'm wrong than from those who agree with me.

Transparency

Disclosure is gaining currency as an addition to journalism. It's easier said than done, of course.

No one can plausibly argue with the idea that journalists need to disclose certain things, such as financial conflicts of interest. But to what extent? Should journalists of all kinds be expected to make their lives open books? How open?

Personal biases, even unconscious ones, affect the journalism as well. I'm an American, brought up in with certain beliefs that many folks in other lands (and some in this one) flatly reject. I need to be aware of the things I take for granted, and to periodically challenge some of them, as I do my work.

Another way to be transparent is in the way we present a story. We should link to source material as much as possible, bolstering what we tell people with close-to-the-ground facts and data. (Maybe this is part of accuracy or thoroughness, but it seems to fit here, too.)

To the extent that we make thoroughness, accuracy, fairness and transparency the pillars of journalism, we can get a long way toward the worthy goal of helping our audiences/collaborators. I don't claim it's easy, but I do think it's worth the effort.

A Newsroom That Fits You

As the overall amount of information and content has increased in recent years, news and media organizations have tried to distinguish themselves from the crowd, sometimes jettisoning their past style, approach and identity. Many media and news organizations now use dramatic language, strong opinion and dynamic personalities to attract attention.

Today, different news organizations may have vastly different approaches to covering the news. Even those that cover the same community or same subject may differ in their focus and tone.

If you want to work as a professional journalist, you should look for a news organization whose approach to the news, reporting style and ethical guidelines fit your own beliefs and personality.

One local TV station may focus on government affairs and what's going on at city hall, whereas another may focus on crime and safety issues. One newscast might be sedate and serious in its tone, whereas another might be dramatic and energetic.

One newspaper may give its readers eye-catching headlines, big photos and shorter articles, whereas another might go for an information-packed front page and in-depth articles.

As the media landscape becomes more crowded, news organizations will try harder than ever to distinguish themselves. Many news organizations are now focusing on niche topics and issues or are radically changing their style of coverage in order to offer something different to consumers of news.

Before you go to work for a news organization, attempt to understand its culture and its approach to news. Study the organization's focus and the style of its coverage. Compare its coverage of a particular story to coverage from another organization. If possible, visit the newsroom and talk to reporters and editors. Ask yourself whether their ethical and journalistic standards match your own.

Finding a newsroom that fits you will help you find fulfillment and success as a journalist.

Elements of STORYTELLING

CHAPTER OUTLINE

CHAPTER 2

You don't want people reporting to you who don't have any sense of the emotional impact of a given moment in history.

—*WALTER CRONKITE*

What Makes a Good Story?

Probably since the days when early humans gathered around a warming fire, people have told stories to entertain and inform each other. From generation to generation, they passed down tales with universal themes of birth and death, love and hate, triumph and despair. No matter what the culture, people remember good stories that touch the heart *and* the mind.

Although the technology for recording and presenting stories has changed over the decades, the basics of good storytelling endure. A successful story should have a purpose and make your audience care about the subject. It should also illustrate a broader truth, a trend or the impact on a person, an issue, a policy or an event.

As media converge, few journalists work on only one platform, such as radio or TV. We need to think as multimedia storytellers. Find the story first, and then figure out the best way to present it.

Think visually

As a multimedia storyteller, the first thing to consider is the video and/or still photos you'll need. What you can't tell with these visuals, you can fill in with **sound bites** from interviews and **natural sound** recorded on location. What you can't tell with audio and video, you can fill in with narration or a **standup**. Veteran NBC News correspondent Bob Dotson refers to this as "writing to the corners of your picture."

Let's say you're shooting a video about a craftsman whose hand-made stringed psaltery (right) are selling well in a failing economy. How can you portray the level of care he brings to his work? If he meticulously keeps track of his orders by hand, you could shoot him writing in a ledger with a fountain pen along with a close-up of his penmanship. And your observations or interviews might reveal that he measures everything down to 1/1000th of an inch.

Not all stories are visual

Some stories lend themselves more naturally to visual treatment than others. An issue-oriented story on reducing air pollution, for example, might be better told with words. You could turn this story into a visual one by riding along with an inspector who monitors air quality and covering the issues through her eyes and voice. Or you could put a human face on the issue by focusing on how air quality has affected the health of one individual or community. Using a real person's story to illuminate a larger issue often provides the human interest needed to hook viewers.

WHAT WOULD YOU DO?

Not all topics make strong visual stories. Sometimes subjects like the first day of school have been covered so much that they become formulaic or boring.

Let's say you're covering a school bake sale. Ho-hum. How could you make this story more compelling visually? One way might be by capturing the behind-the-scenes action of setting up the event.

What other ways could you make this story fresh and visual?

Focus

Focus your story

Even if you have strong visuals, your story won't hang together unless it has a focus. **Focus** refers to the point of your story. It's the thread that holds all the parts together.

One semester a student set out to do a feature story on helicopter parents—well-meaning moms and dads who micromanage their children's lives. The term "helicopter parents" refers to the fact that they hover constantly and swoop in to help whenever there's a problem. But the student ran into trouble because her topic was too broad. She didn't take the time to find an angle or a main character, so she spent a lot of time doing unnecessary research and reporting. She was whirling in so many directions she thought her head would explode.

After she heard Michael Roberts discuss the six ways to focus a story, her headache went away. Roberts, a newsroom trainer and consultant, teaches journalists to tell stories in print, video and multimedia.

As you try these focusing techniques, think about how you can tell the story in a fresh way.

- What ideas, voices and/or people have been left out of previous coverage?
- Who can provide background information or personal experience?
- Should they be on-camera?

> "And by the way, you know, when you're telling these little stories, here's a good idea: Have a POINT! It makes it so much more interesting for the listener."
>
> FROM PLANES, TRAINS AND AUTOMOBILES (FILM), HUGHES ENTERTAINMENT/PARAMOUNT PICTURES, 1987

WHAT WOULD YOU DO?

An idea isn't a story. The sputtering economy is a broad idea. You could go a thousand different ways to show its effects. To turn that broad idea into a story, zoom in on something more specific.

Here's one possibility: Show how more and more students are applying for scholarships and crowding the student aid office.

What other stories could you do on your campus to show the effects of the economic downturn in a fresh, visual way?

What stories could you cover in your community to show how the economy is picking up in a fresh, visual way?

TIMESAVER

Focusing your story before you start shooting makes it easier to decide what to leave out.

Six ways to find a focus

1 Ask a central question. What's at the heart of your story? Set out to answer that question in one sentence or 140 characters (the length of a tweet on Twitter.com). For example:

What's the relationship between helicopter parents and a child trying to break away?

2 What five questions would viewers want answered?

1. Why does someone become a helicopter parent?
2. What motivates helicopter parents?
3. Are they helping or hindering their children?
4. How does this behavior affect other family members?
5. Where can helicopter parents get help?

3 Ask yourself "Why?" five times. Each "Why?" should take you deeper into the story and closer to the central question or premise.

Premise: *Helicopter children sometimes have more problems in school. Why?*

1. Because they depend too much on their parents to help them make decisions. Why?
2. Because they're more connected to their parents. Why?
3. Because of email, cell phones, social networking and other technology. Why?
4. Because parents are fearful and overprotective. Why?
5. Because we live in a scary world.

4 Look for a microcosm. Is there a smaller story, or microcosm, that illustrates the broader theme, issue or trend? With helicopter parents, it could be the relationship between a parent and a child trying to break away. You could show a dad watching TV alone at home, pining in his son's empty room, commiserating with other parents and sending IMs to the child. But if the story is about a son who achieves independence, show him engaged in activities at school and with friends.

5 Find a point of view (POV). Jot down your topic or question, and then list all the people connected to your story. Whose POV best tells the story? Through whose eyes is the story most compelling?

- You could tell a story about helicopter parents from the *POV of parents with an only child.* Provide background and add sound bites from the child, the overinvolved parents and a psychologist.
- Or you could look at helicopter parents from the *POV of one person affected by the problem,* say a sibling, professor or residence hall adviser.
- Either way, you can weave in many of the same facts.

POSSIBLE POVs FOR HELICOPTER PARENTS

- ✓ KID
- ✓ MOM OR DAD
- ✓ SIBLING
- ✓ ROOMMATE
- ✓ FRIEND
- ✓ CLASSMATE
- ✓ CLERGY
- ✓ THERAPIST OR OTHER EXPERT
- ✓ PROFESSOR
- ✓ RESIDENCE HALL ADVISER
- ✓ PSYCHOLOGIST OR THERAPIST

6 Sketch a story map. Write the subject in the middle of a piece of paper. Draw spokes radiating from it. At the end of each spoke, jot down different angles (physical, psychological, social, etc.) and POVs (grandparent, sibling, professor, etc.). Keep adding spokes. A great story might be lurking in the corner, at the end of one of the spokes.

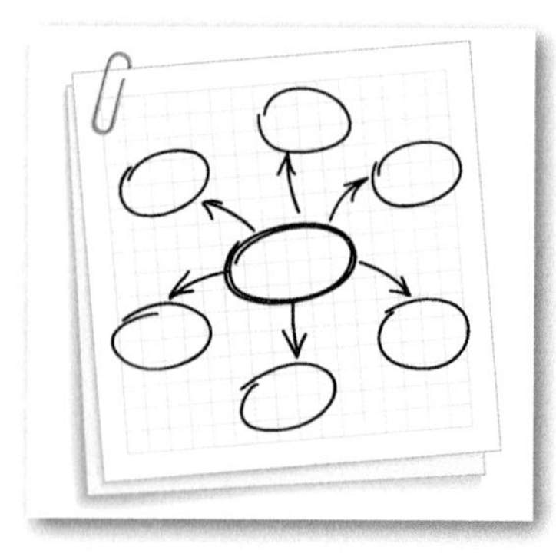

Record your focus

Once you find a focus, boil it down to about a dozen words. Write them in your reporter's notebook. Stick with this focus as you research and report. For the story on helicopter parents, for example, you might write: *One mom launches a Free-Range Kids movement to safeguard children.* Or: *Parents take a Slow Family Living class to relieve guilt about perfectionism.*

Every fact and sound bite should connect to your theme or main character. Having a clear focus will help you stay on target and keep you from collecting a lot of useless information.

Storyboarding

Next, visualize your story in your head or on paper. If you have a photographer, do this together. If you have time, sketch a **storyboard.** This cartoonlike drawing outlines what you plan to shoot, depending on time and resources. You don't need to be an artist. Stick figures are fine. The point is to make a list of the shots you need, especially a strong opener and closer. Think of multiple visuals in different situations that will tell the story.

Things that don't fit the focus of one story might give you ideas for another piece. Or you might be able to use them in a lead-in or tag.

BREAKING NEWS

Now, you might be saying to yourself, *How does this work when I'm out covering breaking news? I won't have time for focus exercises and storyboards then.* With breaking news, begin focusing your story on the way to the scene—in your head, not necessarily on paper.

Let's say you get word of a fatal shooting. Your focus in this case is straightforward. You'll need to get the facts straight about the shooting so you can report them as soon as you go on-air or online. Since you might have only a few minutes after arriving on the scene, begin with the **5 W's**—who, what, when, where and why. Focus on answering those questions accurately. Then ask yourself, "What's going to disappear from this scene first?" If it's compelling video or a witness, that's what you want to record first. Leave the police and public information officers for later.

Once you have the facts straight, look for the central characters who will help you flesh out your story. It could be an eyewitness, a hero who gave CPR, a priest who administered last rites—or the victim's friend.

If you were brainstorming a piece on helicopter parents, for example, you might want shots of mom and dad hovering as their daughter moves into a dorm, shops at the bookstore, walks around campus, talks with an adviser and goes to band practice. But your goal is to capture these moments as they happen. Never stage or set up shots.

Stay flexible

If your story takes a different turn as you're reporting, go with it. There can be many ways to focus a story. If three reporters cover the same story, each one could give it a different angle.

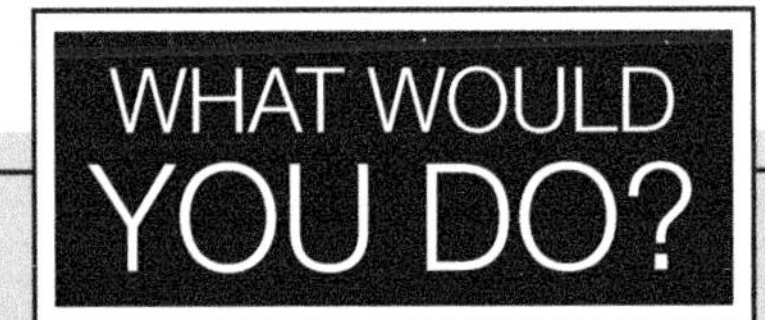

There might be many different ways to find a focus on an event as seemingly mundane as a community garage sale.

Economic: This garage sale is bigger than any in the past because residents are in financial trouble. How could you show this angle?

Legal: The community sought special permission to hold this mega-event. How could you show this angle?

Social: An adjacent neighborhood is complaining about the traffic. How could you show this angle?

Central Compelling Character

Go for the human touch

People are interested in other people. Build your story around what Greeley Kyle, a former TV reporter who's now a journalism professor, calls the **central compelling character (CCC)**. A memorable story builds visuals around this main character. Rarely is this a PR person, government bureaucrat or company official.

Instead, strive to find the **real people (RP)** who will engage your audience emotionally and make them care. The main voices should be those most affected by or involved in an issue or situation because they can describe their experiences. Tell the story through their eyes and with their voices. Let the experts, officials and observers provide the background information.

Motivation

Search for the "why." What motivates your main character? What makes him do what he does? Dig deep. For example, you might discover that a neurosurgeon chose his profession because he had a brain tumor as a child. Or that a homeless man stays off the street during the day by camping out in a U-Haul storage locker.

Capture emotion

Strong CCCs connect emotionally with the audience. According to Al Tompkins, the broadcast/online group leader at the Poynter Institute, viewers remember what they feel longer than what they hear. So get out of the way and let your CCCs tell their own stories! Capture their joy or sadness, anger or empathy, fear or enthusiasm.

Keep your distance

Be careful, though, not to become emotionally involved. After the Haiti earthquake in 2010, some medical reporters who are also doctors cared for suffering victims. Observers questioned whether they should have been reporting stories that also involved them. Should they have picked one role or the other—either doctor or journalist?

Maintain objectivity

Such decisions can be difficult. Your professor or co-workers, news director and producers in the newsroom can help you keep your emotional distance. Talk to them.

IN A TOUGH ECONOMY, THE HOMELESS POPULATION CONTINUES TO GROW. SOME PEOPLE, LIKE ELLIS ECKELS, ARE TAKING UNUSUAL MEASURES TO STAY OFF THE STREET, AT LEAST IN DAYTIME.

ELLIS RENTS A U-HAUL STORAGE UNIT IN DOWNTOWN PHOENIX.

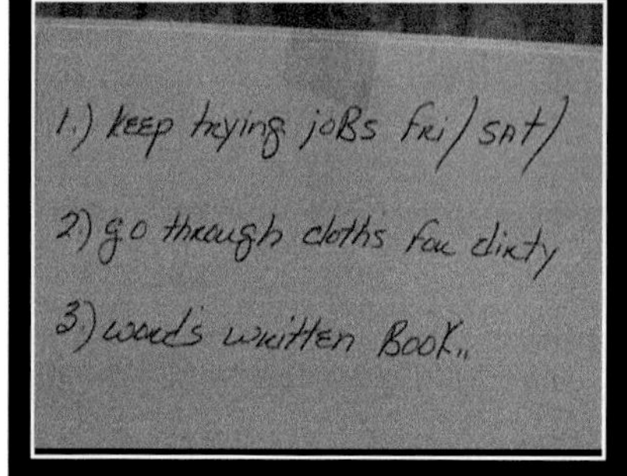

COSTING LESS THAN $100 A MONTH, THE UNIT PROVIDES SHELTER DURING THE DAY, BUT ELLIS HAS TO FIND A PLACE TO STAY AT NIGHT.

NICOLE PEÑA, WITH THE PHOENIX RESCUE MISSION, POINTS OUT THAT STORAGE SHELTERS, HOWEVER, MAY PREVENT PEOPLE FROM GETTING BACK ON THEIR FEET.

ELLIS SAYS HE'S JUST TRYING TO SURVIVE. SOON HE HOPES TO LOCK UP HIS STORAGE UNIT FOR GOOD, NOT JUST FOR THE NIGHT.

Action

Compelling action

Besides a central compelling character, you need compelling action. You could probably produce an acceptable feature story about stamp collecting, but a faster-paced activity such as mixed martial arts (right) or night golf would be more visually exciting.

Try to show your CCC doing something visual or picturesque rather than hanging out. If your CCC is stressed by final exams, however, an appropriate shot might be her taking a break and just gazing out a window.

When shooting action, keep the camera still. Don't pan or zoom. Instead, let the action happen in the frame.

Compelling action

Action in an interview

If relevant, shoot your interviewee doing something while talking to you. This can help put the subject at ease. Remember to put a mic on the person so you can capture spontaneous sound bites. Show the city inspector walking along a row of ramshackle buildings about to be razed or a police officer showing a stash house where illegal immigrants hide for the night (right).

Action in an interview

Action and reaction

Showing both an action and the reaction helps you tell a story visually. At a baseball game, the **action** would be a batter hitting a home run, while the **reaction** would be the joy on the coach's face or a fan tossing his cap in the air. If you were doing a story on an anti-immigration rally, the action would be the protesters marching (right), and the reaction would be mounted police holding the marchers at bay.

It's not always easy—or possible—to get action and reaction shots, especially in sports coverage. One photographer can't shoot a batter hitting a home run at the same instant the coach smiles or a fan tosses his cap in the air. But a quick photographer can shoot the ball sailing over the fence, the runner crossing home plate *and* the crowd cheering. Or you could use a generic shot, such as a fan, mascot or cheerleader, as a transition from one play to the next. You should capture the actual moment, not fake reaction to a specific play. Policies vary, so check with your professor or newsroom.

Action shot (would be accompanied by a reaction shot)

RULE OF THUMB

Make sure the first and last bites of every story are from real people rather than talking heads.

Conflict

Conflict is at the heart of drama. Reuben Frank, a former president of NBC News, instructed network reporters to show drama and conflict in their stories. NBC's Bob Dotson says that any story, no matter what the length, can be broken into four parts:

1. Setting the scene
2. Foreshadowing what's ahead
3. Establishing the conflict
4. Resolving the conflict

Using these guidelines, Al Tompkins of the Poynter Institute dissected the four parts of Dotson's "American Story" about Irena Sendler, a candidate for the 2007 Nobel Peace Prize.

1. Setting the scene: Uniontown, a small town in Kansas
2. Foreshadowing what's ahead: Four local girls want to know more about this Catholic woman from Poland, who saved 2,500 children from Nazi death camps.
3. Establishing the conflict: One conflict involves injustice—the fact that this tiny woman saved so many lives yet is unknown. The second conflict is generational—the assumption that young people no longer care about history versus the reality that these girls from Kansas did care about this 97-year-old woman from Poland.
4. Resolving the conflict: The girls go to Poland to meet Sendler, and then they turn her story into a play back home.

Courtesy of Life in a Jar Foundation (irenasendler.org)

Irena Sendler, a Polish Catholic social worker who saved Jewish children from the Warsaw Ghetto during World War II, meets a Kansas student named Maegan Easter.

Types of conflict

Some types of conflict are **external,** meaning the CCC is in conflict with an outside force:

- Another person (wars, protests, politics, relationships)
- The environment (weather, natural disasters, animals, land)
- Society (values, laws, beliefs)
- Technology

Other types of conflict are **internal,** meaning within the mind or soul of the CCC.

Photo by Kenny Felt, courtesy of Life in a Jar Foundation (irenasendler.org)

Jaime Berndt plays a Jewish mother in "Life in a Jar," the play that Kansas students wrote about Irena Sendler's life.

Fair and balanced treatment

News stories often involve conflicting viewpoints. Be sure to take them all into consideration. But remember that objectivity requires that you don't get involved in the conflict or take sides with either the words you write or the images you shoot.

Surprises

To hook viewers and keep them engaged, build surprises into your story. Surprises come in many forms. They can be stunning visuals, unexpected sounds, memorable sound bites or poetic writing. Or the surprise could be the CCC. Example: An Arizona State University student born with one leg fulfilled a dream by becoming an All-American wrestler.

A surprising twist

In Bob Dotson's "American Story" about Charles Taylor, a Colorado farmhand turned opera singer, the surprise surfaces when we learn that this celebrity is a high school dropout. Music became his salvation, helping him overcome homelessness, alcohol and drugs. Now he sings with the Metropolitan Opera and other major companies.

Grace notes

Simple things, such as a memorable visual or natural sound, can set a great story apart from a good one. Dotson refers to these as "grace notes." At the beginning of his "American Story" about Rex Ziak, Dotson describes trees so old they groan. And, indeed, we hear one of those ancient giants moan. We also see Ziak measure one of the towering cedars with a 38-foot rope, which he sends to a Boston executive who can save the old-growth forest by selling it to the Nature Conservancy.

To compare the girth of the tree with something we're familiar with, Dotson shows the executive circling a car with the same rope Ziak used to measure the tree, allowing the image to tell the story.

BORING	SURPRISING
REPORTER:	**REPORTER:**
AND THEN THE BOSTON EXECUTIVE WALKED AROUND A CAR WITH THE 38-FOOT-LONG ROPE TO GET AN IDEA OF HOW BIG THE TREE IS.	WHAT DID YOU THINK WHEN YOU GOT THIS ROPE IN A BROWN PAPER SACK?
	EXECUTIVE:
	WELL, I WAS VERY SUSPICIOUS BECAUSE I WAS CONCERNED IT COULD BE A BOMB.

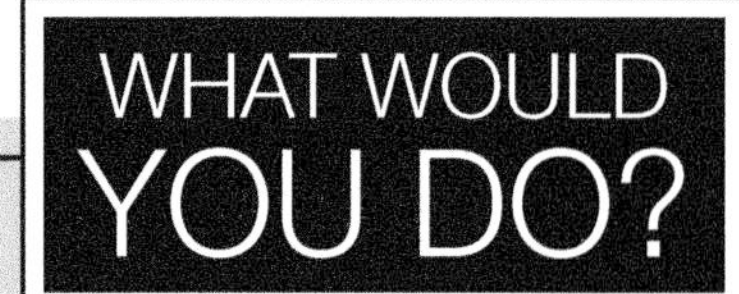

Fascinating facts can add an element of surprise to a story. One way to help viewers understand very large numbers, sizes and amounts is by comparing them with a familiar concept. When French daredevil Michael Fournier attempted a free-fall record from a helium balloon in 2008, he would have plunged 130,000 feet in just 15 minutes. That's three times higher than commercial jets fly.

Let's say you're working on a story about recycling in California. Each resident generates about 6 pounds of garbage a day. That comes to some 240 million pounds a day. Could you compare that huge amount to something your audience will relate to?

Good Audio

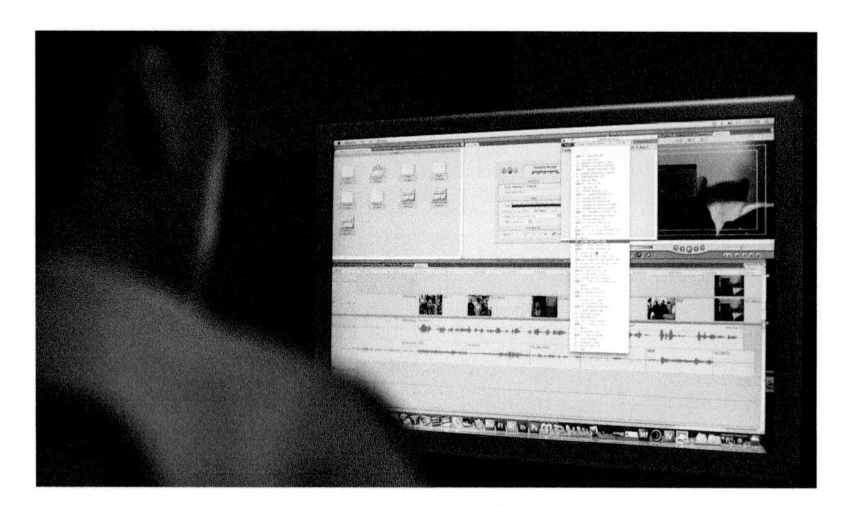

Editing software enables you to integrate video with the reporter's narration, sound bites, natural sound and, if appropriate, music.

We'll discuss audio and video in greater detail in Chapter 6, but here are some key storytelling concepts you should be aware of now. **Sound bites** (TV) and **actualities** (radio) are the broadcast equivalent of direct quotes in print. As a broadcast journalist, you will conduct interviews for background information *and* to obtain bites or actualities to include in your stories. These quotes could be from eyewitnesses, observers, experts or other people knowledgeable about your topic.

Keep it real

Depending on the nature of the story, you might include the voices of at least one official and one ordinary person affected by the story. The ordinary person—a mom, taxpayer or nurse, for example—illustrates the larger theme or trend by speaking from a personal perspective. The official—a sheriff, politician or spokeswoman for the hospital industry, for example—provides the official overview.

Audio complements visuals

Good audio is critical because much of video's power comes from sound. Without it, you might lose your audience. Show the viewer what your CCC is talking about. If he used his wisdom teeth and other recycled parts to build rockabilly bass guitars, include a shot of his choppers. If he lights up when he talks about how he loves to play, also show him plucking the bass guitar.

Silence and natural sound

You don't have to fill every second with words. Where appropriate, allow a second or two of **silence** so viewers can focus on an emotional scene, such as a medic carrying a baby from a crumpled car. If the footage has **natural sound,** let the wailing siren or splashing water play for a half-second or a second without narration. When natural sound is used well, it can transport the listener to the scene.

Music

Music can help the flow of a feature story and enhance a subject such as a parade or rockabilly player, but it shouldn't be used to cover up the lack of sound bites or other shortcomings. Check the policy of your professor or newsroom about using music in a news story.

WORKING WITH MUSIC

MediaStorm (mediastorm.org), a leader in visual storytelling online, offers tips for selecting music:

1. Choose an exceptional piece of music relevant to your subject.
2. Don't play the music for the entire length of your work. Sometimes, dramatic parts are more effective when told quietly.
3. Use music with a strong rhythm, which doesn't necessarily mean a fast tempo. A pronounced beat provides natural edit points.
4. Choose a piece that ends with strong musical phrases.
5. Create an interplay between your narrative and the music. Make the music an integral part of your work, not simply background sound.
6. Learn an instrument. Study music theory. The more you understand, the more adept you become at selecting and editing music.

Pacing

Pacing refers to the tempo and rhythm of a story. Think about one of your favorite songs. A happy song has a fast tempo, while a sad song has a slow tempo. In a similar way, a sad video would be slower paced than an uplifting story. You can speed up the pace with short sentences, quick shot changes and lively music. You can slow down the pace with longer sentences, longer shots, calm music and silence.

Mix it up

Just as your favorite song contains a variety of high and low notes, a compelling video has a variety of sounds. Mix up the **voice track (reporter's narration),** sound bites and natural (nat) sound.

Boring and Predictable

track	10 seconds
sound bite	10 seconds
track	10 seconds
sound bite	10 seconds
track	10 seconds
sound bite	10 seconds
track	10 seconds
sound bite	10 seconds

Mix It Up

track	10 seconds
sound bite	6 seconds
natural sound	1 second
track	5 seconds
silence	1 second
track	7 seconds
natural sound	half a second
sound bite	5 seconds
track	8 seconds

Weave in natural sound

In the script below about old mines, nat sound breaks up the monotony of too much track and helps move the story along.

[PAT KAUTZMAN]	"I thought that was certainly the end of life as I knew it."
[REPORTER]	PAT KAUTZMAN WASN'T ALL THAT WORRIED WHEN HE AND A FRIEND WENT EXPLORING IN AN OLD MINE NEAR YUMA LAST MARCH.
[PAT]	"One of the boards was rusty and couldn't hold my weight . . . and I fell through . . . and that shaft was about 100 feet deep."
[REPORTER]	PAT FELL INTO AN ABANDONED MINE AND LUCKILY LANDED ON A CROSSBEAM ABOUT 20 FEET DOWN . . . BUT AS YOU CAN SEE IN THE PICTURES . . . HE DIDN'T ESCAPE INJURY.

[NAT OF MINE INSPECTOR DIGGING INTO A SHAFT]

[REPORTER]	JERRY TYRA, AN ABANDONED MINE SUPERVISOR HERE IN ARIZONA, IS TIRED OF HEARING STORIES LIKE PAT'S. HE BACKS A NEW BILL IN THE LEGISLATURE.
[JERRY TYRA]	"We could do two things. We can get rid of the old tires and fill up the mines and make them safe."
[REPORTER]	JERRY SAYS IT ISN'T EASY . . . OR CHEAP . . . TO FIND MATERIAL TO FILL UP THE MINES. IN THE PAST YEAR AND A HALF . . . HE SAYS HE HAS FILLED ABOUT 100 . . . LESS THAN 1 PERCENT OF THE MINES.

[NAT OF GAVEL CALLING LEGISLATORS TO ORDER]

[REPORTER]	HOUSE BILL 2290 WOULD ALLOW USED TIRES TO FILL FIVE ABANDONED MINES STATEWIDE . . . A FIVE-YEAR PROGRAM THAT WOULD TEST HOW ENVIRONMENTALLY FRIENDLY THIS OPTION WOULD BE.

[NAT OF DESERT NEAR MINE]

[REPORTER]	THE MAIN SAFETY CONCERN FOR ABANDONED MINES IS JUST HOW EASY THEY ARE TO ACCESS. I'M STANDING ABOUT TWO FEET FROM ONE NOW . . . AND AS YOU CAN HEAR . . . IT'S A PRETTY STEEP DROP.

[NAT OF ROCK DROPPING DOWN MINE TO SHOW HOW DEEP IT IS]

[REPORTER]	WHILE EVEN THIS BILL WON'T HELP FILL EVERY ABANDONED MINE . . . JERRY THINKS EVERY MINE THAT IS FILLED MAKES A DIFFERENCE.
[JERRY]	"You can't fall in a mine if it's full."
	AND PAT HOPES THIS BILL WILL PASS . . . AND MORE MINES WILL BE FILLED UP . . . SO NO ONE ELSE WILL HAVE AN EXPERIENCE LIKE HIS.
[PAT]	"It's an absolute miracle that I'm alive . . . but if the mines were all filled in and there was no way for someone to go in the mine . . . then accidents like this would never happen."

Split sound bites

Another way to prevent monotony is to vary the length of sound bites. You can even split bites into two parts, using the first part as a nat sound and the second part to introduce the person who's speaking.

[REPORTER]	SEVEN THOUSAND FEET UNDERGROUND LIES HOPE FOR THE RESIDENTS OF SUPERIOR.
[LYNN HEGLIE]	"It was one of the largest cities in Pinal County."
[REPORTER]	THIS ONCE-BOOMING MINING TOWN WENT A BIT BUST WHEN THE MAGMA MINE CLOSED IN THE '80S. IT SEEMED AS THOUGH THE TOWN CLOSED WITH IT.
[LYNN]	"With the closing of the mine, the population was almost cut in half."
	LYNN HEGLIE HAS OWNED A SMALL BARBERSHOP IN SUPERIOR FOR THE LAST 15 YEARS. HE SAYS HE ENJOYS THE SAFETY AND SENSE OF COMMUNITY LIVING IN A SMALL TOWN . . . BUT HE NEEDS MORE BUSINESS. HE'S HOPING THAT PLANS TO POSSIBLY REOPEN THE MINE WILL HELP.

Let content determine pacing

This style of writing quick, choppy lines followed by longer lines doesn't work for every story. Use the pacing that suits your story.

Vary the track length

In addition to nat sound and the length of sound bites, the length of the track affects pacing. In the script below about a woman who raises llamas, two-second tracks and quick nat sound get us into the story quickly before revealing the surprise. The story also ends with quick tracks and nat sound.

[REPORTER]	BARBARA PEACOCK KEEPS SOMETHING SPECIAL IN HER BACKYARD.
[LLAMA NATS]	
[BARBARA PEACOCK]	"Come on, big guy."
[REPORTER]	AND IT'S NOT WHAT YOU'D EXPECT TO FIND.
[BARBARA]	"This is Navajo. Here's Hopi . . . Apache . . . Lakota."
[REPORTER]	SHE TAKES CARE OF LLAMAS.
[NAT OF LAUGHING]	
[BARBARA]	"They're wonderful, quiet animals that have a special spirit."
[REPORTER]	BARBARA IS THE PRESIDENT OF THE ARIZONA LLAMA RESCUE . . . TAKING IN LLAMAS THAT PEOPLE HAVE LEFT BEHIND.
[BARBARA]	"They just don't want them anymore. They bought them when they were cute babies . . . and they're not cute anymore . . . and that's probably the main reasons right there."
[REPORTER]	AT ONE POINT BARBARA SAID SHE HAD UP TO 20 LLAMAS IN HER BACKYARD . . . INCLUDING ONES LIKE SINBAD RIGHT HERE . . . CAUSING CURIOUS ONLOOKERS TO STOP AND TAKE A LOOK ACROSS THE FENCE.
[BARBARA]	"All the families with the strollers and on bicycles . . . they'd line up against the fence . . . and of course I'd come out and give them a little talk about llamas and introduce them to everybody."
[REPORTER]	HER HUSBAND DONALD SAYS THE LLAMAS ARE LIKE HIS WIFE'S CHILDREN.
[DONALD PEACOCK]	"She trains pretty good . . . they train her pretty good too. I've got a lot of patience . . . but I don't think I have patience in that area so much."
[REPORTER]	BARBARA SAYS HER HOPE IS TO MAKE SURE EVERY LLAMA FINDS A GOOD HOME.
[BARBARA]	"They're pretty, and they keep the grass mowed. So what if they're just yard ornaments. That's all mine are."
[REPORTER]	YARD ORNAMENTS . . . WHICH BARBARA SAID HAVE MADE HER LIFE . . .
[LLAMA NATS]	
[REPORTER]	RICHER.

Video Sequences

Mini-scenes

An effective visual story is more than a bunch of shots strung together. To tell a story visually, you need to break down the action into multiple **sequences**, or a series of mini-scenes within the larger story. A sequence can have as few as two shots, but typically it has three or four—or sometimes more. Think of these sequences as your story's building blocks.

A sequence of shots from different perspectives gives the viewer a better understanding of what's going on and also breaks up the monotony of one long shot. The BBC, for example, recommends getting five shots, although you don't need to use all of them in the final edit. In a story about a chef, you could shoot (1) a tight shot of his hands, (2) a tight shot of his face, (3) a wide shot of his face and action together, (4) an over-the-shoulder shot and (5) a shot from a creative angle (side, low, high). Another rule of thumb is to shoot 25 percent wide shots, 50 percent medium shots and 25 percent tight shots.

RULE OF THUMB

Look for *both* a strong opening shot or sequence *and* a strong closing shot or sequence.

Wide shot (WS)

Also called an establishing shot, a **wide shot** establishes the relationship of the people in the frame to the location or setting. Use a WS at or near the beginning of your piece to orient the viewer. Avoid static shots of buildings, doorways and signs. If you must use them, show people doing something, such as walking into a restaurant.

Medium shot (MS)

By closing in on your subject, a **medium shot** provides visual focus and eliminates distractions. The closer you get, the more details you capture.

Tight shot (TS)

Also called a close-up, a **tight shot** provides the most detail by zeroing in on a certain feature of a person or object. A TS of a person's teary eyes or tapping feet conveys emotion. Because details fill the screen, TSs show up well on laptops and mobile devices. On these small screens, it's easier to see the details of a person's eyes in a TS than the details of the Grand Canyon in a WS.

High camera angle

Instead of shooting everything at eye height, add variety by moving the camera to a higher position and shooting down. Be aware that high-angle shots put the subject in a weak or powerless position. You can use a high angle to lower the horizon and to avoid distracting elements in the foreground. High angles work well for shooting activities where the action takes place in depth, such as sporting events or a line of traffic.

Low camera angle

Lowering your camera and tilting it upward makes the subject look taller and conveys a feeling of power or superiority. It can also create a sense of awe or excitement.

Broadcast Formats

Taking shape

Radio and TV stories can be presented in various ways. The assignments editor sends the reporter out to cover a story, but the producer determines the format the story takes during a rundown/lineup meeting with the news director and other managers.

The format depends on the news flow of the day. On a slow summer day, for example, there might not be much news. The legislature isn't in session. School is out. A story might become a full **package** in July that would be only a **VO** in January. Each day is different, which makes the news business so exciting.

Reporters have to be ready to respond to the producer, what the day is like and the material available. That means reporters must be ready to shape their stories in any format as needed.

Each newsroom has its own slang to refer to various formats. The following terms are common.

Voicer

This traditional radio story features reporter narration but no **actualities,** or quotes from sources. You'd use a voicer for a city council meeting or similar events that don't have strong audio. This type of radio story is fading in use. Voicers used to run :35 to :40, but they can now be as short as :20.

A MEDICAL HELICOPTER THAT CRASHED ON THE TEXAS COAST TONIGHT KILLED ALL THREE CREW MEMBERS ABOARD. IT HAD JUST DROPPED OFF A PATIENT IN HOUSTON WHEN IT RAN INTO BAD WEATHER. FEDERAL SAFETY INVESTIGATORS SAID THE HELICOPTER WAS TRYING TO LAND AT A NEARBY AIRPORT WHEN IT CRASHED AT 9:30 P.M.

Reader

The reader is the basic building block for more complex TV stories. An anchor (not a reporter) reads the news story in the studio. That's it. No sound bites. No video. The reader works well for short subjects that don't lend themselves to video, such as a city council vote or stock market update.

THE LALAPALOOZA CITY COUNCIL JUST APPROVED A PLAN TO BUILD A 5,000-SEAT FOOTBALL STADIUM AT CENTRAL HIGH SCHOOL. BONDS WILL BE ISSUED TO PAY FOR THE $5 MILLION FACILITY.

VO (Voice-over)

A TV anchor reads news copy while video footage (but no sound bites) rolls. Sometimes the reporter or producer doesn't have a lot of information but finds the story newsworthy. The key is video: If there's no video, then it's just a reader. VOs often tease forward to more complete stories, such as "We'll have more on that at noon."

YESTERDAY, WE TOLD YOU ABOUT THE BRUTAL MURDER OF RABBI MOSHE GOLDSTEIN ON THE CITY'S SOUTH SIDE. TODAY, POLICE ARE STILL LOOKING FOR A SUSPECT. THE VIOLENT STRUGGLE THAT TOOK PLACE DURING THE SLAYING MIGHT HAVE INJURED THE SUSPECT, ESPECIALLY IN THE ARMS, UPPER BODY AND HEAD. THE SHERIFF IS ASKING THE PUBLIC TO LOOK FOR RECENT INJURIES ON EVERYONE THEY ENCOUNTER.

VO/SOT (Voice-over/Sound on tape)

Add a sound bite to a VO, and you have a VO/SOT (pronounced voh-saht). Another VO could follow the SOT to form a VO/SOT/VO. Although most stations now capture video digitally rather than on tape, the shorthand SOT has stuck.

VO/SOTs are used for stories where reporters or producers have a decent amount of information and a good sound bite but not enough material for a long story (package). Like VOs, they can also be used for scaled-down versions of older stories.

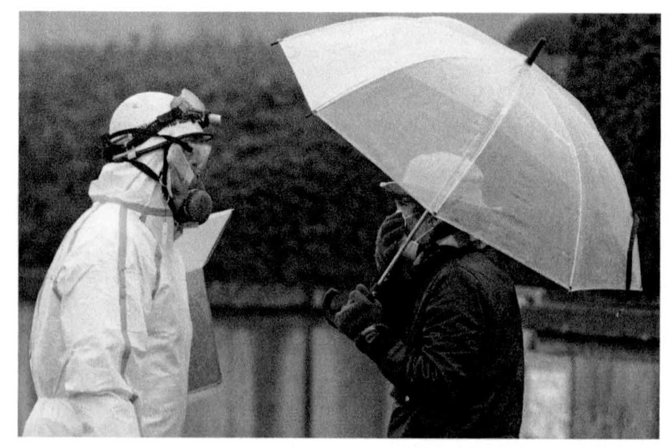

THE BACKERS OF LEGISLATION TO BUILD A SECOND NUCLEAR POWER PLANT ARE PUSHING FORWARD WITH THE IDEA. THE GOVERNOR AND NUMEROUS SENATORS SUPPORT THE PROPOSAL, DESPITE THE NUCLEAR CRISIS IN JAPAN.

"This nuclear power plant will be one hundred times safer than the one damaged in the wake of Japan's earthquake and tsunami."

POS (Person on the Street)

The assignment desk might send a reporter out to get a **POS,** a series of sound bites from people on the street or at a mall or some other place. Let's say there's a story about teacher layoffs, tax increases or another controversial issue. The reporter asks eight to 10 people for their opinions, then strings together the best three or four bites.

BBC Radio produces vox pops (short for "vox populi," or "voice of the people"). These are short (:20 to :40) montages of voices and opinions recorded on location and then woven together.

Wrap or package

Often introduced by the anchor, the **wrap** (for radio) or **package** (for TV) is the big story. It's the staple of broadcast news. The reporter's prerecorded narration, known as track, describes what is going on. The track is peppered with several sound bites.

The reporter often appears on screen at the beginning or end of a package—or sometimes as a transition between scenes. Use this format when the reporter has time to go out in the field and gather video footage, audio interviews and natural sound.

EXPERIENCING NATURE IS SOMETHING MANY ARIZONANS LOVE TO DO. BUT BEING ABLE TO EXPLORE THE DESERT HASN'T BEEN EASY FOR THE THOUSANDS OF PEOPLE IN

ARIZONA LIVING WITH A DISABILITY. THE NEW BAJADA NATURE TRAIL IN SCOTTS-DALE MIGHT CHANGE ALL THAT. IT'S THE FIRST HIKING TRAIL IN THE VAL-LEY THAT'S COMPLETELY WHEELCHAIR ACCESSIBLE.

[REPORTER STANDUP] DENISE LABREQUE, WHO USES A WHEELCHAIR, SAYS SHE CAN'T WAIT TO HIT THE TRAILS.

"I'll come up maybe on a lunch hour and bring a sack lunch and enjoy the squirrels and the hawks and all the other beautiful things that Arizona has to offer."

"It's always been a place that people with any type of challenge couldn't really access, so we set out to build a completely accessible, barrier-free experience in the preserve."

AND WITH COOLER TEMPERATURES ON THE HORIZON, THE TRAIL IS SURE TO ATTRACT ALL TYPES OF NEW VISITORS.

TABLE **2.1** **Components of Broadcast Stories**

The producer considers the day's news flow and the material available when deciding the format of each story.

	Anchor in studio	Reporter in field	Actualities (radio)	Sound bites (TV)	Video (TV)	Usual length
Voicer (radio/TV)	👍	👍				:20 to :40
Reader (radio/TV)	👍					:10 to :40
Voice-Over (VO) (TV)	👍				👍	:20 to :45 or even 1:00
Voice-Over/Sound on Tape (VO/SOT) (TV)	👍	👍		👍	👍	:40 to 1:15
Wrap (radio) Package (TV)	👍	👍	👍	👍	👍	Up to 1:30
Person on the Street (POS) (radio/TV)			👍	👍	👍	:20 to :40

Standout Standups

Why do a standup?

Most reporters like to appear in their stories, but setting vanity aside, a **standup** can add important information if done correctly. A standup establishes a connection between the reporter and the people and places in the news. A strong standup can't be an afterthought. It must fit the context of the rest of your story, so consider these questions as you plan your story: Where will it be used? What will come before and after your standup?

Make sure you have a good reason to use a standup:

- ☐ **To put the viewer on the scene with the reporter.**
- ☐ **To make a transition between themes, places or people.**
- ☐ **To deliver visual information that advances the story. A reporter wearing a parka and shivering with cold doesn't have to use words to describe the conditions in which a Marine unit is serving in Afghanistan.**
- ☐ **To add perspective, analysis or context.**
- ☐ **To illustrate a point for which you have no footage.**
- ☐ **To demonstrate something that is clearer to explain by showing than by telling, such as demonstrating a new bicycle accessory or squeezing water out of a sponge to illustrate how saturated ground sinks.**
- ☐ **To promote an online piece or a more complete broadcast story that will run later. These teases show just enough to grab the viewer's attention without giving the entire story away.**

Not every story needs a standup. It can sometimes be intrusive. A profile of a football star killed in Afghanistan, for example, is dramatic enough to stand on its own. The appearance of a reporter in the middle of the piece would interrupt the focus on the central compelling character.

When to do a standup

It you have a photographer, talk before you leave the newsroom to determine when to do the standup. This is both a visual and an editorial decision.

It can be difficult to know in the middle of your reporting day exactly how you want to begin or end your piece. If you start or end with a standup, you've made that critical decision long before sitting down to listen to your sound bites or log your strongest video. The safest standup, then, is the **bridge,** which links one part of the story to another. If you use a bridge standup, you're free to begin and/or end a story live.

Even if you don't know exactly how your story will play out, by the middle of the day you probably have a key fact or two, even background information for the body of your copy. This information might be just what you need for a standup because it's unlikely to change before your story goes on-air or online.

When trying to figure out when and where to shoot a standup, consider the video you already have or expect to get. Where are the holes? What's the key piece of information you need to include but don't have any video to show it? Perhaps that material can be relayed in a standup.

Where to do a standup

If your shooting schedule allows, shoot the standup last, after you finish your interviews—but think carefully about the location.

The best place to do a standup is on location. If that's impossible, then record it at the studio. Avoid standing in a nondescript place, such as against a brick wall.

How to do a standup

Dress for the situation. A reporter standing in front of the White House will wear business attire, while a journalist reporting about a blizzard will be wrapped in cold-weather gear.

Jot down notes about what you want to say, but try not to memorize or read them. Instead, relax, look straight at the camera and talk to your viewers. Use proper grammar. Enunciate your words. Be careful not to bob your head as you speak.

Let the video roll :05 before **and** after the standup. That will give you flexibility when editing.

Keep shooting until you nail it. Then repeat for good measure.

What to include

Joe Little, a multimedia journalist at KGTV (ABC) in San Diego, stresses creativity. "If you're going to slap a standup onto a package just to see your mug on there, please stop. If you're going to do a standup, make it creative; do something, show me something or at least make it look interesting."

Do something that serves a purpose. Hold up a scorpion. Go out on a small boat like the ones smugglers use. Ride in a salt truck to show how road crews are contending with the winter's worst blizzard.

If you use a prop, it must make sense to viewers. Recently a student shot a story about firefighters in Phoenix. In his standup he wore a firefighter's outfit, but he didn't say anything about the gear.

- A bad standup in firefighter's gear: *Firefighters are finding their job more difficult in today's extreme heat.*
- A better standup in firefighter's gear: *With temperatures approaching 105 degrees, putting on 60 pounds of equipment only makes the firefighter's job more difficult.*

In a standup, student reporter Amber Dixon sniffs a carton of outdated milk to show how special needs kids learn to detect rotten food.

Don't ride the elephant

Get involved. Use props. Engage the viewer, but don't "ride the elephant." In other words, don't do something silly in a feature standup today that might make you less trustworthy tomorrow when you're covering a lead news story.

TABLE **2.2** **Planning a Standup**

Bridge standups give you the most flexibility, leaving you free to open and/or close the story live, with video or with a sound bite.

Type of Standup	Purpose
Open (rare)	Sets the stage for what follows
	Provides background information
	Hooks the viewer
Bridge (common)	Gives additional information
	Explains something
	Acts as a transition
Close	Wraps up the story
	Makes a prediction

WHAT WOULD YOU DO?

You're doing a standup about the increasing number of children who drown in swimming pools each summer. Would you wear a bathing suit? If not, why not? If so, how does it enhance the standup? Would a swimsuit be appropriate for a man but not a woman? Would it be OK if you're submerged in the water?

Putting It All Together

This 1:19 package illustrates many of the elements of good visual storytelling—surprise, strong visuals, a creative standup going from light to dark and natural sound that helps with the pacing.

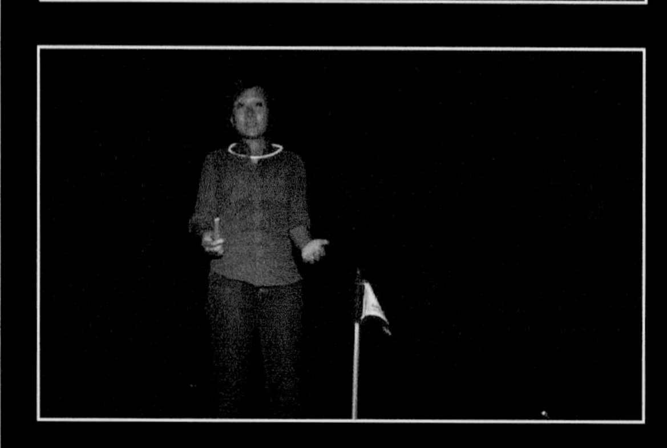

[ANCHOR]	WE ALL KNOW THAT ARIZONA IS WHERE GOLFERS LOVE TO HIT THE GREENS . . . BUT AS MAXINE PARK SHOWS US . . . DAYLIGHT MAY BE AN UNNECESSARY ADDITION TO THE GAME.
[NAT OF GOLFER HITTING BALL]	
[GOLFER]	"Nice ball."
[REPORTER]	AS THE SUN GOES DOWN HERE IN THE VALLEY . . .
[NAT OF GOLF CARTS]	
	THE LIGHTS ON THE GOLF COURSE TURN ON.
[NAT OF GOLF BALL DROPPING INTO CUP]	
	AND THE GOLFERS . . .
[NAT OF THREE GOLFERS HITTING BALLS]	
	COME OUT TO PLAY.
[GOLFER DAVE]	"Oh . . . it's way better at night."
[REPORTER]	NIGHT GOLF IS AN ARIZONA SPORT.
[GOLFER DAVE]	"This isn't serious at all . . . you know. We're just out here to have fun."
[NAT OF THREE GOLFERS HITTING BALLS]	
[REPORTER]	HELD ALMOST ALL YEAR-ROUND . . . WELL . . . BECAUSE IT'S THE DESERT.
[GOLFER DAVE]	"I mean it's 106 in the day . . . you know. At night it's probably 90 right now."
[REPORTER STANDUP]	THE GOLF COURSE LIGHTS THE ENTIRE PLACE WITH THESE GLOW STICKS . . . AND THEY PUT THEM ALONG EVERY FAIRWAY AND IN EVERY HOLE. AND FOR 39 BUCKS . . . EACH GOLFER GETS THEIR OWN GLOW-IN-THE-DARK BALL. BUT LIKE IN THE DAYTIME . . . THE NAME OF THE GAME IS STILL GETTING THE BALL IN THE CUP.
[MANAGER]	"It's fun. It's safe. The only thing you have to worry about is losing your glow ball."
[REPORTER]	MANAGERS SAY IT'S ALL ABOUT HAVING A GOOD TIME.
[MANAGER]	"It's more of a casual, relaxed thing. People don't have to worry so much about their golf swing in the dark, really. Nobody can see it anyways."
[FEMALE GOLFER]	"You know, you play every day . . . and you can see the pins. You can see your distances . . . and this is just totally different."
[REPORTER]	AND THIS GOLFER SAYS HE JUST CAN'T GET ENOUGH OF IT.
[GOLFER DAVE]	"Yeah, I'll be out here next month . . . without a doubt."
[REPORTER]	A NEW TWIST TO A CENTURIES-OLD GAME.
[NAT OF GOLF BALL DROPPING INTO CUP]	
[REPORTER]	IN PHOENIX . . . MAXINE PARK . . . CRONKITE NEWS.

REPORTING

CHAPTER OUTLINE

CHAPTER 3

"In seeking truth you have to get both sides of a story."

—WALTER CRONKITE

In Search of the Source

Up until now, we've discussed the new media landscape and the core concepts of good storytelling. Now it's time to roll up your sleeves and get to work. It's time to report. Once an editor has given you an assignment or approved your story idea, where do you begin? Being a good reporter often means becoming an expert on a new topic in a very short amount of time, so it's important to know how to get started. In this first of two chapters on reporting we will discuss how to tackle several kinds of stories, but each begins with research and sources.

When it comes time to get the story, you can use your cell phone, send an email or put a query out on Twitter. In any case, what you're doing is looking for a source. On deadline, every second counts, so the person you choose to call, text or tweet matters. You need the basic facts, but you also need to put the story in context for your audience. Where do you turn for depth and perspective? You turn to a source.

What is a source?

A source is where the information comes from (Figure 3.1). Typically, we're talking about people. The mayor. The witness to a crime. A health care worker. And yes, even an anonymous source. But sources of information can also be documents, videos, statistics and more. We'll talk about that a little later. The majority of human sources fall into a handful of groups, each with their own pros and cons.

How do you find a source on deadline?

A few years ago in the KPHO-TV (CBS) newsroom in Phoenix, some reporters used to joke about a source they had that was available 24/7. They were talking about Google. Once you have your assignment, yes, the Internet is a great place to start. But when chasing a story, you should quickly cast a wide net.

Getting (at least) both sides of the story

When you're working hard to track down a story, it's easy to get excited if anyone calls you back at all. But you still need to make sure that you've got the whole story. As veteran news director Scott Libin wrote for the Poynter Institute, "It's hard to think of a single important issue journalists cover that has only two sides. We just tend to stop looking after that."

FIGURE **3.1** **Consider the Source**

When deciding which direction to turn in your search for a source, consider the pros and cons.

SOURCE	PROS	CONS
Politicians: The mayor, governor, city council member, school board representative.	Availability; accountable to audience; well versed in issues; sometimes willing to speak off the record.	Media savvy; occasionally looking for personal gain from media attention; skilled at avoiding your questions.
Officials: Agency or department heads; spokespeople for civic organizations and interest groups.	Easy to find; often available to talk; good source of background.	Dry interviews; possibly evasive; not emotionally involved; not conversational.
Private companies and corporations: Public relations personnel; community outreach staff; marketing and advertising staff.	Many look for opportunities for exposure; will be very responsive if story is viewed as positive.	Under no obligation to participate; can be slow to respond if story viewed as negative; records may not be public.
Nonprofits: Advocacy groups, clubs, community organizations.	Rely on donations so welcome exposure; good background information; personal and emotional stories; can put you in touch with people directly affected by issue.	Often push an agenda; need to balance their bias with alternate viewpoints; smaller and less well-funded groups may be slow to respond to queries.
Victims, witnesses: At the scene of events; later, locate through public records and your reporting.	Directly affected by issue; provide human touch to story; often compelling interviews.	May be reluctant to talk or nervous; may act as if they know more than they do.

Libin says that journalists must keep probing and consider other perspectives. "Sometimes the best alternative is the third or fourth or 14th," he says. (Source: Scott Libin, "Leading Beyond 'Both Sides,'" Poynter.org, Jan. 24, 2005. © Copyright 2005 The Poynter Institute. Reprinted with permission.)

Don't let early success in tracking down sources keep you from pursuing the story further.

Whom do you interview?

Even when researching the simplest spot news story, you can generate a long list of possible sources (Figure 3.2). But in the typical 1 minute and 30 second television news story, you rarely have time for more than two or three sources on camera, so both the deadline and the length of the story force you to make some hard choices.

FIGURE **3.2** The Continuum of Sources

Let's say a fire breaks out in a residence hall on campus, and the assignment is yours. Firefighters have evacuated the building, and some students are being taken to the hospital.

There are 11 possible sources you may have access to within the first hour or two of the event. Some you'll find at the scene, including the fire department, police, students and other witnesses. For others—say, the university spokesperson, fire marshal or building inspector—you might have to use the phone. To get interviews at the hospital, you may have to go there. You'll need to decide if you have time for that.

POSSIBLE

Fire department	Provides details of the fire and response as well as preliminary reports of injuries.
Police department	Comments on building evacuations and street closures.
University spokesperson	Explains how many students live in residence hall and how school is responding.
Students from residence hall	Eyewitness accounts from those inside.
Student witnesses outside residence hall	Eyewitness accounts of what fire and evacuation looked like from outside.
Residence hall adviser	Confirmation of student response and effectiveness of evacuation plan.
Fire marshal	Information on investigation into how the fire may have started.
Hospital spokesperson	Confirmation of number of injuries and updates on their conditions.
Injured students	First-person accounts of fire and aftermath.
Building inspector	Background on residence hall's safety record, code violations and recent inspection history.
Parents of students	Concerns they have had about their children's safety on campus; background on students who lived in residence hall; further information on injured students.

Since you need to get the story together as soon as possible and you only have a minute and 30 seconds in which to tell it, you can't possibly interview all of your potential sources. Which sources are the most important? Let's whittle them down.

NECESSARY

Fire department	Expertise is important.
Students from residence hall	Human interest angle of those affected may be most important at first.
Hospital spokesperson	Basic information on number of students hurt, and their condition is crucial to your story.
Injured students	Important to know how students were injured and what their prospects are for recovery.
Parents of students	Will express satisfaction or dissatisfaction with the safety of the residence hall, which may reveal criticism or support of the university.

Now you have narrowed your top sources down to five, but you should still find time to contact at least three additional sources of background information.

ADDITIONAL

University spokesperson	Important source for information on where and how students are being housed and where responsibility lies for what happened.
Building inspector	Background information on the residence hall's inspection and safety history as well as access to records.
Fire marshal	May be able to provide details on how the fire started.

Casting a wide net for sources

SEARCH ENGINES
Great first stop, but stay focused, and don't be led astray by random returns. Look for articles on your subject that could provide background, context or other ideas.

GOVERNMENT WEBSITES
Look for a department or agency that might work with your topic area or play a role in this story.
Is it environmental, judicial or health related?
Check relevant agencies for information and contacts.

VOICES *from the* Newsroom

Deciding whom to interview

Joann Byrd, former ombudsman
Former Washington Post, Washington D.C.

Talking to the usual suspects all the time can make stories predictable and flat. Look for sources who might add a new perspective by asking yourself these questions:

- Who is most directly involved in this story? Who is the central character?
- Who is most affected by what is happening in this story?
- Who is in conflict in this story?
- Who might have more information about this story?
- Who could help me find the right person to speak to for this story?

Evaluate your choices by asking yourself:

- How does this source know what he or she knows? (Is this person in a position to know these things, either personally or professionally?) How can I confirm this information through other sources, through documents?
- How representative is my source's point of view? Is this just one person who complains loudly about the landlord because he or she has a personal problem? Or is this the most articulate voice speaking for an entire group that has serious, legitimate problems?
- Has this source been reliable and credible in the past? Am I only using this source because it's the easy way to go? Because I know I'll get a good sound bite?
- What is the source's motive for providing information? Is this person trying to make himself look good or to make his boss look bad? Why is he talking to me in the first place? Am I being manipulated or spun by this source?

Source: Joann Byrd, "A Guide for Evaluating Sources," Poynter.org, Aug. 13, 2002.

NEWSROOM CONTACTS

Most newsrooms use a centralized computer system that also has a Rolodex function for tracking contacts. This is a valuable tool to find relevant sources other reporters may have talked to before.

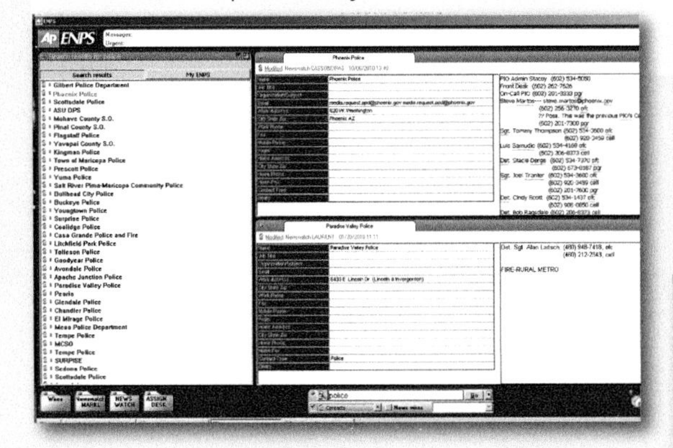

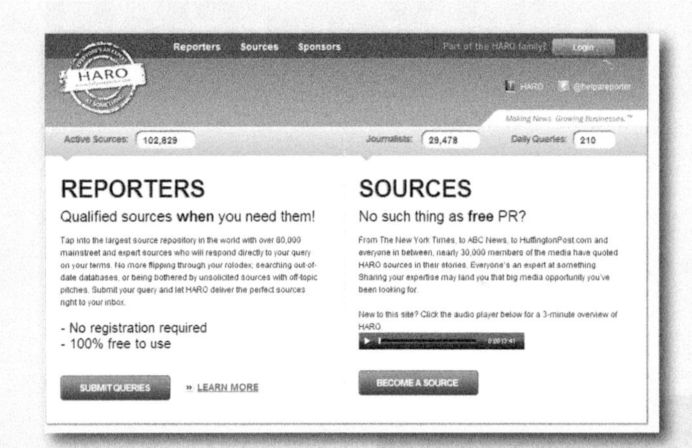

LOCATION SEARCH

Map the address of the location you're reporting about, and see what people or businesses are nearby. You may be able to contact a neighbor for some initial information about what's going on and get a suggestion for where to turn next.

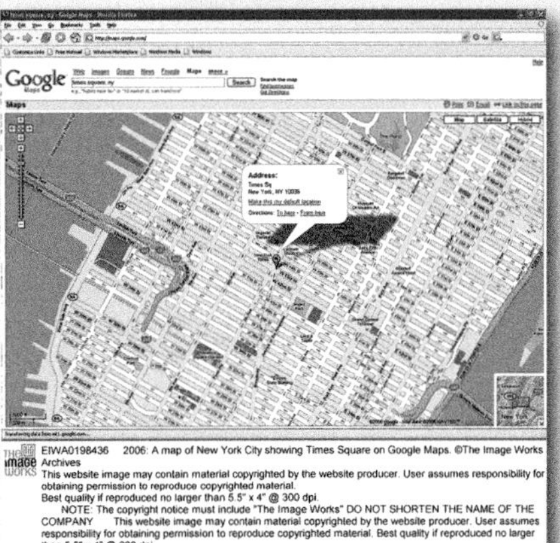

SOCIAL NETWORKING

Using Twitter, Facebook and more, you can let people know what you're working on, and your source may come to you. HARO (Help a Reporter Out) is a unique site designed to match reporters with experts in certain fields.

WHAT WOULD YOU DO?

Your state government is in a financial crisis. The legislature has proposed cuts in state health insurance coverage for children below the poverty level. Now you're hearing from one lawmaker that the issue may go to the full house this afternoon.

a) Do you check the state website for the latest on the legislative calendar?

b) Do you put a call in to the office of the Speaker of the House?

c) Do you grab your bag and head down to the capitol?

Answer:

While *a* and *b* may be worth five minutes of your time, it is worth jumping in your car and heading to the capitol building. Even if the legislation isn't being voted on right away, it's a controversial story, and the only way you're going to stay one step ahead of the competition is to be where the action is taking place.

Build Your Stable of Sources

Ultimately, your best sources will be those you've built over years of reporting. Having strong sources whom you trust and who trust you will also translate into job security. These people will not only tip you off to new stories but will also serve as resources for assignments that come your way.

"The reporter with sources will always be in demand and will get the attention of the competition—and the public officials and whistle-blowers as opposed to the general assignment reporter who comes and goes and quite often is looking to become a full-time anchor," says Bruce Johnson, an anchor and a reporter with WUSA-TV (CBS) in Washington, D.C. He has made a career of being plugged in with sources in Washington, D.C. But, Johnson will be the first to tell you there is no magic bullet when it comes to building a network of sources. It takes hard work.

Freelance radio reporter Rene Gutel began building her own working group of sources years ago. Now, when she's looking for a new idea for a story, she'll tap her listserv members and ask what's on their minds.

A common mistake young reporters make is staying too close to the computer. Veterans will tell you to get out the door and meet people. Get up early and swing by the police station, courthouse or coffee shop on your way to work. Introduce yourself to new people, and always ask for a business card. Even today, those old school methods make sense, especially in small markets. Nick Lough, a reporter for WAFF-TV (ABC) in Huntsville, Ala., still finds time to make face-to-face beat checks at the county courthouse, police station and fire station. "These beat checks are essential to find out what's going on," says Lough. "If we were to just make phone calls, we don't always get everything, and having a personal relationship with these people helps with getting exclusive stories and information down the road."

And don't forget to ask how someone can be reached after hours. Most likely he'll be willing to give you that cell phone number or even home phone number. You might use it right away to confirm a fact or clarify a point, but it could also come in handy years later when you have a story developing at night or on a weekend.

Reporter Etiquette

Under tight deadline pressure it's easy to get short with people, especially if you're searching for that first source who will interview with you and appear on camera. But the tone you use and how you pitch your request are big factors in whether you'll succeed.

Pause for a moment before approaching a source for an interview, and think about what you're going to do. Be confident; too often young reporters sound unsure of what they're looking for and timid, especially on the phone. Taking that minute to prepare for the call will improve your chances. Also, imagine how the conversation might progress. If the source says, "Sure, I'll talk with you," do you know where you'll propose to meet? If the source says "No, I don't have the time today," are you prepared for a second try? Refer to Chapter 5, "Interviewing," for more tips on persuading reluctant sources to talk.

TABLE **3.1** **The Etiquette of Reporting**

DO	DON'T
• Be polite and respectful	• Be abrasive
• Know what you're asking for	• Be unprepared for the conversation
• Speak with confidence	• Appear scared
• Use a firm handshake	• Accept any food or gifts
• Look people in the eye	• Leave if the room is messy
• Thank sources for their time	• Waste someone's time

When approaching sources, always show respect, even if the contact appears evasive or antagonistic. You are the professional, and how you work with sources speaks to your credibility.

VOICES *from the* Newsroom

Building your beat

Bruce Johnson, anchor and reporter
WUSA-TV (CBS), Washington, D.C.

Broadcast journalist Bruce Johnson has been building sources in our nation's capital for more than 30 years. He's built a beat from scratch, breaking stories about city government and more by working his network.

Thinking back to the beginning of your career, when did you realize the importance of building strong contacts?

I was lucky to get my start at WCPO-TV, the CBS affiliate in Cincinnati. The news director was also the anchorman at 6 and 11. Al Schottelkotte was an old school news veteran who cut his teeth as a copy boy at the Cincinnati newspapers. He didn't have a college degree but learned from the pros and in turn passed it on to newcomers like me. Even before you cultivated sources, he said, you had to know your town, its history, its issues, its conflicts, its people.

I just made sure that when assigned to city hall, fire, police or the neighborhoods, I knew my stuff and didn't come across as immature, unsure or afraid. Eventually, I gained trust and started breaking stories. My first was that the basketball coach at the University of Cincinnati had been fired. I used my frat brothers who were the stars on the team as sources. My second story was the new archbishop of Cincinnati. I used my contacts from my days in the seminary to break this story. I later used sources to report that the vice mayor had been padding his payroll and that the police chief was demanding kickbacks from off-duty officers on private security details.

After four years in Cincinnati, I came to D.C. and developed new contacts in very much the same way. I was relentless, hard but fair, and I could be trusted to protect my sources—most of whom had vendettas against the people they were dropping dimes on—but my job was not to be judge and jury, just to ask, "Is it true? Can it be documented? Is it something the public needed to know?"

Has your style of building relationships changed over your career?

It has gotten easier. Most people here know what I do, and they choose to talk to me or some other veteran. I try not to sweat the story that I lose to someone else, but I still want to break every major story. There is nothing better than beginning a story with "Nine News Now has learned . . ." or "We have this exclusive report. . . ." I want every story to be of deep interest and not just filler material, as most have become.

How do you keep those relationships strong?

You have to stay visible. If you start to look like a full-time anchor or disappear from the air for long periods of time, the public forgets you. If your story has a follow-up at 11 that night, you should stay and do it. Don't turn your exclusive over to someone else. Also stay in touch with your contacts through phone calls and emails, just to chat and ask, "What's up?" Sometimes they have stories they don't even realize—or have forgotten about. I don't take my sources to lunch or dinner unless it's necessary or they bring it up. I'm careful about having drinks with them. I never visit their families. I'm not looking to become close friends with sources. Never accept or give gifts. Sexual relations are totally against the rules.

Do your sources regularly appear in your stories, or do you rely on them more for information?

Yes to both.

Have you ever been burned by a source?

Yes—but only once or twice on the air—meaning I've been lied to but realized it before putting the bad info in a report. And when I realized it was a mistake on my part, I made the correction on air.

For a young reporter, what's the key to building a strong stable of sources? Where would you begin?

Start with your beat if you have one. Put in the time. Be visible. Stay late. Let your curiosity and smarts be your calling card, not your looks or salesmanship.

Your beat seems to be the D.C. government. How do you report on potentially contentious issues there while still maintaining strong relationships?

I ask people, "Would you rather have the public hear the bad information from me—someone you trust—or someone you barely know?" People also know chances are I'll be around tomorrow, and that means I'm going to try and get their message—their story—right.

Do you have a system to ensure you're up to speed on the latest going on within the government?

I read everything—newspapers, including small neighborhood papers, and all online dispatches, including the good blogs. I watch the competition—TV and radio.

What's in Your Bag?

You may be paid to work an eight-hour shift, but veterans will tell you the news business is 24/7. Whether you prefer toting a backpack, briefcase or bag, certain indispensable items will help you get the job done day and night.

Most reporters say their smart phone is without question the most important tool today, combining phone, email, Internet and other useful applications like a calculator or map. "I do research on it, have written scripts and blogs on it. I email myself production notes to refer to from the field, and obviously the phone function is important," says NBC News correspondent Mara Schiavocampo.

But for all the high-tech gadgets you can use to stock your office on the go, please don't forget your pens. "You can get away with writing on your hands or having a photographer make calls for you, but without a working pen, you can't write interview notes or a script for your live shot," says Morgan Loew, a reporter with KPHO-TV (CBS) in Phoenix.

A REPORTER'S TRAVEL BAG

Must-Haves

- ☐ Media credentials
- ☐ Business cards
- ☐ Smart phone
- ☐ Pens
- ☐ Pencil (works better than pen in bad weather)
- ☐ Paper (white—for camera white balance)
- ☐ IFB (earpiece)
- ☐ Passport
- ☐ USB drive
- ☐ Energy bars
- ☐ Spare change

For the Extra Pockets

- ☐ Small flashlight
- ☐ Binoculars
- ☐ Gaffers tape
- ☐ Swiss army knife or similar multipurpose tool
- ☐ Hand sanitizer
- ☐ Batteries
- ☐ Audio recorder
- ☐ Sewing kit and safety pins

Ready for the road trip

When an explosion erupted outside the Alfred P. Murrah Federal Building in Oklahoma City in 1995, reporters from across the country raced out the door and to the airport to cover what would become one of the biggest stories in American history. Inside the KNXV-TV (ABC) newsroom in Phoenix, the bomb blast happened just as the day-shift reporters and photographers were making their way into the newsroom. News director Susan Sullivan didn't give the assignment to the best reporter or the photographer with the sharpest eye, but rather to the two people who were most prepared.

VOICES *from the* Newsroom

Don't leave home without it!

What are the little things experienced reporters never leave home without?

Nichole Szemerei, reporter,
WCIA-TV (ABC), Champaign, Ill.

Earmuffs and gloves! The weather can always change drastically. There's nothing worse than trying to do your job when you're frozen solid. Be prepared for the unknown. And spare change. A toll road can be the quickest way to a breaking story.

Zahed Arab, reporter
KLAS-TV (CBS), Las Vegas

Snacks. You never know where you'll be sent and how long you'll be away if breaking news happens.

Linda So, reporter
WMAR-TV (ABC), Baltimore

Sewing kit and safety pin. I have had one too many wardrobe malfunctions, and these really come in handy when you've lost a button that must be in place.

Manny Fantis, executive producer of Digital Content
WUSA-TV (CBS), Washington, D.C.

I'm going old school . . . a Swiss army knife (or a Leatherman) and gaffers tape. When you're by yourself, you are also your own engineer, especially if you're in a bureau. You need to be prepared to repair.

Diana Alvear, correspondent
ABC News One, Chicago

IFB (earpiece). One with a small end and one with a larger end. I never know when I'll have to go live. You'd be surprised at how many sat trucks/photogs do not have a spare one. And Shout Wipes for the inevitable stain on my clothes.

Your Assignment

Most young reporters are classified as **general assignment** when they get on the job. A more accurate description would be "ready for anything" reporter. Each day general assignment, or GA, reporters can be sent in any direction, from a breaking news story or press conference to a light holiday feature. For many reporters, the unknown of what they will cover provides the excitement that brings them back to work each day. It's no desk job.

Assignment: Spot News

Maybe it's a large fire, hurricane or crime scene. There's an adrenaline rush when responding to **breaking,** or **spot news.** But what you do in those first few minutes can make or break your story.

We've talked about using every minute you have. On the way to a spot news story, that means working the cell phone by calling the police, the fire department or a neighboring business to find out what's going on. Also, while you're on the way, the assignment desk can make calls on your behalf. You want to roll up on the scene as prepared as possible.

On the Way

- Call sources, including first response agencies and neighboring businesses or residences.
- Listen to police or fire radio frequencies for information (but this information should not be reported until confirmed).
- Communicate with the assignment desk about any new developments that have come to light or are being reported by other news outlets.

Assess the Scene When you get out of the car, ask yourself, what's most likely to disappear first? Is it the picture of the flames shooting out of the building or the suspect being led away in handcuffs? Don't worry about talking to the officials right away. Capture the video that won't last for long. Then look for witnesses to interview. Do a 360-degree turn. Sometimes the story is behind you. Are there victims or witnesses standing across the street? Sometimes you'll find your most compelling sound a few hundred feet from the scene.

If you're fortunate enough to be working with a video journalist, you can split up. While your videographer captures the best pictures, you can vet witnesses and officials for the interviews you need.

On the Scene

- Capture critical video.
- Find and interview victims or eyewitnesses.
- Look for other sources of video, such as people with cell phones.
- Make contact with officials.

Many items on the spot news checklist (p. 48) can be done via email after you get back to the station (e.g., 911 tapes, police reports and booking photo). While not all reports and interviews will be available right away, get your requests in as soon as possible before you move on to another assignment. Days, weeks or even months later when the information is released, it will provide important new insight for a follow-up report. But some documents are often ready right away, like the initial appearance or arraignment paperwork.

While jailhouse interviews are rare, sometimes suspects will agree, and you won't have the opportunity if you don't request the interview. Creating a file, both hard copy and electronically, in your newsroom computer system is important. You want to be able to exchange information with other staff members who may share in the assignment or one day take over the story. Keep every contact phone number, email and note in that file because you or a colleague may come back to the story when a suspect goes to trial or there's an anniversary of the crime or other significant event.

One of the most difficult tasks will be to locate photos of the victim(s). This can mean knocking on the door of the family or a friend or approaching a grieving person who may be unwilling to talk to you. You may need to explain that using photos and/or video will help people relate to the victim and understand her story.

After the Event

- Locate family and friends of those involved.
- File appropriate public information requests with agencies.
- Leave leads and contact information available for the next reporter.

SPOT NEWS CHECKLIST

Columbus news director Mitch Jacob developed this checklist for breaking news stories to help his reporters stay ahead.

- ☐ Capture video of the scene.
  - Interview relatives, co-workers, witnesses, etc.
- ☐ Look for other sources of visuals of the event.
  - Cell phone video or images, home video, etc.
- ☐ Locate victim pictures.
  - Check with family, neighbors, yearbooks, etc.
- ☐ Check both suspect and victim backgrounds through local courts.
- ☐ Get suspect's booking photo and information from arresting agency or jail.
- ☐ Request initial appearance or arraignment documents from court.
- ☐ Request jail interview with suspect(s).
- ☐ File public record requests with agencies involved.
  - Request 911 tape and/or surveillance tape.
  - Request copies of any video or audio police interviews.
  - Request any search warrants from judge.
- ☐ Use Internet to cross-reference addresses with phone numbers.
- ☐ In the case of a death, request the medical examiner's and/or toxicology reports.
- ☐ If a child is involved, contact child protective services for any available family history.
- ☐ Check Internet and station archives for any relevant stories done in the past.
- ☐ Create a story folder that contains everything you've found, both electronic and hard copy.

Assignment: Press Conference

The governor's office has announced a 4 p.m. press conference to release the details of a budget compromise with lawmakers. The assignment editor has given you some background information, and you're ready to head out the door.

When you arrive at the press conference, take a look around and figure out where you can place your tripod to get the best video. Usually straight across from where the newsmaker will be standing is ideal, but that location isn't always available. If you can't tell where the key players are going to be, then ask someone. Get your technical concerns out of the way. Is there a **mult box,** or multiple input box? Rather than have a half-dozen microphones crammed onto a lectern, many organizations will provide an electronic box to plug your audio cable into that is wired to the lone microphone on the lectern. If not, you'll want to use a small microphone stand to place your microphone on the lectern or table. Once you've checked your audio and addressed any lighting issues, you can start thinking about content.

The problem with press conferences is wading through the mass of information being delivered. It's up to the reporter to figure out what's most important to the audience. What is the newsmaker's agenda? Is he giving out information as fact that others might dispute? As the reporter, it's up to you to ask questions and put the information being offered into perspective. What is the newsmaker's background? That is often relevant to the story and will help your audience understand where he is coming from. If he's a politician, you may need only say that he is a Republican and fiscally conservative. But if your press conference is with an advocacy group, it may take more digging to uncover its background and agenda.

Press conferences typically begin with an opening statement. Listen closely and take good notes. Next, newsmakers typically open the event to questions. Now is your chance to focus your story. Did you hear something in the governor's opening statement that was too vague? Ask a question for clarity. Did she leave out a key detail? Now's your chance to try to get the answer.

Being able to ask good questions means taking good notes in the first place. You may want to use an audio recorder as a backup, but write down key points during the conference and highlight anything that deserves a follow-up question. Other reporters may ask the person an unrelated question, but you should be ready to keep the newsmaker on track.

As part of your note taking, look around the room for details that could add context later. How many people were in the audience? What was their demeanor? What was the newsmaker's demeanor? Look for information that will help your audience understand what it was like to be in the room.

Assignment: Meeting

If you're working a story about poor fire department response times, the flames from a recent fire and an interview with a victim will provide the sizzle. But the steak, or meat, of the story may likely come from a public safety subcommittee or similar meeting. Often unwieldy and boring at the surface, meetings are still an important part of a reporter's life.

Meetings reveal issues that people living in the community want the city council or school board to address. Meetings also expose who is passionate about an issue (and, thus, a good source) and point you toward documents with key background information. Veteran reporters suggest that when story ideas are running dry, it's time to attend some public meetings.

Covering meetings is challenging. There is a sea of information, and your job may be to track one, two, three or more topics at one meeting. Begin your coverage before you arrive by looking at a copy of the meeting agenda online. The agenda will outline issues to be discussed and may also list names of stakeholders who've scheduled time to speak. Identify specific agenda items you want to cover by considering what will affect your audience the most. Residents are concerned about fire department response times, but other interesting topics may also come up, like a garbage rate increase or textbook fee. Perhaps it's a zoning decision on whether to allow a new high-rise or widen a street.

As with a press conference, you'll want to arrive early and set up your gear with time to spare. Touch base with meeting participants or staff members and see if the agenda has changed. Identify members of the public who've come to listen or speak. They clearly care about the issue(s) and may be good interview subjects or even central characters.

During the meeting, do your best to stay focused on the most important topics. The story isn't about the fact that a meeting happened. The story is about the issue and the people affected. Try to limit your shots to sequences that you can use as **b-roll**, and get sound bites that relate specifically to the issues you've identified as key. Again, the best sound will likely come from a person in the audience who cares about the topic rather than a member of the city council or school board. Don't forget to notice the atmosphere in the room. Was it crowded? Were people often upset? How long did the meeting last?

If you have time, get your interviews after the meeting. By then, you will have identified your issues and stakeholders. Rather than rely on what they said during the meeting, pull these key players aside for one-on-one interviews so you can get to the point. Don't forget to get contact information so you can follow up with them later in the day if necessary.

Assignment: Speech

If you're sent out to cover a speech, attending the event is likely only your first stop. As with a press conference or meeting, you will likely need to gather more information than you can possibly fit into your story. But unlike a meeting, where multiple opinions on one issue may surface, a speech will likely focus on only one topic.

To make the most of your assignment, do your work ahead of time. Ask the organizers or agency for a copy of the speech. If it's available, use it to identify key information and sentences that could make for good sound bites. Now familiar with the speech, you can capture video of the most relevant comments, saving you from sifting through all the remarks again later. Also, before the speech, research the person who will be speaking and the sponsoring organization. This background information will help you formulate good follow-up questions on controversial issues and identify other sources you need to interview to balance your coverage.

As with a meeting or press conference, be sure to notice what else is going on around you. Are people protesting outside the speech location? Is the speech well-attended, or is the room empty? And who is in the audience? Have an unusually large number of staff members shown up to listen to their boss' speech? This may be the sign of an important announcement. The audience may be filled with supporters or opponents who could be interviewed following the remarks.

After the speech, you'll likely have the opportunity to ask questions. The quality of your questions will depend on your preparation. If you're up to speed on the issue or person, you'll be able to ask about points he did not address or about complaints made by his critics. If the announcement is about a plan to improve the community, you can ask how it will be paid for or how residents will be affected. If the newsmaker does not take questions following the speech or announcement, then that would be information worth passing along to the audience as well.

PRESS CONFERENCES, MEETINGS AND SPEECHES CHECKLIST

Before

- ☐ Confirm agenda and research topic(s).
- ☐ Call key players or associates to get a sense of what to expect.
- ☐ Shoot video of related locations.
- ☐ Identify any archive video you may need later.
- ☐ Order graphic backgrounds that can be used to explain statistics or present quotes.
- ☐ Get copy of speech.
- ☐ Set up and test equipment, including audio and lighting.
- ☐ Note details like surroundings, audience, other small facts of context.
- ☐ Identify possible central characters.

During

- ☐ Stand near camera.
- ☐ Note time code of possible sound bites.
- ☐ Take detailed notes.
- ☐ Highlight question topics.
- ☐ Ask questions.

After

- ☐ Track down newsmaker(s) or stakeholders for follow-up questions or details.
- ☐ Get contact information for later in the day or evening.

Assignment: The Courthouse

A large building filled with multiple important sources and thousands of documents, a courthouse can seem like an intimidating assignment to a new reporter.

But the motivated reporter will also see opportunity. The justice system of your local community is a source for hundreds, perhaps thousands, of stories.

"I started my morning at 9 a.m. by heading to the Yellowstone County Courthouse and picking up the court docket for the day to see if any of the people we've followed are appearing," says reporter Nick Lough, formerly with KULR-TV (NBC) in Billings, Mont., and now with WAFF-TV (ABC) in Huntsville, Ala. And it's not just the small markets that count on the courthouse to stay in touch with what's going on in the community. Morgan Loew, a reporter with KPHO-TV (CBS) in Phoenix, also reviews new cases making their way through federal court.

These reporters will tell you the key to success inside the courtroom is understanding how the bureaucracy works and where your case stands as it makes its way through the judicial process.

The United States has two basic court systems—federal and state. State courts are usually organized by county and city. Larger jurisdictions subdivide their courts based on the kind of case—criminal in some, civil in others. Cases are also grouped by the severity—felony versus misdemeanor. Some counties may have hundreds of judges and courtrooms, ranging from small claims (where both sides represent themselves without lawyers) to civil and felony criminal courts. Rural jurisdictions may have only one courtroom and one judge, who hears all types of cases.

Besides understanding this organizational system, make sure you're up to speed on the courthouse rules in your local jurisdiction before you head down to the courthouse to cover a hearing. For example, cameras may be allowed in the courtroom, but only if you've requested permission from the judge ahead of time. Yet even if you have permission to bring your camera into the court, you may not be able to operate it in the hallways outside the courtroom. And some courts have rules that interviews must take place outside the building.

In criminal cases, the person who was arrested must usually appear before a judge within 24 hours, depending on your state's laws. Typically called an initial appearance or arraignment, this will likely be your first opportunity to see the defendant, meet the defense attorney and prosecutor, and get a glimpse at the paperwork filed by the arresting officers or probation department.

Before you're ever assigned to a story at the courthouse, take the time and learn how the paperwork (motions, reports, opinions, etc.) is handled in your jurisdiction. For example, you can often find both criminal and civil cases online and check their general status. However, for critical details, you'd need to head to the clerk's office and look up the file. These are public records available to anyone. The file could contain important information and leads, including names of the parties' associates, addresses, crime report and subpoena details. While you're at the clerk's office, make sure to check related cases. For example, was the defendant in your story granted a divorce years earlier? If so, check that file too. You may find information that provides background and context as well as other possible sources, like a former spouse.

If you are following a specific case, track its progress by talking to the key players, including attorneys on both sides, the clerk's office and the judge's office. For example, even though the paperwork may not indicate it, one of the attorneys or the judge's assistant may tell you that a plea bargain is likely rather than a trial.

A court proceeding can bring together multiple on-camera sources. Beyond the attorneys for both sides, you may be able to find relatives of suspects, crime victims or their relatives. All could be key sources for information or compelling, emotional interviews. You may also meet witnesses whom you could interview once their testimony is complete. After the trial, jurors are also possible sources; find out what the deliberations were like and what made an impression on those deciding guilt or innocence. As in any case involving trauma, approach victims and relatives with sensitivity and respect. A trial can be a very emotional and traumatic experience for those closely involved in the case.

Federal court works in much the same way as state court. However, media access is often more restricted. Cameras are typically not allowed in the courtrooms, and often less information is available online. But federal courts still offer opportunities for stories. That's why KPHO's Loew finds the time to swing by the clerk's office and look through logs of new cases.

COURTHOUSE CHECKLIST

Before

- ☐ Look up case file.
- ☐ Identify and contact attorneys to get a sense of what to expect.
- ☐ Submit camera request.
- ☐ Confirm docket information, including time and location.
- ☐ Shoot video of related locations.
- ☐ Identify any file video you may need later.
- ☐ Order graphic backgrounds.

During

- ☐ Identify possible sources, including victims and relatives.
- ☐ Note room atmosphere and key details, like defendant's demeanor.
- ☐ Note time code of possible sound bites (if using camera in courtroom).
- ☐ Write down possible questions.

After

- ☐ Quickly track down newsmaker(s) or stakeholders for follow-up questions or details (if no cameras allowed inside, you may need to position yourself outside the courthouse).
- ☐ Get contact information for future stories.

Social Media as a Reporting Tool

Years ago, journalists defined their careers by the way they delivered news to the public. Newspaper reporters focused on print-style writing. Radio reporters focused on what captivated the ear, and television reporters used pictures to entice the eye. Today's successful journalists must consider themselves platform agnostic—meaning it doesn't matter whether someone is watching your story on television, reading it online or listening to it on a radio or phone. Today the same technologies that help spread the story can also help you research the story.

Tim Vetscher, a reporter at KNXV-TV (ABC) in Phoenix, explains the essential role of the Web to his reporting. Before his morning editorial meeting, he spends about 20 minutes scanning an array of websites and blogs—everything from The Washington Post online to the site of the local college paper. Scanning community sites and online police logs is also part of his morning routine. "I'll also check my Twitter feed, which has several police departments on it, as well as 40 other people who occasionally post newsworthy items," says the veteran reporter. "If I have time, I'll do a quick Phoenix, Scottsdale or Arizona search on YouTube to see if there are any newsworthy video clips posted recently."

And that's all before the first editorial meeting of the day. "After our morning meeting ends, around 10 a.m. or so, I'll usually file my first Web script of the day. Typically it's bare-bones information, just basic facts," Vetscher says. "I've found it's important to get a script on ABC15.com early." How does that help him in his reporting? "Usually I get a feedback email or two during the day, which can sometimes result in an interview or other valuable piece of information that I wouldn't have had otherwise."

Once out the door on his assignment, Vetscher says, "I'll often post on Twitter that I'm looking for help on a particular story. I have a lot of PR types who follow my feed, so they may have a client or someone they know who's an expert in the field I'm seeking."

Social Media: Finding Voices, Facts and Context

Leslie-Jean Thornton, assistant professor, Walter Cronkite School of Journalism and Mass Communication

"Social media" refers to technology that lets information be shared socially—person to person. For generations, reporters have hung around coffeehouses, government buildings and other actual places to find out what people are thinking and doing, what they care about, what's new. These days, information-rich places include such virtual meeting grounds as Twitter, Facebook, YouTube, Flickr and Foursquare.

There are many reasons journalists should know their way around social media. Here are three: The more people you know and the more people who know you, the more likely you are to be able to find information when you need it—and understand it when you get it. The more tools you know, the more likely you'll be to find the people you need when you need them. People increasingly want news to find them, not the other way around. Knowing how to do that with social tools can help you get information where it's needed in the shortest possible time.

If anything's certain about social media and journalism today, it's that change is continual and rapid. Landmarks in the use of information-sharing tools include the 2004 Indian Ocean tsunami in Indonesia and Sri Lanka; the 2005 London bombings; the 2007 California wildfires (Twitter hashtags became popular then); a series of terrorist attacks in Mumbai, India, in 2008; Iran's June 2009 uprising (the first Twitter Revolution); and the February 2011 Egyptian revolution.

Journalists frequently report on surges of social media use. There were 2,250,000 blog posts on Iran in the first 24 hours of the protests, for example. There were also 50,000 to 100,000 tweets per hour referencing Iran, according to trackers. Today anyone, anywhere, can send out information that's also news. Journalists, trained to gather and make sense of information, can use social media as a resource and a tool.

Katrina, Virginia Tech, the Hudson River and San Bruno

Hurricane Katrina, in August 2005, occurred at the beginning of huge changes in how journalists work with the public and each other. When Katrina devastated the U.S. Gulf Coast, Twitter and Facebook weren't part of the news scene. People didn't share photos taken with their phones because they couldn't. The first Blackberry with a camera came out in fall 2006; Apple's iPhone wasn't introduced until 2007.

Blogs, text messages and collaboration of friends and strangers Journalists covering Katrina pioneered modern crisis coverage using social media tools at their disposal: text messages that could get through when landlines and cellular voice services were down, email, online message boards, blogs and continually updated online lists. These became vital public services, locally and globally. They reported news and linked people needing help with those able to give it. Friends and relatives found each other through ongoing lists that were constantly accessible online and publicized through broadcast. The Online Journalism Review counted more than a hundred such lists run by both news and non-news organizations (www.ojr.org/ojr/wiki/katrina/). Photos sent by people caught in or observing the storm and floods gave context and reality to the crisis. Not all the information on these blogs and lists came directly to the journalists, however. Social networks came into play as people outside the hurricane-torn area received urgent or informative text messages that they then conveyed to reporters, who published or broadcast them, continuing the social cycle.

A city unsafe for residents wasn't safe for journalists, either. The Times-Picayune/nola.com, based in New Orleans, fought to stay in production in both print and online, briefly switching to an all-Web format, but finally moved its editorial base to Baton Rouge, La. In another New Orleans example, Hearst station WDSU reluctantly evacuated to Jackson, Miss. For local news operations forced to evacuate their bases, there arose new challenges: How would they stay in touch with the area they were covering? How would they get hometown-specific news out to others who had been forced to flee? News organizations turned to the Internet, particularly blogs and streamed reports. They stayed in close contact with people still on the scene, forging bonds and opening lines of communication through media tools and personal contact. The Times-Picayune and the Sun Herald, of Biloxi, Miss., later won Pulitzer Prizes for public-service coverage. The collaborative community focus of the papers' Web presence during that time was responsible for the Pulitzer committee widening its consideration to online-only work.

Facebook, cell phone video and a university massacre In April 2007, when a gunman shot and killed 32 people, wounded others and committed suicide on the campus of Virginia Tech in Blacksburg, Va., Facebook was firmly established in American culture. Cell phones with video and camera options and email capabilities were popular. Jamal Albarghouti, a graduate student, was walking by Norris Hall (where most of the shootings occurred) when campus officers ordered him to take cover. He did, but he also took out his cell phone and started recording, capturing police reaction and the sound of methodical gunfire against an ominously silent campus background. He sent the video to CNN's iReports, which uses viewer submissions on air and online. Albarghouti's footage, which was shown repeatedly and not just on CNN, informed both the media and the public about conditions in Blacksburg at the very time some of the shootings took place. The video landed on YouTube. Facebook also played a large role in documenting the tragedy. Virginia Tech students began making entries soon after the first shootings, which happened about two hours before the Norris Hall massacre. In the absence of information from university leaders, speculation grew and reports circulated. Facebook accounts were rich sources of information for news-hungry journalists. Use made of some of the resources found there—including pictures of people who had died in the shootings and using words quoted from Facebook walls—raised ethical questions.

Twitter, TwitPic and a plane crash When a crippled US Airways jet slammed onto the Hudson River alongside New York City in January 2009, the first reports were on Twitter. They bested "traditional" news reports by 15 minutes, according to a Wall Street Journal blog. Within minutes of the emergency landing, Janis Krums, a passenger on a nearby ferryboat, took a photo with his iPhone and posted it on Twitter using TwitPic. It showed people from the plane lined up along the slowly submerging wings while others huddled in a life raft, waiting for help. "There's a plane in the Hudson," he tweeted. "I'm on the ferry going to pick the people up. Crazy." Thirty-four minutes later, he was interviewed on MSNBC. About three hours after that, the image had been seen more than 43,000 times on TwitPic alone. It was so popular that the server crashed after 7,000 hits. During the outage, which lasted roughly an hour, there were about 2,000 requests per minute, CNET reported.

He was not the only eyewitness photographer, however, and news organizations knew it. Twelve minutes after the plane went into the icy water, The New York Times "City Room" blog posted an appeal for witnesses and photographs, later producing a slideshow with reader-submitted images. CNN, MSNBC and other news venues featured nonstaff submissions, too. Meanwhile, photos went up at Flickr (search the site for "Miracle on the Hudson River" to see a collection) and other sites. Two years later, a Google image search on "Hudson River plane crash" produced more than 40,000 hits.

Twitter takes lead in explosion, fire coverage A gas-line explosion in a residential area of San Bruno, Calif., ignited a fire that killed seven people, injured dozens and destroyed millions of dollars of property in September 2010. Seconds after the blast, people turned to Twitter to ask what had happened, report what they'd heard and seen and find information. Officials turned to Twitter, too, as did aid organizations (American Red Cross, animal shelters, food kitchens); volunteers; reporters from TV, radio, newspapers, blogs and online-only news organizations; and the company responsible for the blast—Pacific Gas & Electric. Tweeters explained how to use hashtags, told where to go to find interactive resource maps (Google created one and kept it going) and urged people to keep off cell phones so safety crews would have clearer access. Twitter had links to photos, video, documents, news stories and maps. News organizations were heavily involved. In the first 24 hours, there were tweets from 36 online-only news sites and 18 online alert services, along with 29 tweeters who represented TV stations—16 from newspapers, nine from radio stations and three who identified themselves in their profiles as freelance journalists. A hashtag created minutes after the blast, #sanbrunofire, corralled the vast majority of fire-related tweets. Secondary hashtags, like #pets, #ruok (are you okay?) and #imok (I am okay), further organized the flood of information, making it easy for people to search for tweets that included a particular tag. A typical tweet might read: "Take a moment to look at the San Bruno neighborhood before/after: http://lat.ms/c5eRoF. It's shocking #SanBrunoFire." Some tweets cross-referenced to Facebook and the geolocation "game" Foursquare, where people left comments about what they were seeing.

Perhaps because the fires affected a relatively small geographic area that wasn't densely populated, the tweets took on a community aspect. One began to see story lines in the continuing tweets, recognize particular tweeters, find patterns. Where would the food trucks be today? Did emergency services still need blood donations? Was Lily, the dog whose "mommy is in the hospital," ever found? Hector, who worked at Twitter, lost two relatives in the fire. Sympathy tweets poured in. News, via Twitter, became personal as people shared, in addition to updates and alerts, glimpses into their inner lives and concerns.

What it means to you

Social media are not merely venues for reporting. For a reporter, social media offer context, sources and real-time information. The value to you as a journalist, however, depends on three things: your understanding of how social media work, your developed network and your knowledge of how to search and solicit information.

It isn't difficult, but it takes time and effort. Each social network has a culture and a way of behaving. On Facebook, for example, one asks permission to "friend" someone; on Twitter, friending strangers is expected, which gives you immediate access to potential sources and experts. The goal of all social networks is to get people to use them, so signing up and learning the mechanics is generally easy. The important thing is to start. To see Twitter in action, for example, follow lots of news organizations and sources; create lists of contacts and resources; and learn to search and follow hashtags.

Twitter talk In Twitter, a message is most commonly referred to as a "tweet," although sometimes you'll see the original term, "twitter."

A tweet cannot be longer than 140 characters (which includes the sender's and recipient's names).

When replying to someone, the @ sign must appear before the person's Twitter name. The same sign + name combination will show up in the tweet to show who sent the tweet.

If you want to send someone a direct message, type a "D" and then a space in front of the Twitter name. Do not use the @. You can only direct message someone who is following you.

To "retweet" a message (basically, to forward it), write RT or "retweet" in front of the message. Include the previous or original sender's name so that the message can be traced back. It is understood that the message will likely undergo some editing to fit it into the space allotment. Every effort should be made to preserve the original tweet's clarity and meaning.

When responding to a tweet, include enough information that the recipient and others will know what you're talking about without having to search out past tweets.

Avoid "text" abbreviations—LOL, ROFL, "4" for "four"—unless they are easy to understand and are necessary to meet the space limitation.

When including links, use a link shortener such as bit.ly.

To mark a tweet for later reference, save it as a "favorite."

Hashtags were created so that people could search for a particular term, cutting out unrelated information. They are formed with a # sign immediately before a keyword or term: #iranelection was widely used in June 2009. Hashtags are not assigned by anyone; journalists should search on various keywords to discover which ones are being used during news outbreaks. If there are none, start one.

Twitter "lists" are extremely helpful resources. Twitter accounts may be included in lists without your having to follow them. Their tweets can be seen when you look at the list on your Twitter Web page or when you set up a search column for that list on an application such as TweetDeck. Journalists might set up lists according to their beat, for a special project or to see what their colleagues (or competitors) are tweeting.

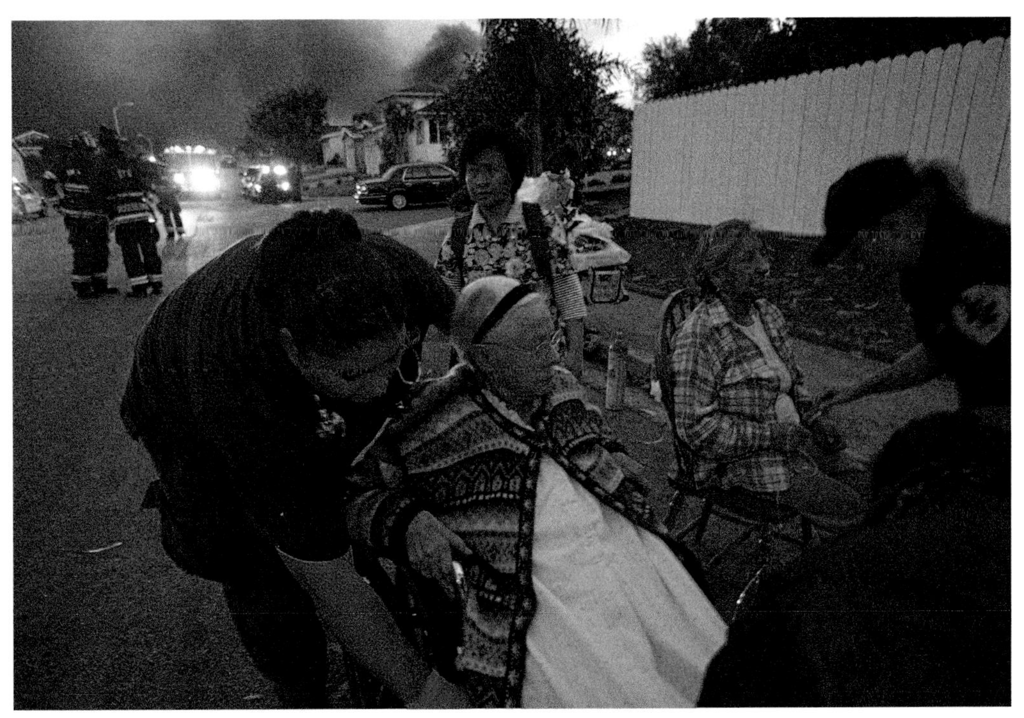

The use of Twitter during the September 2010 San Bruno fire helped the community react and recover, with timely information on topics including food and shelter assistance, blood donations and missing people.

More Responsibility Around the Corner

As technology improves, the responsibilities of journalists will only increase, putting more stress on a career that's already chock full. For example, television stations used to employ artists to handle special graphics for a newscast. Today, that task is often added to the duties of newscast and online producers in both small and large markets. And in the field, **MMJs** (multimedia journalists, also known as "one-person bands" or "backpack journalists") are beginning to handle their own live reports. That means the reporter is responsible not only for conducting the interviews, writing the copy and editing the video, but also for setting up the camera and video feed before appearing on the newscast. Just a few years ago, some television stations might use as a many as three or four staff members for the same task.

ABC News One correspondent Diana Alvear reports from the wedding of Prince William and Catherine Middleton in April 2011.

"Your worth increases with every new assignment or responsibility you take on," says ABC News One correspondent Diana Alvear. "Don't complain. It's the journalists who *don't* work on multiple platforms who will end up with pink slips. Make yourself a valuable player in the newsroom." Janie Porter, a reporter and an anchor with WTSP-TV (CBS) in Tampa, provides a good example of an MMJ. (She is featured in the next Voices from the Newsroom segment.) "Employees like Janie give us more options, which can allow us to put more people out on the streets covering local news," says her former boss, Darren Richards.

Accuracy and Attribution

All the hard work you've put into your story will be wasted unless it's 100 percent accurate. A mistake in your report damages not only your credibility, but the credibility of the whole organization you work for. "Obviously you have to get it right, first," says former Tampa, Fla., news director Darren Richards. "The pressures of the 24/7 news cycle are real, but that's no excuse. You still have to get it right first."

For former Reno, Nev., producer and reporter Gem Gokmen, ensuring accuracy means fact-checking her work and that of her co-workers. "I have to make sure each reporter does what he's supposed to do. I check all scripts for spelling and factual errors, and check video to make sure it matches the script."

ACCURACY AND ATTRIBUTION CHECKLIST

You never want to be the only person to read your copy before it's on air or online. Preferably your newsroom will have a system for proofreading stories. If not, have a co-worker double-check your work to make sure it's both accurate and coherent. NewsLab offers a 10-point checklist designed to help:

❑ **1. Confirm information that could be in doubt**

- Any unattributed information (information that has no name attached to it) is a red flag, demanding further investigation. Even information with two sources may not constitute confirmation, because one source may have learned the information from the other. Always ask: How do they know what they know, and why are they telling me this?
- Make sure that those who claim to be eyewitnesses actually were at the scene and in a position to observe what they are telling you. In breaking news situations in particular, people often sound authoritative when they are only passing along unconfirmed rumors.

❑ **2. Clarify context**

- Make sure the sound bites or quotes you choose fully capture what each person meant to say. In a survey of people who were sources in television news stories, one person in three said important information was left out, and one in five complained that his or her interview was taken out of context.
- If you need to, add information in your narration/track to put comments into context.

❑ **3. Look for what might be missing**

- Review your story with an eye to significant information or points of view that have not been included. Look at each quote or sound bite, in particular, and ask: Who would disagree or take a different position?
- Contact people whose views are not reflected in the story and give them a chance to talk. If they decline, mention that in your story.

❑ **4. Review for focus**

- Make sure your story backs up your lead. Have you overreached or overstated the story?
- Restate the focus of your story, and review the script to see if you have stayed on point or strayed. (A bonus: Doing this will help you find places where you can trim the script to save time.)
- Plug your entire story into a word-cloud generator like Wordle to see if your content reflects your focus.

❑ **5. Check names, places, titles**

- Be sure you have attributed information to the correct source in every case.
- Make sure you have checked the spelling of proper names. If possible, check directly with the source. Press releases can be wrong. Even business cards may not show a current title.

❑ **6. Check spelling, grammar, usage**

- Spelling and grammar count in broadcast news—especially in this age of graphics, closed captioning and Web use. If you are not positive about a spelling, look it up.
- Read scripts out loud to find and fix grammar and usage problems. If in doubt, ask a colleague or check a reference guide.

❑ **7. Do the math**

- Stories with numbers must be checked to make sure the numbers add up. Recalculate percentages, percentage changes, ratios and the like, no matter where you got them. Online calculators make this much easier than it sounds.
- Check with an expert not involved in the story if you have any questions about how the numbers were calculated.

❑ **8. Fact-check graphics**

- Make sure the information you provide in graphics is correct—especially numbers. Call to confirm all telephone numbers and visit all Web addresses.
- Look at the completed graphic before it airs to catch mistakes.

❑ **9. Be precise about pronunciations**

- Make a habit of checking the pronunciation of names and places while you are in the field. Ask people to say their names on tape, so you can go back and listen, if necessary.
- If you are new to an area, be extra careful with names and places that may look familiar but could be pronounced quite differently from what you expect. Nothing raises more doubts about your credibility than mispronouncing a word your audience thinks you should know.

❑ **10. Screen the finished story**

- Be sure that your words and pictures are telling the same story.
- Be sure the narration and sound bites match the finished script and that mistakes have not crept in during tracking or editing.

Source: Courtesy of Deborah Potter, NewsLab

Defeat Deadline Pressure

So you've heard the warnings: Don't miss your deadline. Now how do you ensure you'll make your slot? As you'll learn in Chapter 8, producers **backtime** their newscasts to ensure they end on time. That means that producers calculate from the very end of the newscast to determine exactly what time each story needs to begin.

Imagine trying to create a playlist on iTunes that is exactly 30 minutes long. You would have to time each song down to the second to hit the 30-minute mark. That's what newscast producers do every day. A successful reporter also will backtime his day to help stay on schedule.

It's 9:30 a.m., and you've just received your assignment for tonight's 6 o'clock newscast. You know it takes you about an hour to edit and 30 minutes each to log and write a standard package. Backtiming your day would reveal that you have less than five hours available to report in the field. Stick to the schedule, and you won't miss your deadline.

To backtime effectively, however, you need to break down the process and realistically evaluate each step. How long does it take you to edit a minute and 20 seconds of video? How long to write? How much time will you need to **log** all your interviews and identify key shots? Answer these questions, and you'll know how long you have to gather information.

FIGURE **3.3** **The Clock Is Ticking**

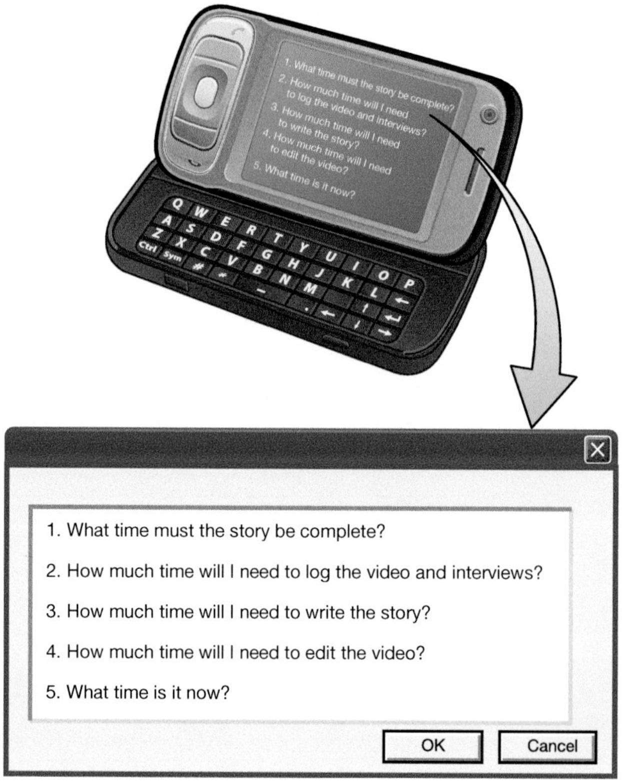

1. What time must the story be complete?
2. How much time will I need to log the video and interviews?
3. How much time will I need to write the story?
4. How much time will I need to edit the video?
5. What time is it now?

OK Cancel

"It's all about time management," says reporter George Lettis of WBAL-TV (NBC) in Baltimore. "Your first couple of years, your scripts will take you two hours to finish. Know your limits. But

FIGURE **3.4** **Backtime your day**
Stick to the schedule, and you won't miss your deadline.

believe me, years four, five and six, you'll log and write in an hour, even less most days."

Fill in the blanks to see how much time you would have to get your story finished.

Add up the total time it will take to complete tasks two, three and four, then subtract that time from the amount of time between now and when the story must be complete. That's how long you have to gather information.

For example, if it takes two hours to complete the tasks and the story is due at 6 p.m., you have until 4 p.m. to gather information. Knowing this, if you are still gathering information after 4 p.m., you will likely miss your deadline.

Working as a multimedia journalist means Janie Porter, a reporter and an anchor with WTSP-TV (CBS) in Tampa, must excel at time management.

WHAT WOULD YOU DO?

It's 3 p.m., and you're racing the clock. Your boss wants you to present a live television report in the 5 o'clock newscast about a new inspection report that reveals that bridges in the city are in terrible shape. You just got off the phone with the head of the transportation department, who's available to talk to you on camera, but he's 90 minutes away.

a) Do you call your newsroom and ask for more time?
b) Do you ask the transportation official if he will be available this evening?
c) Do you ask if you can present your live report from where the transportation official is located?

Answer: C. This is the best of both worlds. You can get the information and then use the live transmission truck to feed part of the interview back to the station in time to use in your live report. If that's cutting it too close, don't miss your deadline. Ask the official if he will be available later, and then you can update your story after your first report.

Log video, transcribe likely sound bites.

3:45 p.m.

Begin writing.

4:15 p.m.

Begin editing.

4:45 p.m.

Story due.

5:45 p.m.

Story airs on newscast.

6 p.m.

Setting Up for Future Success

The reporters who consistently break good stories have a system that works for them, and they stick to it. Some track stories and contacts on their desktop computers. Others prefer loading everything onto their smart phones, while still others keep hard-copy records. Now's the time to figure out what works for you.

Always carve out a few minutes at the end of the day to get organized. Ask yourself some questions:

- Do I have any new contacts to add to my database?
- Should I start a file for any new documents I received today that I may need later on?
- What's the next important date in this story? Have I entered that in my calendar?
- Are there any information requests I need to put in an email or letter before I leave?
- Create your own checklists to make sure you're organized and on top of your stories.
- Create call lists for stories during your commutes to and from work.
- Do your own beat checks during your commute. Call your best sources at the police department or city council to get an idea of what's going on.
- Don't forget to share information you've gathered with co-workers. Another reporter may be assigned to follow up on your story. Don't force him to start from scratch. Leave key information with the assignment desk.

VOICES *from the* Newsroom

Backpack journalism

Janie Porter, *reporter and anchor*
WTSP-TV (CBS), Tampa Bay

WTSP multimedia journalist Janie Porter made news herself in 2009 when she transmitted a live report to viewers all by herself with just a camera, laptop and cell phone.

First, tell us what your job is at WTSP.

I'm a backpack journalist, or BPJ, which means that I shoot, write and edit my own stories. I'm also the weekend morning anchor.

What skills do you employ on a daily basis beyond what a reporter or an anchor would have done 15 years ago?

These days, if I'm "only" providing TV broadcast content, I'm not doing my job. In addition to turning news stories for our television newscasts, I'm also in touch with viewers throughout the day. I use the Web—including my blog, Twitter and Facebook—to tell viewers about stories I'm working on. I even log onto AOL Instant Messenger during newscasts so that viewers can chat with me. Oftentimes, I get their feedback before the story even airs on TV, and depending on the story, I'll use viewer comments as a tag to the broadcast story or to add a new angle to my Web story.

What are the pros and cons of being a backpack journalist?

One of the best parts of being a BPJ is that the story is all up to you. But that's also one of the worst parts. Let me explain.

When I get an assignment, I have full control over the story. I don't spend 30 minutes discussing the direction of the story with a photographer. I don't have to sit through extra questions that I know I won't use. I only shoot the video I need. The day is faster and more streamlined.

On the flip side, because I'm working alone, I miss the chances for creativity that come with working with someone else. There's no one to bounce ideas off of or share in the responsibility of the story. In addition, there is less time to do each job. I can't write my Web story while someone else edits it. I can't make calls while someone else shoots b-roll. I can't do research while someone else loads gear in the news vehicle. As a BPJ, all of these responsibilities fall on my shoulders.

Do you have advice for young journalists looking to get into television news?

Adaptability means job security, and in this downsizing industry, that is priceless.

And please, never tell a news director that all you want to do is anchor! It's OK to want to be on air. That's what I was after when I got started. And I dress the part. I am a BPJ, but you will rarely catch me wearing jeans or flats. Even if I'm writing in-house for the day, my makeup and hair are camera ready. I always want to be perceived as the best for the job I want to do.

But I also want my news director to know that I can do any job well.

A Reporter's Life, Small Market and Large

The typical young television journalist will get his or her first on-air opportunity in a small city, or **market**. The term "market" includes not only the city where the television station is located, but also the surrounding community that is within reach of the broadcast signal. Life in a small market, with a smaller staff, is much different from what a journalist may experience in a large market. Two reporters offer some insight into what their jobs are like in very different markets.

Small Market

Anne McCloy, reporter
KOBI-TV (NBC), Medford, Ore.

What's the biggest benefit to working in a newsroom your size?

The greatest benefit is the amount of opportunity. Our staff is bare bones. We have one to two reporters working on a daily basis. It gives you an advantage to get the live shot of the day (we only have one live truck). Also, we get a lot more attention paid to our stories and performance. Our news director reads and edits our scripts before tracking and watches our stories as they run to give us feedback. She once sat in the booth with me to help me with my voice work.

With so little staff, I've had to learn to do a lot of work in a short amount of time. It's a good thing because I will be able to market myself better as a backpack journalist who can push a package and two VO-SOTs out in a day (sometimes even two packages). We have a half-hour show at 5 p.m. and an hour show at 6 p.m.—a large news hole.

In this changing "you can do it all" world of TV news, how often do you actually shoot or edit your own video?

We do everything ourselves: Come up with the story, shoot the story, shoot the standup, create graphics, write, edit, put CGs in and scramble to get out the door to our live shots with only about two to three hours to put it all together. It's honestly amazing how much we do.

How would you describe the atmosphere in the newsroom?

Our station has a very family-like atmosphere because it's locally owned. You'll commonly see family members coming in to visit. However, there has been a lot of competition between reporters in the newsroom. When I first started, I found it really hard to mesh with everyone. In the beginning I felt people treated me harshly because they were threatened by a new co-worker. Simple things, like who gets the live shot and who gets to use our only wireless microphone, become little points of frustration.

Do co-workers socialize outside work?

Yes. Soon you become pretty close with everyone in a newsroom so small. Everyone goes to watch football games together, and we all go out on the town. It's the way we deal with the stress. It makes it enjoyable to work with people when you build such friendships.

What's the biggest challenge you face each day as a reporter in Medford?

Meeting deadline. I have a terrible fear of missing deadline because I missed it a couple of times when I first started the job. It's a very serious issue, and it's not tolerated. I've got it under control now, but it's still a fear I face. Sometimes I have to make a schedule for myself with detailed deadlines for each task so I know I'll get it done on time. I write out times for logging and writing, and I give myself a deadline for shooting my story. At the beginning, I always shot too much video. The challenge with deadlines in a small market newsroom is you have a lot to do.

If an intern or a new employee asked you what it's like to work here, how would you answer?

Challenging. I am faced with new challenges every day. How do I make a story I've done five times different? How do I get a package done when the press conference is at 4 p.m. with the show at 6 p.m.? At my job, we also face challenges with equipment. With the server it can take a half an hour to send in any clip, and you are expected to send it in no later than half an hour before the show. We also have a production crew full of new people, so you can't always trust them to know what they're doing. However, I have become faster, more confident and better because of it all.

What's the key to survival as an entry-level reporter?

You have to be a strong person, and you have to trust yourself and your instincts. You're thrown out on a story, and you have to come back with something. You have to be creative and pound the pavement to get what you need. You cannot give up because there's no time! The job isn't just 9 a.m. to 5 p.m. It's a lifestyle, especially in a small town. You have to pay attention to your surroundings every day so you know when there's a story under your nose. You have to get out, learn the area and make friends.

It's about coming in with a good attitude, making connections with everyone you encounter and producing the best product you can. Even if you're having a terrible day, you can't let your viewers know it. It's not always easy. It takes a lot of energy. There have been days I come home crying and days I come home elated. Reporting is definitely not all about being on TV. You have to have a serious passion to do this.

Large Market

Gina Silva, reporter
KTTV-TV (Fox), Los Angeles

What's it like to work in a Los Angeles newsroom today?

A lot has changed in the past couple of years. L.A. is quickly becoming much like a small market. We used to have a crew of people to work with: producers, specialized photographers, researchers, bookers and loggers. In the past year, 130 people were laid off. We have one-person crews operating live trucks that used to have two guys. Reporters work up to 12 hours a day on non-breaking news days. It's expected because there aren't enough reporters to go around. If you work for the morning shows, you can easily be assigned up to three stories in one day.

In this changing "you can do it all" world of TV news, how often do you actually shoot or edit your own video?

Our station has not gone in the direction of backpack journalism . . . yet. But friends at KNBC tell me several morning anchors were given small camcorders and laptops and told to go out and shoot, report and edit their own stories. It's only for the station's website, but many believe that will be our future in TV news. I believe only those who can do everything will survive this ever-changing business.

How would you describe the atmosphere in the newsroom?

The morale at our station isn't the best, and it's pretty much the same at all stations in L.A. People are in fear of losing their jobs. There are constant rumors of layoffs. Many of them have come true. Some people are bitter because they don't like the changes taking place, and they refuse to adjust.

Do co-workers socialize outside work?

Yes, co-workers socialize. Sometimes a little too much, and must be disciplined.

What's the biggest challenge you face each day as a reporter in L.A.?

As a live reporter stationed in one location for hours, finding a bathroom is sometimes a challenge! Traffic is a big problem. Dealing with cops trying to keep you out of scenes. Note: You get more with honey than vinegar.

If an intern or a new employee asked you what it's like to work here, how would you answer?

It's challenging but rewarding. If you really love what you do, you'll go with the flow and adjust to the changes. In my case, I love telling stories. If I have to shoot and edit my own reports, I will do that.

I've always loved the creative process that takes place behind the camera. You can see this new process as having more control of your own work. If it all goes wrong, there's no one else to blame but yourself. I really think being happy here is up to you.

You've worked in large markets for more than 15 years. What's the key to survival?

Staying on top of your game, caring about your story, going the extra mile even on stories you know are not Emmy material.

In my case, being versatile has been key.

I work on serious investigative stories, features, silly live shots, anchor, weather, traffic, entertainment and breaking news from a helicopter. I also wash the news vans on Sundays.

SPECIALTY Reporting

CHAPTER OUTLINE

CHAPTER 4

Not only do we have a right to know, we have a duty to know what our government is doing in our name.

—WALTER CRONKITE

The Paper Trail

> "Sometimes you put 100 hours into a possible story that just doesn't pan out, but you know that going into this job."
>
> TAMMY LEITNER, INVESTIGATIVE REPORTER KPHO-TV (CBS), PHOENIX

Getting the story means developing sources, chasing down leads and confirming information. But reporting can go well beyond what you can accomplish in just a few hours. The best reporters take their skills even further by conducting computer-based research, chasing the paper trail or developing an area of interest. Official documents or correspondence will take a news story from opinion and accusation to proof and, perhaps, change.

Often finding the information you need will mean multiple searches of various agencies for public documents. Years ago, this would mean days or weeks of work mailing requests for information or sifting though documents in a clerk's office. Today, more documents are available online than ever before. That means a hunch or tip can take you from a Superior Court database to the County Assessor's Office to the Corporation Commission in less than an hour. Where you begin your document search will depend on the tip or assignment. (See Figure 4.1.)

Organizations outside of government can also help you find what you're looking for. Often watchdog groups will pull together databases for you on topics like government spending, population reports, public safety issues and corporate earnings. Finding the right database can begin with something as simple as a Google or Bing search. The Society of Professional Journalists tracks thousands of available records in the Journalist's Toolbox (www.journaliststoolbox.org).

While some journalists are drawn to the rush of a deadline, patience and organizational skills pay off for those interested in following the paper trail.

In-depth stories can mean collecting thousands of documents, organizing them, and searching for patterns.

FIGURE **4.1** **Following the Paper Trail**

	To find out...	Document needed	Agency
	Who owns the property?	Deed	County Assessor's Office, property taxes
	Criminal background check?	Case file	Superior Court
	Is it a real company?	State registration	Corporation Commission
	Campaign donations?	Donor records	Federal Elections Commission You can find lots of info about campaign donations on www.opensecrets.org, which is run by the Center for Responsive Politics.

Working as a team on investigative stories can provide support and encourage brainstorming.

Your research will often begin online, but ultimately hard copies of documents may be needed to turn your tip or theory into a story.

Freedom of Information

When Tammy Leitner, an investigative reporter with KPHO-TV (CBS) in Phoenix, was glancing through email tips, one story caught her eye. A young woman claimed that after she was in the custody of a local police department, an officer left her outside a convenience store severely intoxicated. Soon after, the woman claimed, she was picked up by strangers, taken to a remote home and sexually assaulted.

Trying to confirm the account, Leitner ran into some roadblocks with the local police agency, so she turned to the power of state law. To find out if the woman's story was true, she filed a public records request.

Soon, the story fell in place because state law required the Tempe Police Department to release the documents that could confirm the woman's story.

What happened to Leitner will probably happen to you. Often an agency that has the document you're counting on for your story does not want to give it up. Perhaps administrators think they don't have to, or they are simply too embarrassed to hand it over. Fortunately for journalists, public records laws are in place to help you.

The **Freedom of Information Act,** commonly known as FOIA, requires federal agencies to release records requested in writing. But the FOIA only applies to federal agencies. It does not let you access court records or Congressional documents. Each state has its own laws that outline rights to acquire state and local records.

Veteran reporters will tell you the downside to the FOIA and other public records access laws: Agencies often take significant time responding to your request. That's why Washington Post reporter James Grimaldi gives this advice to fellow members of Investigative Reporters and Editors (www.ire.org): "Make sure you have exhausted other avenues to obtain records. Check websites. Don't FOIA something you can get by making a phone call or that is already online," Grimaldi says. "Sometimes, the quickest way to get something is just to ask for it—without filing a FOIA." (Source: James Grimaldi of The Washington Post for Investigative Reporters and Editors, Inc.)

States also have open records laws designed to help the public. They are often similar to the Freedom of Information Act but may be either more open or more restrictive. In many states, an organization like the First Amendment Coalition or the Reporters Committee for Freedom of the Press publishes a handbook or online source with details about the state's open records laws.

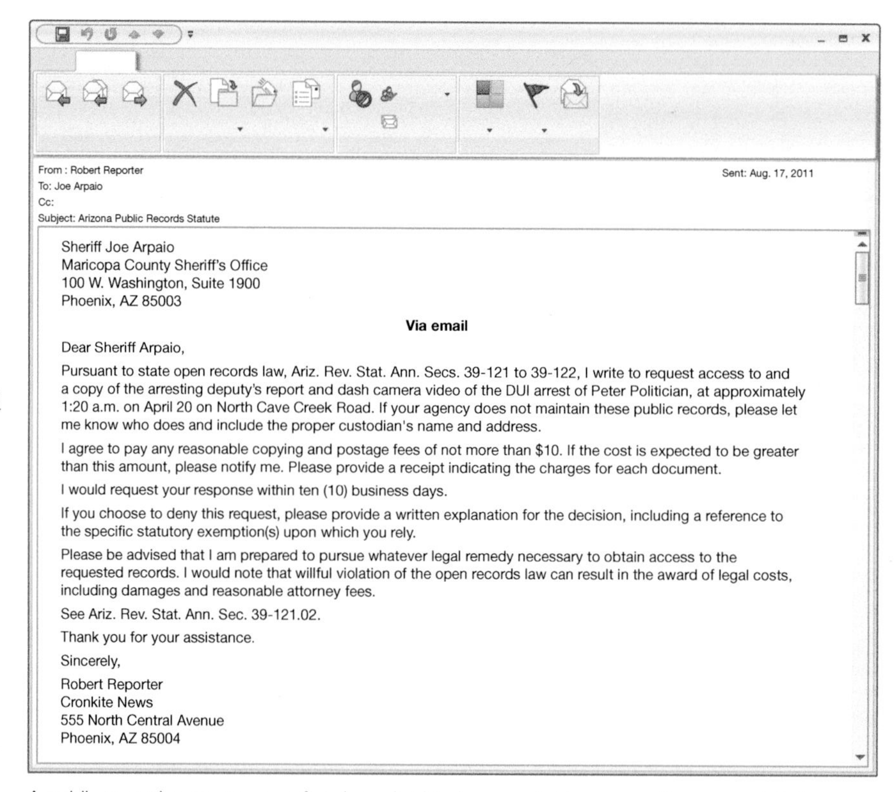

From : Robert Reporter
To: Joe Arpaio
Cc:
Subject: Arizona Public Records Statute

Sent: Aug. 17, 2011

Sheriff Joe Arpaio
Maricopa County Sheriff's Office
100 W. Washington, Suite 1900
Phoenix, AZ 85003

Via email

Dear Sheriff Arpaio,

Pursuant to state open records law, Ariz. Rev. Stat. Ann. Secs. 39-121 to 39-122, I write to request access to and a copy of the arresting deputy's report and dash camera video of the DUI arrest of Peter Politician, at approximately 1:20 a.m. on April 20 on North Cave Creek Road. If your agency does not maintain these public records, please let me know who does and include the proper custodian's name and address.

I agree to pay any reasonable copying and postage fees of not more than $10. If the cost is expected to be greater than this amount, please notify me. Please provide a receipt indicating the charges for each document.

I would request your response within ten (10) business days.

If you choose to deny this request, please provide a written explanation for the decision, including a reference to the specific statutory exemption(s) upon which you rely.

Please be advised that I am prepared to pursue whatever legal remedy necessary to obtain access to the requested records. I would note that willful violation of the open records law can result in the award of legal costs, including damages and reasonable attorney fees.

See Ariz. Rev. Stat. Ann. Sec. 39-121.02.

Thank you for your assistance.

Sincerely,

Robert Reporter
Cronkite News
555 North Central Avenue
Phoenix, AZ 85004

A public records request can often be submitted via email. Be as specific as possible in your request, and be sure to note the state or federal law that gives you access to the information.

TIMESAVER

The Student Press Law Center (www.splc.org) is a wonderful resource for students looking for legal guidance while covering stories. The organization provides details on both federal and state law. SPLC also helps generate assistance in generating letters designed to request records at both the state and federal level.

Open Meetings

Freedom of information laws also ensure that the public (including reporters) has the right to attend open meetings. But sometimes you have to fight for this right. Lawmakers or other officials may simply be unaware that the meeting they are about to have is considered public under the law, or they may be hoping no one notices. In that case, it's up to you speak up and state your objection. First Amendment attorneys suggest keeping a small handbook or card in your wallet explaining state law and what you can say if you're being prevented from attending what you believe is an open public building.

WHAT TO DO WHEN YOU ARE EXCLUDED FROM A MEETING CHECKLIST

- Object to any closed meeting, and request that your objection be recorded in the minutes of the meeting.
- Ask that reasons for the closed meeting be recorded in the minutes.
- If participants plan to hold a closed meeting or discuss a subject in violation of the open meeting law (OML), advise them that any formal action taken at a meeting held in violation of the OML is void.
- If the closed meeting is already in progress, deliver a written objection to the public body and request that the objection be incorporated in the minutes of the meeting.
- Do not volunteer to leave the meeting, but rather let the public body order you to leave.
- Do not refuse to leave a meeting when ordered to do so, but ask first that a public vote be taken on whether to close the meeting and that the vote of each member be recorded in the minutes.
- Never permit off-the-record remarks during a meeting, and never agree not to report certain portions of the meeting.
- If the public meeting is adjourned for an executive session, ask that the head of the public body state the reasons for the executive session. Also, request that these reasons be recorded in the minutes of the meeting. Remember, even executive sessions are usually subject to 24-hour notice requirements except in emergencies.
- Make a written request for a transcript of the proceedings or copies of the minutes. You may report any information you obtain as to what happened at a closed meeting. If you are wrongfully excluded from a meeting governed by the OML, you may seek to void any legal action taken at the closed meeting and obtain injunctive relief against the public body to prevent any further violations of state or federal open meetings laws.

Source: From Daniel Barr, "What to do when you are excluded from a meeting," Arizona Reporter's Handbook on Media Law, 6e, Perkins Coie LLP, © 2007.

Computer-Assisted Reporting

Stephen K. Doig, professor and Knight Chair in Journalism,
Walter Cronkite School of Journalism and Mass Communication

All good reporters learn how to find and interview sources for their stories. But reporters who really want to distinguish themselves from the rest of the newsroom learn how to find and interview data. This important skill is called computer-assisted reporting, or CAR.

Perhaps the first journalist to do a story based on CAR was legendary CBS broadcast reporter Walter Cronkite. He used a UNIVAC computer to analyze exit-poll data for a story about the 1952 presidential election. Since then, increasing numbers of print and broadcast reporters have used CAR to do stories on crime patterns, hurricane damage, criminal justice sentencing, environmental problems, cheating on school test scores, campaign finance, sports injuries, airline safety, malfunctioning medical devices, election fraud and hundreds of other important issues.

You don't have to be a math genius or a computer techie to do good CAR stories. You just need two things—some interesting data and the right software.

Getting the data can be as easy as downloading it from a government website. For instance, information about donors to political campaigns is readily available from state elections departments or the Federal Elections Commission. Many police department websites offer listings of the dates, times and locations of the crimes reported to them. Public school systems routinely post the standardized test scores from the schools they operate. And if the data you need aren't already available on a website, you can use your state's public records laws to request the data in a format that can be loaded into your computer.

As for software, chances are you already have what you need to do most CAR stories: a spreadsheet program like Microsoft Excel. Think of a spreadsheet as smart paper, where your data are in a table carefully lined up in rows and columns. Each column is a different variable, such as NAME, ADDRESS, CITY, STATE, ZIP CODE, OCCUPATION, EMPLOYER, AMOUNT and DATE for a spreadsheet on campaign finance donations. Each row is a different record that includes the information for every donation reported. A modern spreadsheet like Excel can hold more than a million records, with thousands of variables.

A spreadsheet is smart paper because it can do a lot more than just list the information. One of the most useful tricks is the capability to sort the data by one or more of the variables. Good stories can be found at the top and the bottom of well-sorted lists. For instance, sorting a campaign finance table by donation amount in descending order will immediately bring all the major donors to the top. Putting a list of schools in order of their test scores is much more informative than the same list in alphabetical order.

Another important spreadsheet ability is filtering. A filter allows you to focus on just the records you want, such as only the contributions from a particular ZIP code or just the armed robberies that occurred between 9 p.m. and midnight.

Spreadsheets also have a variety of formula-based functions that let you create new information out of the variables already in the data. For instance, given a spreadsheet with total crimes and total population for each city, you can use math functions to readily calculate the crime rate for each city, thus allowing direct comparison of the crime problems in cities of different size. Another example might be a spreadsheet with school test scores from this year and last year; you can quickly calculate how many points better or worse each school did. A school that showed a huge improvement over the previous year could mean a good story about innovative teaching methods—or an investigation into the possibility of systematic cheating.

Spreadsheets also have a powerful tool called a **pivot table** that is useful for finding patterns in data that come in categories, like gender or city or type of crime or date. For instance, a campaign finance pivot table might show you the total dollars collected by each candidate in each ZIP code or which occupations donated the most money to each candidate.

Sometimes there are data stories that require more power than a spreadsheet offers. For instance, imagine that you have a table that lists all the people arrested in your state for driving while intoxicated and another table that lists all the school bus drivers. If both tables have the driver's license number as a variable, you can use a database program like Microsoft Access to link the two tables by the license number, which would give you a list of school bus drivers who have a record of drunk driving. Along with joining different tables by variables in common, database programs also are needed when you have datasets with more than a million records. Many CAR specialists also have learned to use sophisticated mapping software, which will let you answer questions like how many registered sex offenders live within a quarter-mile of elementary schools and day care centers.

If you'd like to add computer-assisted reporting to your toolbox of journalism skills, a good place to learn more is to join the Investigative Reporters & Editors organization at www.ire.org. A student membership to IRE is just $25, and it gives you access to IRE's CAR training materials, including sample datasets and exercises. Work your way through the practice materials or get hands-on training at an IRE conference or watchdog workshop, and soon you'll have a set of skills that will make you a valued member of your future newsroom.

Finding a Focus Area

In Chapter 3 we introduced you to Bruce Johnson, a reporter/anchor with WUSA-TV (CBS) in Washington, D.C., who has made a career of covering city government. It's his beat, or focus area. He makes a point of knowing the players in the city and staying connected so he can be first with a story.

Always a staple of newspaper reporting, beat reporting in television has declined over the years. The number of reporters in the newsroom decreased while market size grew. That made it more difficult for reporters to track one topic when their skills were needed elsewhere each day. But inside the KNXV-TV (ABC) newsroom in Phoenix, technology has helped beat reporting make a comeback.

"The biggest change is that we're saying 'yes' as opposed to 'no' to more story pitches during the editorial process," says News Director Joe Hengemuehler. Moving away from two-person reporter-videographer crews toward one-person multimedia journalists has increased the number of people Hengemuehler has to assign to beats, which range from aviation to crime to tourism. Even anchors have focus area assignments. "It feels almost ancient now to be hamstrung by the notion of having to have two journalists pair up to go get one story," says Hengemuehler.

Whether official or not, finding your own focus area will help you bring strong, fresh ideas to the newsroom each day and increase your own value.

A BREAKDOWN OF ONE STATION'S FOCUS AREA ASSIGNMENTS

At many stations, like Arizona's KNXV-TV, reporters or anchors have more than one topic to track each day. Often a reporter is expected to break stories based on contacts. Some reporters' focus areas center on geographical areas (e.g., Nicole Beyer, Brian Webb and MaryEllen Resendez), while others focus on subjects (e.g., Michael Hagerty and Steve Irvin), and still others focus on a combination of geography and subject (e.g., Jay Reynolds and Lori Jane Gliha).

Nicole Beyer **MMJ** Mesa Scottsdale Apache Junction	**Brian Webb** **Reporter** Phoenix MSCO	**Michael Hagerty** **Traffic** Transportation ADOT	**Jodie Heisner** **MMJ** Health Care	**Josh Bernstein** **Reporter** Government Waste	**Susan Casper** Ahwatukee Surprise Sun City El Mirage Energy
Rebecca Thomas Border Issues Latino Community	**Steve Irvin** **Anchor** Economy	**WX Team** Environment/ Green	**Corey Rangel** **MMJ** Tempe U.S. Marshals DPS FBI	**Joe Ducey** **Reporter** Consumer	**Christina Boomer** **MMJ** Peoria Casa Grande Courts
Tim Vetscher **MMJ** Glendale Maricopa County (County Attorney, Board of Supervisors, etc.) Valley Growth	**Eric English** **MMJ** Northern Arizona (Prescott, Flagstaff, Payson, Wickenburg, Black Canyon City, Grand Canyon) Phoenix	**Dave Biscobing** Pinal County Queen Creek Gilbert State Constitutional Offices (Governor, Secretary of State, Attorney General)	**Rudabeh Shahbazi—MMJ** Anthem Carefree Cave Creek Paradise Valley Fountain Hills	**MaryEllen Resendez—MMJ** Goodyear Avondale Buckeye Litchfield Laveen Tolleson	**Jay Reynolds** **Assignment Editor** Military ATF Eastern Arizona (Gila County, Superior, Globe, etc.)
Lori Jane Gliha **MMJ** Mesa ASU Education	**Chris Sign** **MMJ** Phoenix MCSO Sky Harbor Airport	**Angie Holdsworth** **MMJ** Chandler Sun Lakes State Legislature	**Katie Raml** **Anchor** Tourism Game and Fish	**Kyle Burke** Town of Maricopa Business	

Geographical Focus Areas

Many small-market focus areas are divided not by topic but by geographical area. Entry-level reporters are often assigned to a news **bureau,** which could be as little as 45 minutes away from the main newsroom or perhaps two or three hours away. This can be especially challenging because the bureau staff often consists of one person—you. Finding the story is just one of the challenges facing the bureau reporter, who must also shoot, write, edit, **feed** and perhaps perform live multiple times each day.

Young reporters say making the most of a bureau assignment comes down to staying connected. According to Julie Flannery, a former KERO-TV (ABC) reporter in Bakersfield, Calif., "You have to be a part of that community, talk with the residents. If you don't live there, do your grocery shopping or errands there, go to community events," says Flannery. "Bottom line, make sure people see you in their community and feel like you are accessible to them."

"I've made a point to make friends outside of the station," says Anne McCloy, a reporter/anchor with KOBI-TV (NBC) in Medford, Ore. "My friend at Jackson County tips me off to layoffs and unethical pay raises. My friend at the state office found out she and 150 other people were getting laid off. My car dealer got me an exclusive with a car salesman who was shot during a test drive. My friend who works for the school tipped me off to an H1N1 outbreak. The list goes on and on."

Regardless of topic or location, developing a successful focus area begins with getting to know the issues and people involved. Finding and staying in touch with sources is crucial. Otherwise you're finding out about what's new on your beat like everyone else—through someone else's reporting. Regardless of your focus area, applying certain guidelines can lead to success. NewsLab's Deborah Potter says a focus area is most productive if reporters take on a topic that already interests them. If you have a particular area of interest, let your news director or editor know about it.

Source: Adapted from "How to Build a Beat System" NewsLab.org, Sept. 2, 2009, http://www.newslab.org/2009/09/02/how-to-build-a-beat-system

TIMESAVER

Here are some helpful tips to keep you organized:

- Create story file folders for each working idea.
- Track when and how you contacted sources.
- Keep copies of emails and other correspondence.
- Take notes during phone conversations.
- Finish your workday by reviewing accomplishments and next-day tasks.

HOW TO DEVELOP A FOCUS AREA

Meet the Players

- Attend meetings that are open to the public where potential sources are likely to appear.
- Read previously published stories about your focus area. Note prominent names.
- Meet key and leading figures in your focus area informally to introduce yourself and open a dialogue.
- Always have a supply of your business cards handy.
- Always leave these informal meetings with a plan for a follow-up conversation.

Establish an Information Pipeline

- Sign up for agency email information lists and RSS feeds.
- Subscribe to industry trade magazines.
- Follow potential sources on Twitter, but be sure you're following their business and professional (not personal!) accounts. And see who else is following them.

Create a Focus Area Routine

- Set aside a specific time each week for reviewing your information pipeline.
- Use your calendar software to remind you to check in regularly with key sources via a phone call or email.

Set Realistic Goals

- As a bureau reporter, you might produce a story from your focus area on a daily basis.
- If you're just getting started in a focus area, aim to produce a weekly story.
- Discuss expectations for story production in your focus area with your news director and/or editor.

Popular Focus Areas

Even if a newsroom does not use an official system to assign focus areas, there are typical areas of concentration for reporters that develop over time. Often, this is based on someone's area of interest, expertise or sources. It can even come down to where you live.

Police

A police officer and a cops reporter have plenty in common: long hours, low pay, work outside the building and plenty of reports to read and write. Becoming a successful reporter on the police beat means taking the time to get to know the organization you're covering. How is it structured? Who are the key players?

Many beat reporters make the police station their first stop each morning. There, they can browse through police activity reports for the past 24 hours. Was there a particularly interesting arrest or incident? If you think so, chances are your viewers, readers or listeners would too. If something catches your eye, most likely the department will point you toward the **public information officer (PIO),** who can give you more information. But remember, the PIO is a representative and advocate of the department and may not give you the whole story.

While the PIO or even police chief may be available for an important interview now and then, rarely will they become key sources. Your most valuable sources will be cops who work the streets—the men and women you take the time to get to know. They may be skeptical at first, but after you run into some of the same officers on various scenes or take the time for a ride-along, you begin to form relationships with the officers.

Also get to know the people who work closely with the police department: defense lawyers, prosecutors, victims' advocates, or victims and families themselves. These sources will also have good information about issues you may want to explore. They can also act as sounding boards for reaction when a story comes out of the department.

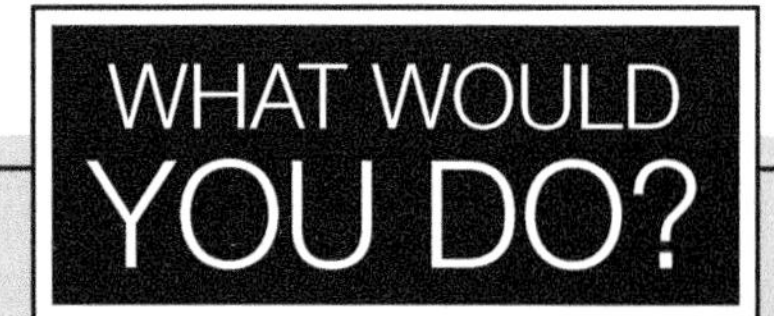

Sometimes a lead may come out of one government department and can be confirmed another way.

You've made a habit of swinging by the police department every morning on your way to work and checking arrest reports from the previous 24 hours. Flipping through the pages, you notice one person arrested for DUI has the same name as a detective in the police department.

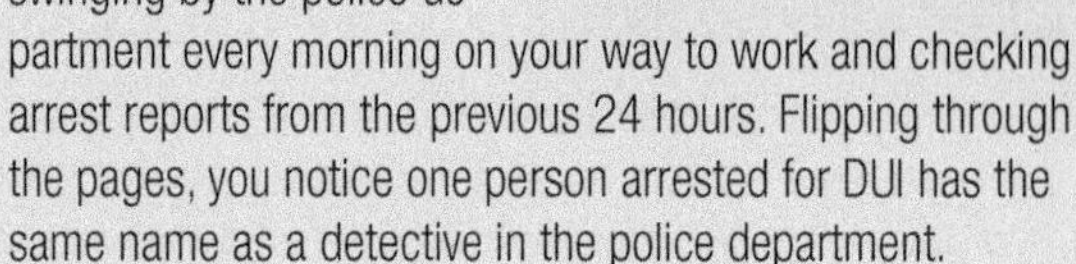

One way to find out if it is the same person would be to track down the detective and ask him directly. How else could you check out this lead?

Court

We talked in Chapter 3 about covering a case inside the courthouse, including where to turn for information about what's going on. Pulitzer Prize-winning Chicago court reporter Maurice Possley offers this advice on how criminal justice journalists can make the most of the court beat:

- **BE PATIENT.** Covering the court beat will require, at times, spending substantial time just sitting and waiting. You will wait for judges to finish their motion call before a trial begins or resumes. You will wait for cases to be called and heard before the case you are interested in is finally called before the judge. You will wait during jury deliberations.
- **BE KNOWLEDGEABLE.** Any reporter on a court beat quickly realizes the difficulty of converting the legal machinations that unfold in court into language that the reader or listener can understand. Many reporters have a lack of knowledge or oversimplify matters, and their reports mislead or misinform the public. A reporter should develop a bank of knowledgeable sources in the law that can be located easily on deadline.
- **BE OBSERVANT.** What happens in the courtroom is more than just men and women speaking words. Particularly in those jurisdictions where cameras are not allowed in the courtroom, you are not just the ears but also the eyes of your readers or listeners. Be descriptive. Bring your audience into the courtroom. Did the lawyer pace during questioning? Did the witness redden, weep, laugh or frown?
- **BE CONCISE.** Avoid jargon. Report with precision. Know what you are writing about. This last admonition would seem obvious, but when you are writing about legal matters, it is always advisable to attempt to understand the legal principle or theory that you are addressing.

  Finally, if you are unsure about something, ask someone who knows. Don't guess.

Source: From Maurice Possley, "Covering the Courts," in COVERING CRIME AND JUSTICE: A GUIDE FOR JOURNALISTS, Criminal Justice Journalists, Chapter 7, found at: http://www.justicejournalism.org/crimeguide/chapter07/chapter07_pg02.html#coveringthebeat

Government

In small markets (and some large), reporters who cover government usually make an important stop on the way into the station. Perhaps it's city hall or the county supervisor's building. It's the stop that leads to the one-on-one connection that makes a reporter successful on the local government beat. The mayor, council members or supervisors may get most of the airtime, but it's the assistants, department heads and other support staff who keep reporters informed about what's going on. Those are people you want to get to know.

What are residents complaining about? Ask the council member's support staff. Which departments are asking for money? Talk to the budget director or deputy. Which county projects are facing serious opposition? Swing by the county attorney's office.

Sometimes the best stories have roots below the city council or county commission level. Subcommittee meetings on issues like public safety, public works and finance reveal important, often contentious issues that are making their way up the ladder. At the very least, a good government focus-area reporter will scan the agendas for these meetings in search of story ideas. If you can make the time, attend. Hand out business cards, and stay connected with sources who work on this level. If not today, it will pay off in the future.

In some states, public records laws can keep you plugged in. In Fort Myers, Fla., one local TV reporter would stop by the Lee County commissioner's office, and when the elected official's office wasn't in use, he was allowed to sift though the opened mail in the in-box. He found letters from upset residents, lobbying groups or other lawmakers or officials—all sources for good story ideas.

Once you've got city hall wired, think about who interacts with lawmakers and departments so you can expand your story idea network. Citizen groups, lobbyists and businesses that do and don't have government contracts all have frequent contact with your focus area and are worth keeping an eye on. But when it comes to working with sources, remember that they often have an agenda, and it's up to you to confirm information before you report it.

VOICES *from the* Newsroom

Brianna Keilar
CNN, Washington, D.C.

CNN Capitol Hill correspondent Brianna Keilar covers perhaps the biggest government focus area of all: the U.S. Congress. But whether it's the town council or Capitol Hill, many of the same rules apply.

What is it like to be covering Congress for CNN?

Before being assigned to the Hill, I'd filled in on every beat in Washington (Pentagon, White House, State Department, Supreme Court and Capitol Hill), but covering the Hill allows a reporter the greatest access to newsmakers. With 435 members of Congress, there is always an abundance of news. And if one person won't talk to you, another will. Reporters walk the same halls that lawmakers traverse, so it allows us the ability to ask direct questions of them.

How did you begin to familiarize yourself with such a large beat?

It's important to check out all of the publications that are specific to your beat. For Hill reporters, that means Congress-specific publications like Congress Daily, Congressional Quarterly, Roll Call and The Hill. I also look at congressional and Washington coverage in The Washington Post, The New York Times, The Wall Street Journal and Politico. I found it helpful to get a broad overview of my beat by strategically reading a few books. Maybe one on the history of Congress, another on lobbying, a biography or two about lawmakers who are big players, and mixed in with all the serious stuff give yourself a humorous primer on Washington culture, such as Dana Milbank's **Homo Politicus.** It was also nice not to have to reinvent the wheel. I work with a team of on-air and off-air reporters on the Hill, and they were instrumental in helping me acclimate to my beat.

How does someone new to a beat get plugged in?

Getting to know newsmakers on your beat, as well as their staff, is essential. They are more likely to give you information if they are familiar with you and believe you are fair. Get acquainted by attending news conferences and asking questions, even if you aren't covering the particular topic *du jour,* so they are familiar with your face. It sounds strange, but loitering in hallways or outside an office is a good way to throw a question at a high-level newsmaker who is not otherwise accessible. If you want to ask about something you don't want other reporters to hear, this is a good route to take. Become familiar with a newsmaker's staff members (a press person or another staffer) by swinging by their offices and calling them frequently. These aides are often extremely plugged in and can be great conduits of information in a

breaking news situation if the public official they work for isn't available for comment. Some of these staff members are able to break down what's really happening instead of talking in the nuanced political or law enforcement jargon that many newsmakers use.

What does it take to keep up with all that's going on in Congress?

A lot of reading, a lot of networking and comfortable shoes. The marble floors are very tough on the feet. When you cover a beat like Congress, you can never really disengage. To be successful, you have to have your finger on the pulse all of the time.

How do you gain sources?

It takes time. Most press secretaries will talk to you if you call them with a question. But they will give you better information if you've developed a rapport. (See my answer about getting plugged in.)

How do you build trust in those sources?

By pursuing the truth and being fair. Most sources realize you have a job to do. And most sources and lawmakers realize it's your job to ask tough questions that may make them uncomfortable. There are many stories that sources or lawmakers would rather you not cover. But if you pursue the facts without an agenda, you develop a reputation as a fair journalist, and sources are more willing to talk to you.

How much does the competition factor into your job? How do you try to stay one step ahead?

There's a lot of competition, especially in the instantaneous age of the Internet and cable news. One of the best ways to stay on top of your beat is by making regular morning and end-of-the-day phone calls—**beat calls**—to your sources. If something is cracking, you can't assume your sources will have time to call you (though after you develop a rapport with them, they will be more likely to call you and tip you off), so you have to be diligent about reaching out often.

What's the biggest challenge for you in this assignment, both professionally and personally?

Professionally: Covering Congress has been a challenge for me because having worked my way up as a general assignment reporter, it's actually the first government beat I've covered. What a way to jump into the deep end of the pool, huh? It's such a big beat that it takes a long time to learn, and it's such a unique culture that it's similar to learning a new language or living in a foreign country. I remember during my first month covering Congress, in a moment of frustration that I wasn't acclimating quickly enough, I asked an accomplished Hill reporter how long it took him to feel that he got it. He told me it took him a whole year. That's when I realized that I needed to have patience and keep putting in the daily work that it takes to learn the Hill.

Personally: Covering Congress is a marathon and not a sprint. I've had to literally schedule time for myself because it's a beat that can become all-consuming. Some weeks are very demanding. Some weeks I hardly sleep. I've found budgeting my personal time and maintaining my hobbies and interests that have nothing to do with my job keep me grounded. It's also important to maintain relationships and friendships off the Hill. People frequently refer to Washington as a bubble with an "inside the Beltway" mentality (a reference to the highway that circles the city). Talking regularly to people outside that bubble gives me a much-needed break and also enlightens my reporting, reminding me what average Americans are really concerned about.

What do you love the most about your job?

I think that covering Congress is like visiting a zoo where there are no bars. Where else can you get so close to the story? We are truly witnessing history.

What's the worst part of your job?

Covering sex scandals. It seems just as soon as one has died down, another pops up. It's important to cover them because there are often questions about whether a law has been broken. If you make laws, you are expected to abide by them, and so there are valid questions that we must ask. But sometimes, after a few days of covering a sex scandal, you can't help but feel that you need a shower.

Do you have some advice for a young journalist trying to tackle a government beat?

- Be religious about making your beat calls.
- Develop good sources across the spectrum: Democrats, Republicans, nonpartisan experts on subjects you'll be reporting on.
- Do a lot of reading on issues pertinent to your beat.
- Accuracy above all else. I can't tell you how many times I have thanked my lucky stars after deciding to make just one more call on a story before rushing it to air, only to realize that there was more to a story than I'd previously thought or even that I didn't have it right at first. You will be defined by your mistakes as well as by your successes. It can be a challenge, especially as a budding journalist, to slow down in an industry driven by breaking news, but it's very important to be meticulous.

Education

Unpredictable sound bites, raw emotion and issues that affect nearly everyone in your audience. We're talking about the education focus area. Whether you're talking about preschool or college, most everyone has some stake in the state of education. Whether it's a parent who has a child in high school or a teacher who's struggling to find a full-time position or a faculty member who has just gotten a big research grant at the local university, most of us have a reason to be interested in school stories.

Covering education means learning to navigate layers of bureaucracy. Getting inside a classroom isn't easy. It often means getting the cooperation of a district public information official, a principal and a teacher. Maybe even permission slips from parents. But this kind of patience can pay off with stories that both educate and inspire. We often talk about finding the human angle to the story or the central character. Who better than a student affected by a budget, policy or safety decision?

When tracking the education beat, make sure you're in touch with the stakeholders from the top down. The state department of education can take the lead on topics like standardized test scores, state budget allocations and teaching credentials. But putting these policies into practice is left up to local districts. Here's where you find those most in touch with the students. Administrators, teachers and parents are all potential sources with ideas of what's going right—and wrong.

Private schools offer additional challenges. Often not subject to public records and open meeting laws, private schools can be more difficult to access. However, on occasion they can be easier because you may have to cut through less red tape to get inside a classroom.

When it comes to story ideas, remember it's about the children. Which schools are performing at an exceptionally high or low level? What separates the good from the bad? Maybe it's funding or parental involvement. In lean times how are administrators able to balance the budget? Is classroom size increasing? If so, what does more children in the classroom mean for the quality of education? Are other programs or extracurricular activities facing cuts?

Covering education is challenging, but a strong story can get the attention of a large audience.

Business and consumer

In the early 2000s, business news gained momentum. This was followed by a series of business scandals, including the Enron and Tyco cases, in which many employees lost their jobs. Together these series of stories brought business news back to the front page and to the top of the newscast. Of course, more stunning—and more newsworthy—was the market crash of 2008. The hows and whys of the economic collapse are still being written.

To become successful covering business means learning how large companies work, understanding the math behind the markets and finding an interest in records and reports. In other words, this focus area isn't for everyone.

Dozens of resources are available to reporters wanting to know more about business and the companies that make headlines. But what will ultimately make your story successful for your viewers or readers is if they understand the information and see the relevance to their own lives. As with those reporting legal and science issues, the business reporter needs to be able to translate industry jargon into terms the typical viewer can understand. Also critical is finding that central character who can explain how the latest business headline on Wall Street affects you 1,500 miles away.

A good business story will explain how events on Wall Street are relevant to the average person.

GETTING STARTED ON THE BUSINESS BEAT

Robin J. Phillips, Web managing editor
Donald W. Reynolds National Center for Business Journalism

1. **Get to know the players.** Who are the major employers in your community? Who are those companies' CEOs? Who owns them?
2. **Dig into data.** The U.S. Census Bureau has lots of information about the economy. Check out the Business & Industry section of www.census.gov for details about business sectors that are important in your county or state.
3. **Understand the local economy.** Find out as much as you can about the local work force. The U.S. Bureau of Labor Statistics, www.bls.gov, is a great resource for data on employment, unemployment, layoffs, wages.
4. **Create a tickler file.** Save Bureau about upcoming events. Keep a calendar of anniversary dates for big stories. Find out about any important trade shows or conferences you'll want to attend. Get the earnings release dates for companies on your beat. Set a reminder in your electronic calendar for the next key date you need to take action on the story.
5. **Be positive.** Budget one good news story or a profile of a company or executive for each week. Ask around about success stories, startup businesses, workers reinventing themselves. These stories will make you and your readers/viewers feel better and may help open doors for you down the line.
6. **Cultivate sources.** Have coffee or lunch with one new source every week. Attend business meetups and mixers. And make friends on Facebook and Twitter with experts in the industries you cover.
7. **Be curious.** Business stories are everywhere. Asking "How's business these days?" often will lead to surprising answers and good stories. Remember to make sure business stories relate to real people and their lives. Make sure you understand so you can explain the story without using business jargon.
8. **Go back to college.** Local universities and colleges do research on economic trends. Find out how and when they release their data. Economic roundtables are a great place to meet new sources.
9. **Go with what you know.** You are a consumer, too. If you notice trends in your personal life, check around. You may be onto something bigger. And that could lead to a good story or series of stories.
10. **Have fun.** Businesses exist to serve people. The beat is not all about numbers.

Consumer reporters rely on many of the same skills as their business counterparts, but they often find themselves working to solve the problems of readers or viewers. In many newsrooms, consumer producers or reporters are often advocates for those who appear to have been wronged by a company or government agency. Ultimately, the journalist works to hold someone accountable and, hopefully, solve the victim's problem.

TIMESAVER

Including the following websites in your own Twitter or RSS feed can help you get a jump on big stories:

- Bizjournals.com—a network of newspapers and websites that covers local businesses. Check to see if your city has one.
- Bloomberg News—financial news around the world.
- BusinessJournalism.org—free training and lots of tips and tutorials from the Donald W. Reynolds National Center for Business Journalism.
- MarketWatch—breaking financial news.
- Wall Street Journal—all things business. The website is not all free. See if your station has a subscription, and get the logon.
- Yahoo! Finance—breaking business and financial news.

Sports

While on the surface it may sound like the most fun focus area and perhaps the easiest, sports is actually one of the most challenging. Not necessarily because learning the rules of the game are as difficult as understanding a Security and Exchange Commission filing, but because sports is about relationships more than any other beat. Keeping a good relationship with athletes and coaches while remaining objective is a constant challenge.

Local teams often offer perks to reporters like free food during the game. You get to know local sports celebrities in a world where access is everything. So when most days mean hanging out at the arena or field and talking about the game, how do you maintain those relationships when you must report about a player's problems off the field? Veteran reporters say ultimately you must do your job and ask the tough questions, even if that means losing access to key sources for a while.

While many young journalists long to be the next sideline reporter for ESPN, finding good sports story ideas means casting your net far beyond the area's top teams. Sports junkies can go online or watch ESPN, so getting someone to watch the local sportscast is a much bigger challenge today. That's why sports staffs are in jeopardy in many newsrooms across the country. News directors and editors are often looking for sports reporters who can find stories relevant to the average viewer.

To make the most of this beat, take time to reach out to high schools and club teams. Special athletes, teams and coaches at this level get little, if any, attention on the national stage, so they'll be interested in sharing their stories. And they are stories that your viewers or readers won't find on espn.com. Is there a special winning (or losing) streak on the line? Is there a story just beyond what most of us see? For example, who's the backup quarterback on the best high school football team? Is he ready to step in should the star get injured? Think beyond scores and records. What are the human interest angles that might entice the audience?

And don't forget to turn around and look 360 degrees for the story. When reporter Elias Johnson, now a reporter with KPHO-TV (CBS) in Phoenix, was working in Des Moines, Iowa, he had to do story after story on the Butler University basketball team, which was performing at a high level. Just when he thought he couldn't come up with another idea, he noticed an old man hanging out around the practice court. Turns out he was a fan who hadn't missed a game in decades and a perfect central character for a human interest piece.

A good sports reporter also looks beyond the teams. Today, budgets and other money issues make up a big portion of the sports world, whether it's a local school fighting to keep a team in the midst of cuts or a professional team grappling with a salary cap. Track new high school and college rules and regulations that might affect local teams. How are school teams performing academically? Is a university grappling with gender equity issues? A well-rounded sports reporter will be able to tackle these issues too. Looking beyond the scores and highlights adds value to the sportscast—and your career.

THE DO'S AND DON'TS FOR SPORTS JOURNALISTS

Rishi Barran, sports reporter and anchor, WBBH-TV (NBC), Fort Myers, Fla.

DO

1. Be original. Concentrating on the obvious storylines is boring and repetitive.
2. Conduct interviews the way you'd ask a friend questions. If you ask a player questions the way you'd ask a nuclear physicist, chances are you're not going to get anywhere. Be conversational.
3. Ask the tough questions when necessary. Don't chicken out because you're worried about covering the same guys every week. You've got to do your job.
4. Take pride in every part of your job. Make sure you can write, interview, shoot and edit like a champ.
5. Push for your department. News directors in general don't understand how important sports are in your community. Persuade them, and stick together with the other people in sports.
6. Do the extra work. Sports departments will almost always have to work harder than the rest of the people in the building. Push yourself to do great work, including special shows if you can convince your management. You'll enjoy your job more if you make it fun, but that requires hard work.
7. Do your research before you conduct your interviews.

DON'T

1. Excessively use sport clichés and catch phrases you've heard from other people. Come up with your own stuff. If you don't, you'll sound annoying.
2. Complain excessively. Nobody wants to shoot high school sports in the rain, but most people in the business have to do things we don't like at times. It's part of the job.
3. Be lazy.
4. Do the exact same stories in the 6 p.m. and 11 p.m. shows (or whatever time your shows air). There's nothing wrong with having some of the same content, but put a different face on it at least. Write different intros and present your highlights differently. If you make one joke in the 6 p.m. show, don't make the same one at 11. You had your moment, but now it's passed.
5. Be intimidated by the competition. You have every right to ask your questions as they do, even if they work for a national outlet. Most of the time, you'll know more about the team than they do, anyway.

WHAT WOULD YOU DO?

Sometimes it can be difficult to cover bad news about people you've gotten to know through your beat.

Let's say you've covered the local minor league baseball team for a couple months now. You've gotten to know several of the players and coaches, and they seem like friends. But now there are accusations that some of the players have used performance-enhancing drugs.

One way to cover the beat would be to go straight to your sources and ask them about alleged drug use.

What other ways could you approach the story?

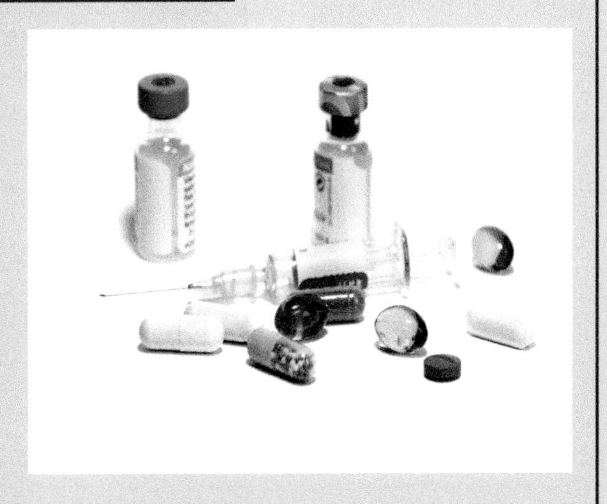

Investigative Reporting

Investigative reporting—it's the sexy side of news. Hidden camera shoots, sources on deep background and risk around the corner.

Each year thousands of young journalists enter the industry in hopes of one day breaking the next big story. Many want to specialize in investigative journalism. In some ways, all stories are investigative. You're uncovering new information and working sources to inform the public. But investigative journalists (sometimes called "the I-team") typically go further, uncovering corruption, government waste and other injustices that deserve public scrutiny.

What separates investigative stories from general assignment stories is often time. A general assignment reporter may have one, two or as many as six hours to prepare a story. Investigative stories take days, weeks or months. Even if your newsroom is too small to afford an official investigative unit, you may still have the opportunity to work on investigative stories. To move this more complicated type of story forward, consider scheduling time to work on investigative stories as you would with any other focus area. Maybe it's one email, document request or phone call each day, but find a way to consistently work on that complex story.

One key to a successful investigative beat is working multiple stories at one time. While the general assignment reporter may be juggling four or five stories, an investigative reporter may have a dozen or so in the works. As you learned in Chapter 3, many journalists are attracted to the business by the daily deadline pressure, so investigative work may not be for them. An investigative reporter doesn't mind long-term projects and can accept that some stories might fall through even after significant work.

HOW INVESTIGATIONS BEGIN

An investigative story may be based on a tip, an event or a document. But getting from tip to solid story can be a long process. First, you must translate that good tip into a theory that will serve as the basis of your investigation.

TIP

THEORY

A new style of highway median barrier fails, causing a deadly accident.

New median barriers do not work properly and put lives at risk.

An anonymous caller claims local police are sleeping on the job on the graveyard shift.

Police are sleeping on the job when they should be patrolling the streets.

A local union claims an airline is failing to approve overtime for maintenance workers.

Lack of timely maintenance is causing delays or other problems for travelers or, at worst, safety problems.

All three of the examples in the "How Investigations Begin" box could become excellent investigative stories. Uncovering a faulty barrier system or exposing police sleeping on the job would call attention to public safety issues. Discovering that an airline's financial difficulties are decreasing the number of planes ready to fly will interest travelers nationwide. As they stand, the theories might be enough to pitch to a news manager for further investigation, but to have enough information to go to air or post online will take significant investigation.

Once you have your theory, it's time to get to work. Let's take the median barrier story.

- Research background: Why did the state turn to this new kind of median barrier?
- Find sources: Who was in favor and opposed to the decision?
- Discover evidence: Is there test data that prove effectiveness?

"Just based on emails alone, there are thousands of leads we begin to investigate each year," says Tammy Leitner, an investigative reporter with KPHO-TV (CBS) in Phoenix. "Sometimes you put 100 hours into a possible story that just doesn't pan out, but you know that going into this job."

Only after you've completed significant research will you have enough information to decide if you've got a story. Sometimes the theory is false, and the story dies. If the evidence is there, however, it's time to move on to additional sources. But before moving forward, come up with a plan. What additional sources appear to be most important? Do you have any video to support the theory? (Imagine trying to do a story proving police are sleeping on the job without video of police sleeping on the job.) What's your timeline for completing this assignment?

And don't forget to stay organized. Investigative reports are often subject to tremendous scrutiny by managers, attorneys and the public. You want to be able to document every fact and every frame of video. Doing this means taking good notes and tracking the course of the investigation. Strong documentation will keep you out of trouble if you end up in court. Reporters never want to cut corners, but nowhere is accuracy more important than in investigative work. You are targeting a person, company or department whose reputations and careers are often on the line, and they sometimes strike back.

RULE OF THUMB

At first, using a hidden camera can often seem like a good way to get the video you need. But the practice brings with it a whole new set of ethical and legal considerations. First, ask yourself if there's another way to get the same video that does not include deception. Next, know the laws of your state. In two-party states, someone has the right to know if she is being recorded. CNN producer Ismael Estrada says, "We don't really use hidden cameras often. If we do, it's a case-by-case basis. We have to call our legal department, our standards and practices department and our fact checkers to make sure we can actually use them and what the laws are in each state that we would use them in. Our only policy is that we discuss any time we decide to use them and come to an agreement whether undercover video is warranted."

Ensure accuracy

Ensuring accuracy means confirming information from multiple sources. Remember, the tipster who sends an anonymous email may have a grudge against the person or place he is complaining about. With that possibility in mind, it's up to you to prove (or disprove) the information before releasing it. For example, if a Democrat gives you a document that "proves" a Republican is violating a campaign finance law, you need to secure the same document from another source, such as the Federal Election Commission. Going to air with just the original document would be reckless and could get you and your employer in legal trouble.

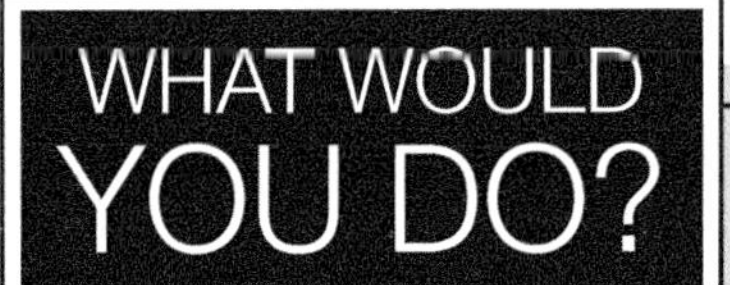

One of the main challenges facing investigative reporters is not having enough video to support the story.

You've been working a story on fake IDs being sold to illegal immigrants. Word is they're being sold inside a local car repair shop. The problem is there's a No Trespassing sign posted in front of the building.

One idea might be to figure out how to legally get a hidden camera inside. How would you go about checking whether that is an option in this case?

Keeping investigative stories alive

Many small-market newsrooms today can barely afford a general assignment news staff, let alone an expensive investigative unit. To remain relevant (and employed) today, would-be investigative reporters must be a viable part of the newsgathering process every day, not just during sweeps or key time periods. Here are some ways to help ensure your I-team's survival:

1. **Lose the I-team attitude.** While investigative reporting is a specialty, you can't forget your responsibility as one part of a much larger news team. Actively remaining a part of the daily discussion and product will remind your news managers that you are an asset rather than a liability.

2. **Attend the morning meeting.** Seasoned investigative reporters approach stories differently than general assignment reporters, who are concentrating on deadlines. How would you tackle the lead story? Is there an angle or a bit of advice you could give to the reporter assigned?

3. **Look for your nugget.** In the morning meeting, look for that element that screams "I-team sidebar." Often it is the document or bit of information the general assignment reporter won't have time to get or perhaps may not know how to find. Prove your value by taking an hour to find a unique public record and suggest it as a live companion report on what your team has uncovered.

4. **Break news.** When the assignment desk is scrambling, don't disappear for an early lunch. Step up and join the fight. CNN senior producer Ismael Estrada says, "Go where they're not. While others are covering the press conferences, etc., go through public records, to neighbors' homes or elsewhere where you can find out more than what public officials will tell you."

5. **Track the public's I-team.** Estrada also makes a habit of tracking U.S. Government Accountability Office reports, as well as state and local auditors or inspectors. These public servants are constantly rooting out public waste. These reports can provide plenty of information for a quick story.

6. **Make the most of your sources.** Morgan Loew, a reporter with KPHO-TV (CBS) in Phoenix, suggests that every time you do an investigate interview, try to get a second quick-turn story out of the same source.

7. **Volunteer to cover regular events.** Stepping up to cover events like the governor's weekly press briefing generally gives you access to rich sources for investigative ideas. Two hours of work toward the day's news coverage could help unearth your next investigation.

8. **Don't ignore court records.** Loew makes it a habit of looking through county, state and federal court indictments at least a couple times each week. He says the documents are great sources for quick scoops or interesting crime trends or angles for future investigations.

9. **Keep in touch.** Don't forget that your friends in other markets face the same challenges. Is a reporter in another city investigating a story that could also be happening in your market?

10. **Stay organized.** Come in early or stay late a couple times each week to get caught up on phone calls, emails, filing and getting stories organized.

INTERVIEWING

CHAPTER 5

> *Interviewing friends is a tough one. Your duty to the interview must transcend your friendship. Occasionally you'll lose a friend.*
>
> —*WALTER CRONKITE*

CHAPTER OUTLINE

5 Stages of Interviewing

OK, so you've scored an interview. Now what? Your next steps will determine whether you get a great interview or barely enough to pull a story together.

The right interviews build credibility and help shape your story. They form the skeleton. The steps described in this chapter will ensure that you conduct interviews that will put some real meat on the bones!

There are five key stages of successful interviewing, which we will explore in detail in this chapter.

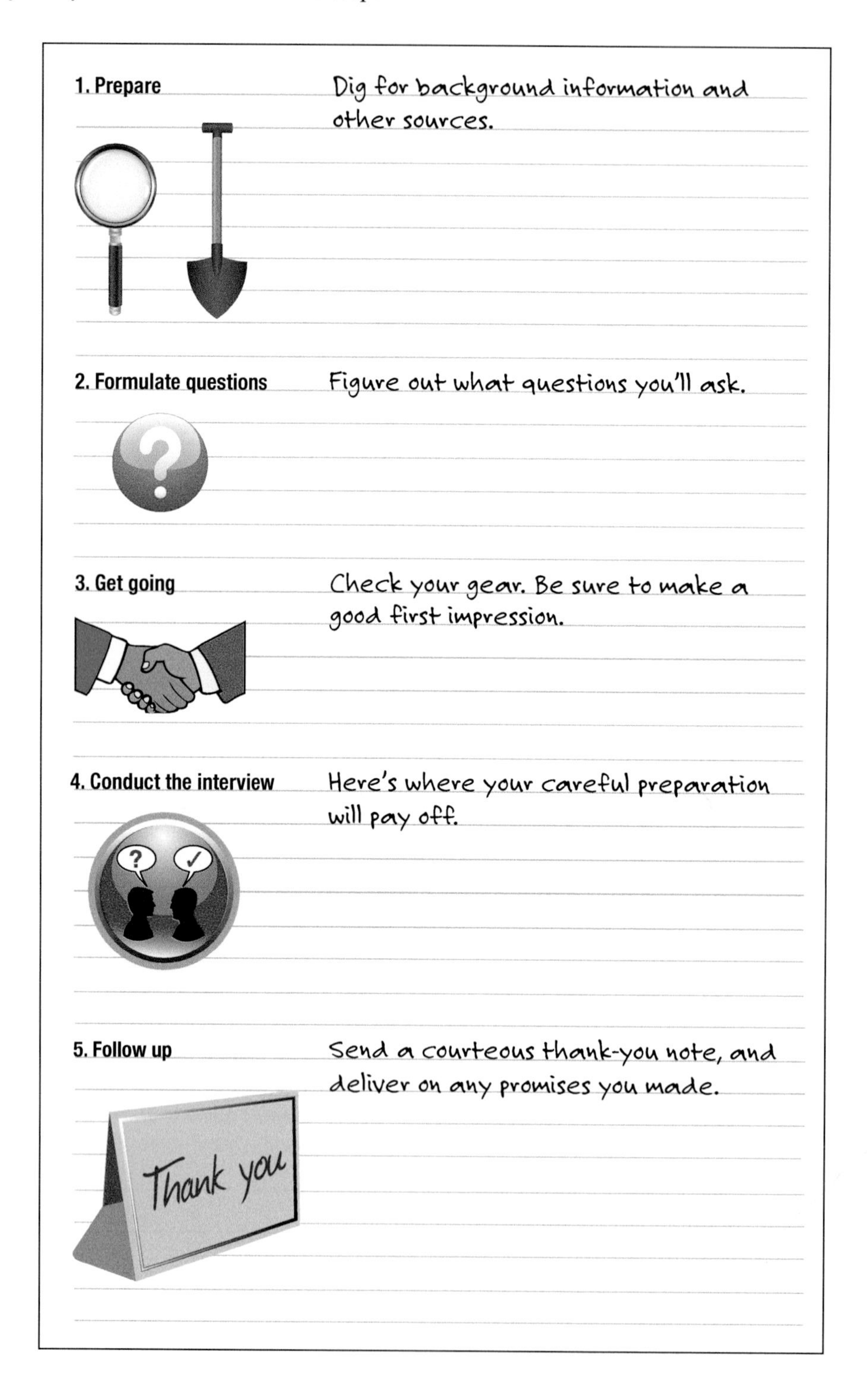

VOICES *from the* Newsroom

Susan Lisovicz, former anchor and reporter
CNN

Prepare

I've done plenty of interviews on the fly, but only out of necessity. Preparation is critical. A person who knows you've done your homework can't push you around. And you'll feel more confident, which is something you always want to project.

When I have a big interview, I go deep into the Internet vault. I'm looking not only for specific milestones in a person's life but also for anecdotes/quotes/observations that can help explain what makes this person tick. When I interviewed Mel Karmazin, the executive who runs SiriusXM Satellite Radio, I quoted Dan Rather, who said Karmazin's management style was "as blunt as a punch in the nose." That's so much more interesting than asking a generic question about his reputation as a tough manager.

Some of the best resources for an interview can be your own colleagues. When I was prepping for my interview with Bill Gates, I called a former CNNer who was a tech correspondent. He was invaluable in walking me through the rapidly changing tech landscape and what made Microsoft vulnerable. It was much more time efficient than reading reams of copy that I didn't always understand.

The cruel reality is that some of your big interviews may come with zero prep time. In this case, if you need help, ask for it.

Formulate questions

Many interviews will have areas that can be uncomfortable. My suggestion is to build the interview before you get to that point. One reason is to establish some rapport. And second, if the interview becomes hostile, you've got something in the rare event the interview ends abruptly.

One question I usually ask is about what keeps you up at night or what concerns you that you think is underreported. I asked the latter of Condoleezza Rice recently. We had talked about the Middle East, but she then started talking about Mexico and the potential of a "failed state" near the U.S. border. Mexico had been pushed aside by other recent crises, and it was insightful to hear someone speak in great detail about what was happening with our neighbor to the south. A lot of guests also like the courtesy of being able to choose the topic.

Get going

Arrive on time or, preferably, arrive early. I make a point of greeting the interviewee almost as if I were host. I introduce the guest to the crew. I make sure the microphone is dressed properly on the guest's lapel. I try to set the person at ease.

I have seen some interesting idiosyncrasies. During a commercial break before a live interview, Ted Turner started pacing back and forth on the floor of the New York Stock Exchange. It was a little unnerving, but I let him do it until the director told me in my ear to stand by. That's when I told—or ordered, actually—Ted to stop pacing and stand next to me.

Conduct the interview

It's your interview. You should control it. Many interviews are arranged because the person wants some editorial control tied to a book, movie or favorite charity. So I start with that point and then move on.

Follow up

I alert the person's staff when the story will air. I make a point of thanking the support staff. I put their names on my contact list. They are often the gatekeepers, and it is helpful if they're on your side. A short, handwritten note makes an impression, especially in the digital age. And I stay in touch with these people.

Types of Interviews

When conducting interviews, your objective is to gather both background information *and* sound bites. **Background information** helps you or your audience understand the story, but it's not necessarily something you'd want to use for a sound bite. On the other hand, carefully selected **sound bites** add credibility, reaction and emotion. Use sound bites to pepper your story with quick reactions from people on the street or in a shopping mall. Sound bites from eyewitnesses at breaking events add real-life drama to a story.

With the pressure of breaking news or a live performance, you have to think on your feet. You won't have much time for advanced preparation. Most stories, however, will be **beat** or **general assignment** reporting, where you'll have time to map out the story. In some cases, stories may take weeks, months or even years to develop. What may begin as a spot news event may over time encompass all six types of interviews. Imagine working in a newsroom when you hear firefighters respond to reports of a plane crash.

Mediated Interviews

Mediated interviews are conducted with the assistance of technology.

PHONE In the race to get information about the reported plane crash, a reporter or producer will pick up the phone to call the airport, fire department or even neighboring businesses to get the facts or an eyewitness account. This source could be put live on the air or recorded. If you can't record a phone conversation, take accurate notes and quickly transcribe them into your computer so you have a solid record.

SATELLITE Satellite interviews provide an option for talking to a source who is far away. Limitations are similar to those of a phone interview. The interviewee can't see you, so you can't show visuals or use nonverbal communication.

INTERNET PHONE (VoIP SERVICES) Voice over Internet Protocol services (VoIP) such as Skype and iChat allow you to make phone calls over the Internet using a high-speed connection. The calls are usually free if the person you're calling has the same service, which saves money on overseas calls. Other than a bit of echo, the sound is usually good. Unlike satellite calls, VoIP often allows for video.

Please describe for us what you can see from the airport terminal right now.

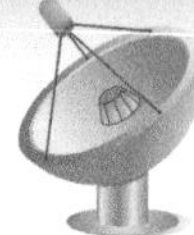

Captain Wilson, you've flown this same kind of aircraft for 15 years. Could you describe in detail what might be going through a pilot's mind during a crisis like the one we witnessed today?

Many of the passengers boarded the plane in New Delhi. What's the reaction at the New Delhi airport to this tragic news?

In-Person Interviews

To convey the immediacy of breaking news, talk to both experts and nonexpert witnesses.

PERSON ON THE STREET (POS) Quick interviews with people at a public place or even at the scene of an event add the nonexpert's reactions or opinions to your story. Keep questions simple for POS interviews. You don't want to provide background that could accidentally taint the interviewee's perspective.

Has yesterday's plane crash affected your confidence in air travel today?

LIVE Q&A Conducting an interview while on the air live is tricky. You need to get the information, keep the interview on track and also be aware of how much time you're taking. Rarely will the producer give you as much time as you want, so ask your top one or two questions first.

What can you tell us about the condition of the victims brought here to the hospital?

IN-DEPTH If you've made an appointment to interview someone, you'll have time to establish rapport with your subject and a higher level of seriousness and reflection. Other advantages are that you can shoot the person doing or demonstrating something. On the downside, it takes time to set up and conduct in-depth interviews.

How does the National Transportation Safety Board begin its investigation of this kind of accident?

Challenging Interviews

Urgent and controversial stories sometimes require reporters to get information from nervous or reluctant sources. This can make for great television, but you have to balance your drive to get the story with knowledge of legal and ethical boundaries.

SPOT NEWS On the scene when news is breaking, you'll have to fire off questions with little or no preparation. Subjects might disappear quickly, so look for potential key witnesses right away. Ask the most important questions first.

CONFRONTATIONAL Sometimes you've called and emailed to request an interview, but your source still declines or even ignores you. That's when you may have to confront him outside his office or knock on his door at home to try and get the information you need. In a confrontational interview the subject will probably be reluctant, argumentative and perhaps even combative. You'll want to ask your most important questions first because the subject could simply walk away—or slam the door.

AMBUSH In an ambush interview the source has no advanced warning that you're headed her way. Unlike a confrontational interview, you haven't called, emailed or made any advance contact with your source. While the promotions department may love this kind of spontaneous ambush, rarely does it get information that truly benefits your audience. The interviewee will probably be defensive and unwilling to answer your questions openly and honestly.

When did you realize the plane was in trouble?

Sir, we've tried repeatedly to get in touch with you. An aeronautical engineer tells us that faulty maintenance was to blame for your airline's crash. How do you respond to those conclusions?

Eyewitnesses placed you and your co-pilot at a bar just an hour before takeoff. Do you want to comment?

May I Quote You?

1. Prepare

An important preparatory conversation to have with interview subjects involves clarifying how you will refer to them in your story. Be sure you and your subjects are absolutely clear about whether you can use their name, show their image on air and quote them directly. If you have any doubts about how to proceed or if your sources are ambivalent about being quoted or pictured, check with your professor or producer.

Anonymous sources

Most sources will allow you to quote them, but some will want to remain anonymous. Sometimes the only way you can get the information is off the record (more about this below). Whistleblowers or people involved in a controversy might not want their name revealed because they're afraid they'll be embarrassed, fired or even arrested. The same is true for those who fear for their safety or that of their loved ones.

Make sure the reason for anonymity is legitimate. Especially with controversial subjects, confirm off-the-record information with another source willing to go on the record. Be skeptical. As the old saying goes, "Even if your mother says she loves you, be sure to check it out."

Verify the source's credibility

To verify that your sources are credible, look online for other articles where they have been quoted. You could even cross-check with other reporters who have interviewed them.

Public records like court documents, campaign donations and property holdings can reveal if a source is who she says she is. If your source says she has a master's degree, check with the university to make sure she graduated with the degree and didn't just attend the school. To see if the source works where she says she works, call the main number at the business or organization.

Check first before you promise

Many stations and websites discourage the use of unnamed sources. Usually the executive producer, assistant news director or news director makes the final decision. Check first before making any promises to your source.

To preserve your credibility and your news outlet's reputation, you must abide by whatever promise you make. Otherwise, you could face legal action.

Understand the ground rules

Some sources assume "off the record" is the same as "not for attribution," while others think it means you can't use any of the information in any form. Sometimes these things aren't very well defined, at least in the mind of your source. Make sure you clarify the ground rules, which are explained below, before the interview begins.

FOUR TYPES OF PROMISES TO SOURCES

On the record

You may use any background information, quotes or sound bites from the source. Clearly identify the person's name and title. Example: *Treasury Secretary Timothy Geithner said, "Our deficits are too high. They will not be solved by future economic growth, and left unaddressed they will hurt future economic growth."*

On background or not for attribution

You can use the information and quote the source, but you can't reveal the person's name or use a sound bite. Instead, use a descriptive phrase. Example: *A high-level source inside the Treasury Department said none of the top officials saw the financial crisis coming.*

On deep background

Former Secretary of State Henry Kissinger pioneered this reporting tool. When someone is interviewed on the basis of deep background, you can use the information but not reveal its source. *Example: The company president is expected to fire 1,200 workers.* Reporting speculation like this, however, can be tricky. The source might have an agenda or intentionally be misleading you. Or the information could be inaccurate. Always double-check.

Off the record

Whistleblowers and bureaucrats often leak controversial information to journalists with the guarantee that their identity won't be revealed. Although you can't use any of this material in any form whatsoever, it might lead to other sources or information.

Examples of the Ground Rules With Sources

ON THE RECORD

OFF THE RECORD

ON BACKGROUND

Prepping for the Interview

1. Prepare

To envision the many kinds of research that go into preparing a story, let's look at how one reporter might research a sports story—the filly Rachel Alexandra's historic victory in the 2009 Preakness Stakes horse race.

Filly wins Preakness

In 2009, for the first time in 85 years, a filly beat the boys in the second race of the Triple Crown. Calvin Borel, a jockey from the Cajun country of south Louisiana, rode Rachel Alexandra to victory. Two weeks earlier, Borel had ridden the winner of the Kentucky Derby. This is the first time the same jockey won both races but on different horses.

Your assignment is to interview Calvin Borel. Right after you confirm the interview, start digging for background information. Don't procrastinate! The Internet makes research easier and faster than ever before, but the news cycle is faster because of 24/7 deadlines and the competition nipping at your heels.

Dig, dig, dig

You wouldn't believe the number of times we've asked reporters what background information they've dug up for a story. They tell us, "I'm still trying to figure it out" or "I have a call in to an expert who's going to explain it all to me" or even "I was going to get more information during the interview." This kind of approach is simply not acceptable or responsible. You must do your research before the interview. Use the interview to fill in the blanks or confirm information.

Your first step

Approach the Internet like an old source on the street. This is where you might find that first juicy lead. Then pound the streets of the information superhighway to back up your angle.

The more you dig, the better informed you'll be and the more you'll come up with questions that no one else is asking. Don't forget to check social media sites like Facebook and Twitter, as well as in-depth databases like LexisNexis.

Subjects to search on Internet

- Calvin Borel
- Rachel Alexandra
- Preakness Stakes and Triple Crown
- National Thoroughbred Racing Association (jockey's bio and official stats)
- Bloodhorse.com (horse's bio)
- Steven Asmussen (trainer)
- Harold McCormick (owner)

Key info: Finding the easy stuff

Your next step

Google or Yahoo can lead to text stories as well as video clips. Don't go to the same source every time. Instead of relying only on CNN or Fox News or The New York Times, check *all* of them. Read different accounts of the same story because each might have a unique angle. Any corrections won't necessarily appear in the original article, so you might have to dig to find the most up-to-date information.

Other places to look

- Videos—YouTube, Google Video, Yahoo Video, AOL Video
- TV—NBC Sports (broadcast the race), ESPN, CNN, Fox News
- Newspapers—Baltimore Sun (the Preakness is run in Baltimore), New York Times, Washington Post, Daily Racing Form
- Radio—NPR
- Magazines—ESPN, Sports Illustrated
- Social media—Facebook, Twitter

Key info: Digging below the surface

How a poor boy from Louisiana Cajun country rose to greatness

Importance of family
Cecil Borel (big brother)
Lisa Funk (his fiancée)

Beyond the Internet
You won't find everything on the Internet. Check your own story archives to see if another reporter has covered the same subject. Talk to seasoned reporters in your newsroom. You can even make allies at other media outlets. One of your best sources might be the sports reporter at the local radio station who doesn't see your story as direct competition. Stations are beginning to share resources and content, especially in small markets.

Public records as sources

- Criminal records
- Sex offender registration files
- Real estate appraisal records

Local court records can be valuable sources. They can give you the upper hand if you know more about the topic than the interviewee thinks you do.

Start calling
After you have the basic background, pick up the phone. You don't have to interview every person on camera. You can talk to sources to gather background material and confirm information before you conduct your on-camera interviews. What you learn on the phone can help you decide what questions to ask—or even what *not* to ask.

People to call

- Steven Asmussen (trainer)
- Harold McCormick (owner)
- Cecil Borel (older brother)
- Ella Borel (mother)
- Lisa Funk (fiancée)
- Javier Espinoza (horse's groom)

Brainstorming
Based on your research and phone calls, brainstorm different angles by drawing an idea map. Next, pick the best focus for your story. When you have a clear focus, you can tailor your questions better. Share the idea map with your professor or producer to make sure you're on the right track.

Key info: Clearing the record

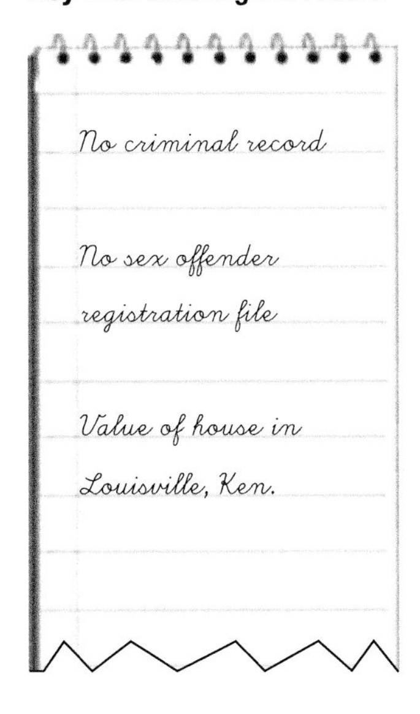

Key info: Related sources

Key info: Possible angles

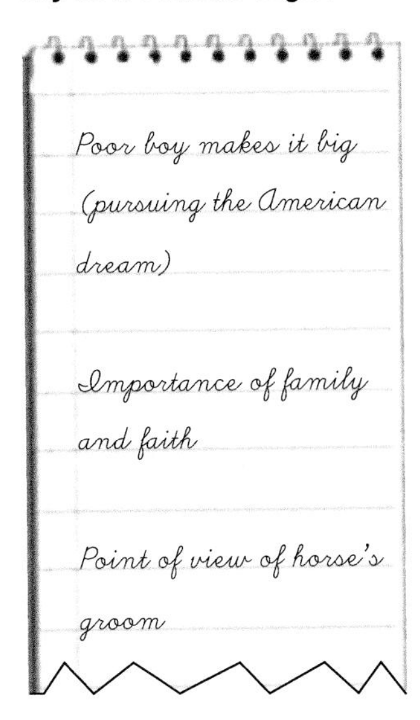

The Heart of the Interview

2. Formulate questions

Now that you've done the research for your story, it's time to figure out what questions to ask. You'll want to come up with more questions than you'll use. Since you might be nervous at the interview, it's a good idea to write down your key questions in an order that makes sense. Type them in a large font so you can read them easily while maintaining eye contact with your subject. Don't feel that you have to stick to your list like a script, however. Go with the flow! As you become more experienced, your interviews will be more like a conversation than an interrogation. For most interviews, the goal is to create the feel of a relaxed conversation in your kitchen.

The right questions

Asking the right questions is an art form that's the key to a successful interview. Like eating an artichoke, it's an acquired skill. Think of this unusual vegetable—the ARTichoke—as a metaphor for the art of asking questions. Why? You eat an artichoke from the outside, slowly peeling off leaves. You start an interview with **objective questions** designed to elicit or confirm facts. The best sound bites come after you've peeled away the first layers, when you subtly change to **subjective questions**. Like the inner leaves of the artichoke, these responses are juicier, tastier and far more satisfying as you slowly work your way to the heart of the story. Chef Christopher Koetke notes, "The artichoke still is a mystery to most. If you grab a thorny variety incorrectly, you might get a nasty poke. To most, getting to the *heart* of the artichoke, its most succulent part, is a challenge." Likewise, your first interviews will be a little rough around the edges, but with practice they'll be as smooth as the butter that artichoke lovers dip the leaves in.

> **RULE OF THUMB**
> The best interviews are the ones where you know the answers to the questions before you start talking, but be open to answers you didn't anticipate. To do this, you must listen carefully to the interviewee's answers.

Objective questions

You'd usually ask objective questions—those that produce facts—at a breaking news scene when you're interviewing, say, the public information officer (PIO). Answers to these questions provide background information rather than sound bites. If you're gathering facts, ask objective questions based on the traditional 5 W's and the H, such as these:

"Who robbed the bank?"

"What did the note to the teller say?"

"When were the robbers caught?"

"Where did they flee?"

"Why did they pick this bank?"

"How much money did they get away with?"

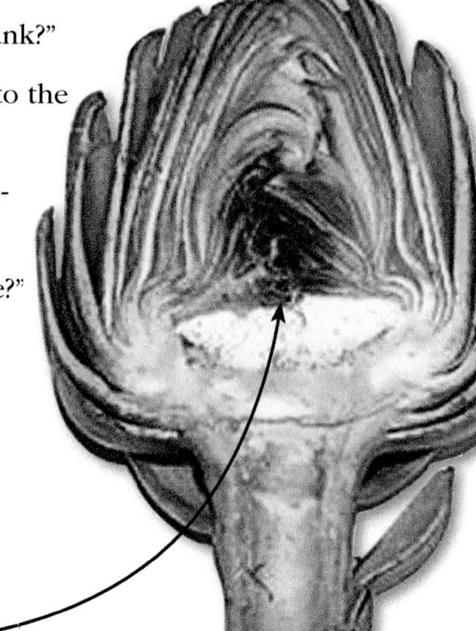

Learning and practicing the "art" of the interview will ensure that you won't "choke" up when you conduct one.

Subjective questions

Most of the time, you'll want to take your interviewees well beyond the most basic information to their subjective thoughts, feelings and opinions. Digging below the surface means asking questions that drive to the heart of an issue. Asking subjective questions of key players, such as victims and witnesses, at a crime scene can reveal insights and emotions that would otherwise go unnoticed. Questions like these might reveal insightful, even emotional, sound bites:

"Describe what you were feeling when the robbers showed you their weapons."

"What was going through your mind when the robber handed you the note?"

The Art of Asking Questions

2. Formulate questions

Don't be a reporter who asks all the wrong questions. These tips will help you get the best out of your interview.

Keep your questions short. Ask simple, direct questions. Treat each question as if it's Twitter length—140 characters. If the question is too long, the subject might forget what you were trying to ask.

> **Too long:** "Mayor Brown, your administration prides itself on concerns with critical issues like immigration, sustainability and economic recovery downtown, but of all these important issues—and surely more—which do you deem to be the number one priority of your administration?"
>
> **Shorter:** "Mayor Brown, what's your administration's top priority?"

Avoid closed-ended questions, like those below, that can be answered with one word: "yes," "no" or "maybe." Instead, ask **open-ended questions** that start with words like "how," "what" and "why." Or encourage the interviewee to describe or explain something. This is usually when you'll hear your sound bite.

> **Closed:** "Were you afraid when you saw the building collapse?"
> **Open:** "Describe what you were feeling when you saw the building collapse."
>
> **Closed:** "Did you see the robber hold up the liquor store?"
> **Open:** "Tell me what you were thinking when you saw the robber hold up the liquor store."
>
> **Closed:** "Are you passionate about this new law?"
> **Open:** "Why are you so passionate about this new law?"

Ask one question at a time. If you fire off two questions at once, the interviewee won't know which to answer first, or she might respond to only one of them.

> **Unfocused**: "How do you respond to the citizens who say the mayor's office is spending money for frivolous things, and by what percentage can you reduce such budget items in the next fiscal year?"
> **Focused:** "How do you respond to citizens who say the mayor's office is spending money for frivolous things?" (Wait for a complete answer. Then, as a follow-up, ask the next question.) "By what percentage can you reduce such budget items in the next fiscal year?"

Stay neutral. Resist the temptation to inject your opinion or anticipate a response.

> **Opinionated:** "You were rather upset by the charges."
> **Neutral:** "What's your reaction to the charges?"
>
> **Opinionated:** "Although you're not going to tell me about the case,..."
> **Neutral:** "What can you tell me about the case?"

Avoid loaded words and phrases. These can influence the listener with their baggage of bias or judgment.

Loaded	Not loaded
scheme	plan
pol	politician
peacenik	pacifist
guerrilla	freedom fighter
tree-hugger	environmentalist
do-gooder	progressive, idealist
ignorant	illiterate
anorexic	slim

Avoid polarizing questions. One example would be "Are you a moral person?" Most people are neither completely moral nor completely amoral but fall somewhere along the spectrum. Plus, few people are likely to answer "no" to such a question. Rather than forcing the interviewee to choose between these two extremes, say instead, "How would you describe your moral standards?"

Always keep an emergency question tucked in your back pocket. We call it a "Madonna question" because you could ask it of anyone—Madonna, a homeless man or a presidential candidate. Asking a question like "What challenges lie ahead?" will give you time to gather your thoughts or jot something down during the interview.

Don't be afraid to ask challenging questions, especially when interviewing politicians, bureaucrats, PR practitioners and others who are used to talking to the press. If you're well-prepared, you can keep probing until they answer your questions and justify their views. Tough questions can be thoughtful and perceptive rather than loud or dramatic. Sometimes these are referred to as "gotcha questions." Mike Wallace of "60 Minutes" perfected this technique. In-depth research allowed him to blow past the smoke screen sometimes put up by politicians and PR practitioners.

Never provide questions in advance. If you share questions ahead of time with the source, the answers will be rehearsed and lack the spontaneity of conversation. For public figures such as company bosses, providing the questions in advance gives PR departments time to help craft an answer that might hide or distort the truth.

There may be rare exceptions, especially if this is the only way to get the interview. Sometimes, for example, government officials or PR practitioners will make it difficult for you to get an interview. When East Germany was still a separate communist country, one of the authors of this book spent time there producing a documentary. To get an interview with the secretary for religious affairs, he had to submit 10 questions in advance. He did so. But once the interview began, he didn't stick to the list.

THE AMBUSH QUESTION

Ask ambush questions only as a last resort. In most cases, you shouldn't need to conduct ambush interviews. But if you've repeatedly contacted an important yet reluctant source and he's still avoiding you, then you should feel comfortable confronting him. However, failing to make any request for an interview and simply ambushing an unprepared source will likely not provide substantive information that's valuable to the viewer.

Before ambushing someone, ask yourself: "Can I get this information any other way or request an interview from this source without appearing unannounced?" Often the answer is *yes.*

Let's say you're doing a story about an overzealous homeowner's association (HOA). You've interviewed upset residents and taken video of the neighborhood. Now it's time to find the HOA president. Typical protocol would have you phone the subject, but you're under the gun, so you drive by his home. You see the man mowing the lawn out front, shirtless. Instead of introducing yourself and scheduling an interview for later in the day, you ambush the man. You walk up, camera rolling, firing questions. Your promotions department will love the fact that you've caught the man shirtless, sweaty and unprepared, but you haven't done your job as an ethical journalist. For one thing, you've done very little to ensure that your viewers get forthright answers to your questions. To achieve that end, you should approach the man, explain your story and ask his permission for an interview either right away or very soon. Let him go inside, get dressed and compose his thoughts.

Once in a while an ambush interview is necessary. Perhaps an investigative television news crew captures someone stealing goods from a Goodwill donation bin in the middle of the night. The reporter doesn't know who this culprit is or how to track him down later, so her only choice is to ambush the person immediately, capture video and ask the tough questions.

If you ambush someone, make sure the video is rolling. Use a hand-held microphone so you can point the mic at yourself when you're asking the tough questions. Often in an uncooperative interview you're holding someone accountable for questionable behavior, so hearing the tough questions being asked is an important part of the storytelling process.

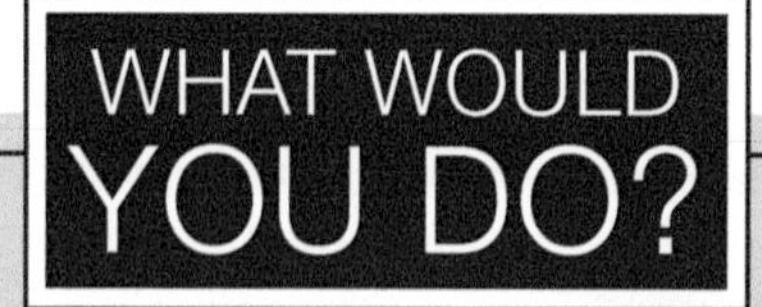

Your source has provided essential information about a local drug dealer but has asked you to use a pseudonym. She fears retribution toward her and her family.

Under what circumstances would you use a pseudonym? What would you tell your viewers? Does using a pseudonym reduce the credibility and verifiability of your story?

If you were a news director, what guidelines would you draw up for deciding when to use pseudonyms?

Out the Door

3. Get going

You've finally set up the interview, done your research and come up with questions. Now you're ready for the interview. As we noted earlier, some interviews can be done by phone, but there's nothing better than talking to your subject in person.

Try to talk face to face

Even if the story is for radio or an online publication, try to conduct the interview face to face because it's amazing what you can find out by showing up in someone's office or home. You can spot details, such as a university diploma or black belt certificate on the wall, family pictures on the desk or maybe a roller derby trophy on the bookshelf. These details might or might not make it into your story, but they can add substance and depth or give you ideas for more questions.

Also, when you do an interview in person, you can pick up on facial expressions, which can tell you a lot. You might note disgust or irritation that you probably wouldn't pick up if you were conducting the interview over the phone.

Location, location, location

If visuals are important to your story, you'll want to think carefully about the setting for your interview. Spot news and disaster stories create their own settings. Features allow you to be as creative as a Hollywood director.

When you have the time, try to meet your subject in the environment most appropriate to the subject matter and where he'll feel the most comfortable. If your story is about a construction worker, don't interview the person inside an office. Meet him at the job site or, at the very least, go outside the office. Even better would be to interview the source while he's working with tools in his hands. Just be sure this doesn't interfere with your interview audio or become a visual distraction.

Think about visual consistency. If most of your story is about something that takes place outdoors, keep it that way. Your story will flow better and save time in the editing process.

Be prompt

All your hard work will be lost if you miss the interview. It's disrespectful to ask someone to give you time—and then arrive late. To make sure you're ready and on time:

- Use a good map. Consult MapQuest or Google Maps.
- Give yourself plenty of time in case you get stuck in traffic or can't find a parking spot.
- Arrive about 15 minutes before the interview so you can set up your equipment and take a deep breath.

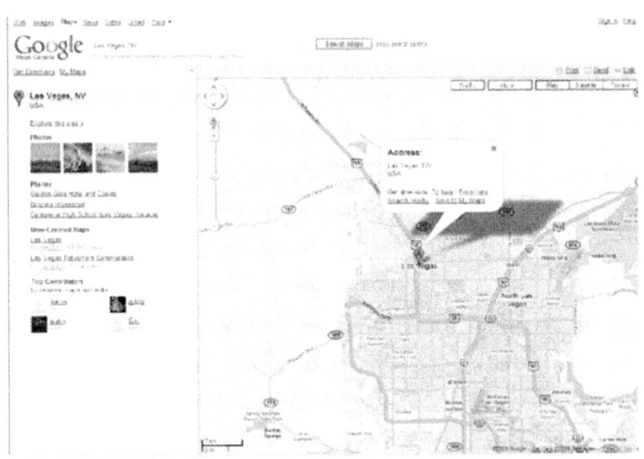

Be prepared

On your way to the interview, think about every possible reaction that might come from the interviewee. Ask yourself how you'd react. That way you're less likely to be caught off guard during the interview, and you'll be able to maintain your professional demeanor and control of the interview.

Dress appropriately

Make a good first impression. If you dress like a student in jeans and a T-shirt, you'll be treated like a student. If you dress like a professional, you'll be treated like one. At the very least, wear tailored pants and a nice shirt or blouse. Guys should also have a tie and possibly a sport jacket. In some cases, however, you'll want to dress the way you think your interviewee will be dressed in order to make her feel comfortable. If you're going to interview a farmer in the barn, wear good jeans and a polo shirt or denim shirt.

Go easy on the cologne or perfume. Some people are allergic to fragrances.

Partnering with your videographer

Map out a visual strategy with your videographer. Talk about the interview. Let her know what you want to get from the interview so she can react accordingly with the camera—zooming into or out from the subject when the subject makes appropriate comments.

Greeting your subject

When you introduce yourself, look the interviewee in the eye and shake his hand firmly. Also shake hands when greeting a person with a disability. People with prosthetics or limited hand motion usually shake hands despite the disability.

Handshakes in other cultures, however, might be limper than the firm American greeting. Or they might be refused. Some Muslim men, for example, might not shake hands with a woman. If you're venturing into unfamiliar terrain, do some background research. Let the interviewee greet you, then respond in kind.

Exchange business cards

This first impression will set the tone for the interview. Exchange business cards, which will ensure that you spell the subject's name correctly and have contact information. You can add the name to your electronic Rolodex as you build your list of sources. Be sure to get a cell phone number, which improves your chance of reaching someone 24 hours a day. (Later, note the date and subject of your conversation on the back of the card.) Then thank him for his time. If he has told you he has only 15 minutes, stick to the limit so he'll be willing to talk with you again.

Call me . . .

If you don't know the interviewee, use the person's title and last name, such as "Dean Callahan" or "Mr. Smith." Let the interviewee say, "Please call me Chris."

Some common forms of address are listed below. For others, check your AP style guide.

COMMON FORMS OF ADDRESS

GOVERNMENT OFFICIALS	
Ambassador	Ambassador (last name)
Cabinet member	Mr. or Madam Secretary
Governor	Governor (last name)
Judge (federal, state and local)	Judge (last name)
Mayor	Mayor (last name)
Representative, U.S. or state	Representative (last name)
Senator, U.S. or state	Senator (last name)
LAW ENFORCEMENT	
Chief of police	Chief (last name)
Detective	Detective (last name)
Police officer	Sergeant or Lieutenant (last name)
HIGHER EDUCATION	
Dean	Dean (last name)
President	President (last name)
Professor	Ask the person's preference
Provost	Provost (last name)
CLERICAL AND RELIGIOUS ORDERS	
Imam	Mullah (last name)
Minister	Ask the person's preference
Priest	Father (last name)
Rabbi	Rabbi (last name)

When interviewing someone in a wheelchair, make sure both the reporter and the camera are at eye level with the subject.

Encountering Diversity

3. Get going

As a reporter, you'll have opportunities to interview people from different backgrounds. If you'll be talking to someone from an unfamiliar culture or whose experiences and opinions may be very different from your own, set your preconceived notions aside.

Cultural smarts

For multicultural reporting, Ruth Seymour, a journalism professor at Oakland University, recommends observing the interviewee carefully and then adjusting your behavior accordingly. "Things go more smoothly if you expect behavioral differences, notice them, and do what you can to honor the other person's comfort zone." Seymour offers eight tips for helping your source feel at ease:

1. **Physical closeness.** Respect the interviewee's personal space. Let her determine how close she wishes to stand or sit.

2. **Saying hello.** When meeting someone from another culture, pause for a few seconds. Let the other person greet you first. Respond accordingly.

3. **Facial expressions.** Follow your source's lead when it comes to smiling and eye contact.

4. **Showing respect.** Address someone as Mr. or Mrs., especially if older, rather than by first name. If you're not sure which is the first name and which the last name, ask the person: "What would it be best for me to call you?"

5. **Touch.** Don't touch anyone unless you're familiar with the culture or have spent time observing who touches whom, where, how long and under what circumstances.

6. **Talking style.** Spend a little extra time with friendly small talk before asking your questions. Avoid contractions and idioms ("Go out on a limb," "Way to go") that might confuse your subject. Talk more slowly than usual, and allow longer periods of silence.

7. **Gifts and food.** Don't reject your host's offer of food or a beverage unless you have a health reason for doing so. Accept small gifts or keepsakes with grace and pleasure. Discuss the ethical boundaries in your newsroom or classroom.

8. **Gender and age roles.** Treat elders in other cultures with respect rather than in a patronizing or familiar way, as North Americans tend to do. Cultures with strict gender roles probably also observe strict rankings of respect based on age.

Source: Ruth Ann Seymour, "Eight Steps toward Cultural Competence," Poynter Report, Poynter Institute for Media Studies, Special Issue, November 2002, Poynter Online, updated March 2, 2011. © Ruth Ann Seymour. This piece was originally published in print and online by The Poynter Institute for Media Studies.

INTERVIEWING A PERSON WITH A DISABILITY

Review these tips from the National Center on Disability and Journalism the next time you interview someone with a disability.

Before the interview

- Ask the person you're interviewing about any specific needs, such as wheelchair access, a quiet place or an interpreter. If you're not sure how to deal with the request, ask the interviewee.
- Schedule plenty of time for the interview. Some accommodations, such as an interpreter, require extra time.
- If a person is in a wheelchair, make sure the interviewing area is physically accessible. Place yourself and the camera at the interviewee's eye level.

During the interview

- Use the same interviewing techniques and manner as you usually do.
- Speak to the person. Maintain eye contact instead of interacting with the interpreter or a companion.
- When talking to someone with a hearing loss, face him. Don't cover your mouth when you speak. Sit so you face the light source and aren't backlit. Talk when the person is looking at you.
- When interviewing someone with a visual impairment, identify yourself and others who might be with you.
- Listen attentively when talking with someone who has difficulty speaking. Be patient. Wait for the person to finish instead of correcting him or speaking for him. Don't pretend to understand if you're having difficulty doing so.

Etiquette suggestions

- Focus on the person rather than the disability.
- If you offer assistance, wait until the offer is accepted. Then ask for instructions.
- Don't lean or hang on a wheelchair or other assistive device. It's part of a person's space.
- Guide dogs and other service animals are working. Don't make eye contact, praise, talk to or pet the animal. This is distracting for both animal and owner.

Source: National Center on Disability and Journalism, Tips for interviewing people with disabilities; www.ncdj.org, Nov. 23, 2009. Reprinted with permission of the National Center on Disability and Journalism.

Setting Up

4. Conduct the interview

Be a team player. Carrying the tripod when working with a video journalist will go a long way toward building rapport. Check with each other when setting up your equipment. Is this a good location? If you're outside, where's the sun? Where are the shadows? What's your audio going to be like? Are there distracting noises?

Put on your mic

Whenever possible, mic yourself as well. You can point the microphone at yourself, use a second lavalier microphone or stand close to the camera microphone. Sometimes stories are better told by using your questions as well as the subject's answers. Doing so can add variety to the narrative flow—the audio part of the script. Don't overdo this technique, however. Vain reporters want to hear their voices all the time asking questions. It also slows down the script. You want the sound bites from the source. Your voice will be on the audio track.

A common mistake is conducting an interview with the microphone directed to the wrong audio input. It's very embarrassing to have to call back later and ask to repeat an interview.

Check your gear

After you've set up your equipment, make sure it's working right. Remember to check your lighting. Do a sound check, and play a little video back in the camera. How does it look? Is the sound crisp?

Relax

While you're setting up your gear, chat with the interviewee. Ask how his day is going. If he went to the same school as you did, talk about that. This will help your subject relax and also give the video journalist an opportunity for **b-roll,** which is the extra footage you shoot to use as cover for your reporting track or during a sound bite.

Even as a student, you're often more experienced with video equipment than the person you're interviewing. If she seems nervous, try to ease her mind about the process. You can joke or talk about the weather. If the source still seems anxious about what she'll look like on camera, you can show her by flipping the camera's viewfinder around for her to see. Remind her that you're there to get information and present her in a professional manner.

If a video journalist is setting up the equipment, use that time to review background information with your interview subject.

Eyes wide open

Note details in the room that could help you write to your video later or that might trigger a response. These conversation points could be a diploma, a sports trophy, a photo of children playing soccer or an interesting souvenir. Case in point: A renowned neurosurgeon wasn't forthcoming during an interview until asked about the photo of his parents on his desk. He then launched into an animated discussion about their heroism during World War II. Their courage had inspired him to become a doctor.

Remind yourself of your purpose

Before you start the interview, remind yourself of what you want to accomplish. Are you looking for facts only, or are you trying to elicit emotion and reaction?

If your topic involves lots of facts and figures but you're looking for emotion and reaction, get the numbers and other background information off camera. Use your on-camera interview carefully. Stay on point. The more you stray off topic, the more tape you're going to have to log and listen to later.

Starting the Interview

4. Conduct the interview

Start by asking the interviewee to say her name and title—and spell it. Jot it down in your reporter's notebook as a backup. You won't be happy if you have to call a few minutes before deadline because you don't have the proper spelling.

Get personal

Chat about the interviewee's personal life. This will put the person at ease and can add context to the story. You might ask about siblings and find out that your interviewee grew up in foster care. She might start talking about how her tough childhood made her want to fight harder to help other kids. Or you might ask someone what he does in his free time and learn that he collects antique tractors. Although you might not use that tidbit in your story, it could lead you to doing a feature story on the growing popularity of this hobby.

If you have only 10 minutes

If your time with the source is limited, ask the most important questions first. Recently a student was trying to interview a state lawmaker who'd been charged with driving under the influence without a license. Ironically, the lawmaker was now co-sponsoring a number of bills calling for tougher DUI laws.

The reporter was told the lawmaker would talk to her for only 10 minutes—probably time for just three or four questions. The student and her faculty editor worked together to figure out the most important questions.

One sure bet: "What were you thinking the night you got behind the wheel of that car after downing several drinks?"

The next question: "Didn't you think of the other people on the road and their lives?"

Then, of course, the follow-up: "Don't you think it's ironic that you're asking for tougher penalties for drunk drivers, yet you got a lighter sentence as part of a plea deal?" At this point the lawmaker might walk out, but at least the reporter would have what she needs.

If you have more than 10 minutes

Let's say you have more than 10 minutes to interview a lawmaker who's pushing for new tax cuts for bar owners. Don't start right off with this: "I hear you were arrested for DUI, and now you're sponsoring a bill supporting bar owners. Why?"

Instead, open with an easy question to make the lawmaker feel comfortable. Ask why she thinks we need this new law. Why is she so passionate about co-sponsoring the bill? Only then should you ask about her DUI—if she hasn't already brought it up herself. If you start with that tough question, you might not get anything from her.

RULE OF THUMB

Don't be afraid to rephrase a question and ask it again and again until you get a satisfactory answer. You might have to ask a question several times to get a good sound bite, especially if the interviewee is

✓ long-winded
✓ wandering off topic
✓ evasive
✓ professionally trained to avoid answering

Listening and Responding

4. Conduct the interview

Listen up!

Ten percent of your job was coming up with the questions. Now, the remaining 90 percent is listening to the answers and responding. The interview *is* a conversation. Focus, listen, react and be interested in making this conversation the best it can be.

Don't feel you have to talk. Silence has amazing power. As humans, we have a natural tendency to fill silence because it makes us uncomfortable. If you ask a question and the person doesn't answer right away, let the silence stretch out. The interviewee will eventually feel compelled to fill it, and this is often when you get really honest responses instead of canned answers.

Often reporters are so intent on asking all the questions on their list that they forget to listen to the responses. They miss opportunities for follow-up questions or emotional responses. Sometimes the respondent will unveil something you didn't know, and if you're not listening, you can't follow up and capitalize on the moment.

Shhhhhhh...

Give visual feedback by nodding your head. Don't talk or murmur encouraging words while the interviewee is talking. The microphone will pick up "Um" and "Yes."

Jot down important things

Record names, numbers, key points and other important information in your notebook, but don't write everything down. If your camera is working correctly, you've got a good backup that allows you to pay attention to your source. Some people like to use a small audio recorder as a backup.

Don't be hijacked!

Stay in control of the interview. Public information officers (PIOs), communications directors, and police or fire spokespeople are well-trained in handling the media and can easily take control of your interview by giving vague answers, refusing to answer questions, or turning the tables and interviewing you. We call this "hijacking an interview." When you get back to the station, you realize you never got any answers at all. That's why it's so critical to pay attention and listen.

Politicians are good at hijacking interviews too. After the president's State of the Union address, members of Congress flood into Statuary Hall to be interviewed by networks from around the world. They'll move from reporter to reporter, hoping to get their reaction back to their own state or district. Time is precious, and the politicians know this. You'll hear a reporter representing a station in Phoenix ask a congressman about illegal immigration, but the elected official gives his opinion on health care instead. The reporter has been hijacked. If the station wants that congressman's reaction to the major news of the evening, then it's going to be on the topic that the congressman, not the reporter, wants to discuss.

Clarify and confirm

An interview isn't going to do you much good if you don't understand what the subject said. If you simply don't get it, say so! There's nothing wrong with asking someone to explain the information and where it came from.

Reporters are often called upon to become instant experts on a topic. They must collect and digest information, then deliver it to the audience in a simple, easy-to-understand format. To meet this challenge, you must be sure you have your facts straight and understand what your sources are telling you.

When US Airways Flight 1549 made an emergency landing on the Hudson River in 2009, the images of passengers standing on the wings of a floating plane captivated the nation. The pictures were everywhere—on television, online and on mobile devices.

In newsrooms across the country and even around the world, local reporters were immediately assigned to figure out how this could happen and how the pilot managed to land that plane on water without engine power. Your first instinct as a reporter would be to track down a commercial airline pilot. But imagine the technical details that could emerge in the interview—differences between the Airbus A320 and the Boeing 737, the role of thrust, what happens to an airplane when an engine fails, what the difference is between flaps and ailerons.

Good reporters aren't afraid to confirm facts or clarify information. Pretending to know more than you do will only get you in trouble. And you can probably assume that if you don't know what an aileron is, most of your audience won't either. Simply say, "Excuse me, but could you explain to me one more time the difference between the flaps and the ailerons?" Or "Is it possible for the engine to be on yet not produce any thrust?"

A good source will understand that you're trying to make sure you're accurate and your audience gets the straight story. Finally, even when you think you've got everything straight, make sure you know how to track down your sources in the hours ahead as you're preparing your report. You might have to clarify information or confirm a fact one more time.

Be polite and professional

No matter what, always be courteous and professional—even if the person you're interviewing isn't. The more you've prepared and the more you know about the person, the more confident you'll be during the interview and the more likely you are to earn your source's respect.

When interviewing someone who appears to be avoiding your questions, it's easy to lose your cool and even become combative.

> **Reporter:** "We have documents that indicate mismanagement of donations."
> **Source:** "You don't know what you're talking about."
> **Reporter:** "Please take a look at page 36."
> **Source:** "You're not reading that correctly."

The next question is key.

> **Combative:** "Yes, I am. You're avoiding the question. Where's the money?" This response will upset the source further and escalate the anger.
> **Constructive:** "If I'm not reading this correctly, please walk me through the documents and explain how you read them."

Don't be afraid to question with confidence, but if you find yourself beginning to argue, remember that you're trying to get the source's take on the story, not advocate for someone else's point of view. Simply note or even record the source's behavior should you need to refer to it later.

QUESTIONING SOURCES DURING DIFFICULT TIMES

In breaking news stories, be especially careful about interviewing victims. You don't want to re-traumatize them with a stereotypical question like "How do you feel?" Such a question can harm the innocent and insult the viewer. Also, it's so open-ended as to be almost meaningless.

Use judgment and compassion. To avoid harm, try a more neutral question, such as "What would you like to tell viewers?" Be open to the possibility that the potential interviewee might simply wish to say nothing. Respect that.

These tips for interviewing victims and families come from the Dart Center for Journalism & Trauma, which helps journalists learn how to cover trauma, conflict and tragedy. You'll find other helpful information on the Dart website: http://dartcenter.org/.

- Journalists can help victims and survivors tell their stories in constructive ways that make for great journalism.
- Sometimes you can't avoid intruding upon someone in grief. If you can't postpone your contact, remember to be sensitive and respectful in your approach.
- Start the conversation with a sincere sentiment, such as "I'm sorry for your loss."
- Don't assume that victims or family members won't want to talk. Often they're eager to share their story and memories with a journalist.
- If someone doesn't want to talk to you, be respectful and polite. And don't forget to leave your business card. At some point the person might decide to talk to a reporter, and he'll likely call the one who made the best impression.
- Make sure the person understands the terms of the interview. Tell him: "This is an interview for a story I'm writing. Your quotes will appear in media coverage along with your name." Remind him of the terms periodically.
- Pay attention to your own emotions during the interview, and let your reactions inform your reporting (while remaining professional). If you find something emotionally stirring, chances are viewers will too.

Be aware of body language

Keep in mind that conversation isn't only verbal. Your source's posture, facial expressions and mannerisms will indicate whether she's interested or impatient. And you, too, are giving signals with your body language.

People can't always control their emotions. If the interviewee shows signs indicating discomfort about a particular question, stay with that topic for a bit. Find out why she cringed when you asked the question.

Remember, however, that you're interviewing, not interrogating. If you see someone fidgeting and avoiding eye contact, he's either frightened about being interviewed or might want to avoid answering the questions.

> **Interrogating**: "Why aren't you answering my questions? Why won't you look at me?"
> **Interviewing**: "I see this is difficult for you, but it's important information. Let's go over it one more time."

WHAT WOULD YOU DO?

It's often difficult to draw clear boundaries about when it's OK to accept gifts and favors. Some decisions are easy, such as not accepting an expensive gift that would compromise your coverage.

But what if you're interviewing someone over lunch, and the source picks up the check? How do you determine if she's merely being nice or if she's trying to curry favor with you? Does it matter if you ate a hot dog or a 16-ounce filet mignon?

What if your source gives you a gift? Should you accept it if it's worth less than $10?

Let's say you're doing an in-depth story in a community where food or small gifts are regularly exchanged. What would you do if your station bans gifts, but in this community it would be considered rude to refuse?

What if a frequent source gives you a gift during the holidays? Would you accept it?

As news director, what guidelines would you develop for gifts and favors?

BODY LANGUAGE: READ THE SIGNS

Your source may be impatient or scared if you notice the following:

- Folding arms across chest
- Staring blankly or shutting eyes
- Scowling
- Pointing one finger at interviewer

Your source may be nervous if you notice the following:

- Nodding like a bobblehead doll
- Slouching or rocking in chair
- Leaning back or toward door
- Drumming fingers
- Jiggling legs or tapping feet
- Fidgeting
- Constantly moving hands or arms

Your source is confident and comfortable if you notice the following:

- Resting hands in lap or on armrest
- Keeping eye contact without staring
- Smiling when appropriate
- Nodding in moderation
- Sitting straight and leaning slightly forward
- Aligning body with that of interviewer
- Keeping head straight or tilting it a little
- Keeping feet still
- Sitting still and relaxed
- Gesturing in moderation

Concluding the Interview

4. Conduct the interview

There's no ideal length for an interview. Sometimes you get the best sound bites in the first five minutes. Sometimes it takes an hour. With practice, you'll learn when you have enough material.

The last question

After you have everything you need, ask the interviewee what else he wants to add. You won't believe the number of times this response ends up being the best sound bite of the interview. Or ask who'd be another good person to talk with about this topic. You might be surprised by the answer. Another way to wrap up is by asking the interviewee to summarize the most important thing you've discussed today.

If you're lucky enough to have a video journalist, ask her if there's anything she'd like to ask. You're a team, and sometimes she'll see or hear something you missed.

Make a graceful exit

The more interviews you conduct, the better you'll get at hearing the sound bite the moment it comes out of your source's mouth. The problem is that your source wants to keep talking… and talking… and talking. How do you extricate yourself from an interview that could seemingly go on forever? Be honest. Say to your source: "Thank you. This has been wonderful. I think I have everything I need. We want to get this story out as soon as possible, so I'll have to get going."

Keep rolling

After thanking the interviewee, make sure you or your video journalist continues to roll. Explain to the source that the formal part of the interview is over, but the camera is still rolling. You might be surprised how much the person opens up after the formal interview is over. You might pick up emotional or descriptive sound bites because the interviewee is talking to you instead of focusing on the camera. If you have a question you really want to ask again, then say something like this: "You know, just let me make sure we got this right. Can you please describe again what was going through your mind when you saw that car coming at you?"

Don't forget b-roll!

Don't leave without your b-roll! Let's say you're talking about the state capital in your package. You want viewers to see shots of the capitol building. When you're interviewing someone at his office, you need to get some cover shots of him, maybe

B-roll of government watchdog website

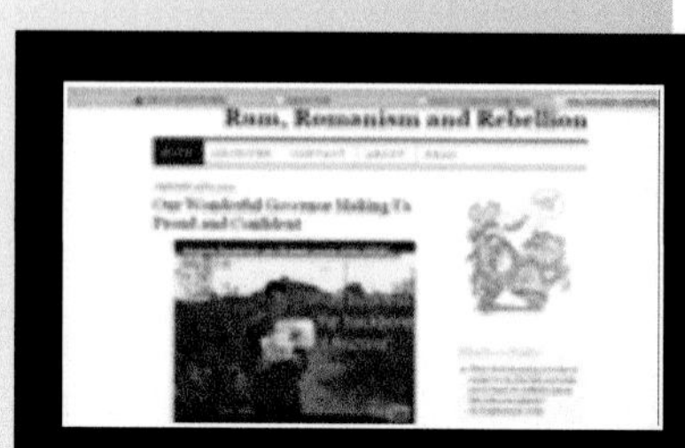

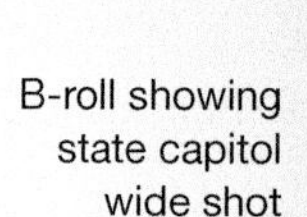

B-roll showing state capitol wide shot

B-roll showing governor medium shot

Interview with blogger medium shot

Hands typing close-up shot

Blogger in action medium shot

working at a computer. If it's a doctor, shoot her working in the emergency room, talking to office staff or caring for a patient—so long as you have the patient's permission. If it's a police officer, shoot him out on patrol.

B-roll adds color to your stories. You'll surely regret sitting down to edit your story and finding that you have no cover video of the person you interviewed. Sometimes this happens when you're in a hurry, but that's no excuse. It takes just a few minutes to get close-ups of him, his hands, his eyes, his computer, pictures on his desk, anything that will help you in editing.

When shooting b-roll, be sure to capture sequences—a wide shot, medium shot and tight shot. This variety of shots will make it much easier to pull your story together than if you have only a bunch of wide shots.

For a story about an Arizona blogger covering state politics, the reporter interviewed the blogger in his "office," which happened to be anywhere he could get Internet access. Along with getting the interview itself, the reporter made sure he had plenty of b-roll to cover his story. He shot cover video of the writer working on his computer, close-ups of the blog and shots at the state capitol building to represent the political stories the blogger was covering.

GUIDELINES FOR INTERVIEWING JUVENILES

Al Tompkins, Broadcast/Online Group Leader, The Poynter Institute

Understanding how young people see the world around them often demands that we hear what they have to say. Adults aren't the only ones with worthy views of news. But interviewing young people raises some of the most challenging questions faced by journalists.

Especially in breaking news situations, juveniles may not be able to recognize the ramifications of what they say to themselves or to others. Journalists should be especially careful in interviewing juveniles *live* because such live coverage is more difficult to control and edit. Juveniles should be given greater privacy protection than adults.

The journalist must weigh the journalistic duty of "seeking truths and reporting them as fully as possible" against the need to minimize any harm that might come to a juvenile in the collection of information.

When interviewing juveniles, journalists should consider:

Journalistic purpose and quality of information

- What is my journalistic purpose in interviewing this juvenile?
- In what light will this person be shown? What is his/her understanding or ability to understand how viewers or listeners might perceive the interview? How mature is this juvenile? How aware is he/she of the ramifications of his/her comments?
- What motivations does the juvenile have in cooperating with this interview?
- How do you know that what this young person says is true? How much of what this young person says does he/she know first-hand? How able are they to put what they know into context? Do others, adults, know the same information? How can you corroborate the juvenile's information?
- How clearly have you identified yourself to the juvenile? Do they know they are talking to a reporter?

Minimize harm

- What harm can you cause by asking questions or taking pictures of the juvenile even if the journalist never includes the interview or pictures in a story?
- How would you react if you were the parent of this child? What would your concerns be and how would you want to be included in the decision about whether the child is included in a news story?
- How can you include a parent or guardian in the decision to interview a juvenile? What effort has the journalist made to secure parental permission for the child to be included in a news story? Is it possible to have the parent/guardian present during the course of the interview? What are the parents' motivations for allowing the child to be interviewed? Are there legal issues you should consider, such as the legal age of consent of your state?
- If you conclude that parental consent is not required, at least give the child your business card so the parents can contact you if they have an objection to the interview being used.

Explore alternatives

- What alternatives can you use instead of interviewing a child on camera?
- What are the potential consequences of this person's comments, short term and long term?
- What rules or guidelines does your news organization have about interviewing juveniles? Do those guidelines change if the juvenile is a suspect in a crime and not a victim? What protocols should your newsroom consider for live coverage that could involve juveniles?
- How would you justify your decision to include this juvenile in your story to your newsroom, to viewers or listeners, to the juvenile's parents?

The Golden Rule for interviewing children

"Do unto other people's kids as you would have them do unto your kids."

Source: Al Tompkins, "Guidelines for Interviewing Juveniles," Poynter.org, August 14, 2002.

Wrapping Things Up

5. Follow up

The research you did beforehand and your professional demeanor during the interview will go a long way toward ensuring the success of your final story. But don't forget that the *last* impression you make on your source is just as important—if not more important—than your first impression. Especially if you'll need to go back to your source to clarify or follow up, be sure that you conclude your interview on a professional and confident note.

Keep your promises

Many interviewees will want to know when the story will air. Explain that producers back at the station make that decision. You can make a good guess, but don't promise anything. You can offer to call and inform the interviewee. If you do promise, make sure you keep your word. You're earning your reputation. Failing to keep a commitment could hinder your future relationship with the source.

Some people will ask you to send them a copy of the story. Most news outlets have a policy to address these kinds of requests. Following the policy protects you from any unapproved use of the video by a person or organization. For example, if your source uses the story to promote a controversial agenda, that could reflect poorly on you or your employer. In that case, failing to follow policy in releasing the video could get you in trouble with your company.

REPORTER'S INTERVIEW CHECKLIST

- ☐ Do your research before the interview.
- ☐ Don't give your questions to your source ahead of time. You want the answers to be spontaneous rather than scripted.
- ☐ Be clear about the purpose of your interview.
- ☐ Check your gear. Discuss the shots and b-roll you need with your video journalist.
- ☐ Help the subject feel comfortable by engaging in chit-chat before you launch into harder topics.
- ☐ Record the person's name, spelling, title and contact info on camera.
- ☐ Don't give verbal feedback during the interview. Be quiet and nod.
- ☐ Listen, listen, listen.
- ☐ Don't look at your notes too often. Keep eye contact.
- ☐ Ask whether the interviewee wants to add anything else.
- ☐ Make a graceful exit.
- ☐ Follow up if you promise to call with information about the airdate.

If you make a copy of a story because a source has been particularly helpful, be sure to give him the version that was actually on air or online. Releasing video that wasn't used in the piece is the equivalent of sharing a reporter's notes and exposes your news organization to criticism about how the story was covered.

Above all, don't make a promise you have no authority to make and can't keep.

Send a thank-you note

A written thank-you note will set you apart from most other reporters, especially if you want to cultivate this source as a future contact.

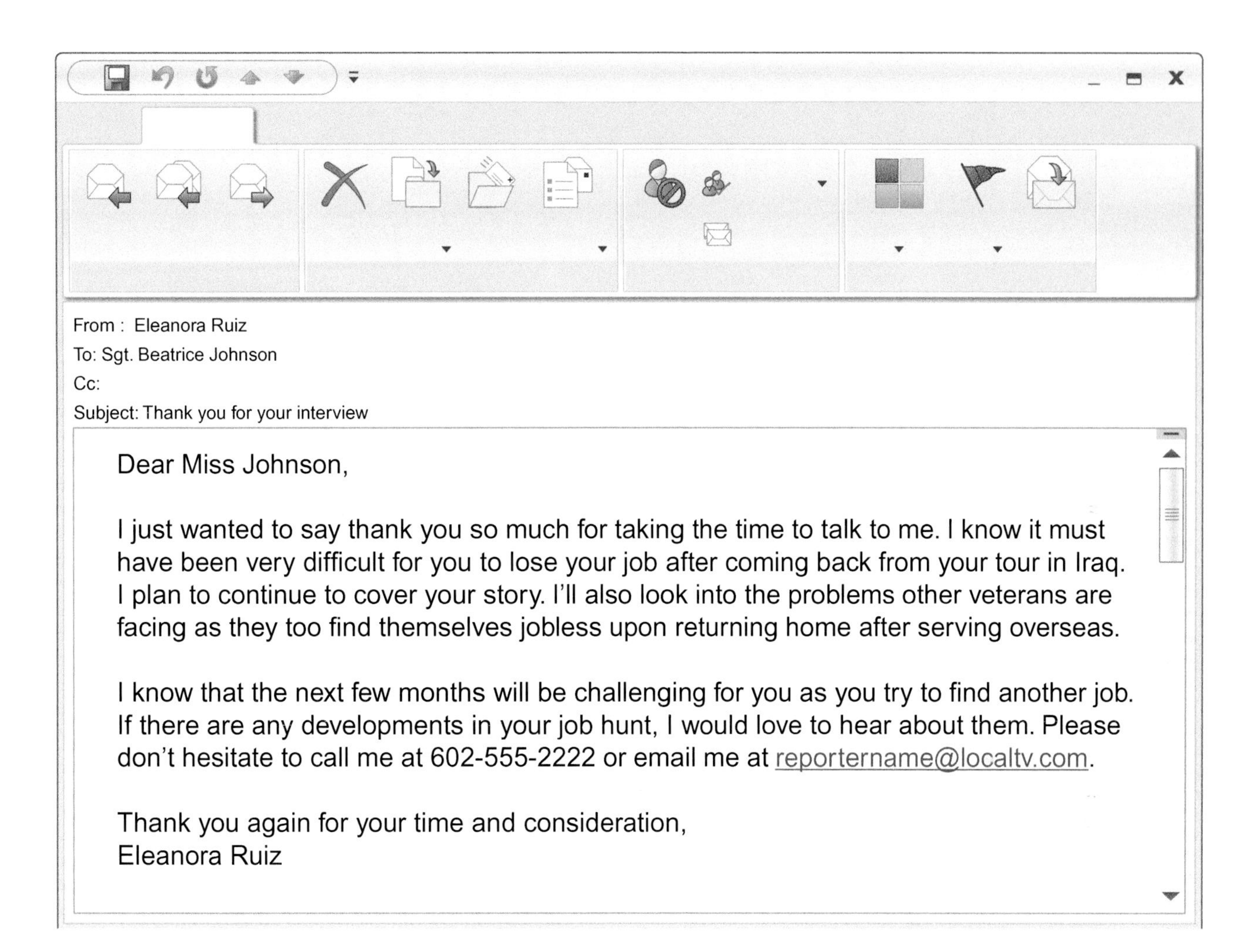

From : Eleanora Ruiz
To: Sgt. Beatrice Johnson
Cc:
Subject: Thank you for your interview

Dear Miss Johnson,

I just wanted to say thank you so much for taking the time to talk to me. I know it must have been very difficult for you to lose your job after coming back from your tour in Iraq. I plan to continue to cover your story. I'll also look into the problems other veterans are facing as they too find themselves jobless upon returning home after serving overseas.

I know that the next few months will be challenging for you as you try to find another job. If there are any developments in your job hunt, I would love to hear about them. Please don't hesitate to call me at 602-555-2222 or email me at reportername@localtv.com.

Thank you again for your time and consideration,
Eleanora Ruiz

SIGHT & SOUND

CHAPTER 6

Contributed by Jim Manley,
Faculty Associate, Walter Cronkite School of Journalism and Mass Communication, and Founder and Director, Manley Films

Contributed by Gilbert Zermeño,
Faculty Associate, Walter Cronkite School of Journalism and Mass Communication, and investigative producer and video journalist, KPHO-TV (CBS), Phoenix

CHAPTER OUTLINE

The Successful Shoot

Shooting video and telling stories is one of the best jobs many journalists can imagine. Why? Because each day you meet someone new, experience something for the first time and have the potential to change lives.

Starting as a multimedia journalist (MMJ) out of college can mean being nervous every time you pick up the camera. Many of the industry's best were also confused and overwhelmed on stories at the beginning of their careers. They sweated a lot, were afraid to make mistakes and, most of all, weren't having very much fun.

Ultimately through trial, error and mentoring, most figure it out. You already know how to use an iPad, laptop and small video cameras. This process won't be much more difficult. Keep it simple, and even the complex stories will become easy to tell. It only took your authors about three years to figure that out. Now they want to share what they've learned with you, so you can avoid the mistakes they had to suffer through.

PITFALLS

Five Common Mistakes

There are five key mistakes most people make when they shoot video.

1. Not using headphones
2. Missing sequences
3. Lack of organization
4. Forgetting to tell the story
5. Failing to be a caring human being

This chapter will explore the basic theories behind quality videography and editing that will serve you well in this era of the MMJ.

One of the most thrilling parts of video journalism is to be an eyewitness to news as it happens. But you can't just stand by and watch. Your job is to capture the images as professionally as possible. Managing the camera, **tripod,** microphone and lights while also tracking the story can seem daunting. But it's possible to shoot great video, gather memorable stories, beat the competition and have fun doing it.

Headphones

Short but true story told by an old-timer:

In the late 1970s, Mick Jagger was about as big as it gets when it came to rock stars. He was granting no interviews, but one video journalist managed to get close to his limo and, while security tried to remove the video journalist, Mick stopped them and let him through. The video journalist got the "best interview ever" with Mick. He proudly took it back to show his news director. Mick looked great, but there was no sound. The video journalist didn't realize that at the time because he wasn't wearing headphones.

If you're not wearing headphones *every* time you shoot video, you will

- not know whether your microphone(s) are working properly.
- not pick up on loud background noise, audio scratches, scrapes and so on.
- eventually lose some extremely important audio you thought you had.

Sequencing

What is sequencing? **Sequencing** is a series of shots that, when edited together, flow seamlessly. Some might refer to it as "matched action." What we're talking about is literally matching the action in the video using a series of shots from different angles. You can begin to collect shots for use in a sequence by shooting several wide, medium and tight shots. One wide, one medium and one tight is a sequence.

Without a variety of shots (multiple wide, medium, tight) you will

- have a very hard time editing a sequence that helps tell the story visually.
- not be able to keep the story visually interesting.
- have random shots that don't relate to one another.

Shooting sequences is easy if you are disciplined about it. The machine-gun approach of shooting anything and everything without thinking doesn't work. The key to being disciplined about shooting sequences every time you cover a story is to consciously make an effort to do it. Soon, you will be automatically shooting sequences for every story. You will have a great variety of shots to pick from when editing, and you will have an enjoyable time crafting your story visually in the edit bay.

EXAMPLE OF A SEQUENCE IN A CLASSROOM

WIDE SHOT OF CLASSROOM Always use a tripod or find a surface to put the camera on to make sure your shot is steady.

Wide shots are best for

- establishing a sense of place
- setting a scene
- opening a story
- closing a story
- transitioning from one location to another

An effective wide shot

- stays steady—always use a tripod or something else solid
- fills the frame of the camera monitor

MEDIUM SHOT IN CLASSROOM Notice that the video journalist has moved to another location in the room and changed the angle of the shot. Simply zooming in from the wide shot location and editing the shots together would create a telescope effect, which can be jarring to the eye.

Medium shots are best for

- showing action
- helping to continue the action in editing from a wide shot to a tight shot
- showing emotion
- recording reactions

An effective medium shot

- stays steady—as with a wide shot, use a tripod or another solid surface
- fills the frame with the action happening

TIGHT SHOT IN CLASSROOM The final shot in this three-shot sequence is a close-up of the white board.

Tight shots are best for

- capturing emotion
- recording reactions
- bringing the viewer closer to the story
- showing texture
- solving difficult situations in editing while maintaining sequence
- gathering great natural sound while you shoot

An effective tight shot

- fills the frame with a close-up of the subject of your sequence
- gives viewers a unique view they may not often get to see

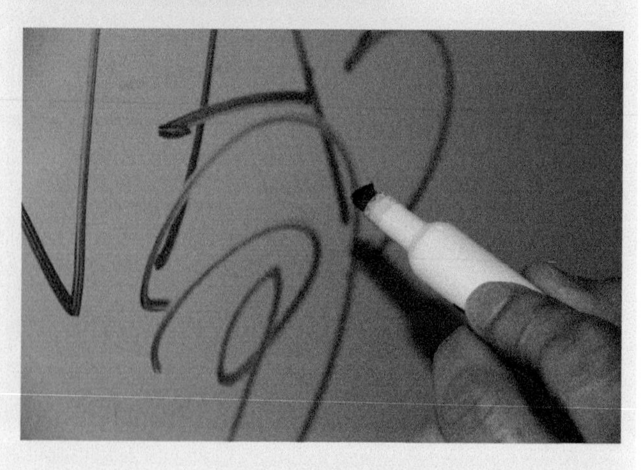

Organization

Divide your story into sections. Why? So you don't get overwhelmed. Even a generally disorganized person needs to stay organized at work as a video journalist. This is one of the most important things to learn how to do and could be the key to going from a nervous video journalist to a successful one. It makes the job fun.

Below is a great way to organize a story about a hot dog-eating contest. The same philosophy can be applied to any story. The basis of this philosophy is preparation and consistency. If you make a habit of preparing a rough outline or wish list of elements you would like to gather for your story, with time you will train yourself so that it becomes second nature. That is important because there are many stories in which you have little time to think ahead. Once you master the art of organizing your story, you will consistently have all the elements you need for every story every time.

Not only that, but your stories will all be memorable in their own way because you have taken the time to think ahead, to think about viewers and what they want to see and hear. Remember we don't do this job to impress other journalists; we do this job to inform, educate and perhaps inspire our viewers.

Section 1: The Preparation

1. **Take five minutes to get wide, medium and tight shots of the person cooking the hot dogs.** Maybe, for example, it's a Lions Club member; maybe it's someone raising money for a charity. Whoever it is, it is action and will be interesting. If you have a wireless microphone, put it on the person while she's cooking. Stay focused and stay organized.

2. **Interview with hot dog cook.** Remember, interview subjects in their working environment whenever possible. For an automotive economy story, you'd want to interview an autoworker along the assembly line, not in the break room. Interview the hot dog cook while she is standing at the grill. It's a great place to ask why she is there and what goes into cooking a good hot dog.

Assuming you shoot just two sequences per minute for five minutes, you will already have 30 shots and one interview.

Section 2: The Spectators

1. **Grab wide, medium and tight shots of people coming in, tables and chairs being set up on the stage and so forth.** Maybe the daughter of one of the contestants is there with a sign that says "Go Dad!" in hopes he wins the hot dog contest. Or maybe the husband of one of the contestants is there to watch his wife win. In any case, there will be an interesting story in the audience.

2. **Interview a couple of people in the audience.** You may find your story within the story there. Don't forget to get a few **setup shots** of your interview subjects. When it's time to write the story, you may want to introduce one of these people, so you'll need to have a few shots of them doing something besides talking to you in a standard interview head shot.

Now, after five to 10 more minutes of shooting, you'll have between 30 and 40 more shots and two or three new interviews.

Section 3: The Contestants

1. **Gather wide, medium and tight shots of the contestants coming in.** Also, look for shots of them getting ready. Perhaps they have a pregame ritual. If you found an interesting story in the audience, find the contestant on the other end of that story.

2. **Interview a few of the contestants, concentrating on the person you will be following the most.** You're telling a story, so make it compelling. Find the most interesting story within the story, and you will have a captive audience. Remember the girl holding the "Go Dad!" sign? Find the dad, and get an interview with him.

In 15 more minutes of shooting, assuming that you've stayed focused and disciplined about shooting sequences, you've gathered at least 30 to 40 more sequenced shots and at least two more interviews. Better yet, you probably have a compelling story already—and the contest hasn't even begun.

Section 4: The Contest

Now just roll on the contest. It's going to happen fast. Usually, you'll want to set your shot before you hit the record button so you don't have a lot of unnecessary or unusable video, but in this case, much as with a rescue or sporting event, you want to keep rolling all the way through. Also, remember to get as many reaction shots from the audience as you can. These will be key in conveying the emotion of the event. Before you start, find out approximately how many minutes the contest takes so you are prepared.

Section 5: The Victory

1 Reaction shots from the contestant you're focusing on. Whether he won or lost, you will have some good emotion. You've given the viewer someone to root for in the audience.

2 An interview with the person you're focusing on.

3 An interview with the family member(s) who were cheering him on.

4 An ending shot—the contestant walking away would be a great one.

Completing the Picture

At some time during the day, you'll want to get an interview from someone describing what's happening. For example:

"Today we're at Coney Island, and there's going to be a hot dog-eating contest."

"There is some tough competition, and, yes, some of these guys take it very seriously."

"We do this for charity, to raise money for kids in need."

If you add it all up, you have a wide variety of sequenced shots and compelling interviews, which can be woven into a very memorable story. The best part is that you had fun because you took a moment to organize your shoot.

Now, in one short hour, you've turned a simple hot dog-eating contest into a compelling story that the viewer will want to watch all the way through. You've captured moments and told a story with your camera. Your shots are steady and flow together like the words of a Pulitzer Prize–winning novel. You are going to have a great time editing this piece because you were focused and disciplined.

Telling the story

This can be summed up fairly quickly. When you are gathering audio and video for your story, you can have all of the sequencing, crisp audio and pretty pictures. But if you forget that you are telling a story that is supposed to be memorable and impactful to an audience, you have not done your job.

Use the tools you are learning in this textbook, and you will always be reminded that storytelling is the most important job you have.

Be a caring human being

You are not just a reporter, a video journalist or a multimedia journalist. You are also a person who cares about accurately portraying the lives of others and the events that happen around them. If you remember that, you will have taken a huge step forward in becoming an excellent journalist.

There are many examples of journalists losing a good story because they chose first to be journalists instead of caring humans. This is one example.

A video journalist was covering the Hurricane Katrina disaster hours after the destruction. More than 30 news outlets from all over the country were waiting in one spot for the authorities to take them into the aftermath. The sheriff chose this MMJ and one other to gather video for all the news outlets present because the mayhem was so severe and he didn't want too many journalists wandering around and getting lost or hurt.

When the video journalists arrived, they found incredible destruction and a few people who had just spent the past several hours clinging to life. The video journalists went in separate directions for a bit. The first found a man and his wife who had climbed into their attic while the water rose almost to the top. They were spared by about an inch.

The first video journalist was blown away by their story and talked to them very briefly with the camera off and at his side. He listened and was genuinely sympathetic to their plight. He could see the dazed look in their eyes. After a couple of minutes, he mentioned that he would like them to share their story with the rest of the world in hopes that viewers could get an accurate picture of the struggle and devastation.

The couple agreed and began telling their story. Then the second video journalist arrived about a minute later. He stuck his microphone in their faces and abruptly asked them, "How do you feel?" The tired and frightened man looked at the second video journalist and said, "How the [expletive] do you think I feel?" The interview for both video journalists ended right there.

Hurricane Katrina evacuees are surrounded by reporters after arriving in Phoenix.

Getting to Know Your Gear

In their first months on the job, most young journalists struggle trying to be good at so many things: video, audio, editing and, of course, actually gathering information and reporting the story. How do you ensure success on each assignment? It begins with getting to know your gear. Working *with* your camera, tripod and microphone should become second nature. That way you'll worry less about the equipment and concentrate more on getting the story.

Cameras

As with microphones and editing programs, there are many different types of cameras in use today. With technological advances, a small camera today can often shoot video just as good as one four times as large and expensive. While they are all the same in many ways, cameras have subtle differences.

Your camera may be overwhelming to you at first, but if you take the time to sit down with it and learn where these key buttons, switches and settings are and what they do, you will have very little problem operating it.

Tripods

A tripod is the place where you mount your camera for steady shots. Most of us already know that. But when do you use your tripod? The answer is

FIGURE **6.1** **Nine Things to Know About Your Camera**

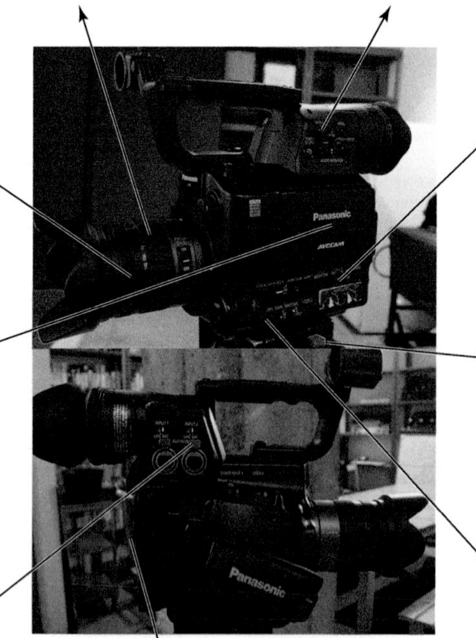

1. **Learn how to turn the camera on.** Yes, we know it sounds elementary, but this is definitely the first thing you need to know. On most cameras, there is a switch near the back of the camera close to the viewfinder.
2. **Find out how the camera fits and locks on the tripod you will be using.** On the bottom of the camera, there is a place to attach a tripod plate. Once the tripod plate is firmly attached to the camera, you can mount it on the tripod. Some tripod plates slide into a notch on the top of the tripod. Others snap into place. In both cases, you want to make sure your camera is securely locked into place before taking your hands off the camera. Furthermore, make sure the tripod legs are tightened down.
3. **Learn how to manually focus your camera.** You might gather the greatest shots ever recorded, but if they're out of focus, they are useless. The focus on your camera is usually near the lens at the front of the camera. You will want to learn how to focus quickly.
4. **Learn how to manually adjust the iris.** It allows light in and out of the camera lens. In darker situations, you would iris up to allow more light into the lens. In brighter situations, you would iris down to compensate for the abundance of light. Your camera will have an automatic iris function, but that is for amateurs and will be very noticeable.
5. **Find the zoom.** It is usually located near the top right front side of the camera. When the servo zoom is on, it allows you to zoom with the camera toggle control. When it is off, you zoom by actually rotating the lens or lens knob. You can also turn off the servo and zoom manually with the lens (usually found near the base of the lens). Don't overuse the zoom. Sequencing is the key to putting together a story that flows seamlessly. Zooming is mainly for zooming into or out of the shots you need BEFORE you press the record button.
6. **Find the headphone jack.** It is in different places on each camera. Most of the time it is located near the back of the camera. Since you will be using your headphones every time you shoot video, you will definitely want to locate the headphone jack.
7. **Go into the menu and see the different functions your camera has.** It might seem a little overwhelming at first, but it's really not that complicated. For example, if you are shooting 16:9 widescreen or if you want to change the frame rate, you will want to look at how to change the **aspect ratio** and **frame rate** in your settings. There are many functions in the menu, and you will find the ones that suit you the best. Open the menu and scroll through the options.
8. **If you're shooting on tape, learn how to load and unload the tape from your camera.** If you're shooting on a disc, card or other form of digital media, learn how to safely load and unload that device.
9. **Learn how to input and output audio.** There are usually at least two **audio inputs** on cameras. Most cameras also have a built-in microphone that is dedicated to one of those channels. You will need to learn how to manipulate the audio on your camera so that you can direct your microphones to output to the desired channel.

simple—almost always. Every MMJ has his or her own style, but one consistent attribute we all share is that we want high-quality, watchable video.

When you use your tripod, your shots will be easier to gather and easier for the viewer to watch. Watch almost any movie or television show, and you will notice that you don't notice the videography. That's because there are no unnecessary movements. Every shot has a purpose and is composed and shot that way for a reason. Even the shows that use hand-held cameras are doing so for a reason. They've chosen this style to enhance the effect of the mood they are trying to create, not because the camera folks are lazy people who don't want to mount the camera on a tripod.

As an MMJ gathering news, you don't want laziness to affect your storytelling. Mounting the camera on the tripod only takes a few seconds. In addition, picking up the camera and the tripod together to move to your next shot takes very little effort. In the long run, you will be much happier when you sit down to edit if you have a purpose for every shot you gather.

Three last things to learn are how to raise and lower the legs on your tripod, how to balance the tripod and how to use the tilt and pan locks efficiently. Once you master them, using your tripod will be easy and enjoyable.

RULE OF THUMB

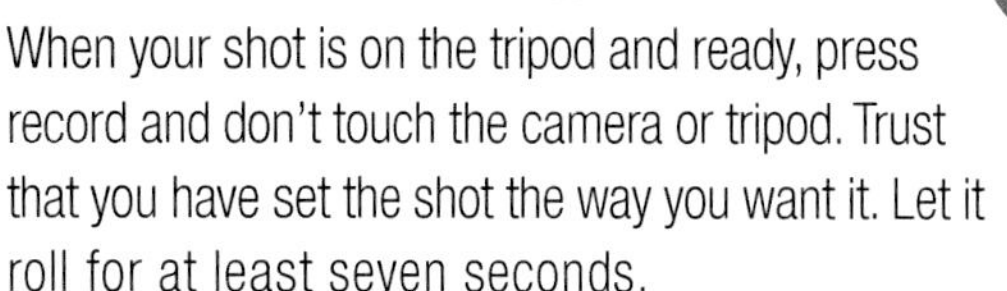

When your shot is on the tripod and ready, press record and don't touch the camera or tripod. Trust that you have set the shot the way you want it. Let it roll for at least seven seconds.

Janie Porter, a multimedia journalist at WTSP-TV (CBS) in Tampa Bay, Fla., prepares to present a live report by herself using Skype.

Lights and interview setup

Lighting an interview subject can be easy for a beginner. As you progress throughout your career, you will expand your knowledge of lighting, and, just like everything else you do as a journalist, you will become more advanced. But for now, let's keep it simple.

Always remember that the person you're interviewing is the most important element in your shot. That may seem elementary, but we've seen many interviews where the background pops more than the interview subject.

To make your interview subject look her best, the simplest technique is to create distance between your camera and the subject and the subject and the background. This separation will help create visual separation between the subject and the background and will allow you to get that clean, crisp shot you desire. Your interview subject will pop and be the main focus for the viewer. In all of these examples, remember never to blast your interview subject with light. The best lighting is simple, even and subtle.

Outdoor interviews in the daytime When you are outside shooting interviews, you want to apply the same concepts for lighting that you do for indoor interviews. But, in most cases, daylight will be your key light, and the sun will act as your backlight. You never want to use direct sun as a key light in your interview subject's face. If you have a reflector, you will be able to reflect the sun back onto your interview subject. You may also have access to a 5600K light (outdoor color temperature lighting). This will help you light the face of your subject. Again, you always want to create separation between the camera, subject and background.

Outdoor interviews at night Techniques for effective outdoor interviews at night can vary greatly, depending on what equipment you have and how much time you have to light. Although we recommend minimal use of a light that mounts on your camera, it can be an excellent resource if used correctly. For example, if your light has a dimmer on it or a mini-softbox, you will be able to avoid overexposing the interview subject's face. You will be able to open the iris more, and the background will be visible (not pitch black).

SIDE BY SIDE

Interview with two lights While using three lights is ideal, if you only have two lights, you can make this interview work in a similar way. With two lights, you will have a key light positioned near the camera, and you can use your second light as a hair light or a background light.

Two lights, front view: hair light (left) and key light (right)

Two lights, reverse view

Note that the interview subject isn't up against the wall. There is separation.

Interview with three lights If you have access to three lights, this will give you a key light, a fill light and a background light (or hair light). In the example below, you can see the key light on the right, the fill light on the left and the hair light on a boom stand behind the interview subject. We turned off all of the lights in the room, but there happened to be spotlights that shone against the background wall. They were on dimmers, so we used this available light to create a subtly lit background.

Three lights, front view: fill light (left), hair light (center), key light (right)

Three lights, reverse view

Types of microphones

Three different types of microphones were used on the story on the following pages about an accident. Each type of microphone should be a part of your equipment every day if possible.

A wireless microphone—plugged into audio channel 1

Use this microphone to

- gather great natural sound from people in your story.
- conduct interviews with people while they are working.

RULE OF THUMB

Wireless mics rely on battery power. Make sure you have backup batteries. Also remember, it is wireless technology, so you will need to closely monitor your audio to make sure there is no signal interference.

A shotgun microphone—plugged into audio channel 2

Use this microphone to

- gather great natural sound from anything that makes noise. Examples include hammers, rivers, blenders and anything else that makes sound.

RULE OF THUMB

You will need to find a good way to mount your shotgun mic on your camera for easy storage and quick removal.

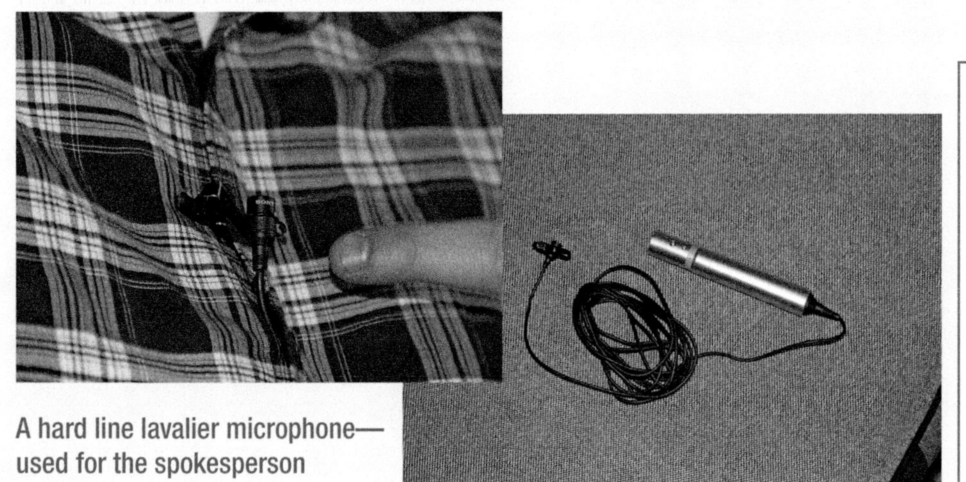

A hard line lavalier microphone—used for the spokesperson interview

Most of the time, you will be using this microphone for interviews.

RULE OF THUMB

Make sure you have power to your microphone. Lavaliers usually have a battery compartment but can also run on phantom power provided by the camera.

Memorable Audio

There are so many things you can do to make your good news story a great news story. But if there is one thing that will make your stories consistently memorable, it is the audio you gather.

We all know that it is necessary in television news journalism to shoot with our eyes, but sometimes we forget to shoot with our ears. Audio drives a story. It helps create the smooth flow that every good story has.

Take a minute to watch any visual medium, and you will immediately *hear* the difference between an average story and a memorable one.

NATURAL SOUND

Natural sound may be the most important tool you will use to make all of your stories memorable. Natural sound is any sound you hear while you are gathering video and audio for your story.

When you gather natural sound and use it effectively in editing, you bring the viewer into your story. You don't want to deprive the viewer of all the sounds, both big and small, that you heard while you were out in the field.

Shoot with your ears as well as your eyes. Listen to what's happening around you while you're gathering the elements for your story, and record that sound.

One shoot, three microphones

We've introduced you to the kinds of microphones available to use in the field and talked about the importance of collecting natural sound along the way. In the following story, you can see what kind of microphone was used:

Ⓦ The use of a wireless microphone is color-coded GREEN.
Ⓛ The use of a lavalier microphone is color-coded BLUE.
Ⓢ The use of a shotgun microphone is color-coded PURPLE.

A video journalist was sent to an accident scene one day to cover spot news. A large truck and a car had collided, and the car had smashed into a telephone pole. Two hospital helicopters and other emergency units were dispatched. When the video journalist arrived on the scene, he did what he usually does. He quickly assessed the situation by looking around while gathering his gear.

As in most spot news, things were happening quickly. That's why journalists are encouraged to break their stories into sections, every time. That way, when spot news occurs, you are ready to roll with the rapidly changing situation.

At the accident scene, the first thing the video journalist did was concentrate on the action: wide, medium and tight shots of the scene. He was particularly careful to get shots of

- [ ] Helicopters landing
- [ ] Blades spinning
- [ ] Emergency crews walking/running
- [ ] Emergency crews working calmly but quickly to extract the people from the vehicle

But that's as far as many average video journalists will go at a given shoot. Yes, they may have gotten a sound bite from a **public information officer** or even an onlooker to go with their story. But in reality, if their story even made air, it probably turned into just a 20-second anchor voiceover.

We all know that accidents happen every day, so it's really not big news.

In this particular case, one video journalist decided it was worth it to go beyond the basic shots and sound. While shooting video of the scene, he listened to those around him. He heard people talking about what had happened, what they had seen and who was trapped in the vehicle.

He heard them talk about a witness who had tried to help pull two kids out of the car but was unable to. He looked around while he was shooting and saw a woman with a small patch of blood on the lower part of her shirt.

Again, never forgetting to follow the action with wide, medium and tight shots, the video journalist worked his way closer to that woman and approached her without the camera. He talked to her person to person, not journalist to witness. After 30 seconds, he told her he would be back after the helicopters departed and would like to talk to her on camera about what she saw. She replied that she would think about it.

But before he left, the video journalist let the witness know that he would like to put a wireless microphone on her to gather some sound of her talking to her friend about what they were watching. She agreed, and he went back to shooting the scene.

As he listened to their conversation through his headphones, the video journalist would spin the camera around every now and then to get video of them talking. He was far away and did not have the camera right in their faces, so they talked as if he weren't there.

Not only did he get a few shots of them reacting, but he also gathered a few shots of other people's faces and gestures—pointing, covering their mouths, a dad watching with his son.

After about 20 minutes on the scene, the video journalist had all of the wide, medium and tight shots he needed to tell the story of the accident scene. The last series of shots was the final gurney going into the helicopter, a tight shot of the blades firing back up, a wide shot of the helicopter lifting off and a final reaction shot (with audio of her speaking) from the woman with the wireless microphone watching the helicopter take off.

After that, the video journalist did a very short interview with the wireless microphone woman. He already had so much natural sound from her that he only needed a little bit more.

He also did an interview with the man who was watching with his son. Finally, he did an interview with the public information officer.

While all the other stations ran a short voice-over on the accident in the 6 p.m. and 10 p.m. newscasts, the video journalist's station was able to lead with a 1:30 package. The package was about the accident, but it went way beyond that.

A big truck plowed into a car. In the car was a mother and her two sons. The mother was trapped in the car, and a bystander (the woman wearing the wireless mic) tried to get her and one of her sons out. She couldn't do it, but the emergency crews arrived to start the extrication with the jaws of life.

The other child had been ejected. Nobody in the vehicle was wearing a seat belt. As you can imagine, it was an ugly scene.

Wearing a lavalier microphone, the public information officer said later that at least one of the kids probably wouldn't make it, and the lack of a seat belt was a big contributor. He also added that the mother and son trapped in the car were thrown around in the vehicle because they weren't wearing their safety belts. They were in critical condition also.

The story followed the events of the accident through a 20- to 40-minute time period.

Viewers watched as the drama of the accident unfolded, but as that was happening, they heard the narration from the woman with the wireless microphone.

She described to her friend what she saw and what she was seeing now. Her reactions added to the urgency and the gravity of the situation.

Other sounds the viewer heard were the police and fire engine sirens, the helicopters, the firefighter commanders yelling orders.

The nucleus of the story wasn't the accident itself. It was a message.

The father who was watching with his son used this as an opportunity to remind his son and others of the importance of wearing a seat belt. He told the video journalist that he often reminds his son that a seat belt can save lives and that the scene unfolding in front of them was a solemn reminder of that. A child who was about the same age as his son was the one who was ejected from the vehicle.

The public information officer also emphasized that point, while the woman with the wireless mic talked about how she hoped she would never see anything as terrible as that again.

The point is, there are stories everywhere. You can look at a story and keep it basic, or you can look at a story and make it memorable. It's hard to accurately describe this particular accident story in text, but it touched a lot of people for many days. Again, on all of the other stations, it was a voice-over and then forgotten.

VOICES *from the* Newsroom

Advice from a network MMJ

Mara Schiavocampo, multimedia journalist
NBC News, New York City

NBC hired Mara Schiavocampo as the network's first digital correspondent. A multimedia journalist adept at working on her own, Mara reports for the "NBC Nightly News with Brian Williams" and other NBC news programs.

1. Slow Down

This may seem counterintuitive, but *slow down.* When you rush, you get flustered, make mistakes and forget things. Make a conscious decision to move slowly and deliberately, like a turtle. Breathe. Think before you act. In the long run, you'll save time by not having to correct mistakes. Plus, when you add up all of that extra slow time, you're probably looking at 10 minutes over the course of the entire day. Slowing down is about being calm while you work.

2. Keep It Simple

Good work can be remarkably simple. I compare it to food: Think of a meal made with fresh, local ingredients, cooked perfectly, like a nicely grilled portobello mushroom. That can be just as delicious as a fancy, complicated dish. You're the grilled mushroom. (I mean that in the nicest way.) Keep things simple. Use your tripod, wear your headphones, shoot sequences. Let the camera do the work by putting most settings on auto. (My exception to that is auto-focus; the camera often focuses on the wrong subject or searches for focus while you're shooting.)

3. Know Your Equipment

Before you take out a piece of equipment, you should know what every single button and menu function does. Every single one. Yes, I'm serious. Sit down with the camera and the manual, and read it from cover to cover. You'll find that you don't need most functions, but you'll also discover some cool things that will come in very handy. But most important, when you're in the field, you'll know what you're dealing with, making the entire experience less intimidating.

4. Content Is King

Do not focus so much on the technical that you lose sight of the editorial. A compelling story that's technically mediocre is far better than a technical marvel with a mediocre story. There's just no competition. Think about it. You've probably watched and loved countless online videos of crappy quality because the content was great. Your priority should be in telling the story the best way possible and finding great characters to tell it through.

5. Audio Is Queen

Do not underestimate the importance of audio. Audio must be good, or people will not enjoy your story, period. If there's an obnoxious hiss or crackle, or an interview is muffled or distorted, the viewer will not be able to focus on anything else. So give audio the attention it deserves. Wear your headphones, eliminate distracting sound when possible (sometimes that means moving yourself), fix audio problems as soon as you notice them. Also, keep an ear out for really strong sounds and infuse your stories with **nat pops.**

6. Available Light

Lighting will make or break your pictures. As an MMJ, you probably don't have the luxury of a fancy light kit or the time to set it up. So use available light to your advantage, and make sure to always follow the basic principles of lighting. Before you set up a shot, stop and look around. Where's the best light? That's where you set up. Is the lighting awful? Can you move a lamp? Can you move yourself (even right outside the room into a hallway or outdoors)? Always think about light *first,* and adjust everything else second.

7. Shooting and Editing

Think of shooting and editing as a tag team; they can support each other. When you're shooting, don't stress about things that you can fix in editing. For example, color correcting, adjusting composition (like centering a shot), slightly boosting audio levels or creating a zoom are all things you can do when you're editing. Knowing that, you can cut corners and save a little time in the field. Aside from fixes, you can also elevate a piece with different editing techniques, and dress it up, if you will.

8. Teach Yourself

If you have a question, just remember that someone, somewhere has found the solution and posted it online. I have never had a question that I couldn't answer by poking around online. And guess what? When you have to search for an answer, you'll never forget it. So don't be daunted by any shooting or editing problem. Just start searching.

9. Swallow Your Pride

Forget to press the record button before your shoot? You'll have to do it all over. Hear a nasty buzz during an interview? You'll have to make your subject wait (no matter how important he or she is) while you fix the problem. There will be countless situations that will bruise your pride, times when you'd much rather keep quiet about your mistake and slink away. Swallow your pride for the sake of your work. You *must* stop and fix problems as you notice them.

10. Honor Your Deadlines

What good is a masterpiece that never airs? What about 90 percent of a masterpiece with a black hole in it? We'd all love to craft a beautiful work of art, but sometimes that just ain't gonna happen. The reality is that we live and die by deadlines, and sometimes you have barely enough time to finish. So don't spend long chunks of time thinking about what word describes that exact shade of blue, what shot would be perfect for that line of track or which take of your standup you liked best. Just finish!

Nonlinear Editing

Today most video editing is done using a computer and shots (also called clips) downloaded from a camera. This is called nonlinear editing. There are many different types of nonlinear editing programs, such as Final Cut, Adobe Premiere, Avid and others. They all have subtle differences, but the concepts of editing remain constant, no matter which program you are using.

On this timeline, the editor has chosen to lay the interview sound down first. Also, notice the yellow bins (or folders) at the top left. These are used to organize the story elements.

First, you want to make sure you keep all of the items you need for your story organized.

Notice in the photo at left there are bins (the yellow folders at the top left). Each bin has a name and a purpose for keeping video and audio organized. Your different bins will almost always include audio, b-roll, graphics, sequences and interviews.

When you import your video into your editing program, in most cases you can decide where you want a certain piece of video or audio to be stored.

If you put your reporter track (voice-over) in the audio bin, your b-roll in the b-roll bin, the interviews in the interview bin and so on, you will stay organized, and you will get your story done a lot faster than if you are disorganized.

After you have a finished a script and you are ready to edit, there are different ways to complete your story efficiently and effectively.

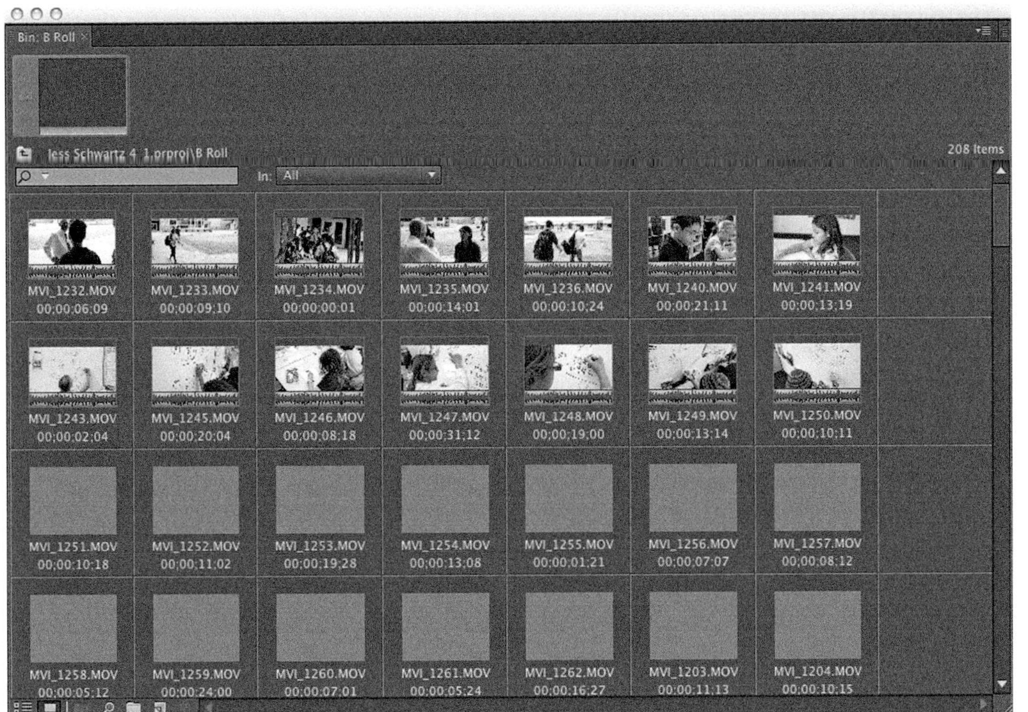

Inside the yellow bin (or folder) labeled b-roll, the editor can choose from a variety of shots.

Voice track first. Some video journalists will put the entire reporter voice track down on the timeline first, then edit around that. In the timeline on the next page, notice how the editor has placed each reporter voice track and sound bite in order but has yet to cover the reporter tracks with b-roll or cover video. One advantage to this method is you'll know early in the edit process how long your story is.

On this timeline, the editor has chosen first to edit together the interview sound and the reporter track according to the script. She will then fill in the appropriate b-roll.

Piece by piece. Some video journalists prefer to edit piece by piece and build as they go. In other words, they like to start at the beginning, laying the first reporter voice track down, then covering it with video and audio, and so on. Some journalists feel they can get a better rhythm going when editing this way, but they won't know how long the piece is until the very end.

You will find out which way works best for you. But no matter how you decide to edit, you will have a pleasant experience in the edit bay if you shoot sequences when you are in the field gathering your story.

Three things to remember when you are editing your news story:

1 If you shoot sequences in the field as we have suggested, then you will consistently have an easier time in the edit bay. You will spend less time looking for shots that fit into your story because you will have gathered video that works naturally together instead of having a batch of random shots that don't relate to each other.

2 Learn how to manipulate the audio on your timeline. It's different from program to program, but your story will benefit greatly if you learn this simple skill. If you learn how to weave (or mix) your audio efficiently between shots, your story will flow much better.

3 Don't go overboard with effects (dissolves, wipes, etc.) just because you can. As with everything else in video production, you should have a reason for anything that you do. This holds especially true for effects. For the most part, in television news there is no reason for affecting video if you have done your job correctly in the field.

- If you have asked the right questions, you will get the proper emotion you need to set the mood of your story.
- If you have shot steady sequenced video, you will have what you need to engage viewers and bring them into your story. You won't need effects to get you from one shot to the next.
- If you have gathered meaningful natural sound, you will have all of the soundtrack you need to help weave your story together without the need of external audio or canned music.

JUMP CUTS AND CUTAWAYS

Jump cuts are two shots that, when edited together, are jarring. For example, if you are gathering video of the basketball player and you are shooting a medium shot of him getting ready to shoot, and then, without moving, you zoom in a bit to get the same shot but a little tighter, that will become a jump cut when you edit those shots together. Instead, shoot your medium shot, move right or left a bit, then get your tight shot. You will immediately see a difference when you're editing. Your stories will flow much better and will be easier for the viewer to watch and remember.

Another example of a jump cut occurs when, during editing, you have the interview shot followed by another shot of the same person in a different place. To avoid this, you will want to gather plenty of transition shots to get you from one place to another. For example, if you have edited a shot from the basketball player, instead of making the next shot a wide or medium shot of him concentrating on the shot, you would want to use a tight shot of the basketball entering the hoop, followed by a wide or medium shot.

It may sound as if it doesn't matter, but avoiding jump cuts and using transition shots are both very effective ways of making your story smooth and memorable instead of a disorganized, jarring story.

A **cutaway shot** can be defined many different ways. If you're shooting wide, medium and tight shots when gathering your video, you will have all of the cutaway shots you need.

If you're shooting an interview, you will want to remember to gather some cutaway shots of the interview subject. For example, if you are interviewing a drummer, you will most likely want to sit him down (or stand him up) with a nice, appropriate background. After the interview, shoot wide, medium and tight shots of him doing his job. Those are your cutaway shots. This tactic allows you to avoid jump cuts in editing and to make your edited video smooth.

THE ETHICS OF AUDIO EDITING

The Canadian Journalism Project offers these ethical guidelines for editing audio, which can be applied to both television and radio.

When editing interviews

The most important rule—never change the meaning of what the interviewee said.

- It's OK, even expected, that you will **cut out ums, ers, long pauses and other examples of verbal stalling**—unless verbal stalling is a key part of the story, as in the case of a politician ducking tough questions.
- It's OK, even recommended, that you will **cut out extraneous words.**
  Before editing: "I think that, you know, that the university should lower tuition fees."
  After editing: "The university should lower tuition fees."
- It's OK to **cut out reiterations** if you can do it skillfully enough to avoid a jumpy cut that sounds either unnatural or like an obvious, audible edit.
  Before editing: "The students in the new program—the students—their families and their teachers will welcome this change."
  After editing: "The students in the new program, their families and their teachers will welcome this change."
- It's OK to **cut out subordinate clauses,** especially to make a clip shorter, as long as it doesn't change the meaning of what they say.
  Before editing: "The police arrested a man, I could see it from across the street, who was carrying a large green knapsack on his back."
  After editing: "The police arrested a man who was carrying a large green knapsack on his back."
- In other words, **it's OK to make edits that help someone sound sharper, tighter, clearer**. It's just *never* OK to change the meaning of what he said.
- It's also OK to use excerpts or clips from an interview in a different order in your story from the way they appeared in the original interview. Similarly, it's OK to ask someone to identify himself at the end of the interview and to use that at the beginning of the interview on the air.
- When using the interview—or excerpts from it—on the air or on the Web, always **identify the speaker** somewhere. No-name clips should generally be avoided.

When conducting interviews for editing later:

- **It's not OK to tell someone what to say**. It is OK to re-ask or, better still, rephrase a question to allow someone another chance to collect her thoughts and answer it again. Often, interviewees are clearer and more succinct the second time around.
- If you want to use the interview—or excerpts from it—on the air, you must **get the permission of the interviewee** in most jurisdictions. Find out what the rules are in your state or province.*
- It is not OK for you, as the interviewer, to record different questions and dub them in or substitute them for the ones you asked during the interview. Sometimes recording what are called re-asks is required, as in television when an interview is shot using only one camera and the questions are recorded again afterward, but the same questions must be used. In radio, **re-asks should almost always be avoided,** except in those rare instances when the interviewer literally chokes asking a question or there is a technical glitch that makes the question inaudible. But in each case, you must ask the same question posed initially and take great care to match the ambient sound. Mismatched background ambience will make it sound like a doctored interview.

*This is not standard practice in the United States.

When recording and using actuality sound in audio reports:

The most important rule—*never* use sound you did not record yourself at the scene or while doing your research. In news, it is not OK to use canned sound effects, sound beds from previous files or fabricated sound.

For example, if you interview a carpenter but fail to record the sound of him at work in his workshop, you can't just record yourself using a hammer at home later and pretend, in your report, that it is the sound of the carpenter at work.

Or if you cover an outdoor protest where demonstrators are singing John Lennon's "Imagine," but a windy day created some mic noise, you cannot just substitute the sound from another demonstration the previous week where different protesters sang the same song.

You can't do either of these things, that is, and honor the first principle of journalism—**accuracy.**

Unfortunately for those of us steeped in news traditions, the rules about using fabricated or canned sound are increasingly broken by people who produce public affairs or documentary radio programming and believe production values are as important as journalistic values. They justify it by saying that background sound beds and key sounds make stories stronger and more interesting for the listener and that sometimes the reporter fails to get those sounds in the field, so they must be added later. Some radio producers believe that if the added sounds don't change the essence of the story, doing so is OK.

But when radio producers add or fabricate sounds, they are, in some ways, deceiving listeners. They are doing much the same thing as newspaper photographers or editors using Photoshop to doctor photos to make crowds look bigger, criminals look more sinister or to erase body parts from train tracks after explosions. When news organizations have been caught doing those things in the past, they have apologized because they know it hurts their credibility, undermines their commitment to accuracy and breaks trust with their readers. Using fake sound in radio may be harder to detect, but it is the equivalent of manipulating photos.

Writing for

BROADCAST

CHAPTER 7

Learn to write. That's the important part, both in print and in broadcasting. The communication requires using the right words. Learn how to do that. You'll get along fine.

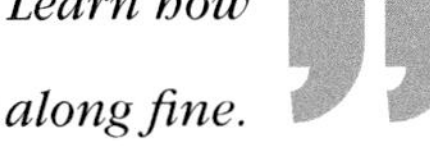

—WALTER CRONKITE

CHAPTER OUTLINE

5 Stages of Storytelling

Writing is about a lot more than banging out a script. The writing process actually began back in Chapter 2, with focusing your idea, and continued in Chapters 3 through 6 with reporting, interviewing and capturing video and audio.

Michael Roberts, a newsroom trainer and consultant, breaks storytelling into five stages: focus, report, organize, write and revise. This chapter will cover Steps 3, 4 and 5. After you've gathered your information and interviews, along with your video and audio, you'll organize everything (Step 3). You don't even start writing until Step 4. The final step is revising.

5 STAGES OF STORYTELLING

1. **FOCUS** Identify a central question or premise.
2. **REPORT** Gather enough information to answer the question or test the premise.
3. **ORGANIZE** Determine the story's central theme, and then plan the story around that focus.
4. **WRITE** With plan in hand, write the story.
5. **REVISE** Revise for clarity and precision, guided by the central focus.

REMEMBERING THE GREAT WORDSMITH

Choking words when a president died. Celebratory words when mankind took one giant leap on the moon. Words that challenged and criticized from a position of credibility. I must have heard thousands of words from Walter Cronkite on the air before I heard him utter a sound in person. That happened when I joined the faculty of the Cronkite School in 2001.

The most powerful words he spoke to me were understated. We had just spent an hour in a lecture hall with 300-plus students—me moderating (me moderating Walter Cronkite!) as he engaged the students on an AP wire feed. Now, at the private faculty lunch (me sitting next to Walter Cronkite!), I asked for an autograph. He wrote: *To Bill who does one fine interview.* It is the finest compliment I have ever been paid in 30 years of journalism.

Fast-forward three years to 2004. While producing a documentary, I interviewed him in his office high in CBS's "Black Rock" tower in Manhattan. He remembered past meetings. More important, he instantly grasped the direction of the documentary about the role of the press in the presidential election. He took me and my crew for a 30-minute rocket ride through the history of the press, the pundits and the people in television news.

Walter was never silenced. That quick mind answered my questions about what makes a good writer. A voracious reader, of course.

"What do you consume for your daily media diet?" I asked.

"I recommend everything from The New York Times to The Washington Post to the tabloids."

"What do you think of the Internet?"

"There is a lot of intelligent, good material there, and there is a lot of junk. Sometimes the junk is the most interesting."

Each time I walk up the staircase in his journalism school, I encounter a six-story window hung with artist-designed stained glass. Sunlight mixes with man-made light.

Every step reminds me of Walter's words. His wisdom: "Journalists must be ever skeptical but never cynical, for cynicism deadens the approach a good journalist should have to a story." Or the words he crafted with personal kindness for the nervous student or professor. Whether delivered from Vietnam or a political convention in Chicago, Walter's words were always teaching about the way it is, the way it was and even about the way it will always be.

"Old anchorman never fade away," he said at the end of his last regular broadcast. "They just keep coming back for more. I will be away on assignment for the next few years."

The window in his school—this staircase of dancing light—allows his dispatches from the field to remain forever with us, warming our hearts and heating up our minds with the fires of truth told in the finest tradition of journalism.

—B. William Silcock

4 WAYS TO GET ORGANIZED

Having a plan is essential to good storytelling. Michael Roberts offers the following suggestions. Experiment until you find what works best for you.

1. **Tell your story to a friend.** Pretend you have only a few minutes to tell a friend what you discovered.
   - How would you convey the excitement of what you learned (the most important points)?
   - What would you say first (the lead)?
   - How does the news affect your friend's life (relevance)?
   - What insights and perspectives will help your friend understand the big picture (context)?

2. **Map your story.** With the information you've researched and reported, redraw the story map you sketched when you were focusing your story (Chapter 2).

Do helicopter parents help or hinder?
Negative effects
Overdependence
Eating problems
Anxiety
Lack of confidence
Fear of failure
POV
Grandma
Sister
Mother
Father
Roommate
Professor
Positive effects
Friendship
Advice
Support
Stay in touch
Improved grades

3. **Develop a theme statement.** Revise the sentence that summarizes the central point of your story. This can be the answer to your central question or a restatement of the central premise. Use the theme statement to determine what material to keep in the story—and what to leave out.

Contrary to popular opinion, students with helicopter parents excel in learning and other activities.

4. **Jot down a rough outline.** With your story focus and length in mind, list key points and ingredients in the order they'll appear. You might have to rearrange the elements a few times until the order makes sense. Include sounds bites, natural sound, narration, graphics and standups. A brief description of each will do.

1. Natural sound open—College kids moving boxes into dorms
2. Bite from mom—"Yes, it will be hard to say goodbye, but we won't be far away"
3. Bite from daughter, who says she'll probably talk to her mom at least once or twice a day
4. Narration—Explains that helicopter parents are never far away from their children because of cell phones, Internet
5. Standup in front of campus psychology building—"But is staying this close to your college kids healthy for them? What's the impact on learning and other activities if the apron strings are never cut?"
6. Bite from psychologist who has researched helicopter parents
7. Narration with graphic—Facts about parental involvement and grades
8. Second bite from psychologist
9. Second bite from college daughter
10. Narration
11. Second bite from mom, followed by one sentence and outcue

Organize

Begin thinking about your script while you're still in the field and the material is fresh in your mind. If a great thought or line comes to you, jot it down right away. Otherwise, you might forget it by the time you sit down to crank out your script.

Make time for multiple perspectives

Several years ago, KPNX-TV (NBC) in Phoenix received a phone call from a viewer who wasn't happy with a story on abortion. The caller had timed the sound bites in the package and said the station wasn't fair because it had given one side a few more seconds than the other. The producer explained that editors don't time everything with a stopwatch. Instead, they select sound bites that make sense and form complete thoughts. The bottom line: People are watching, listening to and reading your work. Make sure you do your job fairly and accurately.

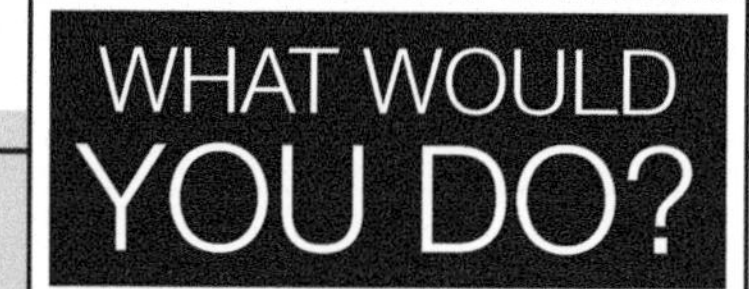

You're covering a rally where pro-immigration protesters outnumber anti-immigration protesters 5 to 1.

How do you give the audience an accurate picture? What is an accurate picture?

Would you give equal time to both sides in order to be fair and balanced? Or would you show five times as many pro-immigration visuals and include five times as many pro-immigration sound bites?

If a scuffle between opposing sides broke out for 10 minutes of the three-hour rally, would you show only that action? Or would you also include the ho-hum footage of people marching? Does including only the dramatic footage represent the entire protest?

Be selective

You've probably collected more information than you can use. Accept the fact that you can't cram everything in. If you do, your story will be so dense that you'll lose viewers.

As you sift through your material, consider all angles and facts. Zero in on what's most important to your audience and advances the story. Focus. Select. Emphasize. In addition, be sure to [Bracket], underline or highlight the key points that must be included in your story.

Anecdote illustrates main character's problem

•

Personal experience, background info and expert commentary reveal wider significance

•

Back to main character to show story's meaning

FIGURE 7.1 **Diamond Story Form**

Select a story form

Story forms provide structure for your stories by helping you think of them in terms of sections. Some common forms are diamond, wine glass, Christmas tree and narrative arc.

Diamond story form This popular broadcast structure begins and ends with a person who is dealing with a problem or an issue. Information and perspectives in the middle explain the story's significance.

Advantages: Best form for broadcast. Puts a human face on a problem or an issue. Can enliven a dull policy story. Background information in the middle of the story can be written ahead of time, even before you've identified your central character.

Disadvantages: The audience must listen to the entire story to understand the main point. Trimming the story likely means taking some background out of the middle to preserve the human element at the end.

Christmas tree story form Introduces a person or place. One or more surprising twists lead to background and context.

Advantage: Surprising twists keep viewers engaged with a long story.

Disadvantages: Takes time and careful planning. Not as effective for short, quick pieces.

Personal experience
SURPRISING TWIST
Background and context
SURPRISING TWIST
Background and context
SURPRISING TWIST
Ending

FIGURE 7.2 **Christmas Tree Story Form**

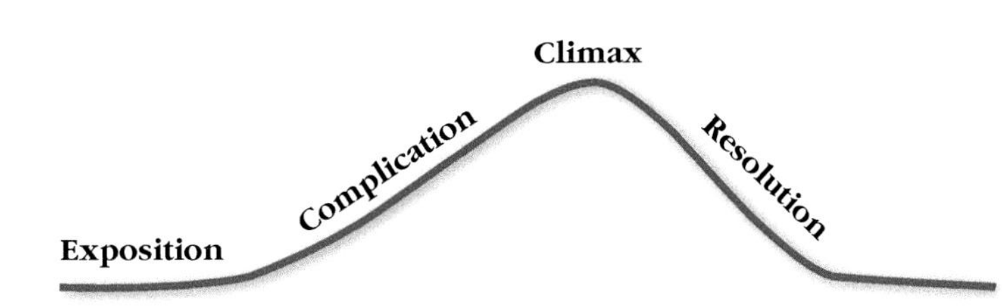

FIGURE 7.4 **Narrative Arc**

Narrative arc The piece begins with a main character who is struggling with a problem or conflict. The tension rises until it reaches a climax, followed by a resolution.

Advantages: Compelling storytelling. Captures viewers at the beginning and holds their attention to the end.

Disadvantage: Difficult to do well.

Most important information
(may be read by anchor)
Transition
•
Chronology
of events
Next
Next
Next
Next
Next
•
Kicker ending
(may be read by anchor)

FIGURE 7.3 **Wine Glass Story Form**

Wine glass story form Starts with a summary lead, like the inverted pyramid. A transition introduces the chronological telling of the story down to a kicker ending. A **kicker** is an awesome line or quote that leaves the viewer thinking, "Wow! What an amazing story!"

Advantages: Conveys complex and dramatic events by double-telling—first with the summary lead and then with the chronological replay. Best for dramatic stories that unfold chronologically. This simple approach can be helpful if you're under a tight deadline.

Disadvantage: Sometimes longer and harder to cut than other story forms.

Write

> "I make some coffee and remind myself that unless I think of something to write about, I will have to get a real job."
>
> —DAVE BARRY, HUMOR COLUMNIST

When you're back at your desk, start writing. Don't lose the feel and immediacy of a story by waiting. The more time that goes by, the more likely you'll forget something really important, or you might miss the opportunity to see the many paths your story could take. Don't worry about making it perfect. You can always delete something that doesn't read well. It doesn't matter how many times you rewrite a line—so long as you're writing.

By weaving audio and video together, you tell a more compelling story than with words alone or sounds alone or images alone. Here are some tips for writing to your visuals:

- Let the visuals show *what* is happening. Use words to explain *why* things are happening.
- Veteran NBC News correspondent Bob Dotson cautions against scripting anything that "your viewers would already know or that the visuals say more eloquently." Instead, add information that helps viewers understand what they're seeing. For example, if the video shows floodwaters rising, don't write something as obvious as this: *The water is rising quickly in Mudville tonight.* Instead, add context and meaning: *The ground is so saturated by six days of rain that the mayor predicts Mudville will be under water by midnight.*
- Look for points where the words match the visuals. These points could be about key people, places, things or topics. If viewers hear one thing while they're looking at something else, they'll be confused. These disconnected shots are called **wallpaper video**. As Al Tompkins, the Poynter Institute's group leader for broadcast and online, points out, "When the eye and ear compete, the eye wins."
- Refer to, or "touch," your video at least once in each section of copy between sound bites or other breaks in the sound.
- Don't go into too much detail about things not in the footage.
- Avoid empty phrases like "Shown here" and "Here we see."
- Don't locate people on screen from left to right, as newspapers do. If you want viewers to look at a particular person, describe him—for example, "The man in the pink leotard."

Weave in sound

People remember what they feel longer than what they learn. Let the sound bites convey **subjective** emotions, reactions and opinions. Example: "The fire ate through the roof in 15 seconds flat. I've lost everything."

Let your script convey **objective** words, facts and figures. Example: "Flames shot 50 feet into the air as a three-alarm fire engulfed a warehouse in Halifax. Some 75 firefighters fought the blaze, which consumed toys, bicycles and skateboards."

Create substantive setups When you introduce a bite or actuality, provide context or perspective that helps viewers understand what they're going to hear. Introduce the speaker's name and title just before the bite or actuality begins. Say something substantive. Don't waste space with empty words.

> **Weak:** President Obama explained what happened like this.
>
> **Strong:** President Obama said he wasn't surprised that Congress vetoed the bill.

Write out bites and actualities Type what the interviewee says in each bite or actuality. This way, you can easily write the text that comes before and after each one. Carefully transcribe the exact words in case you post this story online.

Identify sources Broadcasters rarely quote someone. They'd rather use a paraphrase, a sound bite or

an actuality unless it's a dynamite quote like "I am not a crook" or "I did not have sexual relations with that woman." If you use a quote, though, set it up by saying something like "in her words" or "as he put it." Always identify, or attribute, the source *first.* That way, viewers know who's speaking and can judge the source's credibility, especially for controversial statements.

> **Weak:** "It's a blowtorch we can't get in front of," said Los Angeles County fire inspector Frank Garrido.
> **Strong:** Los Angeles County fire inspector Frank Garrido describes the wildfire that killed a man and destroyed several dozen mobile homes. [Follow with a sound bite from Garrido:] "It's a blowtorch we can't get in front of."

When attributing a source, use the neutral verb *say*. Don't use synonyms like *declare, warn, pronounce* or *assert,* which stick out and can color the meaning of the sentence.

> **Weak:** Earthquake victims cheered when the first relief flights arrived in Pakistan, U.N. officials asserted.
> **Strong:** U.N. officials say earthquake victims cheered when the first relief flights arrived in Pakistan.

You don't need to attribute well-known facts, such as the first president of the United States or the winner of this year's Super Bowl.

Return to the narrative You can transition smoothly from the bite or actuality back to the narrative and also reinforce the message by repeating an important word or phrase from the last sentence.

> **Last sentence of bite:** "That's probably the last of the big profits, at least for now."
> **Transition:** Despite the surge in profits, Exxon Mobil says oil production is down 8 percent this quarter.

Use natural sound: A key to great storytelling

Natural (nat) sound can enhance your radio or TV script in many ways.

At the beginning. Two to three seconds of natural sound will set the mood and grab viewers' attention.

As pauses. Let your script breathe. Viewers need a moment to pause because they're taking in lots of visual and auditory information. Include between half a second and two seconds of natural sound on its own with a strong visual—but without a reporter's track or a subject's sound bite. In a parade story, include a second or two of a marching band. In a story about rockabilly, play a few bars of the music alone.

As transitions. Nat sound can act as a transition from one scene, location or person to another. Introduce the sound just before the cut to the next scene. That way, viewers will know something new is coming.

As an experience. Nat sound puts the viewer on the scene. It heightens realism and believability. Let the viewer experience the crackling flames or chanting protesters or snarling tiger.

Beginnings: Craft the lead

A video piece needs a compelling beginning. You have only a few seconds to hook the viewer by

A GOOD BITE SHOULD . . .

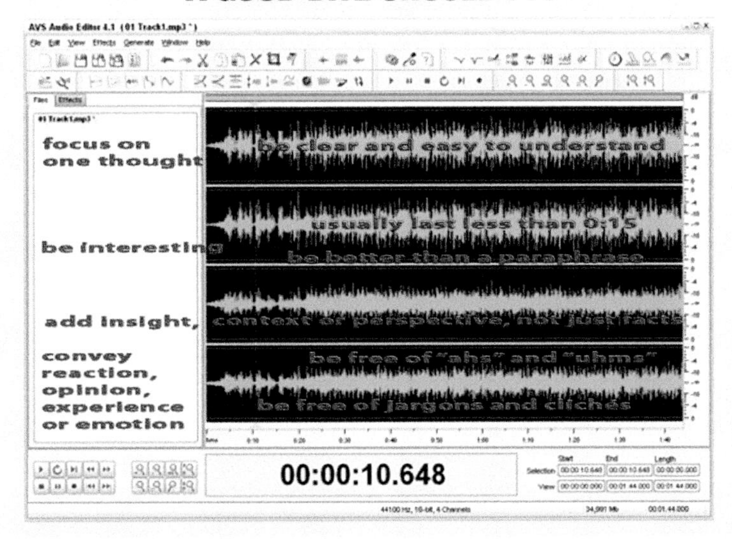

establishing the scene, main character and mood. A shot of a sign or a building establishes a place, but it won't grab your viewer. Instead, look for something strong and visual.

Finding a lead Since broadcast stories don't have headlines, their **leads** do double duty: They grab the audience's attention *and* instantly telegraph the story ahead. Breaking news and major events like a plane crash or flu epidemic automatically attract attention. For other stories, the reporter must find an angle or POV that will intrigue the audience.

Make sure the lead answers the *So what?* question: *Why should I watch or listen to this story? What's in it for me?*

If writing the lead line is stumping you, start with the second line. You might come up with a strong lead by the time you get to the end of the story.

Qualities of a good lead

- **Is it accurate?** If not, you and your news organization will lose credibility.
- **Does it contain some news that's new?**
- **Does it stress the local angle?**
- **Is it an attention-getter? Does it make the viewer care?**
  Boring: The board of trustees decided to have a meeting last night at Kazoo State University.
  Improved: The board of trustees voted last night to raise tuition at Kazoo State University.
  Attention-getting: Kazoo State University students will have to brace themselves for a tuition hike.
- **Is it hyped?** Don't tell your audience that the upcoming story is *bizarre, special, stunning, spectacular, terrific* or *terrible.* If your story is bizarre, let the lead show that.
  Hyped: Although they may not be cute and cuddly, some bizarre critters have become man's new best friend. In Africa giant rats have been trained to sniff out land mines left from previous conflicts. Their noses are more sensitive than mechanical detectors.
  Better: They may not be cute and cuddly, but they have become man's new best friend. In Africa giant rats have been trained to sniff out land mines left from previous conflicts. Their noses are more sensitive than mechanical detectors.
- **Is it clear and concise?** Do the most important points jump out?
  Unclear: A lot of people have decided to vote early in grocery stores in Las Vegas so they can go shopping afterward or else play the slots that are also in the stores.
  Clear: Some Las Vegas residents are voting in grocery stores. Afterward, they can shop for groceries or hit the slot machines a few feet away.
- **Is it a simple sentence or two (subject-verb-object)?** Start with the subject, not a dependent clause or prepositional phrase.
  Wordy: Saving a few of their chores for another day, space-walking astronauts repaired a clogged joint at the international space station earlier today.
  Tighter: Space-walking astronauts repaired a clogged joint at the international space station earlier today.

Types of leads You have many ways to start a story, depending on the topic, immediacy and story structure. Consider these possibilities:

HARD NEWS LEAD: Let's say you're covering the shooting of a local restaurateur in Chicago. The police find the handgun that fired the fatal shot. Lead with a few essential facts—generally *who, what* and *where.* Put the *when, why, how* and other details later in the story.

Example: *Chicago police have found the handgun that was used to kill a local restaurateur this morning. The gun was discovered just a block from the body.*

WRITING A GOOD LEAD CHECKLIST

- ☐ Watch the available video (TV) or listen to the actualities (radio).
- ☐ Review the other material you've collected.
- ☐ Without looking at your notes, jot down the one or two most important things you'd say first if you were telling your story to a good friend. That's the lead. Unlike a newspaper lead, a broadcast lead doesn't include the five W's and H. That would make the lead too long and difficult to follow. A broadcast lead usually lasts about 10 seconds, so you have to grab the audience's attention quickly.
- ☐ Don't reveal how things turn out. Instead, sprinkle the fascinating facts or surprises throughout the story.
- ☐ Keep rewriting your draft lead until it zings.

SOFT NEWS LEAD: After the police make an arrest, you're assigned to profile the shooter. Profiles, as well as features, analyses and investigative pieces, call for soft news leads. These stories are still newsworthy, but they explore a person or an issue instead of breaking news. Keep these leads short and snappy.

Example: *The woman arrested for killing a local restaurateur in Chicago yesterday had everyone fooled. She recently graduated from Harvard with a doctorate in French literature. She rescues injured wildlife. She's 79 years old.*

ANECDOTAL LEAD: This type of lead is a mini-story that illustrates something about the theme or main character.

Example: *Growing up in Chicago, Alfa Romeo was small for his age. Other boys picked on him. When he told his sixth grade teacher he'd be a millionaire one day, she laughed at him.*

Yesterday, the little boy who became a local restaurateur was killed outside his old elementary school.

BLIND LEAD: This lead establishes the main point of the story without revealing a key fact, such as the identity of the main character or central issue. That comes in the second paragraph.

Example: *A local restaurateur was killed last night in the neighborhood where he grew up.*

A 79-year-old woman has been arrested for the shooting of Alfa Romeo, who owns a dozen restaurants.

CONTEXTUAL LEAD: This lead provides insight or ties things together.

Example: *Chicago has regained a title it doesn't want...America's murder capital. Police say the city finished the year with 599 homicides. That's down from 666 last year.*

TRANSITION LEAD: A transition lead links Story 1 with Story 2. If the producer has grouped similar topics together, you can join the two stories with similar words, the theme, the time or the place.

End of Story 1: *Relatives of the slain restaurateur are offering a $10,000 reward to anyone who can provide information about the shooting.*

Example of a transition lead to Story 2 (using repeated keywords): *A shooting of a different nature is keeping police busy in San Francisco.*

Example of a transition lead to Story 2 (using the same location): *Also in Chicago...*

Stay in touch with your producer in case the rundown changes. If it does, the transition might no longer make sense.

Middles: Stay on track

Smoothly transition from the lead to the main part of your story. The middle is where you present the meat of your story by developing your central compelling character (Chapter 2) and any conflict. Don't wander, or you'll lose your audience.

Don't make more than three to five main points. Arrange them logically by thinking about what listeners want to know next. These points do *not* necessarily need to be in descending order of importance.

Keep it simple Good writing is simple and direct. It doesn't try too hard or attract attention to itself. It's invisible. Don't be tempted to overwrite by going to the thesaurus. For a refresher in the art of simplicity, read "The Elements of Style" by William Strunk and E.B. White.

Bloated: *The government came to the decision to replace him with a general of a more belligerent character.* (17 words)
Simple: *The government replaced him with a more aggressive general.* (9 words)

Keep it conversational Radio and TV audiences will hear rather than read the words you write. If they don't understand something, they can't reread the sentence. If you write in a clear, conversational way, listeners will understand the meaning. And newscasters will be able to read your copy quickly *and* clearly.

"Conversational" doesn't mean using bad grammar, slang, colloquialisms or profanity. Instead, it means capturing the casual feel of how people talk.

TABLE **7.1** **Writing and Revising Leads**

Problems with Leads	Possible Solutions
✗ **Longer than three sentences.** *President Barack Obama met Republican leaders at the White House today to discuss health care reform. The Republican lawmakers said the president's reform package is too expensive. They suggested ways to cut costs. The president said he will consider some of their recommendations.*	✓ **Trim lead to one or two short sentences that focus on one or two important points.** *President Barack Obama met with Republican leaders today to discuss ways to trim health care costs. The president promised to consider their ideas.*
✗ **One long sentence.** *Although Democrat Barack Obama dominated digital media during the 2008 presidential campaign with emails, text messages and social media, Republican Mitt Romney is now leading the way with a new smartphone application that supplies his followers with news, quotes and trivia.*	✓ **Trim the lead. Break into two or more sentences.** *During the 2008 presidential campaign, Democrat Barack Obama dominated digital media with emails, text messages and social media. Now, Republican Mitt Romney is taking the digital lead with a new smartphone app.*
✗ **A question lead that sets the audience up to answer "no" and skip your story.** *Have you ever wondered what it feels like to tear your ACL?* (Ummmm...no! An instant turnoff. Viewers want answers, not questions.)	✓ **Rewrite the question as a sentence.** *New England Patriots quarterback Tom Brady will be sitting on the sidelines for up to nine months. On Sunday he tore his left ACL. That's the ligament that passes across the knee joint.*
✗ **A lead that starts with "If you."** *If you like cats, watch this story."* (But what if you hate cats?)	✓ **Rewrite the lead so it appeals to a broad audience.** *When an Ohio man vacated his foreclosed home, he left behind nearly 100 cats. Rescuers have been chasing cats in the Akron house for two weeks. They found cats in the heating ducts, under furniture and mattresses, and in dressers, closets and cabinets.*
✗ **Wimpy space-wasters like *There is, There are, It is* and *It was.*** *It was the growth in imports that ruined his business.*	✓ **Start with strong, active verbs in present tense that put viewers in the moment.** *Growing imports ruined his business.*
✗ **A lead with the name of an obscure person.** *Conan McMurray thought he was being robbed, so he shot Riko Mataki with an assault rifle.*	✓ **Substitute a title or description why the unknown person is newsworthy.** *A detective who thought he was being robbed shot a 10-year-old trick-or-treater with an assault rifle.*

Formal and clunky: *The IRS stated that a number of complaints had been received on Friday, so investigators are now in the process of scrutinizing the possible transgressions.* (25 words)
Clear and conversational: *The IRS said it received a number of complaints on Friday. Investigators are checking them out.* (16 words)

Use active voice It's generally best to write in active voice to show *who's doing what to whom:* subject-verb-object. That's the way we speak. The word "by" is often a clue that the verb is in passive voice.

Passive voice: *The dog was bitten by the rattlesnake.* (object-verb-subject, 7 words)
Active voice: *The rattlesnake bit the dog.* (subject-verb-object, 5 words)

Although passive verbs are wimpier and wordier, sometimes it's OK to use them:

- Use passive voice to downplay the actor or spotlight the recipient of the action: *Barack Obama was elected the 44th president of the United States.*

- When there's a punch line, you might want to put the one performing the action at the end of the sentence for emphasis or surprise: *The gold medal in the one-person luge competition was won by a 6-year-old girl.*
- When nobody cares "whodunit," you might not mention the person performing the action: *Professor Plum has been arrested. Miss Peacock is being treated for a gunshot wound.*
- Passive voice works for phrases normally spoken that way: *Hillary Clinton was born in 1947.*

Use short words and short sentences Since most news packages don't last longer than 1:30, only include relevant information. When writing about a car accident, for example, don't include the make, model, year and color unless this information is pertinent, such as in the case of a hit-and-run.

Use short, concise sentences and short, plain words.

Cut wordiness and redundancy Tighten your writing by trimming unnecessary words and redundancies. Pretend each word costs $50. By cutting five words, you've saved $250!

Avoid redundancies such as "*sum* total," "*end* result," "consensus *of opinion*," "*close* proximity," "killed *dead*," "captured *alive*," "*lifeless* corpse," "*mutual* cooperation," "*ultimate* outcome," "*100 percent* complete," "*exact* same," "at this *point in* time," "*future* plans" and "*small* little."

TABLE **7.2 The Plainer, the Better**

Too fancy	Just right
abrasions, lacerations	cuts, bruises
apprehend	catch, arrest
ascend	climb
attempt	try
commence	begin, start
conflagration	fire
demonstrate	show
facilitate	aid, help
in the event that	if
inquire	ask
locate	find
prior to	before
utilize	use
vehicle	car, truck

Don't ramble Avoid starting sentences with long dependent clauses. You wouldn't say to a friend, "Feeling hungry after working at the computer all morning, I fixed a sandwich for lunch." You'd say something like this: "I was hungry after working at the computer all morning, so I fixed a sandwich for lunch."

Try to keep introductory phrases to five words or less—for example, "a decade ago" or "today in Dallas."

> **Too long:** Although house prices continue to fall around the country, especially in areas where they tripled during the boom, many middle-class families still can't afford to buy a home.
> **Just right:** Although house prices continue to fall, many middle-class families still can't afford to buy a home.

Three's the limit Sometimes you'll include lists in your story. Keep them short by listing only the most important items—and limit those to three.

Go easy on the statistics too. Limit them to three per story and present them so they're easy to understand. Instead of writing "about 87 million Americans have a passport," write "one in every three Americans has a passport."

Keep subjects and verbs close together Listeners find it easier to follow your sentences if the subject is close to the verb (usually subject-verb-object).

> **Long and convoluted:** The government bailout, which remains in flux because Democrats want it modified, would help ordinary Americans in return for bailing out the nation's financial giants.
> **Subject close to verb:** The government bailout remains in flux because Democrats want it modified. The plan would help ordinary Americans in return for bailing out the nation's financial giants.

Tight, bright copy

Good writing makes your stories sing. Ed Bliss, a writer for Edward R. Murrow and an editor for the "CBS Evening News with Walter Cronkite," wrote about the special demands of broadcast writing: "In broadcast news, the challenge is greatest. Nowhere is clarity in writing so necessary; nowhere the clock so tyrannical; nowhere the audience and the responsibility so great. In your hands has been placed

WHAT WOULD YOU DO?

Language keeps changing. So do the terms we use to refer to different groups of people. Today, many homosexual people call themselves "queer"—a word that used to be considered a slur.

Make sure the way you refer to people is relevant to your story. Do you see a problem with the terminology in these sentences?

1. Zelda Fitzgerald is a working mother from New York.
2. He comes from an inner-city neighborhood.
3. Of the 15 families living on this street, all but five are Hispanic.
4. Pablo Morales lives at home with his wife and six children.
5. Jack Johnson is a 50-year-old black man who works at the Library of Congress.

the greatest invention—not the satellite truck or the computer, but the word."

Junk the jargon Stay away from insider terminology that makes sense only to people in a given profession. Jargon includes complex medical and scientific terms, legalese, journalese and cop-speak. A cop might say "apprehend the perpetrator," but you're better off writing "arrest the suspect." Doctors describe heart attacks as "acute coronary events." Scholars might ramble on about "manipulated orientation" and "experimental protocols." Sailors talk about "semicircular deviation" and "gunkholes." Accountants speak of "personnel surplus reduction," which is another way of saying "firing." Don't make your audience work overtime to understand your narrative. Instead, strive for clear, simple language.

RULE OF THUMB

Avoid Weasel Words

Weasel words are imprecise and can weaken your writing. Avoid them.

allegedly	perhaps	recently
almost	possibly	reportedly
basically	probably	somewhat
essentially	quite	totally
extremely	rather	truly
on the whole	really	very

Be precise Murky words send muddy messages to your audience. In the following sentence it's not clear if the boycott helped or hurt sales: *The boycott had an effect on sales.* Instead: *The boycott did not increase [or reduce] sales.*

Descriptions can be fuzzy too. "A thick forest" might mean a grove of pine trees to one person but a rain forest to another. Instead, describe the forest. How tall *is* a "tall building"? If the height is relevant, write "a 110-story building."

Overcome pronoun anxiety A pronoun is used in place of a noun so you don't have to repeat the noun. Don't make your audience guess which noun a pronoun refers to:

> **Murky:** The detective gave her mother *her* ring. (Whose ring? The detective's ring? Her mother's ring?)

Clear: The detective returned *her mother's* ring.
Murky: Put the tray under the bed if *it's* dry. (If which is dry? The tray or the bed?)
Clear: If *the tray* is dry, put it under the bed.

Each pronoun should agree in number with the word it refers to.

No: If a student lives at home, they can earn $4,325 after taxes.
Yes: A student who lives at home can earn $4,325 after taxes.
No: Everybody has their favorite parts of the American dream.
Yes: Everybody has a favorite part of the American dream.

RULE OF THUMB

Avoid Clichés Like the Plague

Clichés are tired phrases that have lost their original punch through overuse. If phrases like those below flow from your keyboard, replace them with something more original:

- A needle in a haystack
- As busy as a bee
- As blue as the sky
- Give the green light
- Sweats like a pig (BTW, pigs don't sweat)
- Level the playing field
- Adding insult to injury
- Every mother's worst nightmare
- Drop the other shoe
- Throw caution to the wind
- As easy as pie
- As white as a ghost/sheet/snow
- Grow the company
- In the nick of time
- Bite the dust
- Blind as a bat
- At the end of the day
- Turn the tables
- Hit the campaign trail
- Nip it in the bud
- It's a whole new ballgame

Simplify punctuation woes Can't figure out where to put a comma when you write a print or an online story? Rejoice! Broadcasters don't use much punctuation, and they don't always follow all the punctuation rules. To show pauses, broadcasters often use ellipses . . . three dots . . . instead of commas.

If you put lots of semicolons, colons and dashes in your copy, your sentences are probably too long with too many thoughts. Simplify!

Misspelling hurts You might think that spelling doesn't matter in a broadcast script. But it does! A misspelled word might cause a newscaster to stumble or mispronounce a word on-air. In addition, many stations post their stories online or run closed captioning for deaf viewers. Misspelled words hurt the station's reputation.

If a word, location or person's name is tough to pronounce, include the phonetic spelling in the script. Cairo in Illinois, for example, is pronounced

FOUR WORTHLESS WORDS

Forrest Carr, news director, KGUN9-TV (ABC), Tucson, Ariz.

These four words can weaken your story—or your résumé tape.

Allegedly

Some writers think that putting the word *allegedly* in a story will protect them from litigation for libel, so they might be tempted to say things they can't support. It won't protect against litigation, however. *Allegedly* means "assert without proof." Another problem is that the word *allegedly* isn't conversational. And it's a sign of lazy reporting. Take the time to talk to sources and dig up facts. Find out who says John Doe is a child molester. The police? His neighbors? A website listing registered sex offenders? Attribute what you learn to the sources.

Suspect

There's no such thing as an "unknown suspect." Call someone a "suspect" only if police know who the person is. Otherwise, refer to the perp as a man, woman, thief, bandit, robber, gunman, gunwoman. Even if the police refer to an unknown person as a suspect, don't you do it too.

Apparently

Avoid this wishy washy word. Find out what happened. Instead of writing that "Smith apparently lost control of his car," look for specific information. Did the steering fail? Did a hit man stage it to look like an accident? Did Smith swerve to miss hitting an extraterrestrial? If no one knows what happened, explain the uncertainty. Example: "The sheriff isn't sure what happened but speculates that Smith may simply have lost control of his car."

Undetermined

Avoid "undetermined" in reference to a robbery or other theft. It's not conversational, and it leaves readers with the false impression that the amount of money that was taken will be disclosed later. It won't.

A worthless sentence

"The unknown suspect allegedly pointed a gun at the teller . . . demanded money . . . and apparently escaped with an undetermined amount of cash."

Source: Forrest Carr, "Four Words That Kill Good Copy," TV PRODUCTION: A quarterly production of RTNDA, Vol. 2, No. 4, October 1995, pp. 1–2.

TABLE **7.3** **Tight, Bright Copy**

Go Easy on the Adjectives	Viewers want solid, accurate information they can trust. Adjectives can make your script sound gushy and hyped. Another problem is that adjectives aren't precise. The word *brilliant,* for example, could mean "sparkling" (like a brilliant diamond), "radiant" (like a brilliant smile), "clever" (like a brilliant idea) or "full of promise" (like a brilliant future).	**Before**: A *shriveled, round* orange **After:** A *shriveled* orange	**Before:** A *heavy rain* flooded the streets. **After:** A *downpour* flooded the streets.
Don't Overuse Adverbs	Use adverbs only when needed. Not every verb needs an adverb. Don't pile on adverbs to prop up weak verbs. Use muscular verbs instead.	**Before:** Students *walked slowly* across campus. **After:** Students *strolled* across campus.	**Before:** The principal snickered *derisively.* **After:** The principal snickered.
	Adverbs can add shrillness to a story—*very* urgent, *highly* unusual, *extremely* serious. Or they can make you sound as though you're trying too hard. Perhaps most important, they can mask imprecision. When you finish your script, type "ly" in the FIND dialogue box. Review each adverb that pops up. Can you delete it or substitute a stronger verb?	**Before:** *The stock market plunge is highly unusual and very frightening.* **After:** *The Dow Jones industrial average closed below 12,000 for the first time this year.*	**Before:** *Relatively few* senators answered the quorum call. **After:** *Seven* senators answered the quorum call.
Ramp Up Your Verbs	Good writing relies on strong verbs, not adjectives and adverbs. Let verbs provide the muscle to power your sentences. When possible, replace *to be* verbs *(is, am, were, was, are, be, being, been)* with action verbs. Type *is, was* and other forms of *to be* in the FIND dialogue box to see where you can substitute strong verbs.	**Before:** The new hospital *is of special benefit* to the elderly. **After:** The new hospital *benefits* the elderly.	**Before:** Students found the results *to be* worth the extra work. **After:** Students found the results worth the extra work.
	One active verb is shorter and stronger than several weak words.	**Before:** The refugees *experienced severe hunger* in their wilderness retreat. **After:** The refugees *starved* in their wilderness retreat.	**Before:** Seattle *displayed a collective grief* over the deaths of the young climbers. **After:** Seattle *grieved* over the deaths of the young climbers.

TABLE 7.4 **Punctuation for Broadcast Journalists**

	Yes	No	What's Used Instead
Colon :	Used rarely, such as before a list		
Quotation marks " "	Used rarely		Actuality or sound bite
Parentheses ( )		👎	Ellipsis . . .
Comma ,	Depends on station		Ellipsis . . .
Dash —	Depends on station		Ellipsis . . .
Hyphen -	👍		
Apostrophe '	👍		
Period .	👍		
Question mark ?	👍		

KAY-ro. Never guess. Online dictionaries provide the pronunciation *and* often a recording of someone saying the word. For unusual personal names, call the person's office, hometown, embassy or consulate.

Use numbers correctly Since your audience will be hearing rather than reading numbers, make them more understandable by comparing them with something people can relate to. This technique will also make your story livelier and easier to understand.

- Instead of "400 square feet," for example, write "the area of a two-car garage."
- Instead of "300 feet long," write "the length of a football field."

HOW TO BECOME A WORDSMITH

Writing is just as important in broadcast journalism as it is in print and online journalism. Good writers make it look easy, but it's tough to make words glide effortlessly across the page. Fall in love with the English language. Words can be poetic or powerful, icy or steely, funny or flamboyant. The more you write, the better you'll get.

Your work will also improve if you seek out good writers to critique your stories.

Accomplished writers are avid readers. Read both the good and the bad (just be sure you know which is which!). Read widely from books (both fiction and nonfiction), newspapers, magazines and poetry.

Like poets, great writers have an ear for the rhythm and pacing of words. You can hone your writing skills by listening to the masters. One of the best was Edward R. Murrow, who reported from London during World War II. When the Germans bombed London in 1939, he opened his broadcasts from the city's rooftops with the phrase "This is London." His words were simple, written to be heard rather than read. He used alliteration, but he didn't overdo it: "The blackout stretches from Birmingham to Bethlehem, but tonight, over Britain, the skies are clear."

Murrow painted pictures with words. Here's how he described the takeoff for a bombing raid on Berlin: "The sun was going down and its red glow made rivers and lakes of fire on the top of the clouds. Down to the southward, the clouds piled up to form castles, battlements." At war's end he wrote about the liberation of prisoners from the Buchenwald concentration camp: "It sounded like the handclapping of babies, they were so weak."

Source: From Edward R. Murrow, World War II CBS World News Broadcasts, 1938–1939. Copyright © CBS News. Used with permission.

Endings: Go out strong

Have your ending in mind before you start editing so you know where your story is headed. Mindy McAdams, an online journalism professor at the University of Florida, says a strong, satisfying conclusion has two parts: "The **climax** is the destination, the place you're taking the audience, in a straight line from the opening. It will come near the end of the story, but afterward, you also need to provide *closure*. Make it feel *complete*. That's the **resolution.** It's the cherry on top of an ice cream sundae."*

End on a strong note Just as you started your story with a strong visual, end with a strong visual as well. That's what your viewer will probably remember.

Work as hard on the last line of your story as on the first. This is what the listener will remember.

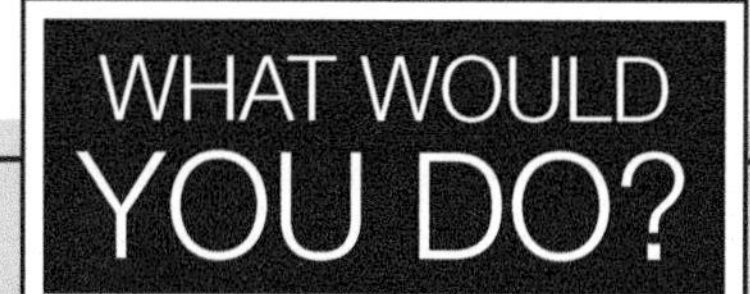

One of your colleagues has asked you to look at the draft of a script about cowboys rounding up wild burros. It needs editing. Keep in mind what you've read about wordiness, adjectives, adverbs and verbs.

The wild burros came at a run out of a thicket toward a flimsy veil of jute netting. Four cowboys in a hovering helicopter follow closely behind, pushing the burros hard.

400 pounds of frantic burros, looking for an escape, races passed, hooves clattering wildly across the desert cobble. Then the burros and cowboys became a tangle inside an explosion of dust at the mouth of the trap. Gary Cook, a cowboy from Springville in Utah, hurls a loop quick as a snake around a jack that balks.

Seven burros are a good catch at approximately $500 a head.

When enough burros had been caught in the trap, another was built downstream.

Don't revisit, rehash or summarize what you've already covered. Here are a few ways you can finish with juice:

- Come full circle. Give your story a sense of closure by echoing the person, place or thought you started with. Let's say you begin with a patient undergoing an experimental treatment for cancer. You could wrap up with the patient's prognosis if the treatment doesn't work.
- End with natural sound and a few words, such as "The high cost of gasoline means many Chinese won't consider buying American cars" and the sound of a car revving up.
- Leave your audience with a revealing anecdote or memorable fact that reinforces your main point. You could conclude a story on space-walking astronauts like this: "Chris Cassidy's experience as a Navy SEAL means he'll attack problems boldly, even when he's floating 220 miles above the Earth."
- Offer a solution to a problem raised in your story. For a consumer piece on how to settle credit card disputes, you could end with what to do if all else fails: "If you're not satisfied with your current company, go elsewhere."
- Address what will happen next, such as "The Supreme Court will hand down a decision tomorrow."

In general, ending with an actuality or a sound bite is the lazy way out. Use this technique only if the bite is so powerful it makes you laugh or cry. At the end of a story about children resuscitated after drowning, a mother of a developmentally disabled son says, "I just wish I could let parents know how hard it is to keep on going after your life has forever changed."

*From "Tell a Good Story with Images and Sound," MindyMcAdams.com, March 19, 2009; http://mindymcadams.com/tojou/2009/rgmp-11-tell-a-good-story-with-images-and-sound

TABLE **7.5 Numbers**

Newsroom styles vary, but many operations use hyphens to link all the parts of a number (both words and figures) with the noun it modifies: eight-days, 53-cats, two-thousand-140-miles. Other than dates, don't use more than three digits per number: ten-thousand-923-horses, two-million-547-thousand-dollars. Write out *dollar* and *percent* instead of using the symbols *$* and *%*. Consult the "Associated Press Broadcast News Handbook."

Use Words	Use Figures	Use Both
One through nine *three-mountains*	10 through 999 *53-brides*	Amounts over a thousand *17-million-stars* *five-thousand-500-dollars* *15-thousand-troops*
Thousand, million, billion, trillion *six-million-dollar-man*		
	Years *1950, 2010*	
Dollars, cents, percent, degrees, **not** $, ¢, %, ° *five-million-dollar-diamond* *15-cents* *55-percent*		
First through ninth *June fifth*	10th and above *June 12th*	
Decimals one through ten *12-point-three*		
Fractions *one-half* *two-thirds*		
Number at the beginning of a sentence *Twelve dogs barked.*	Year at the beginning of a sentence *2008 was an election year.*	
	Time *4 p-m or 4 this afternoon* *4:30 a-m or 4:30 in the morning* (NOTE: a-m and p-m, not a.m. and p.m.)	
	Sports scores *behind 42-to-21* *7-to-3*	
	Addresses *32-0-1 Escalante Ridge Place*	

Revise

Your first draft won't appear on-air. Nor, probably, will your second or third revision. The more you rewrite, the better your story will be. Even professionals don't get it right the first time.

Don't toss your drafts. You might want to salvage something from an earlier version.

Put it away, and then revise

If you're not facing a deadline, let your story sit for a few minutes or even several hours. You'll be amazed at the silly things you notice when you look at it with fresh eyes.

Read your script out loud

Make sure it sounds natural and conversational. Reading it aloud will help you hear the parts that sound rough or wordy or just plain nerdy.

Language that works in print or online might sound confusing or embarrassing when read out loud. To avoid confusion, use context to distinguish homonyms like *ladder* from *latter* and *lacks* from *lax*. Beware of double meanings. Think of how embarrassing it could be if you wrote about a golf tournament where a lobbyist played "a round" with a former president of the United States.

REVISION CHECKLIST

CONTENT

- ❑ Does the story highlight the most important points?
- ❑ Does it provide insights and perspective?
- ❑ Does it make people care about the subject?
- ❑ Does it include trends or issues that help the audience understand the big picture?
- ❑ Is it fair and complete? Are all sides of an issue included?
- ❑ Have you used diverse voices to represent the community in terms of gender, ethnicity, religion, age, physical characteristics or occupation?

ACCURACY

- ❑ Did you double-check the spelling of the name of every person and company? Is it Katherine or Cathryn? Smith or Smythe? (Remember that a version of your script will probably appear on the Web.)
- ❑ Did you run a spell-checker? When in doubt, look in a dictionary. Pay attention to homonyms, such as *they're, there* and *their.*
- ❑ Have you verified job titles, dates, ages, places, facts and figures?
- ❑ Did you point out any shaky sources or disputed facts?
- ❑ Do the facts or claims in sound bites accurately reflect what the source said and convey what was meant?

STRUCTURE AND STYLE

- ❑ Is the lead concise, clear and intriguing?
- ❑ Does the middle of the story support the lead?
- ❑ Does the story end on a strong note?
- ❑ Does each sentence flow logically into the next one, linked by transitions (words such as *and, but, also, meanwhile* and *like)?*
- ❑ Are sentences and paragraphs short? Is there one thought per sentence?
- ❑ Are most sentences in present tense and active voice with strong verbs?
- ❑ Have you cut jargon, clichés and unnecessary adjectives and adverbs?
- ❑ Have you fixed grammatical and punctuation glitches?
- ❑ Do all the elements—your script, sound bites or actualities, natural sound, visuals and the newscaster's delivery—work together to create a seamless narrative that will hold the audience's attention?

Style Guidelines

Make your copy conversational by capturing the feel of how people talk without copying their speech exactly. Avoid copy that's wordy, irrelevant, tricky for the newscaster to read or difficult for the audience to understand.

TABLE **7.6** **Troubleshooting Common Style Problems**

Problem	Solution
More than one theme or POV per story	Focus on one theme or POV.
Several ideas per sentence	Strive for one idea per sentence.
More than one comma per sentence	Tighten or break into two short sentences, with each conveying just one thought.
Sentences longer than 20 words in hard news leads or 25 words in the rest of the story	Tighten or break into two short sentences. Incomplete sentences (fragments) are OK if not overused. So are a few long sentences if they're easy to understand.
Long introductory phrases (more than five words)	Shorten introductory phrases to five words or less, or flip sentence and begin with subject.
Passive voice (The tree was hit by the car.)	Unless you have a good reason to use passive voice, switch to active voice. (The car hit the tree.)
Past tense *(said, sent, arrived)* except when necessary (The store was robbed. The cost of living rose.)	To convey immediacy, write in present tense *(says)*, present progressive *(is sending)* or present perfect *(has arrived)* as much as possible.
To be verbs *(is, are, was, were)*	Substitute strong, active verbs.
Alliteration (His feet flailed like a furious fox.) and sibilance (Six snakes slithered south.)	If you don't spot alliteration and sibilance while writing, you'll hear them when you read aloud.
Formal phrases *(has not, it is, do not)*	Use contractions, which are more conversational *(hasn't, it's, don't)*, except when emphasizing something. (The dean says he does *not* want to offer that course.)
Decimal places, such as 12.3	Round off numbers with decimals. For decimals below .5, round down. For .5 and above, round up.
Large exact numbers, such as $74,574	Round off, for example, to almost $75,000.
Too many facts and figures	Include only the most important facts and figures.
Middle names and initials	Use only if requested by the source, if a person's middle name or initial is well known (John F. Kennedy, Lee Harvey Oswald) or to distinguish between two people with the same first and last name (George Bush).
Last name only in first reference	Use complete names on first reference except for well-known people, such as the president or pope. Use last name only on second reference.
Addresses	Use only if relevant to story. Spell out all the words *(north, south, street, avenue, road)*.
Ages	Use only if relevant, such as in an obituary, or if unusual, such as a 16-year-old who graduated from college. If used, put the age before the name (16-year-old Dr. Doogie Howser).
Long titles (Deputy Undersecretary of Defense for Civilian Personnel Policy)	Shorten titles (a Pentagon official, the governor's spokesperson, authorities)
Courtesy titles *(Mr., Mrs., Ms., Miss)*	Follow your station's policy. Some stations, for example, put *Dr.* in front of a medical doctor's name.
Unfamiliar abbreviations *(M-S-G-T)*	Write out unfamiliar abbreviations. *(M-S-G-T* stands for master sergeant.)

Radio and TV Scripts

Follow your newsroom or class preferences for formatting scripts. Some common guidelines follow.

FORMATTING CHECKLIST

- [ ] Leave wide margins (2 inches or so) at the top and bottom of the page—and an inch on each side.
- [ ] At the top of each page, put a slug consisting of your name, the date and sometimes the time.
- [ ] Double-space or triple-space your copy for easy reading.
- [ ] Indent paragraphs and use capital letters (uppercase) for all the words to be read aloud. That makes it easy to see what's meant to be spoken.
- [ ] Type ### at the end of each story.
- [ ] Put each story on a separate page so the rundown can be easily changed.

Radio scripts In most of today's newsrooms, computers help you format scripts and even time them. TRT (total running time) indicates the length of a piece of media. Reporter Mark Brodie wrote this script for KJZZ, the NPR affiliate in Phoenix.

RADIO SCRIPT

Slug →	AZ Vaccine
Reporter →	Brodie
Date →	10-1
Announcer →	ARIZONA WILL SOON GET ITS FIRST SHIPMENT OF VACCINE FOR SWINE FLU. THE STATE HAS PUT IN AN ORDER FOR MORE THAN 70-THOUSAND DOSES OF FLU-MIST, WHICH IS A NASAL SPRAY. K-J-Z-Z'S MARK BRODIE REPORTS.
TRT →	:53
Reporter →	THE STATE WANTS TO MAKE SURE HEALTH CARE WORKERS ARE THE FIRST IN LINE TO GET THE VACCINE . . . KIDS UNDER FIVE AND PEOPLE WITH UNDERLYING HEALTH PROBLEMS WILL BE AMONG THOSE VACCINATED NEXT. WILL HUMBLE, INTERIM DIRECTOR OF THE STATE HEALTH DEPARTMENT, SAYS UP TO A MILLION MORE DOSES SHOULD BE ON THEIR WAY TO ARIZONA BY MID TO LATE OCTOBER . . . WITH MORE TO FOLLOW BY THE END OF THE YEAR.
Actuality →	*(This represents about 1.5 percent of the total vaccine that we expect to get between now and January . . . so it's a very small amount . . . but it's also a useful test in terms of measuring our ability to execute this throughout our mass vaccination plans.) :16*
Reporter →	AROUND 37-THOUSAND OF THE DOSES COMING TO THE STATE WILL BE ALLOCATED TO MARICOPA COUNTY . . . BUT THE COUNTY'S PUBLIC HEALTH DIRECTOR SAYS THAT'S LESS THAN HALF THE NUMBER OF HOSPITAL WORKERS IN THE STATE'S MOST POPULOUS COUNTY. HE'S HOPEFUL THOSE WITH DIRECT CONTACT WITH PATIENTS WILL GET VACCINATED FIRST.
	FOR K-J-Z-Z, I'M MARK BRODIE.

# # #

Source: Mark Brodie, "AZ Vaccine" broadcast, KJZZ, October 1, 2009. Used with permission of KJZZ.

TV scripts A script for a television newscast includes video, audio, natural sound and the words to be read out loud. No matter what format your professor or station uses, the technical information must be clear, correct and aligned with the corresponding change. Remember that changes work best at the beginning of a sentence or phrase.

SCRIPT FOR A TV PACKAGE

↓ **Slug**	↓ **Reporter**	↓ **Date**	↓ **Time**
Hate Group	Phillips	6/12	Six

Anchor

THERE WAS ANOTHER SORT OF PROTEST IN THE VALLEY . . . BUT THIS TIME IT INVOLVED A GROUP OF NEO-NAZIS WHO SAID THEY WERE MARCHING AGAINST ILLEGAL IMMIGRATION.

MEMBERS OF THE NATIONAL-SOCIALIST-MOVEMENT SAID THEY WERE MARCHING ON THE CAPITOL TO STAND AGAINST ILLEGAL IMMIGRATION.

BUT AS TOBY PHILLIPS SHOWS US . . . THERE ARE MANY WHO SAY IMMIGRATION IS JUST A COVER FOR FEELINGS THAT RUN MUCH DEEPER.

(Package)

[TAKE PACKAGE OUTCUE: A PLACE FOR EVERYONE

DURATION: 1:30]

[CG in 0:09 to 0:18:DUET 2 LINE\Toby Phillips\CRONKITE NEWS]
[CG in 0:29 to 0:36:DUET 2 LINE\Bill Straus\ADL REGIONAL DIRECTOR]
[CG in 1:09 to 1:13:DUET 2 LINE\Jeff Schoep\NSM LEADER]

[TAKE NAT/ VO]

THE BEAT OF A DRUM . . . LEADS THE WAY AS MEMBERS OF THE NATIONAL-SOCIALIST-MOVEMENT DESCEND ON THE STATE CAPITOL . . . PROTESTERS HELD AT BAY BY HORSES AND LINES OF POLICE.

[TAKE SOT
NAME: NSM member shouting into microphone]
"This is our country."

[TAKE SOT
NAME: standup]

"The NSM behind me say they are here to promote a white America and say they are just against illegal immigration while all the other groups say they are here just to promote hate."

[TAKE SOT
NAME: Bill Straus]
"The level of hate in Arizona right now is very high."

[TAKE VO]

BILL STRAUS WITH THE ANTI-DEFAMATION LEAGUE SAYS THAT THE N-S-M IS A HATE GROUP AND THAT OTHERS LIKE IT ARE SPREADING ACROSS ARIZONA.

[TAKE SOT
NAME: Bill Straus]

"Border issues have brought a lot of attention to Arizona . . . particularly from white supremacist racists. Let's face it . . . this is where the business is."

[TAKE VO]

HATE GROUPS HAVE BECOME SO PREVALENT IN ARIZONA THAT THE A-D-L HAS A REGIONAL OFFICE DEVOTED SOLEY TO OUR STATE.

[TAKE SOT
NAME: Bill Straus]
"The targets are usually African-Americans or Jews . . . most recently the Hispanic community."

[TAKE VO/GRAPHIC]

ACCORDING TO THE SOUTHERN POVERTY LAW CENTER . . . WHICH TRACKS HATE GROUPS . . . THERE ARE CURRENTLY 19 KNOWN GROUPS IN THE STATE . . . AND N-S-M IS JUST ONE. AGAIN . . . THEY SAY THEY MARCH AGAINST ILLEGAL IMMIGRATION. THEIR WEBSITE SAYS THAT ALL NON-WHITE IMMIGRATION SHOULD BE STOPPED . . . ILLEGAL OR NOT.

[TAKE SOT
NAME: NSM commander]

"We aren't a hate group. We're a white civil rights organization. The swastika is a symbol of white people."

[TAKE VO]

A SYMBOL THAT N-S-M FLEW PROUDLY AT THE CAPITOL . . . BUT THE SYMBOLS WERE DENOUNCED BY OTHER DEMONSTRATORS.

[TAKE SOT]

"We're out here saying we don't want swastikas flying at our state capitol. We don't want that in our community."

[TAKE VO]

A COMMUNITY THAT CONTINUES THE BATTLE TO FIND A SPACE . . . FOR EVERYONE.

(NATS)

Toby Phillips. Cronkite News.

(On-camera tag)

THE N-S-M SAYS THEY ARE PLANNING MORE MARCHES AROUND THE COUNTRY. TO TRACK HATE GROUPS IN OUR STATE AND TO LEARN MORE ABOUT THEM . . . [CG:DUET 2 LINE\splcenter.org\MORE INFORMATION] VISIT THE SOUTHERN POVERTY LAW CENTER'S WEBSITE AT S-P-L-CENTER-DOT-ORG.

###

PRODUCING for Broadcast

CHAPTER 8

> *The person who sits here is but the most conspicuous member of a superb team of journalists—writers, reporters, editors, producers—and none of that will change.*
>
> —*WALTER CRONKITE*

Contributed by Melanie Asp Alvarez, Faculty Associate, Walter Cronkite School of Journalism and Mass Communication, and Executive Producer, Cronkite NewsWatch

CHAPTER OUTLINE

So, What's a Producer?

Let's start by explaining the difference between a **producer** and a production crew. People who work in production work in the studio as camera technicians, audio technicians, technical directors or directors—in other words, they work on the technical production of a show. But a newscast producer is something very different. A newscast producer creates the vision. There are several different kinds of producers, such as a show producer, a field producer or a story producer. A show, or newscast, producer creates the vision for the entire show—not only organizing the show but also doing the majority of the writing. A field producer sets up a story in the field, shoots it, comes back to the studio to write it and then has an anchor or another reporter track the story. The field producer also edits the story. The job of a field producer, then, is to produce a story for the anchor or another reporter. Most of this chapter focuses on show producers.

Producer Vision: Your Greatest Show on Earth

Producing a daily newscast takes a true ringmaster—someone who creates and plans a great show, sketching out each performance to the tiniest detail, keeping all the components in check, making sure all the participants are prepared and then watching the show unfold, megaphone in hand, whip at the ready, as the astonishing, mesmerizing and death-defying acts play out for the audience. OK, so maybe on a good day you can expect a newscast to go off without a hitch. But it takes a *lot* of work every day. And that's why the newscast producer exists.

FIGURE 8.1 **The Producer's Three-Ring Circus**
The area where Content, Production and Execution intersect is Producer Vision.

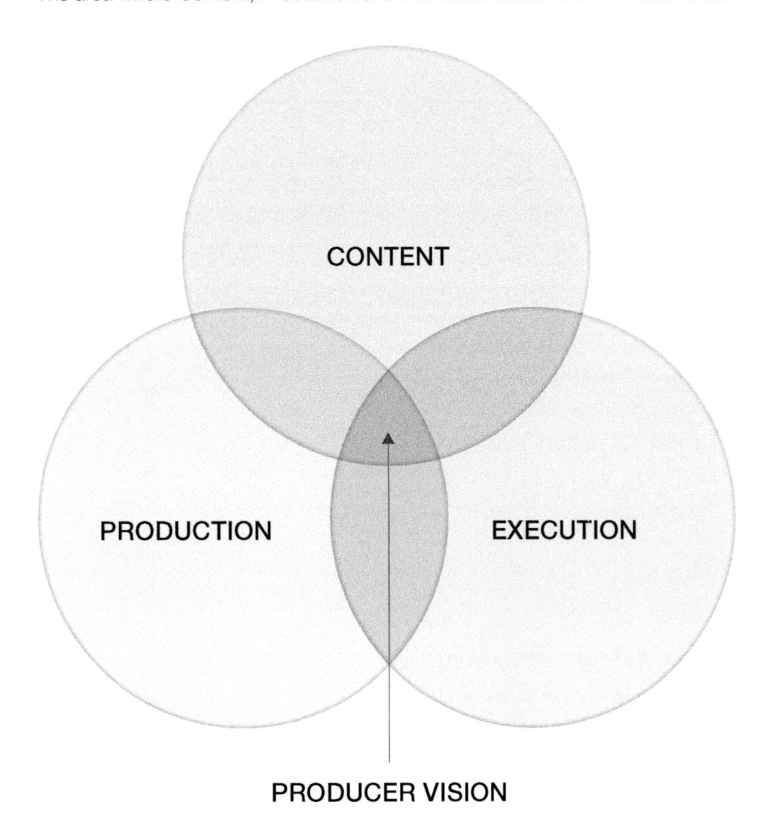

The producer is the one person responsible for the vision of how the entire show comes together—blending content, production skills and execution skills to create a compelling, informative newscast.

It is the news producer's job to create the overall vision for the newscast. To do that, the producer must select, organize and write the editorial content (packages, video, sound bites, readers, teases), support that content with the best production elements available (graphics, on-screen text, live shots, studio/newsroom presentations) and oversee the execution of the newscast with planning and communication throughout the day (among managers, reporters, anchors and the production crew). The producer must also provide confident leadership as the key decision-maker, final timekeeper and main go-to person in the control room during the live newscast.

The responsibilities we have just outlined apply equally to online, TV or radio producers. Producers are responsible for the content and the look, no matter what the medium. In radio, producers might not be concerned about visuals, but they are concerned about using natural sound and interviews to help paint a picture in the minds of the listeners. They also have to produce newscasts throughout the shift, changing the content to keep pace with the latest developments and trying to keep it fresh for the listeners, who are tuning in and out.

An online producer, like a broadcast producer and radio producer, is concerned about sound, video and the printed word. The online producer is also concerned about writing headlines that will draw readers, as well as packaging stories—deciding whether they should include still pictures, video or just words. Creating a great headline for online news is just as important as teases are for broadcast and radio producers. The headline and the tease have to grab viewers' attention and convince them to stick around and read or watch more. Overall, the job of the producer is to develop a vision and then figure out how to get everyone else to buy into that vision and help pull off the show.

Content

A producer's day begins with questions about content. What stories are going to go into today's newscast? What stories will the viewers want to see? The decision-making and news judgment should start not upon arrival at the newsroom, but much earlier. If you are the producer, you must activate your Producer Vision just as soon as you open your eyes for the day.

Ideas for getting ideas

To be a producer, you must have a passion for news, for always learning something new, and you must be motivated to work around the clock to achieve this goal. Producing can't be turned off when you leave the station for the day. Everything you see, hear or read has the potential to become a story in your newscast.

Turn on the TV

When you wake up, turn on the morning news shows. This will help you find out what happened in your neighborhood, your state and the world while you were sleeping. Any stories you see that morning could become a bigger story in your newscast later in the day.

Go online

With the TV still on, begin searching the Internet. There are many great stories online that never make it to a newscast. Make sure you know about them. Where should you look online for story ideas? You can Google anything with your state name in it, and you can check in with your social media contacts on Facebook or Twitter to find out what people are talking about.

Explore potential story ideas

More information means more potential story ideas. A story you see about a neighboring state might trigger an idea. For example, let's say that highway police in another state have stopped patrolling the roadways between midnight and 6 a.m. because of budget cuts. In fact, they are only called out for emergencies, which mean longer response times. "Hmm," you might think. "I wonder if that's happening in my state." After checking, you find that it is, so you request paperwork from the police agencies and follow your story. A story like that would affect anyone in your state who uses the highways. Great story, and good information for your viewers and listeners.

PRODUCER CHECKLIST: FROM WAKE-UP TO MORNING MEETING

- ☐ Turn on the TV.
- ☐ Go online.
- ☐ Explore potential story ideas.
- ☐ Read newspapers, including community papers.
- ☐ Listen to talk radio in the car.
- ☐ Start visualizing graphics.
- ☐ Check in with the assignment desk.
- ☐ Check in with producer from the previous show.
- ☐ Begin mapping out show on a notepad.
- ☐ Attend the morning editorial meeting.
- ☐ Firm up your plan.

Read, read, read

After you have listened to the TV news shows and checked online, read the newspapers—and not just the big local ones. Also look at small community papers. They often have great stories that deserve wider coverage or reveal trends. You might notice similar stories—say, about homeless people spending their days at the local public libraries in two different neighborhood papers. Could this be a trend? A story like that could develop into a major investigative piece.

Turn on the radio

Now you're in your car, heading for work. Don't mindlessly listen to music to pass the time. Instead, tune in to your local radio news station. You can also listen to talk radio or even sports talk to see what is going on in the world. On talk radio, you get a sense of what's on listeners' minds. You can also use this time behind the wheel to visualize a list of stories for your show. This is the fun, creative part of your job. As a producer, you get to pick from the stories you have at your fingertips.

FIGURE 8.2 **Finding Story Ideas**

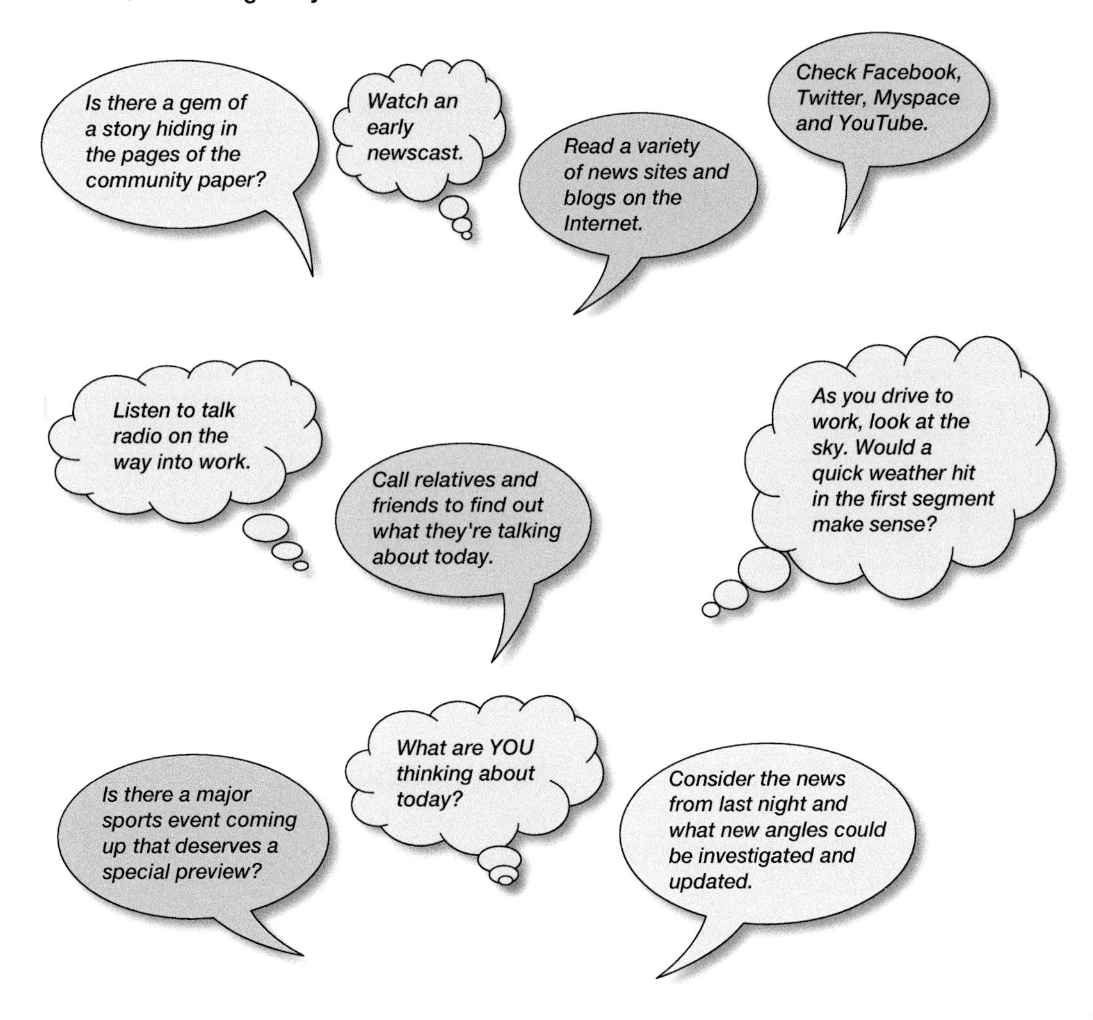

Start visualizing graphics

As you begin to see how your show could come together, you can start thinking graphically. Visualize how you might include live shots or how you might present a **talker story,** meaning one that doesn't have great visuals but still should have a place in your newscast. Not all stories have to be hard news; they just have to be interesting. Maybe it's a hero story, or one about a child who created a unique business in her basement, or a video on YouTube that had a million views in just one day. These are stories the viewer, listener or reader will remember long after the newscast has ended. As you consider the possibilities, your mind is clicking away with ideas!

Check in with the assignment desk

When you arrive at the newsroom, your first stop is the assignment desk, which is the hub for story coverage. The **assignment editors** listen to police and fire scanners for breaking news. They also maintain the **daybook,** which is a list of planned news events throughout the day. The daybook also lists the crews that are working that day and any scheduled shoots. In other words, the daybook gives you an outline of potential stories. The assignment editors also control the news crews. A priority is to talk to them about planned events for the day and breaking news that happened overnight. Some of these stories might appear in your newscast as **VOs** or **VO/SOTs,** so it's nice to know exactly what you will have.

Check in with producers

The next step is to talk to the morning show producer. This person has been working at the station overnight, and she or he can tell you what happened during the wee hours, what great pictures or sound you might have for later and what stories you will probably want to follow.

The hand-off from one producer to another is critical in this 24/7 news industry. Something that might not fit in your show might work well in the next one, and you need to share this type of information with each other.

AP ENPS Messages: Urgent: AP-AZ--KFGZ-AZ Hazardous Weather Outlook

DAYBOOK [02/15/2011]

Story Slug	Segment	Crew	Status	Location	Story Log Preview	Assgn Info	Object Placehol
READY TO RUN				TEMPE	ASU SOFTBALL-MYLAN PHAM		
ABORTION BILLS		STEVE		STATE CAPITOL	HEARING ON ABORTION BILLS		
NW REPORTERS		MORGAN		CONTROL	MORGAN--EGYPT SKYPE INTERVIEW		
FOOD BILL BATTLE		LISA		TUCSON	LISA SHOOTING FOOD BILL BATTLE		
SECURITY MEETINGS		JOHN		PHOENIX	SECURITY CHANGES AT		
HEALTH FORUM		SIERA		STATE CAPITOL	RURAL HEALTH FORUM-		
GAME AND FISH		NANCY		PHOENIX	GREY WOLF MEETING		
ASU BENEFIT		CHARLIE		PHOENIX	Nursing benefit for asu		
SPRING TRAINING		MARCIE		SCOTTSDALE	spring training begins talk to S.F. Giants		
BORDER EXPO		SIERA		PHOENIX	border expo begins in Phx. with		
EXPECTED					"WEDNESDAY"		
DAYBOOK					Feb. 15. 8 a.m. to 3:30 p.m. RURAL		
WORKING				PHOENIX	PHOENIX SUNS TICKETS-MYLAN		

Screen shot of the Essential News Production System (ENPS), an electronic daybook system.

Map out your show on a notepad

Now you begin to start drawing out your show more specifically on your notebook. Of course, the news is constantly changing, but you always have to have a basic plan and then be prepared to change it as the day evolves.

Attend the morning meeting

A well-functioning newsroom is one in which everyone brings fresh ideas and resources to the morning editorial meeting. And the morning meeting is a key time to hone that Producer Vision. As the news team shares its ideas and plans for the day, a producer can sketch out what a probable newscast could look like.

For example, the editors and planners at the assignment desk will likely come with a full list of community events, news conferences, court dockets and Freedom of Information Act documents, also known as FOIAs. They'll also have video of overnight crimes and chopper shots of rush-hour car wrecks to offer. The **news director** might come with a plan for a special investigative report tied to the state budget cuts. One reporter might have a brewing exclusive on a possible hospital closure downtown. The **executive producer** might have a **network tie-in** that must air before prime time. A photojournalist might ask to do a **natural sound package** on this afternoon's annual Mighty Mud Mania event.

Firm up your plan

Now you start to actually formulate your plans. Here's a look (below) at how a producer could map out the typical content discussed in a morning

FIGURE **8.3** **A Producer's Story Grid Based on the Morning Meeting**

A-block

- 2 or 3 reporter-driven "day of" news stories
- National story tie-ins with local peg
- Several hard news VOs, VO/SOTs & readers
- First weather hit
- Super-tease to best stories of the B-, C- and D-blocks

B-block

- Highly teasable human interest or feature reporter package
- Consumer, health, business or other franchise-related stories
- Must-see video of the day

C-block

- Lighter teasable reporter package
- National weather video or environmental story
- Weather full forecast

D-block

- Sports (generally produced by sports anchor/staff)
- Kicker: short, fun or memorable story
- Goodbye from news team, teasing to next newscast

At the morning meeting, producers, reporters, assignment desk editors and managers discuss story ideas for the day's newscasts.

meeting. With a paper divided into **blocks,** or segments of the show, with the first segment being the A-block, followed by the B-block and so on, the producer can create an early look at the eventual format for the **rundown,** considering the flow of stories as well as where teases and commercial breaks will go.

Producers need to ensure there is solid news content throughout the show, and they can do this as they divide content between each news block. Placing morning meeting ideas into a grid like this also allows a producer to see the holes in content. For example, the grid might reveal that the show has some great feature stories (B-block) but no obvious lead story. Or maybe the show has all hard news and nothing teasable for the lower blocks. Mapping out the Producer Vision early will help avoid shortfalls in content later in the day.

What's the big idea?

There is a major difference between an idea for a story and an actual story. Three little words can mean all the difference to a producer: Is it turnable?

In other words, which story pitches from the morning meeting can be made into stories? Ideas that are vague or not well fleshed out probably won't make it. But ideas with thought behind them, maybe a little research and perhaps even a pre-existing contact have a much higher probability of being turnable, meaning they can be turned from ideas into news packages that day.

Qualities of a good producer

A good producer is flexible, a good communicator, a team builder and a good listener. No two days are alike, and no two newscasts are alike.

Anticipating change Because newsgathering is such a dynamic process, a producer must be extremely flexible. A lead story can change a dozen times a day, depending on events in the community, state, country and world. Plans for great feature stories fall through. Tapes with the video for a great kicker get lost. A good producer must roll with the changes and be very comfortable with making decisions on the fly.

Communication

Once the plan is sketched out on paper, a producer needs to have face-to-face talks with reporters, assignment editors, anchors and managers to ensure everyone is on the same page. The point here is to

IS IT TURNABLE?

Weak idea: "It's hot outside. We should do a story about how hot it is."

- *Too general, no focus, big-time "duh" factor.*

OK idea: "It's hot outside. We should do a story about people who have to work outside in this heat today."

- *Added thought puts an emphasis on people and provides a situation.*

Better idea: "It's hot outside. We should do a story about people who have to work outside in this heat today. I read on today's city council agenda about a proposed shutdown on road construction if the temperature exceeds a certain point."

- *Relevant research adds a new dynamic with wider implications.*

Turnable idea: "It's hot outside. We should do a story about people who have to work outside in this heat today. I read on today's city council agenda about a proposed shutdown on road construction if the temperature exceeds a certain point. I've already talked with a councilwoman and a construction worker who are ready to go on-camera for interviews."

- *It's now a story with background and contacts that can turn today.*

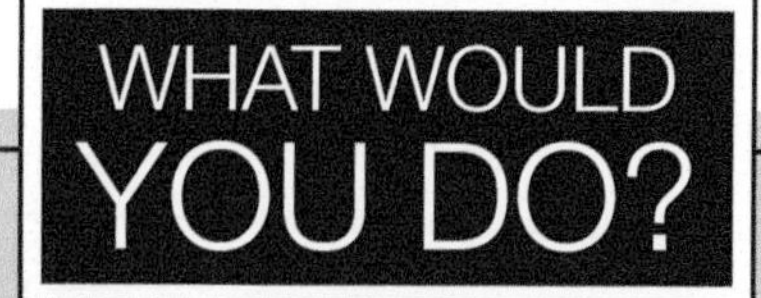

Here's how a topic might be developed during a morning meeting. Someone says that everyone is talking about swine flu dangers, so we should do a story about it.

Well, that's pretty broad. It's a topic, not a story. We need to focus and clarify what the story might be, not just toss out an idea. Now you can begin to use your skills as a journalist. This is the most exciting phase of the process because you're starting to hone in on the actual story.

How do we move forward from the idea to the actual story? The producer might ask the reporter if he has looked at how hospitals are preparing to handle the number of cases expected in intensive care units during the flu season. Or he might suggest a story on options for parents who can't afford to take a week off work with their child.

The producer might then begin to envision a sequence: First, graphics on the projected number of swine flu deaths, followed by a quick VO on what local hospitals are doing to prepare and then perhaps a live shot of a reporter presenting options for child care. In this way, the producer has taken a broad topic like swine flu, envisioned the nuts and bolts and then narrowed it down to a great **sidebar** piece.

eliminate the newscast-crippling claim that "Nobody told me!" Producers, much like circus ringmasters, are loudmouths and should not be ashamed of that fact.

The news team needs to know

1. which reporters are going live, which will be presenting from the set, which will be assembling just a straight package.
2. which story is the planned lead.
3. which stories need tease video and/or sound.
4. what the producer sees as the main emphasis for each story.

That fourth point is critical. Very often, reporters leave the building without understanding what their stories should be. For example, a reporter is assigned to cover a suspected drug ring at a local high school. The facts of the case—the who, what, when, where and how—are already established in a police news release. Moreover, the producer has included those facts in the introduction to the story, complemented with a nice map and full-screen graphic, before the anchors pitch out to the reporter and the reporter begins telling her story. Unfortunately, the reporter assumed those basic facts were the whole story and so is now stuck repeating all the same information the producer included in the introduction. A good producer would have avoided such an unprofessional embarrassment by clearly communicating with the reporter that the assignment was to get a **sidebar** on parent, student and school reaction to the arrests rather than the nuts and bolts of the story.

Using the same example, a good producer will always invite the reporter to deviate from the

RULE OF THUMB

A producer has to have a backup plan—and a backup plan for your backup plan. You cannot plan your show and think it will look the same eight hours later. It could change five minutes before the newscast. It's best to plan on nothing working out the way you plan. That way, you are surprised if it actually does, and you are prepared if it changes.

planned assignment if something better comes along. That is, even if the reporter heads out the door to get a basic reaction piece, that reporter could wind up with an exclusive interview with the undercover police officer who posed as a high school student to bust the drug ring. The reporter should be allowed to trade up from the original assignment with an even better angle for the story. When the producer and reporter communicate about this change, the newscast plan can be amended, the headline tease and reporter intro can be rewritten and the emphasis of the lead story can take on a whole new life. So the reporter should communicate the new information with the producer as soon as possible. The more time the producer has to make changes, the sooner the adjustments can be made, and the smoother the show will be.

Wearing "elephant ears"

In addition to being a good communicator, the producer must be a good listener. The police scanners at the assignment desk could be a producer's early clue to a rapidly changing news day. An overheard conversation between a reporter and an editor about missing file footage could have a big impact on the newscast. Hearing the news director talking about a story that just crossed the wires could mean an imminent change in the content plan for the day.

In short, producers cannot afford to exist in a soundproof bubble. From cable news and satellite feeds yapping in the background to the steady alerts of urgent news updates piling up in the breaking news queues of the computer, producers need to have their ears open in a state of constant newsroom awareness.

Production

> **PRODUCER CHECKLIST: CREATING THE SHOW**
>
> - Prepare the rundown.
> - Produce it up.
> - Pick your lead.
> - Produce your segments.
> - Create variety.
> - Use strong writing.
> - Be a tease.
> - Throw a good toss.
> - Anchor your anchors.
> - Anticipate change … again!
> - Hand it to the magicians.

Prepare the rundown

The only way to ensure that everyone on the news team can "see" the Producer Vision is by putting all the information in one place—the rundown.

The two most popular computer software programs used in newsrooms across the country to compile the rundown and provide newsroom communication are **ENPS,** which was designed by the Associated Press, and **iNews,** which was designed by Avid. Both systems support the sometimes overwhelming flow of information in a newsroom, complete with interfaces for scripting, newswire services, internal messaging, calendar-based planning, contact Rolodexes and, most important for producers, rundown creation and maintenance. Simply put, these programs organize scripts, graphics, video and on-screen text in one place.

The rundowns are also programmed to "talk" to the teleprompter, meaning the program can transfer the scripts to a clear screen in front of the studio camera lens for the anchors to read.

So when a producer creates the rundown and puts in **story slugs,** he or she creates one giant controlling document—a spreadsheet in which every column, every line and every notation tells a different part of the news team what to do and when to do it during the live newscast. The rundown is absolutely central to a newscast producer. Clarity in that rundown will help ensure a successful newscast.

Produce it up

It is now time to begin building the technical side of the rundown. Once a producer has the content plan from the morning meeting and a designated newsroom computer system up and running, it's time to build the rundown. Line by line, every element of the newscast needs a slot in that giant spreadsheet. Every newsroom has its own rundown lingo to denote those elements.

The list of notations in a rundown can go on for pages. Also, new options for shots, live locations and graphics can be created daily, limited only by the producer's imagination and the technical capabilities of any newsroom.

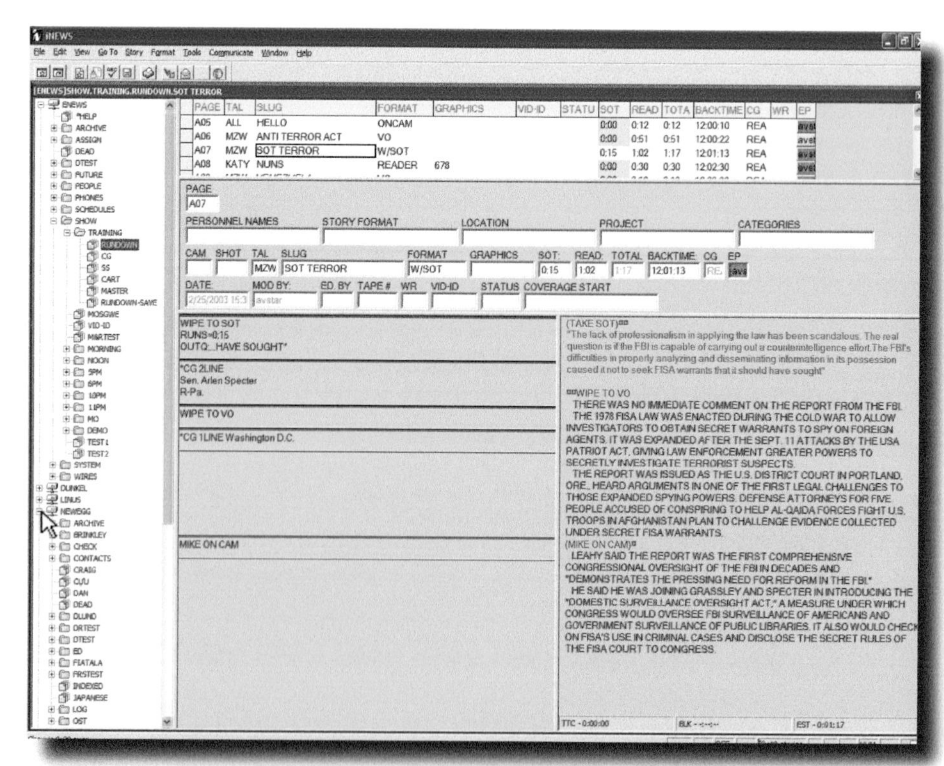

On this iNews screen, the entire newsroom file system flows vertically at the left.

RULE OF THUMB

Newsroom Lingo

- MCU, CAM or ONCAM for a standard anchor head-and-shoulder shot
- VO for an anchor or reporter "voicing over" a piece of video
- SOT for "sound on tape" that the anchor or reporter will pause to hear
- PKG for a prerecorded reporter or anchor package that includes a voice track over video interspersed with natural sound and sound bites
- OTS for a shot of the anchor with an "over-the-shoulder" graphic
- LIVE or REMOTE to denote a reporter going live from a location outside the studio
- WXWALL or CKEY for weather anchor or other talent presenting from the chroma key green or blue screen in the studio
- 2SHOT, 3SHOT, 4SHOT to note how many anchors or reporters in a single set shot
- 2BOX, 3BOX, 4BOX to request a graphic with boxes to show an anchor on set side-by-side with one or several live reporters in the field
- FS-GRPX or STILL to call for a graphic that encompasses the whole screen

A producer must become fluent in the language of the rundown, and encourage all colleagues to do the same. That way, anyone in the newsroom can glance at the rundown and understand the producer's vision for any given story, segment or show.

One newscast may start with flashy graphics, music and an announcer's voice. Others begin with a series of headlines that tease to the best stories and video of the day. And still others get right into the newscast on a quick two-shot of the anchors, who say, "Welcome, and here is our top story."

The style and tone of the newscast are designed to complement the branding and image of a news station. But once certain basic guidelines are met, the Producer Vision sets the tone, energy, and flow of the newscast through story selection, pacing of story formats and live elements, and strong writing.

Good producers not only write the day's news stories along with reporters, but they are also responsible for matching graphics and video to the words and sound. They must also create a flow in the newscast, making it comfortable, interesting, and easy to watch and listen to.

Pick your lead

You have figured out what is going to go in your newscast. Now you must decide which story will go first. Which do you think is the most important story of the day? You want something that will grab your audience, something compelling, informational and memorable. Although sometimes you've got an obvious story of the day, other times the decision is not so easy.

Some stations pride themselves on leading with breaking news every day, and they follow that formula every day. Others might prefer to lead with a consumer story or an item of community news if that's the most interesting story of the day.

Produce your segments

The challenge doesn't end with choosing a good lead. You need to consider all your stories and how they fit together. In other words, you need to consider the flow.

Rundown X	Rundown Y	Rundown Z
High-Profile Murder	New Gas Tax Hike	Hail North of Town
New Gas Tax Hike	High-Profile Murder	New Gas Tax Hike
Charity Sand Castle Contest	Carjacking Crash Update	Governor's Budget Exposé
Carjacking Crash Update	Hail North of Town	High-Profile Murder
Governor's Budget Exposé	Charity Sand Castle Contest	Carjacking Crash Update
Hail North of Town	Governor's Budget Exposé	Charity Sand Castle Contest

Here are three ways a producer could build a list of stories in the A-block for a typical 5 p.m. newscast. Note that each comes from a unique Producer Vision.

Rundown X goes by the stereotypical news cliché "If it bleeds, it leads," starting the show with a murder investigation. But how will the producer make a good transition from murder to taxes? *(Please* don't even think of resorting to that other cliché about death and taxes!) The next story, a charity fundraiser about sand castles, sticks out as odd in the middle of that block, and it would be tough for an anchor to make the turn from the sand castles to the carjacking crash update. Plus the first weather hit is in a standard spot at the bottom of the block, but a hailstorm makes the weather report a bit more important on this news day. Rundown X just doesn't seem well thought out.

Rundown Y leads with the story that likely affects the widest chunk of the audience. Viewers drive, and viewers pay taxes. Next, the two crime stories, if kept short, group well together. The weather story comes a bit higher in the block, offering a natural break for the change of subject. In this rundown the investigative report on the governor's budget is sunk lower in the block, perhaps in hopes of using a strong tease in the headlines to keep viewers through the first few minutes of the newscast. Rundown Y appears to have more method than does Rundown X.

Rundown Z goes with a good safety net for many news stations. Weather is often the most compelling story of the day; it affects *everyone* and often has great video with real people reacting to it. A tally of hailstorm damage estimates could segue well into a block of two money-related stories. The crime stories could segue into the sand castle contest, say, if the contest were to benefit young victims of crime. In Rundown Z it seems the producer has not only considered the newsworthiness of each story but also balanced it with a flow, much like that of a good conversation. It starts with what everyone's talking about and then transitions from topic to topic.

The toughest part about crafting the best rundown is that "best" is extremely subjective. Producers, reporters, managers and viewers can and will disagree on which flow makes the most sense. The most important thing is for producers to have a good reason for placing stories in a particular order and to make sure the scripts mirror that reasoning. Anybody can stack a heap of content into the empty spaces in a rundown. It takes a producer's judgment, creativity and strong writing to craft it into a good newscast.

WHAT WOULD YOU DO?

Here is a list of possible stories for a show. Choose which story you would want to lead with, decide how you would present the stories (live shot, PKG, VO/SOT, etc.) and discuss why you made your choices.

- Marijuana proposition passes, legalizing medicinal marijuana
- Crime stats in your city skyrocket 25 percent, according to an FBI report
- Dream Act is being put on fast track in Congress
- Construction begins on train connecting two new communities
- Groundbreaking takes place for new security institute at nearby university
- Local major league hockey team moves out of city

VOICES *from the* Newsroom

Matt Hamada, producer
KPHO-TV (CBS), Phoenix

I am the kind of producer the production staff dreads. That's because I am always looking for ways to push the envelope with how I present the news. I love to see my anchors moving around and getting up from behind that boring desk. If your TV station has a big set with lots of positions, you have to take advantage of them. I think anchors read the news better when they are standing up. It makes them appear to have more confidence, and that will extend to the stories they're telling. Think of your news set like a big toolbox filled with tools. Which ones will you use to build your newscast?

That toolbox is also filled with your vocabulary. Anyone can tell you about a murder investigation or a budget battle with lawmakers. Your job as a producer is to use language that sells the story you are telling while selling your station's branding and personality. I always try to remember that the people at home are just like me, so I try to write just the way I talk. Plain and simple.

Here's a great tip I was given when I started producing: Start a story in your head by pretending to talk to a friend and say, "Hey, guess what I just heard..." and then start writing your story. It works almost every time.

You cannot ignore the basics of producing. Facts, proper English and common sense are essentials to telling the news of the day. But what will make you stand out from the competitors across the street is how you tell the same story they are—only yours looks, sounds and feels better.

Live shot of a reporter using side graphics to help support parts of her story.

AP ENPS

Messages:
Urgent:

NEWSWATCH MASTER [09/28/2009 15:00]

Pag	Story Slug	Segment	Anchor	Est Duratio	Actual	Graphic
A1	SHOW OPEN	VO	ANCHOR		0:00	
A2		MCU	ANCHOR		0:00	
A3		LIVE	REPORTER		0:00	
A4	BUDGET CUTBACKS	PKG	REPORTER		0:00	
A5		T-LIVE	REPORTER		0:00	
A6		MCU	ANCHOR		0:00	
A7	NEW LAWS	PKG	REPORTER		0:00	
A8		T-MCU	ANCHOR		0:00	
A9		MCU	ANCHOR		0:00	
A10	SHOOTING	PKG	REPORTER		0:00	
A11		T-MCU	ANCHOR		0:00	

Here is an example of a bad lineup. A rundown that has three packages in a row will feel chunky, so varying the story formats is important. In this rundown an anchor tosses to a reporter package and back. This is not a very creative way to present this news to your audience.

AP ENPS

Messages:
Urgent:

NEWSWATCH MASTER [09/28/2009 15:00]

Pag	Story Slug	Segment	Anchor	Est Duratio	Actual	Graphic
A4	BUDGET CUTBACKS	PKG	REPORTER		0:00	
A5		T-LIVE	REPORTER		0:00	
A6	NEW LAWS	MCU	ANCHOR		0:00	
A7		VO	ANCHOR		0:00	
A8		MCU	ANCHOR		0:00	
A9	NEW GUN LAW	VO	ANCHOR		0:00	
A10		SOT	ANCHOR		0:00	
A11		T-MCU	ANCHOR		0:00	
A12	ABORTION LAW CHALLEN	MCU	ANCHOR		0:00	
A13		OTS	ANCHOR		0:00	
A14	SHOOTING	PKG	REPORTER		0:00	
A15		F.S. GRA	ANCHOR		0:00	
A16					0:00	

This is a much better rundown. Under the segment column you can see it has better rhythm. It starts with a live shot and a package on budget cuts, then goes to a VO, VO/SOT, reader, reporter package and full-screen graphic. This variety will be much more appealing to your audience.

Live shot of a reporter with an over-the-shoulder graphic that helps visually tell the viewer what the story is about.

Create variety

Newscast viewers have extremely short attention spans, and they are armed with the dreaded remote control, ready to find something else to hold their interest if the newscast cannot. Content can only hold an audience so long, so using the production elements in a newscast creatively is the producer's next challenge.

Leading with a reporter live on location is always a good bet to showcase the top story. But graphics can also complement and support the statistics in the anchor's introduction or reporter's live wrap-up to his or her package or video story.

A good producer can boost production values by creating an OTS, or over-the-shoulder graphic for one story, like the shooting, and asking a photographer to shoot some video to support another story, like the gun law. You can even move the anchor off the set to do a brief presentation at a computer monitor for a third story if it relates to a particular website.

Just as important is including a variety of voices, but avoid ping-ponging between anchors in a series of quick back-and-forth reads.

Use strong writing

Of all the responsibilities a producer has in creating a newscast, good writing is perhaps the most integral. Good writing leads us from one story to the next, tying the pieces seamlessly together, whether it is writing a voice-over between reporter packages or a story that the anchor reads on-camera with no visual elements. But what makes for good writing in a newscast?

As you learned in Chapter 7, good writing is conversational. It connects a viewer to the newscast and piques a viewer's interest quickly. It is also concise, conveying information efficiently without wasting a viewer's time, and it maintains a balance of emotional highs and lows. Good writing consistently matches the video or graphic seen on-screen or the story being heard on the radio. It keeps viewers tuned in. It is truly the heavy lifter that supports the Producer Vision.

All the information, tips and examples presented in Chapter 7 apply to the producer's job. But several components of broadcast writing are specific to the role of producer, namely the **teases** and **tosses.**

Be a tease

Write good teases. As its name implies, a tease flirts with the audience. It's a short description that gives just enough information to entice viewers to keep watching until the story runs later in the newscast. Teases usually open a show and then appear periodically during the newscast.

Like good leads, teases doesn't summarize the story or give away the best part. They can ask a question. Or promise something that will benefit the patient listener. Or give a reason to care about the subject. Doing that well in less than 10 seconds isn't easy.

Throw a good toss

Writing strong tosses is an art. As its name suggests, a toss refers to the hand-off from one newscaster to another. If it's not delivered well, it will fall flat, and the audience will leave. The toss can take several forms:

Snoozer: The name of the next anchor or reporter, such as "Over to Bill."

Boring: The name of the next anchor or reporter and the subject, such as "Over to Carolyn Carver for the weather."

Interesting and informative: A tease about the next story and the person covering it, such as "Turning back the clock could be good for your heart. Reporter Emily Graham explains why."

Dueling anchors: With two anchors, one can read the first part of the story, then toss to the other.

Switch from one anchor to another at a logical place, such as the transition from one location to another.

(***anchor 1***): "For 66 games in a row, the Carl Hayden Falcons left the field as losers."

(***anchor 2***): "But as Luis Leon shows us, tonight these players finally walked off as winners."

RULE OF THUMB

Write the tease in present tense and active voice. Don't be trite or too clever. It shows. Don't hype the upcoming story or promise something you won't deliver. And make sure the tease matches the video.

Anchor your anchors

Another way a producer's writing role differs from a reporter's is that producers are usually writing scripts for someone else to say, so they have to write with the anchors' and reporters' knowledge and comfort in mind. Some anchors might not be comfortable saying the word *blaze* but feel better saying *fire*. So, you want to write with that anchor's style in mind. Or an anchor might trip over certain words. If you know what these words are, you can avoid them. Some anchors might deliver emotional

Effective teasing — SIDE BY SIDE

A tease that tells too much: Turning back the clock tonight could be good for your heart because you get to sleep an extra hour. That story is up next.

Better: Turning back the clock tonight could be good for your heart. We'll tell you why after the break.

A tease that tells too much: Another airline just announced it's charging for carry-on bags. Why you might want to avoid flying Frontier Airlines. The story is next.

Better: Sick of paying extra fees? We will tell you which airline you might want to avoid next time you fly.

A tease that tells too much: If your child has asthma, you'll want to know how yoga will help your child breathe easier.

Better: Air pollution and dust storms can make life miserable for kids with asthma. But one school says it's found an activity that can help kids breathe easier. That's straight ahead.

From his work station the producer (right) can speak to the anchors and reporters, as well as the director and production crew.

story lines better than others, so you want to make sure you choose the right anchor to deliver that line. Producers must take all these variables into consideration when putting a show and a script together.

As producers write and rewrite, they must also communicate with their anchors about everything from the appropriate tone for a specific story, to pronunciations of certain words, to opportunities to improvise and show some personality. Producers should make sure anchors review the entire rundown and read and revise their scripts well before the newscast.

Anticipate change . . . again!

Be flexible. When it comes to writing a newscast, a producer must remember that change happens. A script that is written and marked "complete" at 2 p.m. may need to be rewritten and tweaked a dozen times before it airs at 5 p.m. Details of a story change from moment to moment. New information comes in unexpectedly.

A good producer must be constantly looking for ways to update a story. A producer must check the wires, check the video feeds, check with the assignment desk, check with reporters, check the competition—all in an effort to keep the newest news in the newscast. When rewriting a story, always remember to update the leads and teases to include and allude to the latest information coming into the newsroom.

Once you select the stories for the A- and B-blocks, think about their intros, tosses and teases with your overall vision for the show. Do this even before the stories are complete, even though you may need to go back and revise them later. A producer who stays ahead of the game and ahead of deadlines can better handle all the inevitable changes in the final hours before the live newscast.

> **RULE OF THUMB**
>
> Turn the rundown upside down. A producer can often write the newscast much more efficiently from the bottom up. Generally the kicker and feature stories in the C- and D-blocks are based on events or issues that will not necessarily change over the course of a news day, so write those stories and the teases for them first.

Hand it to the magicians

The rundown is complete, reporters are working furiously to meet deadline, scripts are nearing completion and the clock is ticking ever closer to the start of the show. It's almost time to hand things over to a marvelous group of magicians: the **production crew**.

For all the envisioning, planning, writing and revising up until this point, it is the newsroom production crew that makes a newscast happen. The **newscast director** leads a team of technicians with a wide range of tasks: punching the buttons on the control room video switcher, manning the studio cameras, controlling the audio levels, lighting the talent, rolling the video, creating and inserting the graphics and ensuring that all a producer's hard work comes to fruition in a nice, clean, error-free newscast.

A producer's face-to-face conversations with the production crew and, most important, with the newscast director need to begin at least several hours before the newscast is slated to start. A director needs to be able to visualize the newscast plan just as proficiently as the producer.

That director needs time to then assign duties to his crew, such as preparing the cameras for a special newsroom live shot. The director also needs to complete a production version of the newscast rundown, complete with line-by-line notations for studio camera assignments, audio cues, video playback channels and notes for the floor director on cueing the talent. That newscast director must also print all the scripts in the newscast, reviewing and marking production cues within those scripts, well before the newscast begins.

VOICES from the Newsroom

Stephanie Ingersoll, producer
KPNX-TV (NBC), Phoenix

The toughest part of the transition from college to the real world is responsibility and decision-making. You could say that about any profession, but producers take it to a whole new level. Ultimately, they are responsible for the entire show. Anchors, reporters, directors, production staff—they are all pieces of the puzzle. The producer is the one who puts it all together. The producer is the architect of the show, and if something doesn't go right, the producer figures out why so that it doesn't happen again.

The producer is also responsible for making sure that everyone knows what's going on and that everyone is on the same page. Good communication skills are the most important tools a producer can have.

A producer is also responsible for the reporters. As I once heard someone say in the newsroom, "We live in a world of Producer Vision." Producers visualize how they want a story to be told and how they want the show to look. To achieve those things, the producer needs to constantly communicate with the reporters. The reporters might write and deliver the package, but the producer gives direction.

Decision-making is another responsibility for producers. They decide on story content and what they want in the show. The producer decides on what to lead with and must have a plan to back it up. A bit of advice: Go with your gut feeling. If you know which one is the big story of the day and there is no question about it, lead with it! Producers also have to have backup plans, though. If plans A and B don't work out, what are plans C and D? I learned quickly that the producers always needs to be three steps ahead of themselves.

Finally, if you want to be a producer, you have to be comfortable with change. Things happen so fast in a newsroom that everything can blow up. Breaking news is our friend. Sometimes when nothing is going on, I pray for breaking news. Seriously! The thrill of not knowing what's going to happen is part of the challenge, but you have to be flexible. Every afternoon at 2 p.m., we have a rundown meeting where producers present their shows. Sometimes the show that eventually goes on the air looks nothing like the show that was on paper, and a producer needs to be OK with that. Not only should producers be comfortable with change, but they also need to be fast at making those changes.

If you like change, a little bit of stress (maybe a lot of stress at times) and a fast-paced working environment, then producing will be very rewarding for you.

As changes to the newscast come, as they inevitably will, producer-director communication becomes even more critical.

If a reporter gets a new SOT for a live report and the producer adds it into the rundown, the director needs to know about it.

If the outcue and total running time for a package change after the director has printed scripts, the director needs to know.

If the producer decides to switch the anchor who is reading the story from one to the other, the director needs to know. Added elements, dropped stories, rewrites of scripts, inserted **super times**—the list of possible changes that need to be communicated borders on infinite. Suffice it to say that the producer-director relationship, with consistent communication between the two, is one of the most important in the newsroom when it comes to getting a newscast on the air.

> "The director/producer relationship is incredibly important to the success or failure of the show. While it is the producer's vision and style that drive the newscast, it is the director and production team who execute it and make it a reality. Because of this, communication is key. It is vital that all members of the production team, from director to floor director, understand the rundown and the flow of the show that the producer has spent all day crafting. There is nothing better than watching that communication in action and creating a show that everyone is proud of."
>
> —JIM JACOBY, TELEVISION PRODUCTION MANAGER, CRONKITE SCHOOL OF JOURNALISM AND MASS COMMUNICATION

Time for Execution

PRODUCER CHECKLIST: EXECUTION

- ❑ Hit the air!
- ❑ Be ready to deal with breaking news.
- ❑ Be ready to deal with problems.
- ❑ Get off the air on time!
- ❑ Fade to black and regroup.
- ❑ Complete the hand-off.

Hit the air!

"We're ready," says the producer as she grabs a headset and makes the long, steady march to the control room. Members of the production crew glance up from their duties as she enters the dimly lit room. The newscast director checks the clock as the seconds count down to execution time. No, not *that* kind of execution. It's simply time for the newscast to hit the air!

As much as a producer has done to get a newscast to this point, execution time—when the show goes live—brings on a whole new set of responsibilities and challenges. And producers never really know what those challenges will be. The live broadcast production atmosphere is extremely fast paced; it requires quick thinking and split-second decisions, a keen eye (and ear) for detail, a calmness and confidence in control room communication and the ability to keep things on schedule.

The newscast director (left) talks to the technical director about changes in the newscast.

Be ready to deal with breaking news

In a perfect world, the Producer Vision would play out exactly as it was planned in the rundown. But part of the challenge, and fun, of news is that it continues to happen, and it has no problem breaking right in the middle of the show.

Producers must be able to add a breaking news item to the newscast while the newscast is already under way. The process usually begins with an alert, perhaps a call from the assignment desk or an urgent Associated Press wire story. The urgency of the story will have a lot to do with how that story gets on the air. It's up to the producer to use news judgment and quickly formulate and enact a plan without compromising the quality of the newscast.

BREAKING NEWS SCENARIOS

Extremely urgent: Major natural disaster, major plane crash with casualties, school shooting with casualties, imminent threat to community with mass evacuations

- Immediately get information on the air, even unscripted.
- Anchors ad-lib from wires and updated desk notes.
- Take live phone calls, maps, newsroom updates, live shots as available.
- Give precedence to coverage over all other content and breaks.

Urgent: Amber Alert, sudden death or resignation of high-profile person

- Write a quick script, place story in rundown at the next convenient slot—for example, following the next package or right after the next commercial break.
- Tell director and anchors about added story, run it with breaking news and an over-the-shoulder graphic, also known as an OTS or **stinger.**
- Use a graphic and a quick music break to transition from an anchor to a reporter.
- Revisit the story again with any additional information later in the newscast and promise continuing coverage.

Semi-urgent: Arrest made in previously reported crime investigation, bad crash shuts down highway at rush hour

- Write the script, but take time for the newsroom to provide the file video or live camera to support the story.
- Add and air sooner rather than later, but not in a rush that could lead to mistakes.

Be ready to deal with problems

A well-prepared, level-headed producer can navigate a newscast through the perilous waters of so-called technical difficulties. Most problems can be dealt with by creating backup plans and with quick and simple communication in the control room.

In the case of a full-on newscast meltdown, like the video switcher crashing or the microphone dying in a single-anchor show, the easiest and cleanest thing to do is go to break and regroup during the commercial.

FIGURE **8.4** **Producer Action Plans**

Problem	Plan	Action	Result
Lead PKG is suddenly not available to air two minutes before newscast.	Have a backup lead story selected from the existing options in the rundown.	Instruct production crew and anchors to skip to designated page in rundown.	Viewer does not know this was not the planned lead story.
Live reporter loses IFB just before planned live report; no communication with producer or director.	Skip over any live reporter who has no way to hear cues.	Instruct director and anchor to skip toss to live report and toss straight to PKG. During PKG, tell director to come out to MCU, and tell anchor to read reporter's tag.	Viewer still gets information without risking putting an unprepared live reporter on air.
SOT will not roll after reporter has already pitched to it.	Have a set of quick code words established with directors, anchors and reporters.	Tell director, "Go to live tag." Instruct reporter over IFB, "No sound, read tag."	When acted upon quickly, a slight pause and calm recovery will go unnoticed or be forgiven by most viewers.
Wrong OTS graphic is punched up.	Quickly remove from the shot any graphic or font that is wrong or contains an error.	Tell director, "Lose OTS." Director tells technical director to drop the graphic from the shot and camera operator to center up for an MCU or straight shot.	Viewer may see the initial error, but when it is removed cleanly and smoothly, the production crew is subtly acknowledging to the audience that they are correcting the error.

Get off the air on time!

If you ever had to keep a newscast on time, you know how crucial 30 seconds can be. When a producer winds up with only 30 seconds until the end of the show and one full minute of content left for the anchors to read, it's a problem. But good producers know how to squeeze their way out of newscast timing problems.

A producer's eye is always on the clock. Newsroom software programs like iNews and ENPS provide computer-assisted backtiming, calculating how much time a show is "over" (too much content) or "under" (not enough content) as the newscast progresses line-by-line through the rundown. Good producers must also be able to monitor content duration versus the time left in the show by sketching it out on paper, as one cannot always rely on a crash-free computer.

COMMUNICATING A DROP

When a producer calculates that the show is going over the time limit, content planned for later in the newscast needs to be dropped.

Say at the end of the A-block, a producer determines that the block ran 45 seconds longer than planned. During the first commercial break, the producer looks at the B-block and decides to drop the story at B6, which is a 20-second reader, as well as the 25-second VO at B7. The producer tells the director that pages B6 and B7 are dead or dropped. The director confirms the drop to the rest of the production crew. The producer then must tell the anchors the same thing through **IFB** (also known as an intercom system) and use the computer to "float" or "kill " those pages out of the rundown so those stories will not appear in the prompter, in video playback, or as a graphic or font on-screen. Once this all happens, the newscast should be back on time.

Keep in mind: The preceding is a long explanation of a swift process that happens within a matter of a few seconds during the live newscast.

Fade to black and regroup

The show is done! When the newscast ends, the best producers take off their headsets, look their news colleagues in the eye and thank them for an intense day of work, no matter how the show went. A few kind words can go a long way in mending and maintaining good working relationships between the editorial side of the newsroom and the production team. After all, everyone has just been through a pressure cooker of an experience.

At the post-mortem meeting, usually a casual gathering immediately following the show, the team briefly reviews the newscast that just aired. They discuss highlights, offer critiques and consider lessons learned. And they revisit the three rings of our metaphorical circus.

Complete the hand-off

The post-mortem meeting may be over, but as producer you still have work to do. You must do your hand-off to the next producer in line, and you will likely need to post shows to the Web as well. As part of your Web-related responsibilities, you may have to rewrite some text stories and cut some video. Producers must be multitalented. You must be comfortable with writing and storytelling for all platforms, whether it's television, radio or online. Journalism today is all about multitasking and getting the news out to as many people as possible in as many ways as possible.

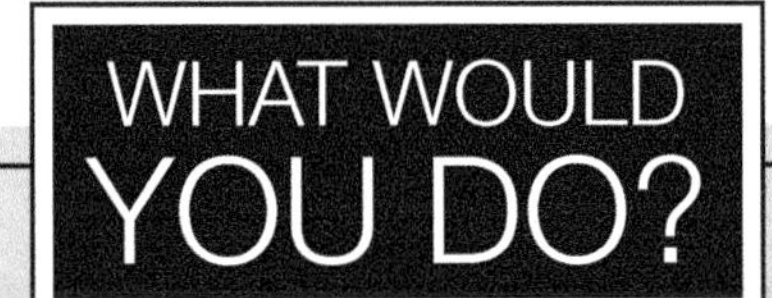

Let's say every script in the newscast took five seconds longer than anticipated, and that adds up to a minute of extra time you had not counted on. It is now 5:27:45, and the show must end at 5:29:30. You have 2:30 of sports left in the show: a 20-second VO about the local sports team in playoffs, a 45-second VO/SOT about the local high school baseball team being slapped with NCAA violations and a 1:25 PKG about how the local college women's basketball team had adopted a child with a life-threatening illness, and he led the team out on the field. What would you do to make sure you get off the air on time?

BOOTHING THE SHOW

Key responsibilities of a news producer in the control room, also called the booth, can be spelled out the Cronkite way:

Communicating with anchors and reporters, and ensuring they get **standbys** and cues

Reacting to problems with an immediate plan

Overseeing the production crew along with newscast director

Nitpicking any mistake, any typo, any loose wire, any fly-away hair: Get it fixed!

Keeping in control, calmly but commandingly

Information gathering and then communicating any changes during breaking news situations

Timing the newscast

Expecting the best but prepared to handle the worst

VOICES from the Newsroom

Evan Dougherty, producer
KGO-TV (ABC), San Francisco, Yahoo Sports

As a sports producer, I produce multiple sportscasts during the week, which involves creating a rundown, writing, editing, creating graphics, checking facts and so forth. I also have to coordinate with reporters, photographers and assignment managers to decide what stories to cover.

I love it because I get to watch sports and get paid for it! No, seriously, I love telling the stories of each game. Each night there's something in the world of sports that makes you say "Wow," whether it's an amazing catch or a fan running onto the field and making the crowd go wild.

Don't go into the job thinking you're just going to offer highlights and sound bites.

Some of the best stories I have done and seen have been about sports people but not necessarily what they're doing on the field. Great stories with great characters make any story memorable, especially a sports story. It is one way to get a non-sports fan to watch your sportscast, and we all know the goal is to make your show the one people are watching!

FIGURE 8.5 **Post-Newscast Meeting to Discuss Show**

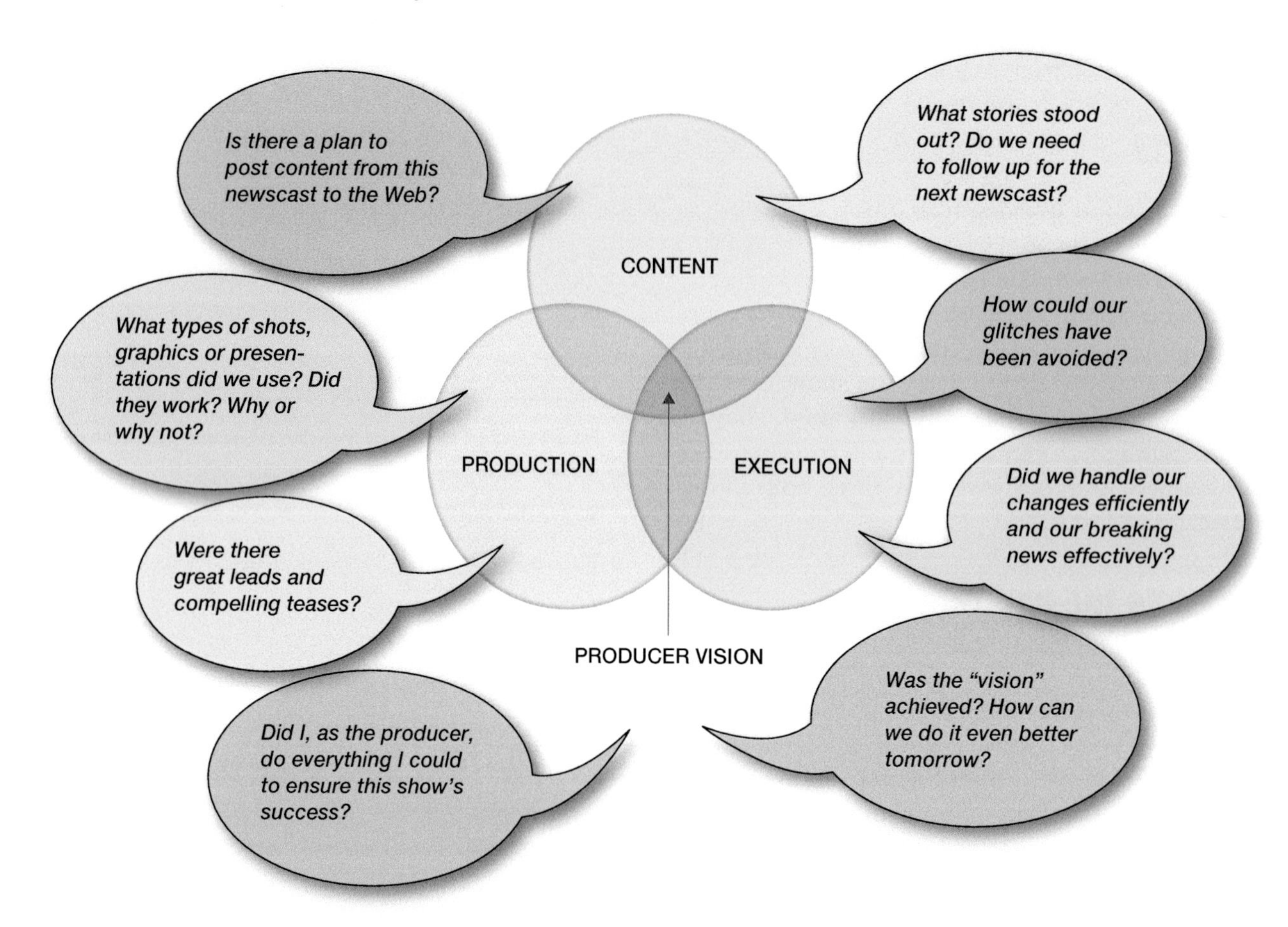

VOICES from the Newsroom

Amanda Goodman, producer
KRQE-TV (CBS), Albuquerque, N.M.

My goal has always been to tell great stories—you know, the kind that make people feel something, the kind that people are talking about the next day and, if I am lucky, the kind of story that moves people to action. In the beginning, I thought I would be doing this primarily through packages on TV.

My education was geared toward television news, as were my internships and even my first job out of college. However, times have changed—and so has the industry, and in order not only to survive but thrive, I have had to adapt.

That is where the Web producing comes in. I was hired as a part-time reporter because that was the only position available at the time, but I pushed my news director to train me on the Web so that I could get more hours and learn a new set of skills in the process. It was a decision that paid off. The Web is all the rage at almost every station across the country, and I now have the experience and skill set to walk into any newsroom and make an impact immediately because of my Web producing.

Boothing the Show: The producer has a plan in place, but at any moment during the live newscast, the plan may have to change.

Beyond the Newscast

This chapter has focused on the circus atmosphere a producer works in while putting together a daily newscast for a typical commercial news station. But producers play roles that go far beyond producing the standard half-hour show. Local, network and cable outlets have producers for specific segments and beats. In the newsrooms are sports producers, weather producers, investigative producers, Web producers and special projects producers. Outside typical newsrooms are documentary producers, series producers, segment producers, commercial producers and promotion producers. In the end, the aspects of producing discussed in this chapter apply to all types. The goal of all these people is to create a vision for content, production and execution and to see it through into reality, whether on the air or online.

When the show is over, the producer's work hasn't ended. It continues to the next show and on the Web. In many shops, the producers are responsible for writing stories and cutting video for the Web. Online or digital media is an extension of the show. The two work hand in hand to get information to viewers. Everyone in the newsroom has to get that information out to viewers, not just the reporters.

Jobs in the newsroom used to be separate, but that is no longer the case. There's overlap everywhere, and you must become comfortable producing for online as well as for on the air. Well-rounded producers should have a dictionary at their fingertips, as well as the Associated Press stylebook, also known as the AP stylebook, for both broadcast and online text. Both will become your best friend, so become acquainted with them!

Don't worry. In Chapter 10 we'll dig a little deeper into writing and producing for the Web so you'll feel more comfortable. But remember: The key is great storytelling. So long as you have the basics down, you'll do just fine, whether on the air or online.

HOME | ABOUT | STORIES | NEWSWATCH | NEWS21 | CRONKITE | CONTACT

TOP STORIES

ATF agents, family blast gun-trafficking investigation that let guns "walk away"

By Cristina Rayas

Phoenix-based agents blasted the Bureau of Alcohol, Tobacco, Firearms and Explosives in congressional testimony for the bureau's "Operation Fast and Furious," which let suspects get away with guns in the hopes that larger gun-trafficking networks would be revealed.

Federal officials get committee grilling over management of wildfires

By Nick Newman

Medical marijuana challenges Arizonans on multiple perspectives

By Cronkite News Staff

Opponents vow not to back down from fight over land-exchange bill

By Matthew Trotter

SPECIAL REPORTS

Emergency-action plans lacking for some Arizona dams

Owners of dams considered high and significant risks in the event of failure must have emergency-action plans on file with the state. A Cronkite News review found that 14 dams aren't in compliance with a law on the subject.

—*Lauren Gambino*

THE LATEST

- Proposal to require E-Verify nationwide cast as a jobs bill by supporters
- Giffords released from hospital, to remain in Texas for treatment
- U.S. Supreme Court declines to intervene in Salt River ownership fight
- Congress takes another run at long-delayed Resolution Copper

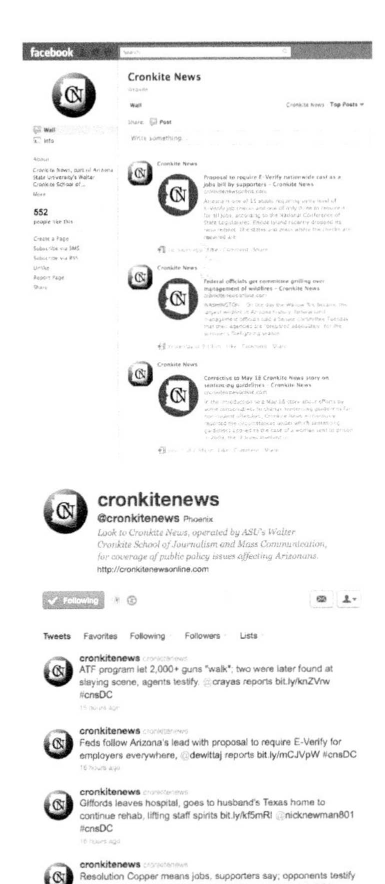

Content does not just live on the air. It must also live online. Part of the goal is to drive as many eyes as possible to your content, whether on TV, on the Web or on mobile phones.

ON-AIR, ON-CAMERA

CHAPTER 9

> *A downside to celebrity is the autograph seeker who, getting your signature, turns to a companion and asks: 'Who is he?'*
>
> —*WALTER CRONKITE*

CHAPTER OUTLINE

Tough Skin, Tearful Moments

Have you ever had an all-access VIP pass to a rock concert? Backstage, after the show, you meet band members in the green room, still sweating from all the bright lights and highly energized by their performance in front of thousands.

Look around. You spot a lighted makeup table, hair supplies and costumes used to maximize the experience. These items might turn you off from the perfect image that appeared live on stage and on the giant video screens just 20 minutes before. Slowly you realize all this attention to detail was necessary so that *how one looks maximizes the performance and doesn't get in the way of what one wants to share.*

The same principle applies to reporting TV news, online stories or VOD (video on demand) services. Old school print reporters scoff at all the fuss required for TV types to get ready for a broadcast. They smirk watching a reporter gear up for a live shot in front of the courthouse. A small mirror is used to double-check that the hair looks perfect and professional just minutes before going on-air.

We don't want to train nor encourage what Eagles singer Don Henley called "the bubble-headed-bleach-blonde who comes on at 5," but even Walter Cronkite knotted fashionable ties (which he often auctioned off for journalism scholarships), wore professional makeup nightly and early in his radio career learned how proper breath support enhanced his delivery style.

A professional style enhances the substance of journalism presentation. It adds to credibility. Prepare yourself, though, for criticism of your professional style from audience members, colleagues and even your boss. You will need a tough skin in the TV news business, not only to deal with such uneducated observations but also to handle more personally sensitive moments when a news director demands you change from brunette to blonde before she will move you to the weekend anchor slot or tells the sports guy to "*never* wear that jacket and shirt combination again!" You can't ignore how you look and sound if you expect to find success in a video-driven medium where one minute the audience watches "American Idol," then flips a channel to see Hollywood actors, and flips again to land on a credible newscast. The same studio lights make all three look their best. Like it or not, you are part of a media landscape that requires you to pay attention to how you look and sound. Ready to learn how?

In this chapter we share the vocal and visual steps it takes to put on a professional broadcast news performance. For those in radio we cover proper breathing and vocal techniques needed to sound credible on-air. TV news adds the visual dimensions of skin, makeup, hair and the professional costume (what to wear on the air) that affect the look. This is critical in the era of high-definition (HD) television, where powerful cameras and transmission signals share with millions of viewers exactly what you look like, right down to the flake of dandruff on your shoulder. The old adage that "The camera doesn't lie" has never been more true.

Developing a healthy self-image

Before we head into the heart of this chapter, pause and think about the concept of self-image. Sherrie Johnson, a global youth leader, says, "Our self-image helps us define ourselves—and leads us to act according." Your visual and vocal image play a key role in building the self-confidence critically needed to appear credible and confident on-air in front of thousands of people. One way to build and maintain self-confidence is to recognize your own strengths.

Eleanor Roosevelt's insight is memorable: "No one can make you feel inferior without your consent." Part of a healthy self-image is knowing who you are and what you do right—giving yourself permission to feel confident. Plenty of people, especially early in your career, will tell you what you're doing wrong. Sadly, in a bustling, deadline-driven newsroom, far fewer will offer positive feedback. You're going to need to develop thick skin. As inspirational writer Marvin J. Ashton said, "Proper self-image is a basic ingredient of pride in one's self." Without personal pride, you will never have the confidence needed to succeed in the intensely competitive field of television news and other online, video-driven platforms.

Putting yourself on the air can be a thrilling high, but when you make a mistake, it can be a depressing low. To get through the rough spots, self-esteem is critical. One tool we've found that helps is to create a private list—we call it the "I am not a geek" sheet. Think of this note to yourself as similar to a self-affirmation statement. Use paper or a large Post-it, and put it on your bathroom mirror or inside your reporter's notebook. When the day from hell descends, when it seems everyone has something highly critical to say about how you write, how you sound or what you look like, reread your "I am not a geek" sheet. It's a reminder that you *do* have self-worth, and that reminder can help you regain your self-confidence.

Eleanor Roosevelt, who exhibited a healthy dose of self-confidence, became a powerful role model for women in public life.

The role of news consultants

Even though a journalist's self-confidence can sometimes be shattered, it can also be built up, for example, when consultants hired for that purpose visit your newsroom. Your website, TV station or ownership group may ask a news consultant to share advice on how to improve the newscast and increase ratings. Visiting in person a few times per year, the consultant frequently monitors air checks of the reporters' and anchors' on-air work to provide feedback to news directors.

We suggest you learn all you can from what they share because the station is paying them a hefty fee to improve the look of the broadcast. Stay humble enough to accept an outside opinion, and treat consultants with respect. We are confident that, as you mature in the news business, you will be able to recognize and provide your own suggestions for how to improve the look and feel of the newscast. You'll even get good at critiquing your own performance.

THE "I AM NOT A GEEK" SHEET

Answer the following questions, tuck the responses in your notebook and pull them out when you think you've really blown it.

- ☐ List one thing you do well. List another.
- ☐ What does your mom/dad/significant other like about you?
- ☐ What is the greatest thing you have accomplished so far?
- ☐ Write down a recent compliment from a peer.
- ☐ What's the nicest thing you recently did for someone else—stranger or friend?
- ☐ List one thing you like about yourself.
- ☐ List another.

The T word—talent

Because the early days of television news adapted many words and slang from live entertainment productions as well as the movie business, some terms, which at first might seem silly when talking about journalism, have stuck as labels. Anyone who appears on-camera, from a field reporter to a studio anchor, is referred to by the production team as **talent.** It is a friendly term. Take it with a grain of salt, and make sure you've paid your dues through knowledge about the news not to be stereotyped as the "dumb talent." Your interpersonal relationships off camera with those who never appear on camera—the studio crew and the editorial team of assignment editors, producers and writers—must be earned. Don't assume that because you're talent, you have more knowledge than others. Just because you're called talent does not mean you are talented. Earn your colleagues' respect. Know your facts. Know your journalism.

Williams Hawes, in "Television Performing: News and Information," notes the critical importance of building personal relationships between talent and crew. "A performer is well advised to be reciprocally cooperative and generous. If the staff likes a performer, it often gives an extra measure of devotion to make that performer look good; but if a staff dislikes a performer, the reverse may result. For instance, as a performer you may not need a rehearsal, but keep in mind your crew may need it."* And remember that even though someone might have fewer years of formal education than you do, that's not a reason to disrespect her work.

Building a relationship of trust with your camera operator in the live truck or with your floor director in the studio is vital to accurate communication. Those in the studio might not consider

What do news consultants do? What is their value?

Dr. Craig Allen, associate professor
Walter Cronkite School of Journalism and Mass Communication

We put those questions to Dr. Craig Allen, a well-known broadcast historian whose book "News Is People" includes a look at the spreading influence of news consultants.

News consultants play a wide-ranging role in television news. Several firms engage in news consulting. The largest is Frank N. Magid Associates, based in Marion, Iowa. Named for its founder, whom "Time" magazine in 1977 called "the nation's leading television news doctor," Magid created the action news format and developed ABC's "Good Morning America."

News consultants help TV newsrooms with the business side of journalism. Their goal is to help client networks and local stations improve ratings, top competitors and earn greater amounts of money. Consultants work most closely with managers and news directors. Depending on the needs and ratings objectives of a client, consultants can provide a variety of advising services, including set design, graphics, promotions, lighting, camera angles, on-camera demeanor, clothes, makeup and hairstyle.

Newsrooms most often seek consultants in order to obtain links to the viewing audience. Consultants exert their greatest influence as providers of audience research. This research can be very important, as it can determine the careers of on-air anchors and reporters. As with actors and performers, the media industry gives U.S. news anchors and reporters Q Scores—that is, quotients measuring their popularity and familiarity. News consultants conduct the focus groups and surveys from which these Q Scores are derived.

Consultants further influence careers by maintaining large talent banks that contain résumés and audition videos of anchors and reporters. Networks and stations use talent banks in order to test and select on-air personnel.

News consultants have been blamed for advising tabloid news and for formulas that cause TV newscasts to look alike. Critics frequently complain that news consultants such as Magid exert too much behind-the-scenes power. On the other hand, consultants have improved numerous news operations worldwide. Their clients have won major broadcasting and journalism awards.

*(Source: Focal Press, 1991. Copyright Elsevier, 1991.)

themselves journalists, but they are professionals. Their ability to give you accurate camera changes and time cues will help you perform the journalism functions flawlessly. Take interest in the crew's hobbies or home life. It may seem like an intangible, but strong personal relationships of trust between the talent and the crew are vital when a live studio broadcast is on-air and the pressure is on. The longtime "CBS Evening News" anchorman Dan Rather often used to catch updates on baseball game scores with his studio production crew during the commercial breaks of his broadcasts.

WHAT WOULD YOU DO?

Sometimes, anchors are labeled by their newsroom colleagues as prima donnas because of their perceived inflated egos. Yet the off-camera relationship with the rest of the news and production team is critical to the on-air performance. An anchor's response to her colleagues' pertinent observations is critical to building a relationship of trust with the entire news team.

Let's say your station bought a new series of billboard ads to announce your promotion to the main news slot. They're displayed prominently all over town. You must learn to handle both compliments and criticism.

- How do you respond or react when the weekend anchor makes an envious comment about the new billboard ads?
- How do you respond or react when the assignment editor jokes that they didn't get your hair color right in the big billboard ad on Main Street?
- How do you respond or react when a photog compliments you about the new ads, saying, "It makes me proud to point out to my friends where I work"?
- How do you respond or react when the photog above reacts positively (not with envy) about the ads?

Successful Role Models

John Cameron Swayze was the first anchorman (1949) of an NBC newscast. He later became famous as the pitchman for Timex watches on TV commercials.

Chances are, you're pursuing a broadcast news career because once upon a time you stood in front of a bathroom mirror pretending to anchor a newscast, or your parents videotaped you at age 7 imitating a news reporter, or a high school English teacher inspired you. No doubt your own broadcast news role models differ from your those of your parents and especially your grandparents. In the early days—the 1950s and '60s—newscasters were typically white males with deep voices. That pattern changed long ago, but sometimes the myths about a certain look or sound remain.

Professional standards exist. We will explore those in just a couple of pages, but focus now on who your role models are and why. Are your choices based on physical appearance, voice quality or the empathy that seems to emanate from the screen? Is what appeals to you based on how the newscasters phrase their questions, on how they engage and banter with an interviewee or on the level of knowledge and background that becomes evident in an unscripted breaking-news situation? Is it OK to have one role model for on-air performance aspects and a different role model for knowledge and understanding of the issues? What do you think?

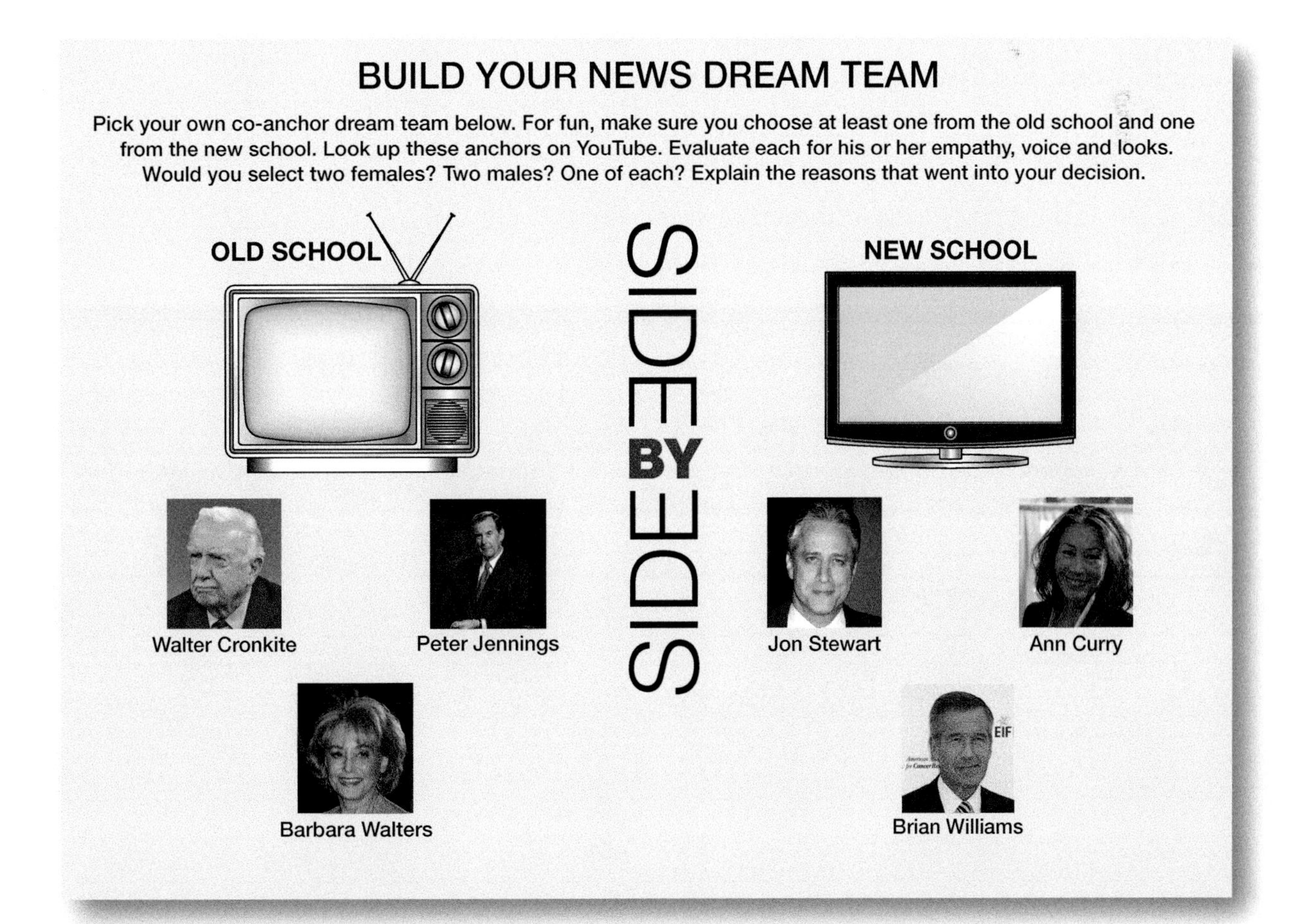

The Key to Credibility

Three components combine to create an anchor's credibility image on a TV newscast: the voice, the visual image and how the news is communicated. William Hawes notes that the message aspect must "convey honesty and rationality." The credibility factor in delivering the news is a direct result of what you know. What you know is based on what you read. You can't fake knowledge. An actor can deliver words and pretend he's an anchorman, but there is an intangible meta-world created between the professional news anchor and the audience as stories are told. When the audience says, "That guy looks as though he knows what he is talking about," it is because he does. He has earned the chance to read convincingly about the story's events and details by constantly combing through websites and wire services for background knowledge. We call this credibility.

Improving your media diet

Just as a kid in school learns about the proper foods for establishing good eating habits, as a newscaster you must pay attention to your media diet. Tom Rosenstiel, director of the Project for Excellence in Journalism, wrote about the importance of a good media diet.

"With a finite number of hours in a day, and a huge number of media sources available, where will you spend your time? And to what result? Power is shifting from the journalist setting the agenda, to the consumer becoming their own editor—deciding what their media diet will be," Rosenstiel said. "We're in the fast food news culture, where you've got a huge buffet."

As an anchor or reporter you set the example of healthy media habits for your audience. Increasingly, you're being asked to blog about your stories. A healthy diet allows you to enrich what you write because you have a deeper understanding of complex issues. The audience and your bosses expect you to taste new websites and sample new sources.

Assignment: Improving your media diet

This assignment will help you evaluate your current media diet and set goals for better news-reading habits.

1. Spend 24 hours tracking your current media consumption:
   - What you read (on social media like Twitter and Facebook's wall, on websites and in printed newspapers and magazines)
   - What you watch (TV news)
   - What you listen to (podcasts and radio)
   - What you interact with (websites, games).
2. After the 24-hour tracking period, write a summary of your current diet of media consumption and set improvement goals (think of a gym workout).
3. At the end of a month, complete another 24-hour tracking of your media intake and review your progress. What has changed?

Empowering Your Pipes: The Voice

The broadcast journalist's secret weapon is her voice. As old as the storyteller, the voice is a vital communication tool in the reporter's toolbox. But what makes a good voice for delivering a radio newscast, tracking the audio for a TV news package or recording a podcast? If a reporter has a savvy news sense, writes well and looks credible on-camera but has a squeaky or annoying voice, can anything be done to make improvements?

Absolutely! While this section will not be able to provide an individual voice analysis to help you find your optimum performance level, it does offer guidelines on how all reporters and anchors can use their voice effectively to deliver the news.

- Avoid broadcast gear
- A healthy voice
- Breathe! Just breathe!
- Script marking and the prompter
- Meaning-laden words
- Ad-libbing
- Co-anchor chemistry

Avoid broadcast gear The old school perspective for a radio or TV newscaster was that the voice should be a deep, bass-sounding male voice. Even today, many young broadcast journalists try to artificially force their voice into a lower pitch range in order to speak with what they think is an authoritative sound.

We call this going into broadcast gear, where you mimic the Ron Burgundy character from "Anchorman" or a character your parents may recall—Ted Baxter from "The Mary Tyler Moore Show," a sitcom about a TV newsroom. Don't go there. Broadcast gear sounds forced and faked. To be honest, some of us are just born with better pipes or a more naturally pleasing speaking voice.

While you can blame genetics if your voice isn't silky smooth, there are several things you can do to achieve your optimum performance. Remember, the voice is just one tool in the reporter's toolbox. Many a successful TV reporter with a less than perfect voice has developed another tool, such as crisp writing, communicating with gestures, a credible appearance and, most important, knowledge of the news. Credibility comes about via the entire set of tools used to communicate. If you perceive that you have a weakness in one aspect of news delivery, you can compensate by excelling in another.

A popular CBS sitcom from the 1970s, "The Mary Tyler Moore Show" featured Moore as a local TV producer in Minneapolis. To her right are the show's anchorman, Ted Baxter (played by Ted Knight), and real anchorman Walter Cronkite.

A healthy voice Just like the gears in a machine need oil to stay lubricated, so does the human voice box need fluids to function properly during performance. Maintaining a healthy voice requires good eating and wise drinking habits. Here are some obvious do's and don'ts.

DO

- Always keep your throat moist by drinking plenty of water. Some anchors drink tepid warm water with a little lemon juice in the final 30 minutes before airtime. This seems very effective for keeping things loosened up.

DON'T

- Don't eat chocolate or drink milk products one hour before going on-air or before tracking audio in the sound recording booth. These can coat your throat and hinder you from producing optimum sound.
- Don't smoke. The worst thing you can do for your voice and your body is to smoke.

Born in Canada, Peter Jennings was a longtime anchor of ABC'S "World News Tonight with Peter Jennings." Tragically, he died of lung cancer in 2005.

A false culture once existed in the broadcast business that smoking cigarettes will lower your pitch and make you sound credible on the air. In truth, tobacco smoked or chewed can lead to cancer. Two of the profession's most famous anchors, Edward R. Murrow and Peter Jennings, both died of lung cancer. Don't follow in their tragic footsteps—don't smoke!

Breathe! Just breathe! The single most important thing you can do to maintain the quality of your delivery is to learn how to breathe properly. Breathing provides the power to make all the amazing aspects of your voice work. Proper breathing is critical to a good delivery. Think of an old-fashioned pipe organ like that played in "The Phantom of the Opera." An organ has stops, or mechanisms that admit pressurized air to the pipes. Each pipe is a different size. As air passes through them, different sounds are produced.

In a similar way, human voices have a different type of pipes, called vocal cords. Sound is created as air passes across the vocal cords, causing them to vibrate and creating what is called the resonance of the voice. In pipe organs the air to produce the sound comes from pumping the feet. For human speech, people don't need to pump their feet, of course. Instead, a muscle called the diaphragm expands and contracts, forcing air to pass over the vocal cords and produce sound.

It's critical to understand how the diaphragm works in order to improve your optimum broadcast delivery.

Place your hands under your rib cage. As you push in, exhale. You're feeling the work of your diaphragm,

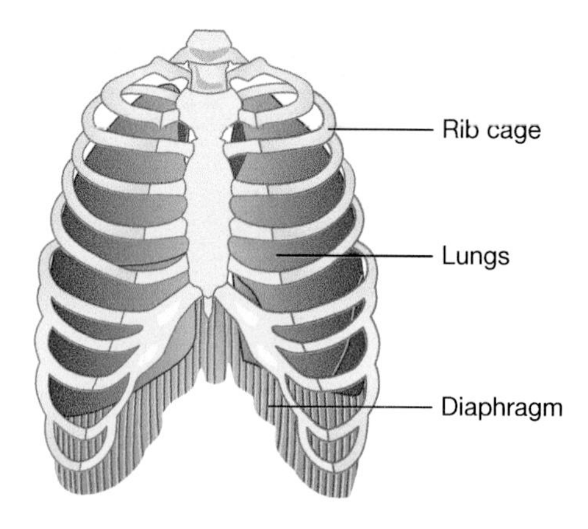

or the thin sheet of muscle under your lungs that extends across the bottom of your rib cage. Now relax your abdominal muscles, allowing your diaphragm to descend. Your abdomen will expand, creating more room for your lungs to fill with air. Inhaling with full, deep breaths using the diaphragm muscle helps generate air flow. This creates a friction that opens up the vocal cords to produce sound through the mouth.

Finally, inside your mouth is an amazing instrument—your tongue. The tongue is the articulator that allows the precise production of the smallest unit of sound, called a phoneme. We learned how to make sounds, and eventually words and sentences, as a very small child.

As a child, you learned speech patterns by imitating those around you—your mom and dad, siblings, neighbors, teachers and friends. If those voice models you imitated spoke perfectly crisp and clear English, then, all else being equal, you probably do also. But if your role models had their own accents, regional dialects or poor speech patterns, then that can affect the way your voice sounds and the way you pronounce words.

Voice expert William Hawes notes: "In order for you to determine whether you have standard speech, you must be able to hear a proper model and compare your speech with it. If you cannot hear a standard sound and tell there is a difference, then you will be unable to change your speech. Some sounds are subtle and require listening to a voice model and practicing under a capable coach. . . . You will be able to eventually hear the difference and make a change for the better. This process can be quite slow depending upon how deeply ingrained the errors are in your speech."

Script marking and the prompter The news script, or what is often simply called copy, needs to be rehearsed before performance. Just as an organist might mark sheet music in pencil to remind him how to perform a piece, a broadcaster marks the copy to indicate particular words to emphasize.

In the studio and in some field locations, teleprompters, sometimes called autocues (especially in England and other European countries), generate words electronically on a two-way mirror in front of the camera. Thus, it is difficult to mark the copy. But whether you are an anchor on the news desk or a reporter in the recording booth, even with a prompter you still have the hard copy of the script—the physical piece of paper that matches what is on the electronic prompter screen. Mark the hard copy! You should read it out loud more then once and mark it to maximize the delivery potential.

Meaning-laden words Script marking is highly personal. One effective way is to highlight keywords with a black permanent marker, which shows up easily under the bright studio lights. Certain words should receive more emphasis than others. Dr. Anne Utterback devised a technique called "meaning-laden words." Here are the steps.

1. Go through the news copy and highlight (or underline) just three or four keywords in a 25-second news reader. These can be nouns or verbs. Think of them like newspaper headlines—just the three or four words that tell the story.
2. When you deliver the copy, make these meaning-laden words stand out in your delivery by giving them extra emphasis or pausing just slightly before them.
3. You can apply the concept of finding meaning-laden words beyond the 25-second news readers to each graph in a longer script of a news package or even a documentary.

Ad-libbing When there is no written script, the anchor or field reporter must ad-lib, or simply communicate in clear and concise sentences what they are thinking. This is something you cannot practice. It comes from inside, based on how much you have absorbed the story. Ad-libbing is an art that takes doing it many times to become good at it.

Co-anchor chemistry Chemistry describes how the audience perceives the interpersonal relationships among the talent on set. The casual chatter between stories or pitching to commercial breaks, weather or sports is the few seconds where your personality shines. Viewers get to know you and build a relationship of trust with you. Good chemistry with co-anchors can carry a newscast.

Working on a set with a co-anchor team takes practice. Consultants suggest several tips:

- Look at your co-anchor when she is reading, but don't stare.
- Glance back at the camera.
- Create a conversational feel, as though there are three people in the living room—you, your co-anchor and the viewer. The camera lens is the viewer. Think of telling a story as having a

FIVE PROMPTER TIPS

Learning to use a teleprompter takes practice, especially so you don't look like a deer in the headlights. ABC News anchorman Peter Jennings was perhaps the best at making the prompter disappear. He appeared to be sitting across the couch from you in your living room, maintaining conversational eye contact.

1. Look down on names and numbers (a Jennings trick that added to credibility).
2. Look down at the end of every story. Briefly pause. The viewer knows you are changing stories.
3. Keep the copy flat. Holding it at an angle causes the studio lights to reflect on it and distract from what you're reading.
4. Being as familiar with the copy as possible ensures that you can deliver it competently even if the prompter fails. It will!
5. Mark the news script for meaningful delivery.

A teleprompter is an electronic form of a cue card that allows the anchor to look directly into the camera and read the script. The audience, however, can't see the words.

three-way conversation rather than as broadcasting to thousands of people.

- At the end of your solo delivery, give a slight glance at your co-anchor, as if you were tossing her the ball in a sports game. You're telling viewers to shift their attention from you to your co-anchor. Do it subtly but with confidence.

Techniques for voicing a news package for TV or online

Aleksandar Miladinovic, reporter
B92 Television, Belgrade, Serbia

Aleksandar Miladinovic demonstrates voicing into a large mic covered with a muff that enhances the sound by reducing background noise.

Your voice in the news package is very often your signature, and the audience should be able to recognize you and your style of voicing your packages. It is very important to make your voice sound as perfect as it actually is.

Just like the anchor, you should not eat anything at least an hour before reading your voiceover because some residuals of food can make you cough and thus have to read over and over again. This is especially critical when you are pressed for time as the newscast is about to begin.

If you are in the recording booth, try to stand while you read because your diaphragm needs to be free. That way you'll have enough air to finish sentences without trouble. But if you have to sit, at least keep your back straight. Don't read too fast or too slow. Stress the keyword in every sentence, and think about the meaning of your text. Don't keep your mouth on the microphone, and don't shout—that's what the microphone is for. You need to be convincing that you have mastered the topic. And if you make a mistake—don't panic! You'll waste more time panicking than simply starting the whole block of script from the beginning.

Voicing in the field can be more difficult, as there are many more distractions that fight for your attention. Do your best to isolate yourself. You can get away from the noise by tracking inside a car or in a room without people. Make sure the location is silent but does not produce an echo. The audience needs to hear your voice-over only once, not an echo repeated dozens of times.

My trick is always to have a bottle of water with me. A dry throat often comes when you're nervous. But be careful. You don't want that water to go the wrong way and make you cough.

Most important, stay focused. Focus and a supportive crew calm my nerves and inspire me to do my best.

VOICES *from the* Newsroom

Brent Goff, senior business anchorman
DW-TV, Berlin, Germany

Success in delivering the news begins in the newsroom. I make it a point to be involved in every story, and that includes writing all of my copy. An anchor tells a story better when he is also the narrator. Don't let others craft the narrative for you. I have had one producer in my career who mastered my writing style. That is a luxury. Don't depend on it.

Today's news studios can be sterile and rather dehumanized. Everything is automated, and it's just us anchors. It is important to always remember that we are having a conversation with the people on the other side of the teleprompter. I am not talking *at* my viewers. I am talking *with* my viewers.

I've been lucky in my career: I like my co-anchors on and off the air. The viewers detect tension and friction very easily. A professional anchor knows it is in his or her best interest to have a genuinely congenial relationship with the person who shares the news set.

Newsrooms are loud, busy and the worst forums for concentration. Yet that is where the art of precision thinking and writing is best learned.

The Visual Self: Makeup & Hair

Christi Schreiber, president/CEO
Colour Basis, Irving, Texas

For this section we invited one of America's most respected and widely used television news on-air talent consultants, Christi Schreiber, to share her advice on skin care, makeup and hair. Her company, Colour Basis, is in high demand as TV news companies adjust to broadcasting in high definition. Schreiber's role is to teach on-air talent how to maximize their best features and polish their overall appearance. Schreiber says, "It is a process, not an event." (For more information, visit Colour Basis at colourbasis.com.)

The HD factor

High-definition television broadcasts have a resolution up to six times greater than standard definition and digital. The clarity can be shocking, for good or for bad. Your appearance in HD will either draw people in or be a barrier to their connecting with you. It's not about being great looking; it's about looking great and not being distracting. Unpolished talent with too much or too little makeup is obvious to most viewers. Don't overlook or minimize how critical your overall appearance is to your success on-air to broadcast TV.

The difference is in the details: stray hairs sticking out all over your head, lint and hair on your jacket, makeup on your collar, food in your teeth and untrimmed nose hairs. You have to train your eye to see the details in your appearance like never before. What you see in the mirror is what the HD camera sees—and then some! Every little detail, pore, scar, blemish and bad (or good) makeup application will be seen. But once you know what to look for, how to prepare and how to make proper corrections, it's not as horrible as it seems. An HD television newscast becomes a powerful experience with the proper lighting, set and polished appearance of the talent.

RULE OF THUMB

Wash your face *at least* twice a day with a facial cleanser. No exceptions. *Never* use body soap!

Skin care

Your face is part of your marketing packaging. Taking care of your skin and body is taking care of your brand. Great skin is the first key to looking great on-camera.

Proper cleansing The first step of good skin care is cleansing or washing your face. *Never* use body soap to wash your face. Your facial skin is more delicate than your body and needs to be treated accordingly.

One of the best facial cleansers on the market is Cetaphil. You can find it in your grocery store or drugstore. It is the number one cleanser (and moisturizer) recommended by dermatologists. It's very affordable and great for all skin types, even super sensitive, for men and women.

What Skin Type Do You Have?

There are four skin types:

OILY: Larger pores; skin shines most of the day; breakouts are frequent. Needs cleanser designed for oily skin and oil-free, light moisturizer for surface dehydration.

DRY: Small pores; skin feels tight or sometimes itchy; flaking is normal. Face never has shine. Needs creamy cleanser and heavier, penetrating moisturizer.

COMBINATION: T-zone is oily with larger pores; blackheads common, with normal to dry cheeks. Center of face shines most of the day. Needs a thorough cleanser with medium moisture designed for combination-to-normal skin.

NORMAL: Pores unnoticeable; no real tightness; flakiness or high shine areas; occasional breakouts. Needs a gentle cleanser and light moisturizer (oil-free if you have regular breakouts).

Moisturize Step two is moisturizing your skin. All skin types should use a moisturizer daily. If you have oily or acne-prone skin, use an oil-free moisturizer designed specifically for your skin type. Cetaphil manufactures terrific moisturizers, as does Neutrogena.

Be sure to keep your skin protected during the day with a sunscreen of no less than SPF15. Most daily sun exposure happens on your way to and from work when you don't even think about being exposed. Photo aging caused by sun damage is the hardest to correct. It adds many years onto your appearance, and overexposure to the sun can lead to deadly skin cancers. No tanning beds either. Spray tan if you think you must have some color!

Eye cream Step three is eye cream. Preventive maintenance is crucial for preventing aging around your eyes. It is never too soon to start using an eye lotion or cream. They are heavier than moisturizers and are formulated specifically for the delicate eye area. There are many great choices out there.

Makeup

> "The difference between great makeup and scary makeup in HD is about 15 strokes: Blend, blend, blend!"
>
> —CHRISTI SCHREIBER, COLOUR BASIS

Wearing makeup is necessary for on-camera work for both men and women. No exceptions. With the clarity of broadcasts, it is important that any shine, skin discolorations or imperfections are corrected to limit viewer distractions. Think of it as part of your job uniform, something you automatically wear when you go to work on-camera.

There are many types and brands of makeup available. Shopping for the right products can be a daunting experience, especially if the person helping you has no HD television knowledge. The most important things to consider in your makeup for HDTV, whether it be foundation, shadows or powders, is the pigment (color particle) quality, color and texture. I get asked a lot if there is really that big of a difference in the various makeup lines. The answer is yes. The difference is normally based on the pigment quality, color and texture as well as the ingredients used. You need to use products that match or complement your skin tones and are matte (no shine or sparkle). Check out each section on the next page for more specific information on the different products needed for on-camera application.

These guidelines apply to field reporters as well as on-camera reporters. Even though you are in the field, out in the elements, it is important that you are put together and polished for your on-camera pieces. Never leave on an assignment without all of your appearance products. Make sure you have a good mirror for application and/or touchups in the truck. If there is no visor mirror, buy a mirror and keep it in your personal kit.

> "Wearing makeup is necessary for on-camera work for both men and women."
>
> —CHRISTI SCHREIBER

The basics: Makeup application for men and women, in studio and field reporting

BOTH: Apply foundation, either in airbrush or powder form. If you are using a powder foundation, be sure to apply with a brush, *not* a sponge. Sponges apply foundation too thickly and are a breeding ground for bacteria. It looks more natural to have several thin layers when applied with a brush as opposed to one thick layer obtained by sponge application.

BOTH: Conceal under eyes with a specially designed concealing product a shade lighter than your skin tone. If you have superdark circles, start with a corrector that is orange in color to neutralize the blue. Follow with your skin tone concealer.

BOTH: For your foundation makeup (skin tone color applied to your entire face), pigment quality and color are very important, as is texture. You need to use products that match your skin and are matte (no shine). There is a buzz about mineral makeup. It's great for your skin, but most have too much sheen for on-camera, so avoid this as your on-camera work makeup. Airbrush makeup is the ultimate in foundation makeup application and is the first choice for HD. Colour Basis offers airbrush, as well as an alternative, HD Powder Makeup. Both are oil-free with great texture and weight. Once the makeup is on your skin, you don't feel it, and you don't look made up. That is the goal.

MEN: Eye definition. Apply a *very* thin line of taupe-colored eye shadow just under the iris (the colored part of the eye) if you have really light hair and eyelashes. This will help give some eye definition without looking made up. The trick is the line must be right at the lower lash line and very thin.

MEN: Brow definition. Light blond or silver brows need added color to help eyes pop on-camera. Darker brows sometimes need correction from scars or areas where brows grow unevenly. Tweeze, wax or thread mono brows, guys. Get rid of hairs at the bridge of the nose.

MEN: If you have superdark beard shadow, you will also need the same orange-colored corrector in a thin layer to neutralize the beard before applying foundation. If you have a dark, fast-growing beard, you will need to shave and apply makeup just before your show or first on-camera appearance. It is possible you will have to shave and reapply your makeup in between shows if you are on for an extended period of time.

MEN: Lash definition. Apply brown mascara to your top lashes only if you have superlight eyelashes. Do not use for lengthening, just to add color by gently pressing the mascara brush to the lash as opposed to coating it from lid to end of lash for lengthening. Be careful not to apply too much, so it doesn't appear feminine.

BOTH: Apply finishing powder. Always, no matter which foundation formula you use, set or finish your makeup with a shine-controlling powder.

BOTH: Apply contour color, which is a neutral reddish brown. Make certain there is *no* sparkle, sheen or orange tone in the color. The whole idea of contouring is to add dimension and shading to the face just under the cheekbones. Contour color can also be used around the hairline to lower a high forehead, under the jawbone to slim the jowl area and on the sides of the nose for an instant nose job.

WOMEN: Define and maintain your eyebrows. They make a huge impact on your overall appearance and cannot be ignored. If they are thin or uneven, fill in for balance.

WOMEN: Define eyes with color. Apply eye shadow and upper liner with two to four colors, depending on eye shape. It is important that your eyes are bright, clear, defined and open to connect with your audience.

WOMEN: Apply cheek color just above your contour color directly on your cheekbone. This is the most challenging area to properly blend in HD. Blend, and then blend a little more.

WOMEN: Remove facial hair. If you have facial hair on your upper lip and/or noticeable peach fuzz on your cheeks and jaw line, it needs to be removed. Even if the hair is blonde, it holds more makeup and can appear darker in those areas. Threading or razoring is the preferred method, as waxing can be harsh, removing additional layers of skin as well as causing breakouts.

WOMEN: Define your mouth with lip liner for added definition and long-lasting wear for your lipstick. Gloss is optional. If you choose to wear gloss, dab it only in the center of your lips. HD tends to exaggerate shine.

BOTH: Touch up shine during show commercial/segment breaks with your finishing/shine control powder. You should check yourself during commercial breaks or just before your segment. This is your responsibility. No one is going to do this for you.

RULE OF THUMB

NEVER change your hairstyle or color without approval from your news director. You may even be asked to change your hairstyle or color. It is important to remain open and flexible to management or consultant recommendations.

Hair

Hair for television news needs to be consistent. It should not change from day to day and should be manageable. Gone are the days of stiff anchor hair, although it still needs to be properly styled, look touchable and have some movement. Your hair should be cut in a style to flatter your face shape and work with the texture of your hair. Using the correct products in your hair is also very important for a finished look. Seek professional help when choosing a new style. If you color your hair, be sure to have a standing or regular appointment for root touchups. Don't try to go an extra week or two without recoloring because it will show.

Men

- Keep your hair above your collar in back and trimmed around your ears.
- Be careful not to go too short. Hair typically looks a little shorter on-air than it appears in person.
- Do not wear hair too long, as it looks unprofessional. Keep it fairly conservative for TV news.
- Have a standing or regular appointment for your haircuts. No one should be able to tell you just got a haircut. If so, you either went too short or waited too long in between cuts.
- Do not use gel. It makes hair look thinner than it is, dries too shiny and can flake on your jacket, which shows in HD. Use a pomade or wax instead.
- Use wax to lay down individual stray hairs.

Women

- Your hair length should be determined by your face shape, hair texture and thickness. Your hair should remain above the bust line in all cases. You don't want your hair to be cut off in your closest shot.
- You must have a style, not just one-length, not-sure-what-to-do-with-it hair.
- Backcombing is a must even if you wear your hair straight. It's not about having big hair. Backcombing gives structure to hair and yields a polished look. Ask your stylist for a lesson if you don't know how to backcomb your hair. A proper comb is necessary for best results.
- You must be consistent with hairstyling. No day-to-day changes with on-camera hair for television news. Entertainment television is a whole different ball game. For success in television news, keep your hairstyle consistent. If you are not good at styling your hair, invest time practicing and consider a lesson with your stylist to learn the tricks of the trade. Part of your job is to make your hair look good on-camera.
- Do not use hair lacquers for added shine. Hair too shiny in HD looks like artificial hair.
- Supercurly hair does not work well on-camera, especially if you are dealing with a green screen. Soft curls and waves are better, depending on style and hair texture.

Field Reporters

- Consistency is also important for you, but it can be challenging out in the elements.
- Ladies, do *not* fall into wearing a ponytail or hair up in a clip for field shots. This should only be done in bad weather situations, such as high winds and rain.
- Rarely should men or women in the field wear a ball cap. Again, this is only in bad weather situations and should be a station-issued or -approved hat.

The Visual Self: Wardrobe

Michelle Fortin, faculty associate
Walter Cronkite School of Journalism and Mass Communication

Michelle Fortin spent nearly a decade working in television newsrooms across the country, both behind and in front of the camera as a field producer at KTVK in Phoenix and as an anchorwoman for KHGI (ABC) in Kearney, Neb., and WMTW (ABC) in Portland, Maine. Her advice? "Being on-air is never about being the most beautiful or trying to catch the viewer's eye. In fact, it's the opposite. You want to present yourself in an attractive and pleasant manner, but never in a way that distracts from the primary purpose—which is to tell a story, someone else's story. It's about the story, not you or what you wear. This applies whether you're a street reporter or the 6 and 10 anchor."

Men

- Buy two well-fitting suit jackets when first starting out. Pair them with nice slacks/trousers, non–button-down-collar shirts and ties.
- Change up everything but the suit coats. Viewers won't notice.
- As for jewelry—a watch and a wedding ring. That's it. *Nothing* more. No earrings. No piercings.

COLLECTING A WARDROBE

- ❑ Invest in a few nice pieces that you can mix and match with other items in your wardrobe rather than just buying lots of pieces on sale or at discount stores. HDTV will show all the flaws.
- ❑ Keep an eye out for sales and stock up.
- ❑ Open an account at a consignment store.
- ❑ Find what colors look good on you, photocopy them, send them to your mother and have her carry them in her purse so when she buys you something, it's also something you can wear on-air.

Women

- Discipline yourselves to buy only double-duty clothing—items you can wear on the air and off. (Don't buy anything you cannot wear on-air.)
- Avoid patterns, silks/satins, colors that wash you out, white and pastels.
- Focus on contrasts—black suit coat with pink shirt, blue shell with brown cardigan and so on.
- Keep jewelry simple—one ring per hand (nothing big), watch only, no bracelets, simple necklaces (not bigger than pearls), earrings the size of a nickel or smaller.
- *No* headbands or other hair accessories (other than an appropriate hat for weather conditions in the field).

Live From the Study

Lena Sadiwskyj, vice president
News & Operations, WVLT-TV (CBS), Knoxville, Tenn.

Lena Sadiwskyj's experience in multimedia journalism and management spans more than 30 years. Before becoming VP of News & Operations for WVLT-TV in early 2011, Sadiwskyj was editor-in-chief for a mobile technology company where she developed the content strategy for Taptu, a social news app for the iPhone, Android phone and iPad. In her TV leadership roles, Sadiwskyj has managed and mentored newsrooms in cities such as Dallas, Phoenix and Orlando, Fla. She has also written and produced documentaries and videos for business, government and academic clients.

I started my career in a role we'd now call "associate producer" and worked my way up at the network I'd watched and admired since I was a teenager—the Canadian Broadcasting Corporation. During my 10-year career in Toronto and Halifax, I was fortunate enough to cover some incredible stories as a producer, investigative reporter and fill-in anchor.

As a news manager, I have hired hundreds of anchors and reporters. The ones who really stand out in the newsroom make real connections between their stories and the viewers. They're curious and competitive, with a passion to give all they have.

Whether you're in New York or Glendive, Mont., you are the face of your station. Many of your viewers have already seen the news on their iPads, their mobile phones or the Internet, but they're making a choice to watch and hear it from you as well. They're looking for what they can't find online—more than the facts. So it's your job to bring out the heart of the story and make it real. Sometimes, when you're under intense pressure, your professionalism is critical. If something goes wrong, don't panic. As long as you are in control, the viewers will have confidence in what you're saying, will keep watching and will come back for the next newscast.

Brian Curtis, the main anchor at KXAS-TV (NBC) in Dallas, had all those qualities as well as superior smarts when I met him while teaching journalism at the University of Missouri. He'd become even more driven by the time I hired him as an anchor/reporter in Birmingham, Ala. A multiple Emmy winner, Brian has done everything from live Olympics coverage to investigations to breaking news in the country's fifth largest market. So how does he prepare? "I have developed some habits and rituals right before the show. I'll take some deep breaths and focus; this is a live performance." And even though he usually has a co-anchor, Brian makes sure he knows what's in the entire newscast. "Being a good listener is the key to building credibility and the team. I may not have every story, but my co-anchor's reads (stories) are my listens. So, in effect, every story is mine; I am involved in the whole newscast. Being involved is the key. You have to go through life with your eyes open. My job has homework. I stay engaged all day, whether I am in the newsroom, the house or the gym. I can't imagine how difficult it would be if I didn't know what was going on until after I walked into the newsroom."

When it comes to looking comfortable and confident, take a look at your favorite weather anchors. They talk for three minutes or so without a prompter, so they have to be prepared. In Tucson, Ariz., KGUN 9 (ABC) chief meteorologist Erin Christiansen does four nightly TV newscasts as well as some radio reports. She says once she has produced her weather segment, she clicks through her maps and graphics and talks out loud about the key points. For Erin, this ritual isn't just a rehearsal; it's what helps her develop that critical connection with the viewers: "People tell me that when they watch me do the weather, they feel as if I am talking to them at the grocery store. The great thing about weather is that you can speak off the cuff and let your personality show. It helps to have a conversation with someone in the studio during the commercial break, so when the break ends, I just continue that conversation with the camera."

Jan Tennant made history in 1974 as the first woman to anchor *"The National,"* CBC's flagship newscast. She's retired now but still has that great voice and precise diction: "There are technical skills to be learned—the pitch of the voice, the clarity of enunciation. You need to know how to sit or stand and how and when to breathe. It's important to finish the thought right through to the period at the end of the sentence." Jan always came to the newsroom with positive energy and questions about what was going on. Most of the time, she already knew what the big stories were; she just wanted to make sure we had put them in the newscast. She brought an honesty and credibility that went beyond the set:

"I met the queen in 1982, when the Canadian constitution was being repatriated. I was introduced as a news anchor. Her Majesty chatted about how complicated the world of television is with the lights, cameras, endless cables. I added, 'Just be yourself.' And the queen said, 'Yes, exactly.' So how do you be yourself? It's like being a good actor. You are not pretending, but it is a performance. The viewers have to be able to look into your eyes and see that you are true. No automatic pilot. For a time there was a popular notion to look away or down as if you were thinking. Fortunately that seems to have passed away. Thinking is good. Pretending to think is bad."

At KIMA-TV (CBS) in Yakima Wash., David Klugh has the dual role of assistant news director and main anchor. David has more than 20 years experience as an anchor and reporter in major markets, including Indianapolis, Milwaukee and Tampa. He says it's essential to take time to make the newscast fit your way of speaking. "Even the best producers don't write the way you talk. I take the 30 minutes before the show to make the reads (stories) work for me. Then I circle my name at the start of the story and draw a line over my co-anchor's reads. I look at how her scripts start and end, so I can make logical segues or transitions." Whether you're reporting, field anchoring or on the set, you need to know your story. But, David warns, don't know it by heart. "Never memorize a script. The quickest way to stumble and not be able to recover is to have memorized the words, because if you lose your place, you'll have trouble trying to recover. If you don't understand the story, you will never look comfortable telling it on set, and you will lose the confidence of the viewers."

Live From the Field

Stories delivered live on location have become the mainstay of TV news. More and more the audience is comfortable with a live shot that sometimes has less-than-perfect picture quality. You might take these shots with a cell phone or even on a webcam or via Skype.

Unlike the studio, where there is maximum support—studio set and lights to make you look your best, a full production team, co-anchors—reporting live from the field or from your desk often takes place under minimal conditions. As one reporter told us, "You are on the spot. There's no teleprompter, and it's an experience that some J-schools simply can't prepare you for." Nervousness is normal, and practice is the only way to overcome it.

Eric Chaloux, reporter, KCTV5 (CBS), Kansas City, Mo.

Before every live shot, I stop and tell myself to "own the story." It's a little nerve-calming and story-focusing technique I learned from a veteran "newsy." It's helpful during breaking news. When time is your worst enemy, it's important to have focus and authority in what you're telling the viewer. Whether you've had all day to work the story or just five minutes from when the live truck arrived, you need to "own the story."

You picked the information for your report for a reason. Now the live shot needs to set it up and deliver it home. Before you go live, you need to be an expert in what you say. If you don't feel it, believe it or own it, then the viewers can tell. Their trust in you is earned when you own the story.

Chris Wright, reporter, WDRB (Fox), Louisville, Ky.

I try to keep live introductions and tags to my packages relatively short—usually two brief sentences. Anything longer than that, and there's always the chance you will run out of breath. While it may seem natural to rehearse the shot as many times as possible while you are waiting to go on, don't do it! Go over it once or twice. If you try to memorize every single word, your chances of stumbling increase exponentially.

As long as you get your point across and use the correct roll cue to video, there is nothing wrong with ad-libbing a bit. If you do mess up, just keep going. The viewer likely will not even notice your flub.

Finally, do not get discouraged by a poor live shot. It happens to everyone at every level.

Justin McHeffey, weather anchor, KMOT-TV (NBC), Minot, N.D.

During the first few months of your new job, a degree of nervousness is expected. You're human, after all. But with practice, like anything else, you become comfortable speaking conversationally, as if an old friend wanted to hear about your weekend. This is the communications business, and weather forecasting in particular embraces the delivery of information with a friendly-sounding voice.

No matter what weather software you're using, it's always important to focus locally. Viewers depend on your daily and weekly outlooks so they know if they should wear a sweater or reschedule the backyard barbecue. Once you've created your show based on what's most important, now it's time to take notes. Think about what points you should highlight on each slide. When you write down phrases and concepts, it registers in your mind so you're never at a loss for words. Don't just describe what it's going to be like tomorrow. Also tell your viewers why (i.e., low pressure over Idaho is sending rain and cooler air our way for the weekend).

Here's a tip on preparing your voice and presence for the camera: While the last commercial plays on TV before you're on-air, make yourself laugh as though you had just heard a hilarious joke. Expect quizzical stares from the anchor and floor director, but don't worry about them. This final burst will increase your positive energy and reduce nerves at the last second.

Five minutes before you go on-air, make sure all content is updated. It's amazing how quickly things can change, especially during severe weather. If you're still not completely comfortable on the green screen, it helps to visualize or even practice where you want to be standing. For instance, don't block the temperature map (people at home will yell at the TV). Also, become friends with both the production crew and the anchors. People watching the newscast can easily spot disingenuous banter. Say something relatable when you toss back to the desk. And above all, be yourself and show your passion for the weather.

Emily Schmidt, freelance reporter, CNN Newsource, Washington, D.C.

I owe my on-air news skills to my first boss, who said he wanted me to fill in for the weekend weather segments. I thought he was crazy, as I knew next to nothing about maps and forecasts. It turned out to be a great move—not so much for my meteorological training, but for learning to find and use my voice. With three minutes and 30 seconds to fill a weathercast, my style changed from scripting to storytelling. Going live began to feel more like a conversation with viewers instead of a report to viewers. It was terrifying at first, but eventually I learned to trust what I knew and how to explain it.

I haven't done a weather segment for years, but those skills still matter in every live shot. When arriving on breaking news with just minutes to gather the facts, I take a few literal and figurative deep breaths, and then I begin to simply shape a conversation—telling what I know, what I don't know and how I'm going to go about finding more information.

When things get especially complicated, a mentor once told me to think of script tracking and live shot delivery like reading a children's book: Simplify, slow down and showcase the words that matter by slightly lowering your voice. It's all a way to make memorizing sentences less important than thinking about how to tell a story from beginning to end. It's all preparation so that when someone asks, "What's the weather today?" you are ready with an answer they'll remember.

Writing and Producing for THE WEB

CHAPTER 10

> *The Internet can be highly informative, but, of course, there is an awful lot of junk there. Sometimes the junk is the most interesting.*
>
> —WALTER CRONKITE

CHAPTER OUTLINE

24/7 News Cycle

Today's journalists must plan and prepare stories for multiple platforms. Especially at the smaller stations where most graduates start working, you'll both write and produce content for the Web. You might find yourself writing a blog, producing Web video, preparing podcasts and using social media to post breaking news.

As consumers' viewing habits change, the Internet is becoming increasingly important in TV newsrooms. Instead of watching the news in the morning, after work and before bed, people consume news throughout the day on the Internet and mobile platforms.

Many stations use their websites for on-demand viewing. They offer live streams of news conferences and cover breaking news on a level never conceived when the only outlet was TV or radio.

Deliver news quickly

Today, with the growing popularity of social media, immediacy is even more critical. When an earthquake shook Mexico on April 4, 2010, within *seconds* people were reporting their experiences on Twitter and Facebook. It took several *minutes* for CNN and ABC to report the tremors. The news outlets even used several tweets to show what people were saying and how widespread the quake was.

Anchors, reporters, producers and even news directors update viewers directly via Facebook, Twitter and other types of social media. These moment-to-moment updates are the modern news ticker of information, with a seemingly limitless reach around the world.

People don't want to wait. It you don't have what they want, they'll go to a competitor. Delivering news is still a business. Without customers, stations will go under. The trick is to retain your existing audience, compete for new customers and grow.

Deliver news often

Your followers will keep checking back only if you offer something new several times a day. You can file breaking news as an online bulletin, a blog post and/or a tweet. Upload pictures from the field. These days you're your own promotions department marketing yourself and your content.

Deliver news on multiple platforms

Not only do your followers want news now, but they also want it delivered on multiple platforms—radio, TV, websites, mobile phones and digital devices such as the iPad. It's like an extended family with many generations. One family member might watch the nightly network news on TV, while another checks what friends are saying on Facebook, and yet another receives news alerts on a mobile phone.

To reach all those family members, you need to be where your audience is. Keep in mind that today, your audience is global. An estimated 5 billion people worldwide have mobile phones.

USING SOCIAL MEDIA

Journalists use social media for

- story ideas.
- breaking news.
- beat checks.
- brand development.

Because it is

- immediate.
- concise.
- a different form of writing.
- a good multimedia tool.

And they use it

- to promote blogs, columns, breaking news.
- as a barometer to see what people are talking about.
- to find new sources.

And while using it, they remember to

- be personable and as human as possible.
- respond to people who are asking questions or giving feedback.
- share information, not just promote it.

Remember that social media is a conversation. Give-and-take will help you in the long run.

Producing for Digital Media

Tips, eyewitness accounts, photos, videos, viewer comments and reaction are all instantly updated during the day. Social media, too, provide an immense flow of information and ideas to supplement the standard newscasts and keep content fresh for viewers around the clock.

Producers can lead the charge in tapping into these venues. Here's how it works.

Old way versus new way

The assignment desk editor has just confirmed that the governor is resigning because of personal issues.

Producers can't be responsible for *every* aspect of this integrated coverage plan, but they must be aware of the potential for a stunning multiplatform approach to any major story using the power of digital and social media.

PITFALLS

Along with these new opportunities come the inevitable pitfalls. It's hard to know what information can be trusted in cyberspace. It can be difficult for producers to distinguish personal updates from those delivered by newsroom staffers who represent a legitimate news outlet. And who is to say how much is too much when it comes to one-on-one interaction with viewers? How well do such conversations translate to solid content and coverage decisions? Objectivity—a cornerstone of journalistic ethics—comes under scrutiny quickly in an arena as transparent as social media.

Producing the OLD way	Producing for DIGITAL media
• Run a crawl and/or do a brief special report report about the governor's resignation.	• Update the Web with a breaking news banner, photo montage of the governor and a list of links to the last 10 news stories related to the governor. • Make sure your lead reporter is tweeting live from the state capitol. • Send out a Facebook status update to inform voters and ask what they think about the governor's resignation. • Set up a Web link to a bio of the lieutenant governor. • Have your investigative reporter start tweeting teases to his exclusive exposé, which led to the resignation in the first place. • Get a live feed from the state capitol streamed online, and then stand by for the televised special report.
• Start changing the rundown for the newscast that starts in three hours.	• Start changing the rundown for the newscast that starts in three hours.

News on the go

More and more viewers want to get their news on the go, and news stations are finding ways to reach them via cell phones and hand-held digital devices with live or quickly syndicated sources. As these mobile formats evolve, producers will have to create content and tease to it effectively across all platforms while interacting with thousands of viewers at a time. In short, producers will no longer merely create a half-hour newscast. They will act as the creative force behind an integrated news source—selling a news identity that transcends the type of media the viewer is using.

Online media policy

To help avoid the pitfalls, news outlets must establish an online media policy. Some points to consider:

- What takes precedence—getting information online quickly or gathering video and interviews for later newscasts?
- Will you hold exclusive video for a later newscast or post it immediately to the station's website? Sometimes you might choose to hold video until the later newscast because of competition.
- Who will post content through social media? How often on a daily basis versus breaking news?

- Is there a time to stop producing content for social media? If not, who's responsible for round-the-clock updates?
- Should anchors be the voices of the station, or can others ghostwrite under the station's identity—for example, on a blog?
- What's the overall tone of your social media identity? Some news organizations go for a casual, conversational style, while others keep stricter journalistic standards.
- What's the newsroom's main goal in online media integration? Once a mission is defined (e.g., "Attract more viewers for newscasts" or "Use as a news-gathering source"), it will be easier to focus on the when, why and how of getting the job done.

Online media guidelines should be reviewed and updated on a regular basis. The news station's leadership team determines how its content will be presented in these varied formats and what type of news identity it hopes to create on a global platform. It's often up to producers to ensure that this mission is fulfilled.

VOICES from the Newsroom

Christina Caron, managing editor
ABC News

Christina Caron oversees six ABC News on Campus college bureaus and mentors about 30 paid student reporters. She works closely with the students to edit and vet their reporting, then delivers their broadcast and text material to ABC News' various platforms.

What skills does a successful Web producer need?

Web producers need to be organized and detail oriented while working quickly and accurately. They're experts in coordination—whipping up headlines, ordering images from the photo department, coordinating with the Web video producers to bring in relevant video and shepherding stories through the writing and editing process.

How do you bridge the gap between video reporters and text reporters?

In the ABC News on Campus program we ask our broadcast students to write text pieces from time to time, and we ask our print students to try shooting a package. In this way the students are truly engaging in media convergence.

How do deadlines work on the Web?

Deadlines depend largely on the type of content being produced. Breaking news deadlines are always ASAP, of course. Feature story deadlines can stretch out for days. In general, most producers and writers at ABCNews.com typically turn out an original story every day or at least every other day, in addition to their other responsibilities. Editors review stories on a rolling basis throughout the day.

How important is the headline?

The right headline is crucial to selling a story on the Web. At ABCNews.com some stories are posted on the home page or in a section index, without an accompanying image. In these instances the headline becomes the readers' only introduction to a story. If the headline isn't clickable, the story will tank, regardless of how well crafted or thoroughly researched it is. If a headline is also accompanied by an image, then that image is just as important, if not more so, than the headline.

The 24/7 news cycle thrives on updates via Twitter and Facebook.

Story Planning for the Web

Online stories that are less time sensitive—such as in-depths, features and profiles—take more time to plan, produce and polish than breaking news pieces. If you don't have multimedia skills, partner with a Web-savvy classmate or colleague. It generally takes a team to create multimedia and interactive elements.

Storytelling on the Web

The most effective online stories are conceived as Web projects from the get-go. Before you start a multimedia project, figure out the best way to tell different parts of your story. Which part can you best tell in words? With audio? As a slideshow or video? As a quiz, timeline or animation? Also write down the visual elements that will enhance the online version of your story—fact boxes, checklists, Q&As, diagrams, timelines, maps, polls, scans of original documents and/or supplemental interviews.

Make sure all these elements complement rather than repeat each other.

> "If you don't know where you're going, you'll end up somewhere else."
>
> —YOGI BERRA, NEW YORK YANKEES

Fitting all the pieces together

In 2009 the Sarasota Herald-Tribune named scoundrels in an in-depth investigation of the massive house-flipping mortgage fraud schemes that operated in Florida for most of the past decade. The paper's website made good use of online tools, including interactive maps and social network analysis. This project was a finalist for the Pulitzer Prize for Investigative Reporting.

RULE OF THUMB

Mix one part broadcast with one part print. Stir in multimedia, interactivity and links to other resources—and you've got online journalism. Users are active participants who select the order in which they vew the information presented.

TABLE **10.1** **The Right Medium for the Story**

This action or information	Works best in this medium
Hear and see main character	Video, audio slideshow
Show action	Video, animated graphics
Freeze action	Photos
Convey strong emotion	Radio, podcast, video, natural sound, music, photos
Create a mood	Radio, podcast, music, natural sound, photos
Listen to a first-person account	Radio, podcast, audio slideshow
Hear natural sound	Radio, podcast, video, audio slideshow
Illustrate things you can't see, such as outer space, or how things work, such as a computer chip	Static or animated graphics (can combine with text, photos, audio and video)
Show locations	Map

Writing for the Web

To make sure timely information appears online, reporters in the field not only report stories for the newscast but also call in a headline and a few paragraphs for the Web. In addition, news outlets are increasingly encouraging their reporters, anchors and columnists to maintain blogs, update Twitter accounts and post to Facebook throughout the day. The practice connects journalists with an audience that increasingly relies on social media.

Online challenges

Posting updates online can present challenges. "The key with social networking is not making your friends/followers feel as if they're being slapped with ads for your stories all the time," said anchor/reporter Janie Porter, who is active on both Twitter and Facebook for WTSP-TV (CBS), Tampa, Fla. "To accomplish that, it's imperative to be a real person and not a news machine."

Being that real person instead of a news machine can mean giving viewers or readers a window into your personal life. But revealing too much personal information can become a safety risk. "I'm as much a social media addict as anyone else on this planet," said Syleste Rodriguez, an anchor/reporter at KPNX-TV (NBC) in Phoenix. "I share almost everything, but there are still things kept for only those whom I consider in my circle of trust."

Be neutral

Ethical guidelines call for journalists to remain unbiased, so how much is too much? "I draw the line at personal opinion," said Catherine Anaya, an anchor with KPHO-TV (CBS) in Phoenix. "I don't mind talking about my personal experience, but these social media sites are still public forums, and as journalists we have a responsibility to remain objective."

Even online, journalists must remain neutral on issues. Otherwise, you're jeopardizing your credibility. As a young journalist, your reputation is your most important asset, so protect it by remaining unbiased and credible. "We can't make statements of opinion that might give the impression that we're in any way, shape or form biased," Anaya said.

Breaking news

Breaking a news story online can drive traffic to the website and tease to a news story coming up in the newscast. It can also generate information from the community that can strengthen the story.

The Web is all about speed and immediacy, but never sacrifice accuracy in the race to be first.

Improving scannability

Think in a visual way as you organize your story. Dividing a story into sections, for example, breaks up long blocks of gray text. Here are other ways to improve the scannability of your Web story.

- Include a summary deck below the headline. Provide enough information to entice someone to read the story that follows, but don't repeat the lead.
- Use bold **subheads** to break up a long story. Subheads summarize what's in the section that follows. Put them where there's a logical break between sections. Make subheads informative rather than clever or cute.
- Highlight important points with lists, bullets (•) or numbers.
- Emphasize keywords with bold type.
- Add an intriguing **pull quote.** Also known as a callout, a pull quote is a sentence or quote that's pulled out of the story and set in larger type (see page 190).
- Put relevant information in a sidebar (see page 195).

Attracting readers

Even though space is unlimited on the Web, people have limited time and patience. They'll read stories that are interesting, relevant and presented so it's easy to find news and information.

You want people to find your story when using Google, Yahoo or another search engine. The Web headline and news story on the next page include keywords that people will use when searching for the story: Governor Jan Brewer, Alice Cooper, Arizona, dine out, restaurant.

Put the most important information up top. The inverted pyramid works well because you can keep adding updates to the top. Blend the new information into the existing copy.

Summarize the story in a nut graph explaining what happened, what made it happen, its context, why viewers should care and how big a deal it is.

Try to make the story relevant to your audience. What's in it for them?

Write clearly and concisely. Include specific details. Explain why this information is important.

Governor Jan Brewer, Alice Cooper urge Arizonans to dine out for the common good

By CHRISTINE ROGEL,
Cronkite News Service

PHOENIX (Thursday, Sept. 10) Gov. Jan Brewer took the stage Thursday with rocker and restaurateur Alice Cooper to convince Arizonans that dining out is good for the state.

Announcing a three-month public-awareness campaign called Dine 4 AZ, they said going to restaurants supports businesses and helps preserve jobs. Brewer noted that restaurants generate 10 percent of Arizona's tax revenues.

"We are working hard to lead the Grand Canyon State forward and out of this recession, and Dine 4 AZ fits perfectly into our plan," she said. "Please treat your family to a meal, and we'll get through this together."

Participating restaurants are offering coupons, discounts and promotions at Dine4AZ.com.

"People come to Arizona to have fun. And it's our responsibility not to gouge the audience, not to gouge the customers—just to give them a great time," Cooper said.

Shamrock Foods Co., a Phoenix-based food distributor, is sponsoring the campaign. With more than a quarter million employees, Arizona's food-service industry is vital to the state's economy, said Stephen D. Chucri, president and CEO of the Arizona Restaurant Association.

"We've been hit hard by unemployment, immigration issues and rampant foreclosures in our housing market, but with the Dine 4 AZ initiative we can all do some simple things to get our economy rolling again," he said.

Arizona businesses offering food and drink shed 6,300 jobs during the year ending in July, including a loss of 4,500 jobs from June to July, according to the state Department of Commerce.

Marshall Vest, director of the Economic and Business Research Center at the University of Arizona's Eller College of Management, said he doesn't expect the Dine 4 AZ to have a large impact.

"All of these campaigns are a feel-good type of effort to get people to think about how their actions and purchasing decisions make a difference," Vest said. "So I think it's beneficial, but I think the overall effect on the economy would be pretty small."

The news conference was held at Alice Cooperstown in downtown Phoenix. Cooper said business at his restaurant has been consistent, mostly because of its proximity to the US Airways Center and Chase Field.

His advice to restaurant owners: Stay consistent and do what you know best. For example, if you make a great pizza, then continue to make a great pizza.

Prepping a script for the Web

It usually takes less than 10 minutes to convert a TV script to a Web story. Just follow these easy steps from Cory Bergman, former director of digital media at KING-TV (NBC) in Seattle and the founder/director of LostRemote.com, which analyzes how technology is changing television.

- ☐ Combine the text elements—toss, lead, sound bites, ending. Delete redundancies. Lead with a strong sentence or two.
- ☐ Remove all the technical directions.
- ☐ If necessary, switch from all caps to caps and lowercase. Fix the capitalization.
- ☐ Switch the sound bites to quotes. Double-check the attributions.
- ☐ Change ellipses to commas. Remove unnecessary hyphens from numbers. Change sentence fragments to full sentences.
- ☐ Delete any direct references to audio and video. Add description to help readers visualize a scene.
- ☐ Add any important details that didn't appear in the original version.
- ☐ Smooth the rough spots so the story reads well from start to finish. Add paragraph breaks in appropriate places.
- ☐ Add links to relevant references and multimedia.
- ☐ Run a spell-checker.

Source: Adapted from: "Converting TV Scripts to the Web: A Handy Ten Minute Checklist," Cory Bergman, July 30, 2006, Committee of Concerned Journalists website, accessed at concernedjournalists.org/converting-tv-scripts-web

TV Versus Online Scripts

Elias Johnson, a reporter at KPHO-TV (CBS) in Phoenix, wrote both the TV script and online story below about Arizona State University freshmen moving into dorms.

SIDE BY SIDE

TV Script

Elias Johnson went back home to check up on the new batch entering ASU . . . Elias, how was it?

Marya (ad-libbing what's going on) You had to feel for those freshmen living on the third floor . . . but thanks to a company hired by ASU to help . . . saying goodbye was the hardest part.

It's moving day . . .

Sandy Farmer—Scottsdale family
"Moving in."

Laurie Daly—Chicago family
"We are moving our daughter in."

Susan Armstrong—Mom
"A freshmen . . . my baby . . . last to go."

Time for moms and dads like Susan Armstrong to say goodbye to their college freshman . . .

Susan Armstrong—Mom
"I shouldn't be doing this. I'll start crying."

And hello to the Arizona heat . . .

Susan Armstrong—Mom
"I hate the heat. I was born and raised in it."

Some deal with it better than others . . .

Dillan Armstrong—Las Vegas freshman
"Used to it . . . so I'm not really too worried about it."

Laurie Daly—Chicago family
"In Chicago we have the humidity . . . this is the dry heat."

This year ASU student services is making the move a little easier . . . free of charge

Vin Peseski—University Student Services
"We are moving in approximately 10-thousand students campus wide."

And two giant forklifts will handle the hard part.

Vin Peseski—University Student Services
"One person actually came up and kissed me as I walked by . . . so I don't know if that's going to go over real well with my wife at home."

Just when the temp seems unbearable . . . future Sun Devils find motivation.

Robert Farmer—ASU freshman
"The change . . . new people."

Dillan Armstrong—Las Vegas freshman
"Girls."

If only it were that easy for mom . . .

Sandy Farmer—Scottsdale family
"It is my first one out of the nest . . . so I have to say . . . pitter-patter on the heart."

Online Version

ASU Students, Heat Move In

10,000+ Students Move Into Dorms as Temps Rise Above 110

By Elias Johnson

TEMPE, Ariz.—It's moving day.

"We are moving our daughter in," said Laurie Daly from Chicago.

Time for moms and dads like Susan Armstrong to say goodbye to their college freshman.

"I shouldn't be doing this. I'll start crying," Armstrong said.

It's also time to say hello to the Arizona heat.

"I hate the heat," Armstrong said. "I was born and raised in it."

Some deal with 112 degrees better than others.

"I'm used to it, so I'm not really too worried about it," said ASU freshman Dillan Armstrong.

"In Chicago we have the humidity," Daly said. "This is the dry heat."

This year ASU Student Services is making the move a little easier—free of charge.

"We are moving in approximately 10,000 students campus wide," said Vin Peseski with University Student Services.

Two giant forklifts will handle the hard part.

"One person actually came up and kissed me as I walked by, so I don't know if that's going to go over real well with my wife at home," Peseski said.

Just when the temp seems unbearable, future Sun Devils find motivation.

"The change, new people," said freshman Robert Farmer.

"Girls," Armstrong added.

If only it were that easy for mom.

"It is my first one out of the nest, so I have to say pitter-patter on the heart," said Sandy Farmer from Scottsdale.

VOICES *from the* Newsroom

How do you turn a broadcast script into a text story?

Christina Caron, managing editor
ABC News

Converting a broadcast script into a story involves close collaboration between the writer and producer. Often, it's best for producers or correspondents to write the Web story because they've done the reporting. But if a producer or correspondent doesn't have time to write the text piece or produce Web extras, then the writers at ABCNews.com lend a hand.

The broadcast script provides a skeleton for the text. The writer then fleshes out the script, adding additional quotes and finding information that might have come to light since the script was written (things change so fast, and the Web needs to be as up to date as possible). The writer must also come up with a lead that works in print. A broadcast lead often doesn't work as a text lead because the script relies on imagery or vocal intonation to get a point across. In addition, it's often necessary to expand the SOTs selected for broadcast scripts. Sometimes SOTs are chosen because the character was particularly emotional at the time, and sometimes they're greatly abbreviated or not full sentences. So not only do the visual aspects need to be included in the text if possible (i.e., the character teared up), but the rest of the quote (if applicable) should be included as well.

In general, text pieces for the Web ought to reflect the most recent information at the top of the story to tell readers right away what the story is about and why they ought to continue reading. Broadcast pieces, in particular magazine-style pieces, can spend an entire act leading up to the most recent news available because their emphasis is on narrative storytelling, with several twists and turns.

Writing Web headlines

Newspaper headlines can be pithy and clever because subheads, photos and sidebars provide context. On the Web, however, search engines might not find your story unless the headline summarizes the main point as clearly as possible. **Search engine optimization (SEO)** means writing a headline and using keywords that will make your story appear high in the list of search results. Most Web searchers don't look beyond the first page of results.

Here are ways to optimize your stories so search engines will rank them high in the results:

- Put *keywords* in the headline. *Think like a Web searcher.* If your mother wanted to find your story, what words would she type into Google or Bing?
- Include *proper nouns,* such as names and places.
- Use *simple words that summarize your story.* Don't be clever. Skip puns, poetry and plays on words.
- Put the *important words up front* because search engines weight them more heavily. The more words you put before the keywords, the less effective your headline will be.
- If relevant, put the *geographic location up front.*
- *Spell out words.* Don't abbreviate street, New York, governor and so forth.
- Keep *headlines shorter than 20 words* for best search results.
- Repeat the *headline keywords in the first few paragraphs* to reinforce that the story is about what the headline says.
- Put *keywords in hyperlinks.*
- Look at *Google's Keyword Tool* for keyword ideas: adwords.google.com/select/KeywordToolExternal
- *Link to related stories and items* on your site.

Writing sidebars

One way to break up text is with a **sidebar.** These stand-alone information boxes relate to the subject of the story but don't repeat it. They provide a new perspective or additional information. The extra work you put into writing a sidebar can make your Web story richer, more interesting and more helpful to your readers.

- A sidebar is *not* a list of quotes from the story.
- A sidebar is *not* a quote or an excerpt from the story.
- A sidebar is *not* something that took five minutes to compile.

Types of sidebars Sidebars can take many forms. This list isn't exhaustive.

- Annotated bibliography or list of resources
- Checklist, such as things to take on a winter hike
- Top Ten list
- List of links to related stories
- Fascinating facts
- By the numbers (statistics)
- Tips or expert advice related to the subject of the story
- Definitions
- How-to guides, such as how to prevent mold in your house
- Travel information
- Quiz (a story about stress could include a quiz on "How Do You Handle Stress?")

Tips for writing a great sidebar

- Come up with a fresh idea.
- Write a clever title.
- Include a short, snappy intro.
- Write tight and bright.
- Surprise, inform and/or entertain the reader.
- Add subheads, numbers or bullets to make the information stand out.
- Double-check the accuracy of all information—facts, statistics, quotes, tables and so forth.
- When appropriate, use humor if you can do it well.

This sidebar accompanied a story about vineyards in Arizona's wine country. Notice the subheads, short paragraphs and lively writing.

HOST A WINE-TASTING PARTY

Be the toast of your social circle by inviting people over to sniff, swish and spit. A wine-tasting party is a low-stress way to have a get-together in your home while giving your friends a chance to become wine connoisseurs. These tips will make heels click and glasses clink.

Wine

Serve enough varieties to suit a full range of tastes. Have at least six bottles—three whites and three reds. Start with the lightest white and gradually move up to the heaviest red. This will keep the flavors of a strong wine from overpowering a lighter wine.

Cheese and chocolate

To bring out the flavor notes of the wines, pair each bottle with a cheese or chocolate.

Bread

Put out chunks of French bread for guests to nibble on between bottles. This will cleanse their palates and prepare them for the next wine. Drinking water in between tastings helps too.

Pens and index cards

Clearly label each bottle of wine, cheese and chocolate. Give guests pens and index cards so they can make notes about what they taste and pairings they like and dislike. Provide lists of terms and taste descriptions so guests can translate the sensations that tantalize their tongues. The point of the party is to become savvier wine connoisseurs, but if people get too tipsy, have designated drivers.

—LYNH BUI

Blogging

Blogging gives you another way to communicate with your audience. Some of your followers might provide useful information and even become sources. In addition, writing on a regular basis makes you a better writer and editor. You'll also gain practice in finding and linking to reliable online sources.

Writing great blog posts

Mindy McAdams, an online journalism professor at the University of Florida, recommends these ways to keep your writing fresh and sharp:

- *Have something to say*—and say it well.
- *Write short sentences and short posts* so your blog is quick and easy to read.
- *Read other blogs.* The more you look at other blogs, the better your own blog will be.
- *Use an RSS reader,* such as Google Reader, to subscribe to other blogs. This is more efficient than bookmarking them.
- *Include at least one link* to another blog or website. The blogosphere is all about *connecting*. Your links to other blogs (and your thoughtful comments on those blogs) will increase your visibility as others link to your posts.
- *Write good link text.*
- *Use keywords in the headline and text* of every post.
- *Don't steal other people's text.* If you like someone's post, quote a brief excerpt and link to it.
- *Include images* with photo credits and interesting, informative captions.
- *Run a spell-checker and proofread* before you click PUBLISH.

RULE OF THUMB

If you're blogging for a news outlet, check your company's policy about issues like conflict of interest and expressing your opinion.

Blogging will help improve your research skills. To write informative posts, you need to research your subject thoroughly.

FINDING OTHER BLOGS

Google's Blog Search blogsearch.google.com/ points to the latest buzz on any keyword or topic.

Technorati technorati.com/ indexes blogs by topic, allowing you to find, for example, blogs dedicated to politics, technology or sports. It also lists the most popular terms people are blogging about and features a Top 100 list.

IceRocket icerocket.com/ is another good place to look up blogs on a particular topic or search for posts by a specific author or within a certain time period.

Promoting your blog

Serena Carpenter, an assistant professor at the Walter Cronkite School of Journalism and Mass Communication, suggests some simple things you can do to reach a wider audience and encourage people to follow your blog:

- *Write timely posts* about things that people need/want to know about. Even better, *break news.*
- *Post regularly,* especially on weekdays, so your followers keep coming back for new or updated content.
- *Allow people to comment* on your blog postings.
- *Comment on other bloggers' posts* related to your topic. This encourages them to comment on and about your blog.
- *Include an About/Contact Me page.*
- *Add your blog URL* to any Web page with your name on it (e.g., LinkedIn, Facebook, Twitter).
- *Promote your posts* on Facebook, MySpace, Twitter, StumbleUpon and other social networking sites.
- *Cross-promote your blog* on sites like Open Salon open.salon.com.

Video blogging

Instead of writing a blog, some journalists keep video blogs, or **vlogs.** By incorporating video footage, audio, still images and a little text, vlogs enrich the blogging experience. You can record video footage with a camcorder, a digital still camera that shoots video or even a cell phone camera. As with a written blog, update your video blog frequently. On some sites, viewers can leave comments under videos.

Links

The ability to link from your story or blog to other websites, stories and blogs sets the Internet apart from other types of media. Make sure your links are relevant to what you've written about. You can also link to relevant audio or video clips—or even embed them in your posts.

Link to specific content Make links as specific as possible. It's more helpful to link to a specific page within a site than to a home page. A link to the home page of CBS News isn't helpful because (1) anyone can find that page without your help and (2) the contents of that page will probably change in a few hours.

Links are more valuable when the linked content is provided by someone with expertise or a unique perspective. The content of some personal Web pages has little value because the author lacks qualifications.

Link text Mindy McAdams points out that links are more valuable when your text describes the content the user will find. The words *Click here* or *This link* don't tell anything about the linked content. Where will you go? You don't know!

This is good link text: *Lyndon gives 10 tips for writing blog posts.* Why is it good? Because the text lets you know what to expect if you click on the link.

Good links According to Columbus (Ohio) Dispatch staffers, a good link should do the following:

- Be trustworthy.
- Be credible.
- Be relevant.
- Be authoritative. Link to a foundation, government agency, organization or individual regarded as a leader in the field.
- Deal with a related subject but in a new or different way.
- Provide background and context.
- Add understanding.
- Broaden content.
- Expand on the topic with information you couldn't fit in a news story.
- Offer tangible information, such as locations or FAQs (frequently asked questions).
- Provide further detail.
- Work. After you publish your post, double-check the link to make sure it works.

Source: From Chip Scanlan, "H Is for Hypertext: What Makes a Good Link," poynter.org, Aug. 6, 2007. Reprinted with permission of The Poynter Institute.

Webcasting

When you broadcast live video or audio on the Internet, you're webcasting. During breaking news or special events, live webcasts distribute information quickly to an Internet audience. Unlike covering a live event on television, which can require heavy planning and lots of staff, webcasting can be set up by just one person in a matter of minutes.

Types of webcasting

Live webcasts come in many forms. Some are produced with graphics, video and anchors, much like TV newscasts. Often, these webcasts are an actual simulcast of live TV and radio programs. In other instances, webcasts are produced like TV and radio programs, but they're prepared exclusively for the Internet.

A second type of webcasting distributes raw audio or video without any production. These webcasts are often more popular than produced webcasts because they offer the audience a perspective not regularly seen on TV. They also allow the audience to connect directly with breaking news or special events because they provide a raw look without editing or anchor narration.

Because webcasting is live, viewers must be in front of their computers to watch. The Internet thrives on on-demand content, so successful webcasts are either archived for later viewing after their initial airing or transcribed into Web stories for later reading and searching.

Webcasting tips

If you're webcasting a planned event, take the time to test your audio, video and lighting equipment ahead of time. Although you can webcast with inexpensive equipment, use the best microphone and video camera available.

During the webcast, stay focused. It's easy to lose concentration when you're covering breaking news or a live event. Make sure you're not too close or too far from the microphone. Monitor the audio to ensure high quality. Put the camera on a tripod, and use a good lighting kit. If the quality is poor, viewers will tune out.

Web videos

It takes time and talent to create a slick package for the 6 p.m. newscast. Although Web video can be highly produced, much of it is gritty and shaky. Compare David Pogue of The New York Times with Walt Mossberg of The Wall Street Journal. Both are seasoned journalists. Both produce weekly video reviews of products and services. Pogue's carefully edited pieces usually involve several locations, scripts, music, titles, transitions and sometimes other actors. Mossberg, on the other hand, records his reviews at home on a cheap webcam without a script. Other than opening credits with music, closing credits with music and screen shots of products, Mossberg's videos have little or no editing.

Mossberg's fans accept his less polished reviews not only because he has expertise and experience but also because Web viewers are tolerant. They accept varying levels of quality, including video shot with cell phones. Web viewers crave authenticity, such as breaking news or a look behind the scenes.

Raw video for breaking news Viewers also don't seem to mind sacrificing slick productions for an unedited look at breaking news. News websites like washingtonpost.com run unedited footage from The Associated Press and other sources.

No reporter track Some powerful online stories rely only on visuals and sound. No reporter track. To pull this off, you must plan carefully:

- Focus. Think about the structure. Storyboard.
- Collect plenty of sound so you can create a coherent narrative. You can't use your own words to fill in the holes.
- Make observations instead of asking questions—"Wow, what a mess!" instead of "How much did the fire damage your house?"
- Talk to people in different locations. Record while they're doing something.
- If you have time, conduct a formal interview in a quiet spot.

Audio slideshows

In most local TV newsrooms, reporters and producers don't usually put together audio slideshows for the Web. Photos with audio are much more common on larger network sites and newspaper sites.

You'll find excellent audio slideshows in The New York Times' award-winning multimedia series called "One in 8 Million." Each audio slideshow features one of New York City's 8 million residents. As you watch, you're sometimes not even aware the photos aren't moving because the audio works so well with the pictures.

MEDIASTORM

A master of multimedia storytelling on the Web is Brian Storm, the founder of MediaStorm mediastorm.org. MediaStorm productions incorporate as many different types of communication as needed to convey a message:

- Audio (music, natural sound, narration, sound bites)
- Words
- Visuals (video, still photography)
- Maps (still and animated)

MediaStorm productions are unpredictable. There's no formula. They've been compared to magazine articles that move, books that talk and a combination of documentary photojournalism and National Public Radio.

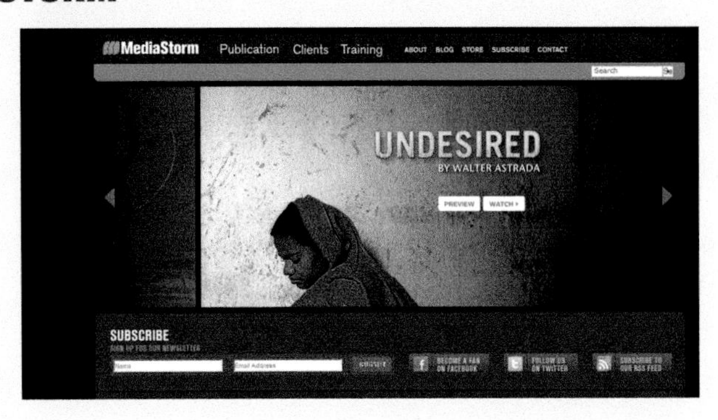

Whether you're working with still pictures or video, always keep in mind that you're a storyteller.

Shooting a 1:30 audio slideshow Many of the principles that apply to shooting good video also apply to shooting still photos for an audio slideshow.

- Work the situation. Shoot lots of images—wide, medium, tight, details, from up, from down.
- Capture the moment. Never ask anyone to move or pose. Never rearrange objects.
- Show people doing something.
- Pay attention to emotion, lighting and composition.

Editing and producing a 1:30 audio slideshow

Some people lay down the audio track first because they find it easier to match the photos to the sound. Other people edit the photos first. That way they have an idea how the sound needs to flow so they know what audio to leave in and what to take out. Either way, save the original audio files in case you need to go back later and make changes.

Make sure you have enough strong images to match the audio. You face a problem if you have great photos of a chef preparing cheesecake, but all she talks about in the interview is filet mignon.

- Select your best 15 to 20 photos. Make sure they tell a story.
- Include a strong opening or establishing shot, a strong closing shot and lots of details.
- Edit tightly. Avoid redundancy.
- Shorten long filenames. Make sure they're lowercase. Don't include spaces or weird characters, which can cause problems with some software programs.
- Save photos as JPGs with a resolution of 72 pixels per inch (ppi). This is a good habit to develop when prepping photos for the Web.
- If necessary, crop and adjust the photos.
- Don't erase anything from a photo.
- Don't add anything to a photo.

Podcasting

The word *podcast* has several meanings. The *pod* comes from the iPod—Apple's brand name for the portable music device no doubt plugged into your ear as you read this. The *cast* comes from the word *broadcast,* only instead of being distributed over the airwaves, a podcast comes to the listener via the Internet.

Content versus creation The word *podcasting* can be confusing, as Mark Briggs points out in "Journalism Next," because it "can mean both the content and the method of delivery." Thus, you might have a selection of favorite podcasts saved on your iPod to listen to in the car. In this case, it's about content. You could also create your own series of programs and distribute them on the Internet. In this case, you'd be podcasting. "The Digital Journalist's Handbook," by Mark S. Luckie, defines a podcast as "an audio or video series distributed over the Internet for playback on a computer or portable audio player."

Podcasting traditionally refers to audio only. Yes, you can create a program on the Internet using video, which is referred to as a *vodcast*. But that word hasn't caught on as quickly, and sometimes podcast has come to mean both.

Permanence Whether they're audio or video files, podcasts can be downloaded to iPods, MP3 players, iPads, cell phones or computers. Unlike a radio program, which disappears after it's aired, podcasts can have an eternal shelf life. You can download and listen to them anytime, anywhere.

You can subscribe to regular podcasts on iTunes or other websites that host podcasts. Some podcasts are radio programs aired earlier in the day, such as NPR's "Fresh Air" interview program hosted by Terry Gross. Other podcasts are created just for the Internet.

Often, a podcast sounds exactly like a radio news or public affairs program. That's because it's built around sound, and the medium is driven by audio, not video.

Podcasting tips

The three keys to a successful podcast mirror the elements that make a radio program listenable and that build a loyal audience.

- Compelling subject matter. Just as with any type of news medium, the topic has to be interesting.
- Quality audio recordings. This includes both the interview (sound bites) and the sound in the natural environment (nat sound).
- Clean, crisp writing delivered with a credible voice.

Dueling Web Identities

When stations are trying to reach their audience, the first thing they have to do is figure out who their viewers and readers are.

KPHO, the CBS affiliate in Phoenix, serves a local audience. The station wants its viewers and readers to know it's on top of local news. It focuses on hyperlocal stories so people know what's happening down the street or around the corner.

It's a different story for a major website like CNN.com. Its community is the United States and the world. CNN tries to make sure its global audience finds interesting stories about communities not only across the country but also around the world. CNN can't be as hyperlocal as local television websites like KPHO, but it can try to inform its readers about news worldwide.

Both websites are important. One is no better than the other. They offer different types of news stories to different audiences. The Web enables viewers and readers to stay tuned into what's happening in their neighborhood as well as around the world.

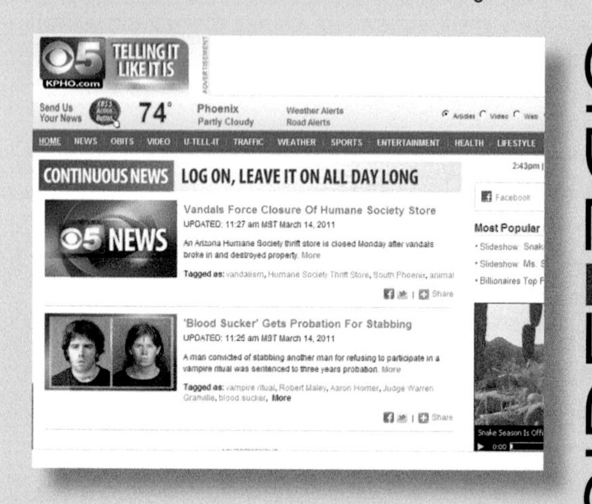

SIDE BY SIDE

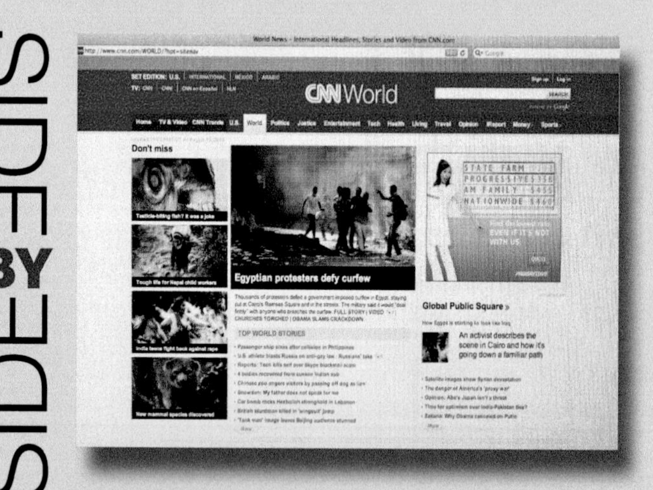

Building Community

Websites have become an integral part of news operations. Years ago, when the Internet was beginning to grow, many stations only posted videos from their newscast online. But they learned that viewers wanted something different, so they had to figure out how to augment the newscast or provide something that would stand on its own. In other words, give viewers a reason to go online to continue the story.

Supplemental information

Successful stations view the Internet not as competition but as another tool to engage viewers with supplemental information that can't be aired because of time constraints—everything from streaming live news to posting unedited video interviews. When reporters put news packages together, they can't fit everything into a minute or a minute and a half. A lot of times that means interesting interviews are never aired. But with the Internet, reporters can put several minutes of the interview online. If viewers wants to hear more from the governor or a business leader, for example, they can watch the complete interview online. These interviews add depth to the story.

At the end of a broadcast piece, the reporter or anchor should tell viewers to go to the Internet for more of the interview. Just saying you have "more information" doesn't work. Tease with words like this: "Go to our website to hear more from the governor about her next goal for curbing illegal immigration along the border. She'll talk more about the controversial virtual fence."

Additional depth can also come in the form of graphics. Let's say you're doing a story on prison overcrowding. You might have come across interesting information about the prison population, such as the number of repeat offenders and violent criminals. You don't have time for this detailed information in the newscast, but it adds depth and information to the online story.

Traffic and weather Another way to build viewership is by providing up-to-the-second information on traffic and weather, which you don't always have time to do on-air. Viewers can program their own "newscast" by picking *what* they want and *when* they want it. Weather is important, so why not make it available every minute of the day? Some stations even have a "bus stop" forecast, so you know whether to wear a heavy coat or short sleeves.

Viewer-generated content

Not only can you use the Internet to deliver more information, but you can also foster loyalty by encouraging viewers to become an active part of your community, not just a bystander. Let them upload videos and photographs. Encourage them to post comments to be read on-air.

Hear Me Out

Is new economic plan right for Arizona?
HEAR ME OUT: Some say Arizona Governor Jan Brewer's new economic development plan is just what the state needs, while others disagree. Whose side are you on?

Should AZ restrict firearm magazines?
HEAR ME OUT: Some say Arizona should restrict large-capacity firearm magazines after the Tucson shooting, while others say that won't help. Whose side are you on?

Should AZ's education funding get cut?
HEAR ME OUT: Some say cutting the education funding in Arizona should not be an option, while some say it has to be done in midst of a budget crisis. Whose side are you on?

ABC15.com in Phoenix has a weekly segment called "Hear Me Out," where it presents a hot issue along with two opposing sides and invites readers to comment.

Many stations conduct online polls that give people a chance to sound off by voting and writing comments about a particular topic. Often these comments are mentioned on the air. CNN brings viewers on-air through online comments, whether they're using Facebook, Twitter or the comments page. Viewers become part of the coverage.

Some of the most popular spots on the Internet are weather photos uploaded by viewers. They get a kick out of seeing what's happening in their neighborhood.

Some stations devote sections to high school sports where viewers can post videos or photos of local games and, therefore, take some ownership. This shows viewers you're interested in what's going on in your own backyard. Although you might not have reporters or photographers at the game, this open invitation helps build community. You've created a gathering place.

Community is built in both directions. The station delivers content that viewers find interesting, and the community uploads information and feels a part of something.

Legal STREET SMARTS

Contributed by Daniel C. Barr, Partner, Perkins Coie LLP, and Faculty Associate, Walter Cronkite School of Journalism and Mass Communication

CHAPTER 11

> *I am dumbfounded that there hasn't been a crackdown with the libel and slander laws on some of these would-be writers and reporters on the Internet.*
>
> —WALTER CRONKITE

CHAPTER OUTLINE

Know Your Boundaries

Posted signs shouldn't be ignored.

Capturing video of children on a playground will likely require school permission if you're on school property.

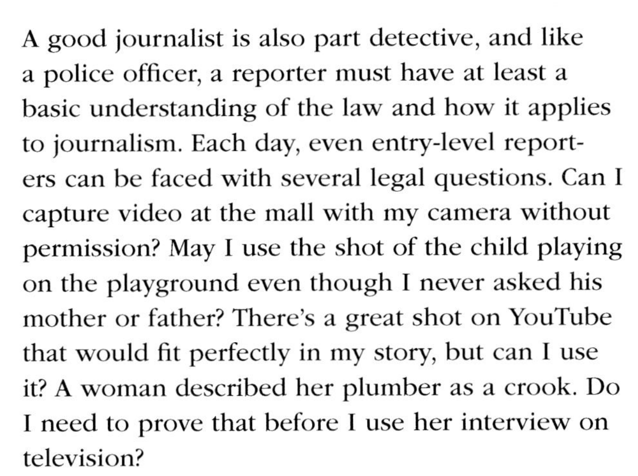

A good journalist is also part detective, and like a police officer, a reporter must have at least a basic understanding of the law and how it applies to journalism. Each day, even entry-level reporters can be faced with several legal questions. Can I capture video at the mall with my camera without permission? May I use the shot of the child playing on the playground even though I never asked his mother or father? There's a great shot on YouTube that would fit perfectly in my story, but can I use it? A woman described her plumber as a crook. Do I need to prove that before I use her interview on television?

Just because you may not have a lot of experience doesn't excuse you from responsible, legal journalism. In this chapter, we'll discuss some of the basic concepts that will help you identify and avoid common legal pitfalls for journalists.

Trespass

Generally, trespass is an unauthorized entry onto private property. Just as you would not walk into someone's home, fenced backyard or nonpublic areas of an office without permission in your private life, you may not do so under the guise of newsgathering. We'll talk about this in more detail when we discuss intrusion. For instance, you cannot walk uninvited into the backyard of a famous athlete to see who is attending his Saturday evening cookout just because some of your readers or viewers would be interested in knowing who was there.

Can I use the shot?

As a general rule, you may capture video or photograph anything and anyone in a public area. No one has any reasonable expectation of privacy to anything he or she does in a public place, and you do not need permission or a signed release from him or her.

For example, the owners of a restaurant or shopping mall can restrict or prohibit camera use because those areas are private property. Likewise, school officials can restrict or prohibit photographs of children on school property because access to school property is often restricted during school hours. However, those officials can't prevent you from capturing video of children on an outdoor playground if you can easily see them while standing on *public* property. The degree of someone's reasonable expectation of privacy on private property is specific to each situation.

You may also photograph a person who is located inside a private home if he or she can be seen from a public area. For example, if someone is standing by the window inside his or her home and can be seen from the street or sidewalk, he or she cannot claim that you invaded his privacy. However, if the person inside the private residence can only be seen by peering inside the window or entering private property, taking a photo of that person could be considered an invasion of privacy. This same principle applies to the use of hidden cameras.

JUST BECAUSE YOU'RE A JOURNALIST DOESN'T MEAN YOU CAN BREAK THE LAW!

The First Amendment does not give reporters the right to violate laws such as trespass, privacy or contract in order to get a story. Almost 40 years ago, the U.S. Supreme Court stated in Branzburg v. Hayes, 408 U.S. 665, 691–92 (1972):

It would be frivolous to assert . . . that the First Amendment, in the interest of securing news or otherwise, confers a license on either the reporter or his news sources to violate valid criminal laws. Although stealing documents or private wiretapping could provide newsworthy information, neither reporter nor source is immune from conviction for such conduct, whatever the impact on the flow of news. . . . The Amendment does not reach so far as to override the interest of the public in ensuring that neither reporter nor source is invading the rights of other citizens through reprehensible conduct forbidden to all other persons.

Make sure you have your supervisor's permission before promising a source confidentiality.

Use of confidential sources

The use of confidential sources, ranging from unattributed quotes to deep background, is a necessary tool of reporting. For more information see Chapter 5, "Interviewing." But a reporter's promise of confidentiality to a source may create a contract, which may give rise to an action for breach of contract if the reporter reveals the source's identity.

In Cohen v. Cowles Media Co., 501 U.S. 663 (1991), a political consultant named Dan Cohen offered documents relating to a candidate in an upcoming election to reporters on the condition that those reporters keep Cohen's identity confidential. Despite the reporters' promises, their newspapers identified Cohen as the source of the documents. On the day the articles appeared, Cohen was fired.

Cohen sued for breach of contract arising from the reporters' failure to keep his promise of confidentiality and won a damage award of $200,000. The U.S. Supreme Court upheld the verdict.

The lesson? Reporters should not promise confidentiality without the permission of an editor and should, when doing so, make sure the source clearly understands what is and is not being promised. Moreover, any promise of confidentiality should be recorded on tape or in writing. And for the source's protection, the confidentiality agreement should be kept in a secure place.

> "Use of confidential sources isn't something taken lightly. All we have in this business is our word, and once you've violated that trust, it's impossible to get it back. Using confidential sources should be done in conjunction with your editors and management, as the company is also on the line."
>
> —ISMAEL ESTRADA, PRODUCER, CNN

Copyright in the Digital Age

A **copyright** is a grant of ownership to authors of certain types of literary and artistic works. Under copyright law, no one but the owner can copy, publish and sell the copyrighted work for a limited amount of time. Copyright protection extends only to the expression of an idea or concept, not to the idea itself. For instance, a story, song or poem about religion, politics or science would be protected, but not the religious, political or scientific idea. Likewise, facts are not protected by copyright, so an article or broadcast story about a news or sporting event is protected, but not the facts about those events. Copyright laws are relevant to journalists in several ways:

Copyright ownership

The author of the work owns the copyright. In many cases, the author will be the person who created the work. However, when the work is **made for hire,** the employer is considered to be the author and the owner of the copyright.

A work is made for hire if it is (1) prepared by an employee within the scope of his or her employment or (2) specially ordered or commissioned for use as a contribution to a collective work. Freelance journalists usually own the copyright to their work, and the media entity they sell it to holds only contractual rights to it. But freelancers transfer the copyright to the media entity if (1) the work was specially ordered by the media entity, (2) the work was created as a contribution to one of the types of works listed in the copyright statute and (3) the parties agreed in writing that the work would be made for hire.

Infringement

You infringe a copyright if you reproduce, adopt, distribute, publicly perform or publicly display a protected work. You need not copy the entire work to infringe a copyright. A substantial paraphrase or even a small portion can also be considered an infringement if the portion is qualitatively substantial. For example, unauthorized use of even the first few notes of a famous song can constitute copyright infringement.

TABLE **11.1** **Length of Ownership**

Work Created	Copyright
3/1/89–present	A copyright notice, ©, is not necessary to preserve an author's exclusive rights. Almost everything that was originally published online does not need a copyright notice to be protected. However, any work published before March 1, 1989, must have been published with a proper notice.
1/1/78–2/28/89	Life of creator(s) plus 70 years. For works made for hire or anonymous works, copyright protection will last for the shorter of either 95 years from the date of publication or 120 years from the date of creation.
1/1/23–12/31/77	Protected for 95 years from the date of publication if the work was published with a proper copyright notice.
Before 1/1/23	In the public domain. A work in the public domain is no longer owned by anyone and can be used freely without fear of infringement.

Movie reviews fall under fair use.

FAIR USE

Book and film reviews are a classic case of fair use. Here, the reviewer may quote from the copyrighted book or show clips from the copyrighted film, and the purpose is to comment or critique, not to sell. There is no set rule for the number of words or seconds you may use of a copyrighted work to fall under the fair use protection, but it cannot be a substantial amount of the work.

PARODY

In Campbell v. Acuff-Rose Music, 510 U.S. 569 (1994), the U.S. Supreme Court noted the importance of parody as a mechanism for criticism and a means of "shedding light on an earlier work, and, in the process, creating a new one." In Acuff-Rose the rap group 2 Live Crew parodied Roy Orbison's "Oh Pretty Woman" by copying the repeated bass riff and the words of the first line. The Supreme Court held that parody can be a defense even when it is for a commercial purpose and that "a parody must be able to conjure up at least enough of the original to make the object of its critical wit recognizable."

The group 2 Live Crew had to go to court to defend a parody.

Exceptions to the infringement rules: fair use and parody

According to the doctrine of **fair use,** you can use certain material without infringing on the copyright. In the context of a **parody,** you can also use certain copyrighted material. Four factors determine whether use of copyright material is fair use or parody:

1. The purpose and character of the use, including whether you are using the material for commercial or nonprofit educational purposes.
2. The nature of the copyrighted work.
3. The amount and substantiality of the portion used in relationship to the copyrighted work as a whole.
4. The effect of the use on the value of the copyrighted work.

No one of these factors determines whether a work is fair use or parody. All four must be considered.

RULE OF THUMB

You are more likely to run into copyright problems if you copy the most memorable part of the work.

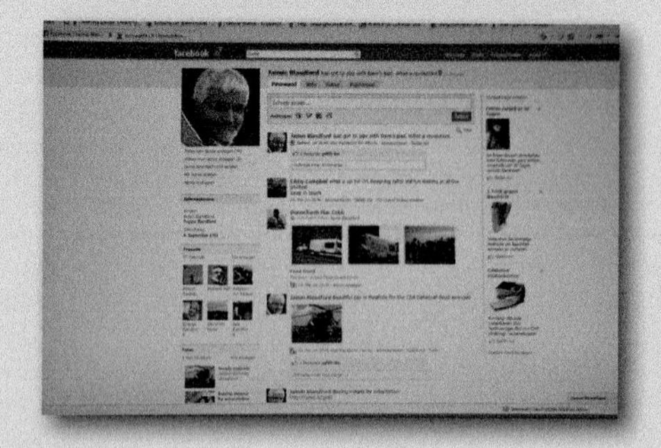

Working a story about a teenager murdered on school property, you are frantically looking for information on deadline. An intern at the station shows you the victim's Facebook page, which is filled with sad comments from friends and touching photos that would be perfect for your story. Trying to find the page yourself, you realize it's marked "private," and you realize the intern only accessed the page because she's "a friend of a friend."

If you can't view the page, would you face legal consequences by using the intern's access to help your story, since the victim intended the page to be private?

FIGURE **11.1** **Common Myths About Copyright**

IT'S ONLINE!

"I found it on the Internet" is not a defense against copyright infringement. Material on the Internet is as copyrightable as any other kind of work. Nor is the lack of a copyright notice a defense. It is not necessary for a work to have an explicit copyright notice for it to be copyrighted. Indeed, you rarely find a copyright notice on material that was originally published on the Web because such notice is not required for anything published after March 1, 1989. Unless you know that the work is in the public domain (for instance, it was published before 1923), assume that it is still under copyright. And the rules are no different for YouTube. If a journalist takes infringing video off YouTube, then the journalist is infringing as well. But if the creator of the video is voluntarily posting it on YouTube, then that person is giving it away to the world for free.

I GAVE THEM CREDIT!

Some people mistakenly believe they can use all or part of a work—say, a photo in a magazine—if they credit the source, the author or the photographer. This is not true. Acknowledging the creator is not protection against a claim of infringement. When in doubt, the most prudent course of action is to seek permission from the copyright owner. Do not use copyrighted work if you cannot find the copyright holder or if you have asked the copyright holder for permission but have not received a response.

QUICK FIX?

Some people believe that they'll be fine if they simply remove copyrighted material from their website when a copyright holder discovers it and complains. But taking down the material—no matter how quickly—is not a defense against infringement.

HYPERLINKS, CUTTING AND PASTING

Hypertext linking to another website does not infringe on the copyrighted material of the linked website, even though the Web page that is called up by the link was created by the original author. But unauthorized cutting and pasting of content from one website to another would constitute copyright infringement.

Defamation: Libel and Slander

You've been assigned to check out an alleged scam. It's fall, and one of your station's viewers has called to complain about a local heating and cooling company that's overcharging for preparing heaters for the cold winter months. During the interview the victim calls the repairman a crook on television, and your copy describes his business as a scam. Now that repairman claims your story has harmed his reputation; he's making a claim of defamation. If he says this harm appeared in written form, he's making a claim of **libel**. If he claims you defamed him in speech—say during a TV or radio broadcast—he's making a claim of **slander**. What would make his claim a valid one in the eyes of the law?

Elements of defamation

- **The repairman claims you made a statement of fact.** A statement of fact is something that can be proved true or false, such as the repairman has seven complaints filed against him with state regulators. It cannot be considered a statement of fact if it is one of the following:
    - *A subjective impression.* Whether someone is funny or rude is a subjective impression and cannot be proved true or false. So is whether a movie is entertaining or boring or whether food is tasty or bland.
    - *Humor and/or satire.* The tenor of the speech negates the impression that the statement could be viewed as factual. If Jon Stewart makes fun of the repairman on "The Daily Show," it's clearly meant to be funny and is not necessarily truthful.
    - *Figurative or hyperbolic language.* Calling someone a "jerk" or a "turkey" is not a statement of fact.
- **He claims the statement is false.** For example, the repairman says that he has never charged anyone for work that was not performed, as you reported in the story, and that you have defamed him by claiming so. However, statements that are true or substantially true cannot be defamatory. A statement is substantially true if it is inaccurate in only some minor detail, such as whether someone received a speeding ticket for driving 90 mph as opposed to 75 mph. The fact is that he violated the speed limit and got a ticket for it.
- **He claims that the statement you made was about him or about a small group he is part of.**

A fair and accurate report of what is said during an official proceeding will protect you from defamation.

For example, the statement "all repairmen are crooks" does not refer to any individual repairman or repairmen. A 1998 libel case brought by a cattle ranchers' organization against talk show host Oprah Winfrey was dismissed because Winfrey's statement about mad cow disease, "It has just stopped me cold from eating another burger," did not specifically identify any of the plaintiffs.

- **He claims that you communicated this defamatory statement to a third party.** For example, he says that you harmed his reputation by describing his business as a "scam" to others in the newsroom. No matter how hurtful or false the statement may be, it is not defamatory if you said it only to the repairman.
- **He claims that this statement lessens his reputation.** In other words, the statement must expose him to disrepute, contempt or ridicule, or raise a question about his honesty. Accusing someone of embezzlement can lessen his or her reputation; falsely stating that someone is a world-class violinist cannot.

PITFALLS

Defamation Trouble Spots

Be careful! A person can also claim defamation under these often-overlooked circumstances:

- If a reporter republishes somebody else's defamatory statement—even if that statement is reported accurately. So, using the repairman example, even though the interviewee called the man a crook, you as the reporter are still accountable for the accuracy of the information. This holds true unless the statement was originally made in an official proceeding or public document. So if you found the words *crook* or *criminal* used in a state regulator's report, you would not be held responsible for the accuracy of the information.
- Letters to the editor are a common source of defamation by republication. But operators of websites such as nytimes.com cannot be held liable for reader comments that are posted in reaction to a story, so long as the website operator does not edit them. As a result, The New York Times, which could be held liable for publishing a defamatory letter to the editor in its newspaper, cannot be held liable if the same letter is posted by a third party on its website.
- If, in trying to provoke a response, an interviewer makes a defamatory claim to a source about someone else, even if the claim is never published. Example: "I have heard that Joe Repairman is a crook. What is your reaction to that?" The rumor about Joe Repairman's scam turns out to be false. Therefore, the reporter's question has defamed the repairman.

Defending yourself from defamation

Your news story cannot be deemed defamatory if it is a summary of official proceedings. A fair and accurate report of what is said in the proceedings of a governmental body such as the legislature, the city council, the school board or a court is immune from a libel or privacy lawsuit.

✗ **DEFAMATORY:** "In interviews outside the courthouse, former customers say the repairman is a crook."

✓ **OK:** "During a hearing this morning the Arizona Registrar of Contractors called the repairman's actions 'criminal' and cited him for violating state law."

Your news story cannot be deemed defamatory if it is a summary of public or court documents. A fair and accurate report of the contents of public documents is allowed, even if the statements contained in those documents turn out to be false.

✗ **DEFAMATORY:** "Initial appearance papers from the court clerk's office reveal the suspect had a vial of cocaine in his possession at the time of his arrest." The initial appearance papers, however, do not include the word "cocaine" but instead say that the suspect had a "vial of an unknown drug." The drug turns out to be a legal drug for which the suspect has a valid prescription.

✓ **OK:** "Initial appearance papers from the court clerk's office reveal the suspect had a vial of cocaine in his possession at the time of his arrest." If the court documents state the presence of cocaine, you, the reporter, are protected, even if it's later proved the suspect didn't have cocaine in his possession at the time of the arrest.

Your news story is less likely to be deemed defamatory if it corners public people. If your story involves public officials or public figures, you are less likely to be accused of defamation. **Public officials** include all elected officials or government employees who have, or appear to have, substantial responsibility for the conduct of government affairs. **Public figures** are individuals who have assumed roles of special prominence in society or who occupy positions of power and influence, such as Oprah Winfrey, Lindsay Lohan or Tiger Woods. Such people are called "pervasive" public figures. A second and more common type of public figure is an individual who voluntarily injected himself into a matter under public scrutiny. These people are called "limited purpose" public figures. In some instances, an individual may involuntarily become a limited purpose public figure through his involvement in a matter of public importance or controversy. Examples might include an architect involved in constructing a controversial publicly funded building, a scientist involved in a public dispute over fluoridation of drinking water or an organized crime enforcer who had turned state's evidence against a crime boss. It can be difficult for such people to claim slander or libel because they are now well-known to the public whether they intended to be a public figure or not.

✗ **DEFAMATORY:** A story about an ugly neighborhood dispute contains one homeowner's false statement that his neighbor, who is neither well-known nor a public official, is an alcoholic.

✓ **OK:** A story about an ugly neighborhood dispute involving the mayor contains one homeowner's false statement that the mayor is an alcoholic. The mayor has been seen intoxicated at several past events, and neither the neighbor nor the reporter believes the statement about the mayor's alcoholism is false.

As a public figure, actress Lindsay Lohan has less protection against defamation.

> "Of course, the best way to avoid becoming the target of a defamation suit is to simply make sure the information you're reporting is true."
>
> —MORGAN LOEW, INVESTIGATIVE REPORTER, KPHO-TV (CBS), PHOENIX

Privacy

The press is overstepping in every direction the obvious bounds of propriety and of decency. . . . [M]odern enterprise and invention have, through invasions upon [man's] privacy, subjected him to mental pain and distress far greater than could be inflicted by mere bodily injury.

So, when do you think those words appeared in the Harvard Law Review?

2010? 1998? 1936? 1890?

The right of privacy was introduced in an 1890 article in the Harvard Law Review. In words that could have been written today, Samuel D. Warren and Louis Brandeis (who later became a U.S. Supreme Court justice) penned the quote above as part of their famous article "The Right to Privacy," 4 Harv. L. Rev. 193 (1890).

We've all seen the images on air or online—the paparazzi following a Hollywood star through an airport or along a public street. There's little expectation of privacy in these very public places. But what if the same star is lounging by the pool in his own backyard? Should a photographer in a neighboring tall building be allowed to snap a photo of him? And does a famous star have any less right to privacy than anyone else? Journalists must have a clear understanding of someone's right to privacy in order to stay out of trouble themselves.

Even celebrities like Paris Hilton are entitled to certain privacy rights.

Like defamation, privacy violations are **torts,** wrongful acts for which an injured person may bring a lawsuit to recover monetary damages. Unlike defamation, which addresses harm to reputation, privacy focuses on a subject's feelings, such as mental anguish and distress, from having been exposed to public view. Public exposure doesn't need to be defamatory to invade someone's privacy.

There are four ways someone could find himself or herself the target of a privacy suit:

1. Publicly disclosing private facts
2. Portraying someone in a false light
3. Intruding on someone's privacy
4. Misappropriating a name or likeness

Public disclosure of private facts

Certain kinds of private facts—medical conditions, family history, financial condition, anything to do with sex—can be of great public interest and, once in the news, tend to become the subject of privacy lawsuits. To prove that your news story publicly disclosed private facts on these or other topics, plaintiffs must show five elements:

1 You made a public disclosure. While defamation requires only that a statement be made to one person who is not the plaintiff, in privacy cases the matter must have been communicated to the public at large.

The Case A reporter investigating an elected official tells the person's neighbor, "I hear your neighbor, Councilman Jones, stole $10,000 in public funds."

> **PUBLIC DISCLOSURE** Because the statement was only said to one person, this does meet the criteria of publicly disclosing private facts.
> **DEFAMATION** Even though the information was only said to one person, if false, the reporter could be the subject of a defamation suit.

2 You disclosed private facts. While prior secrecy about a fact does not matter regarding a defamation claim, it goes to the heart of a privacy claim. If the fact in question is already known or in the public record, it cannot be considered private.

The Case Looking up a 6-year-old divorce file at county court, a reporter discovers that an elected had an addiction to prescription drugs, ich he has since overcome. The journalist revealed the information online.

DEFAMATION If the information is true, the elected official has no basis for a defamation suit.

PUBLIC DISCLOSURE Even though the public was not aware of this information, the elected official has no basis for a public disclosure of private facts suit either, because the information is already in the public record as part of his divorce file.

3 You identified the plaintiff. Readers or viewers must reasonably be able to understand that the offending communication is about the plaintiff. As with defamation, the statement must be about a specific person.

The Case A reporter cites an unidentified source who claims that several players on the local college football team take steroids and other perfomance-enhancing drugs. There are 85 players on the football team.

DEFAMATION Because there are 85 players on the team, a particular player could not claim that the allegation about illegal drug use was about him. The situation might be different if the same allegations were made about a basketball team with only eight or nine members.

PUBLIC DISCLOSURE Same analysis as for defamation.

4 The disclosed fact would be offensive to a reasonable person. The publicized information must be offensive to a person of ordinary sensibilities—not a hypersensitive or unreasonably sensitive person. Also, the disclosed fact must be such that the writer or broadcaster should have realized that it would be offensive. A photograph of a couple kissing in a public place is not offensive to a person of normal sensibilities.

The Case In the course of a story about obesity, a news report captures a picture of two obese men lounging at a public pool.

DEFAMATION Offensiveness is not an element of defamation. The photo accurately shows the two men at the pool, so there are no grounds for a claim of defamation.

PUBLIC DISCLOSURE While perhaps offensive to some, the appearance of obese men in bathing suits would not be considered offensive to someone with ordinary sensibilities.

5 The disclosed fact is not newsworthy. Information of legitimate public interest cannot be considered private.

Many state courts look at three factors to determine whether published facts are newsworthy: (1) the societal value of the facts published, (2) the depth of the article's intrusion into the claimed private matter and (3) the extent to which the party voluntarily achieved a position of public notoriety.

The Case A reporter receives medical documents in the mail that reveal the governor is taking the prescription medication Viagra®.

DEFAMATION The documents are real and the information is correct, so the governor has no basis for a defamation suit.

PUBLIC DISCLOSURE Unlike, say, information about a bankruptcy or other financial difficulties, the governor could question the societal value of such information becoming public. While the governor achieved a position of public notoriety by running for office, medical information is often considered to be private.

RULE OF THUMB

As a journalist, if you are sued for disclosing private facts, you can't defend yourself by claiming the facts are true as if it were a claim of defamation. It is the *truth of the statement* that makes it damaging.

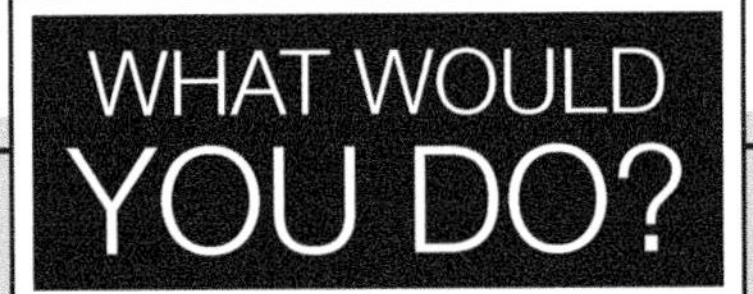

Working on a story about elementary education, you see children playing after school hours on a playground at a nearby school. Standing on the public sidewalk, you capture video of the kids playing. One comes over, and you interview her on camera. She says she's 9 years old.

Hours later, the girl's mother calls the newsroom demanding that you not use her daughter's interview or video, claiming you violated her right to privacy.

How would you respond to the mother's request?

False light

Claims of false light against journalists tend to come up when someone says that you falsely attributed an opinion or statement to him or her—or that you used a photo of someone with a wrong or misleading headline, text or script. Say you use a photo of a spelling bee champion to illustrate a story about victims of child abuse, or you use a file photo of a mother with her child to illustrate a story on a mother abandoning her children. Perhaps your televised report about an increase in AIDS cases clearly shows a woman walking down the street who does not have the disease. All of these subjects might have a false light claim. To prove a false light claim, they would need to show four elements.

1. **You made a public disclosure.** Was the photo printed, posted or put on air?
2. **The disclosure is false or creates a false implication.** As with defamation, a true statement cannot constitute a false light claim. However, certain true facts can create a false implication if a crucial fact is omitted. For instance, you create a false implication if you write, "Joe was drinking at work" but neglected to say that Joe was drinking water.
3. **You identified the plaintiff.** Remember, simply avoiding the use of someone's name doesn't mean she can't be identified. Could a friend or relative figure out who's in the photo or video?
4. **The disclosure would be offensive to a reasonable person.** (See previous discussion regarding public disclosure of private facts regarding what is offensive to a reasonable person.)

Intrusion

Say you're accused of eavesdropping on a private conversation or looking through the windows of someone's house to gather information—or even going through someone's mail. Even if you don't publish a story using that information, the person can make a claim of intrusion. To prove it, however, he or she has to show four elements.

1. You engaged in unauthorized, intentional intrusion or prying into the plaintiff's seclusion.
2. You intruded into a private matter.
3. The intrusion would be offensive to a reasonable person.
4. The intrusion caused anguish or suffering.

Misappropriation of name or likeness

This is also called the "right of publicity." Claims of misappropriation come up most often in the context of advertising, when someone's image is used without his or her permission to promote a product. To prove misappropriation, plaintiffs have to show two elements:

1. **You appropriated the plaintiff's identity or persona.** For example, an advertising agency hired a singer to sing "like Bette Midler" for an automobile commercial after the real Bette Midler rejected an offer to sing her signature song for the commercial.
2. **You used the plaintiff's identity or persona for your benefit.** In the example of the advertising agency using someone to sing like Bette Midler, the agency would get the benefit of having the customer wrongly believe that Bette Midler is endorsing its product while not having to pay Bette Midler to provide the endorsement.

FIGURE **11.2** **Violations of Privacy**

	Public disclosure of private facts	False light	Intrusion	Misappropriation
Elements	• Went public • Disclosed private facts • Identified plaintiff • Offensive to reasonable person • Not newsworthy	• Went public • Made a false implication • Identified plaintiff • Offensive to a reasonable person	• Pried into plaintiff's seclusion • Intruded into a private matter • Offensive to a reasonable person • Caused anguish or suffering	• Appropriated plaintiff's identity or persona • Used it for your benefit
Examples	In a story about a zoning commissioner, you reveal that he attended psychological counseling after getting into repeated disputes with his wife.	In a story describing recent sex crimes against children, you show a picture that identifies one child who was not a victim.	Snooping around a single councilwoman's car, you notice a pregnancy test sticking out of a grocery bag and ask her if she is pregnant.	A phone company puts orange drapery over a map of the United States to show its coverage area, implying it has the endorsement of the artists who created a similar exhibit in Central Park. The company did not seek the artists' endorsement.
			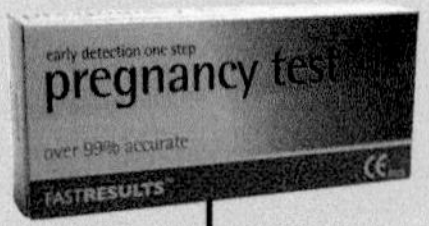	
To avoid trouble	Make sure that the information you are reporting is relevant. The commissioner can argue that his marriage counseling has no effect on his ability to do his job and, therefore, is not newsworthy.	Look at each photo and piece of video closely to make sure words and pictures match. Take time to double-check quotes and attribute information.	Remember you are protected by what you can see or hear while on public property or in areas of public access on private property. Stay within your boundaries, and report only what's newsworthy.	Do not imply that a famous person endorses a product or event when he does not.

PITFALLS

Be aware that misguided zeal to get a story might land you (and your organization) on the wrong side of the law.

- Entering someone's property without his or her permission may also violate criminal trespass laws.

- Accompanying law enforcement executing a search warrant on private property can constitute intrusion. While the search warrant gives law enforcement permission to enter private property, it does not give reporters the right to enter with the police, nor does it give the police the authority to allow reporters to accompany them inside the private property.

- Journalists may be liable for intrusion if they misrepresent themselves to obtain highly sensitive information.

- Although the majority of states allow reporters to record phone conversations with sources without their consent, the following 12 states require the consent of both parties: California, Florida, Hawaii, Illinois, Maryland, Massachusetts, Minnesota, Montana, New Hampshire, Oregon, Pennsylvania and Washington.

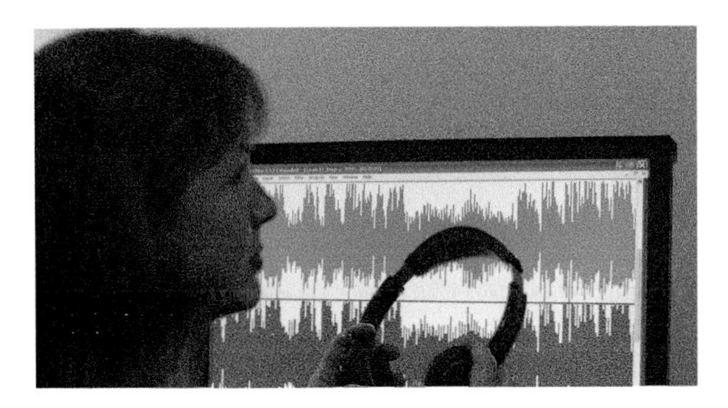

- Photographing an area of an office or a store that is not accessible to the public, customers, clients or patients can constitute intrusion.

Charting Your ETHICAL COURSE

CHAPTER 12

> *Ethics must be reintroduced to public service to restore people's faith in government. Without such faith, democracy cannot flourish.*
>
> —*WALTER CRONKITE*

CHAPTER OUTLINE

Walter Cronkite and Ethical Journalism

"Journalists must be ever skeptical but not cynical, for cynicism deadens the approach a journalist should have to a story."

—WALTER CRONKITE

Jon Stewart's "The Daily Show," "The Colbert Report" and thousands of blogs, YouTube posts and Twitter links use humor and cynicism to help us understand the day's events. Your parents grew up on a different kind of news—fact based, opinion free. The foundation of the news they watched was not cynicism but a healthy dose of skepticism. The careful gathering of facts, packaged into a newscast where objectivity was paramount, became the high standard for each broadcast. Walter Cronkite ended each "CBS Evening News" broadcast with the famous words "And that's the way it is." His closing tag was a benediction on the day's events.

A distraught woman is photographed after receiving shocking news. Whether rushing to cover breaking news or delivering an investigative story, you must never forget that you are affecting individual lives. Build into your reporter's toolbox a solid set of ethical guidelines. The impact of a tragic event or scandal lingers far longer than the single story you produce that day. Your ethical decisions could affect friends, families and loved ones long after you have moved onto your next job in another market.

Cronkite delivered the words with such authority that, coupled with the newscast viewers had just seen, the experience created a powerful meta-world of trust between the anchorman and the viewer. This meta-world is based on the sometimes elusive, even difficult-to-define concept called credibility. Sticking to the objective presentation of facts as opposed to offering opinions enabled the newscast to achieve credibility. The result for Cronkite was that national opinion surveys named him "the most trusted man in the United States."

How did Walter Cronkite earn the audience's trust? It took time and work as he covered the key turning points in recent history—from the Kennedy assassinations to a man walking on the moon to Watergate. With each story, big and small, night after night, year after year, Cronkite held true to the traditional values of journalism. **Values** are the beliefs we hold deep in our hearts, while **ethics** refers to a code that guides our conduct. Journalists have formal professional codes of ethics that are written down, as well as more personal, unwritten codes. We will explore both types in this chapter.

What Is an Ethical Journalist?

U.S. networks (ABC, CBS and NBC) and cable news organizations (CNN, FOX and MSNBC) have formal ethics codes all journalists must follow. Sometimes local television and radio stations have written codes as well. But for the most part, local news directors rely on the ethics codes devised and promoted by three professional journalism organizations. At the end of this chapter, we have reprinted the three formal ethics codes.

Professional journalism organizations

Here's a brief look at the background of the big three professional journalism organizations:

- **SPJ,** or the Society of Professional Journalists: The code applies to print, broadcast and multimedia journalists. SPJ was founded in 1909 as a journalistic fraternity (Sigma Delta Chi) at DePauw University. SPJ's mission states that a free press is the cornerstone of our nation's liberty. spj.org

- **RTDNA,** formerly known as the Radio-Television News Directors Association, now the Radio Television Digital News Association: In an effort to broaden its membership to include online journalists, in October 2009 RTNDA became the Radio Television Digital News Association. The original organization was started in 1946 for managers in broadcast news. Today, RTDNA draws more than 3,000 worldwide members working in electronic news. rtdna.com

- **NPPA,** or the National Press Photographers Association: The NPPA was founded in 1946 in an era when the press was fighting the government over camera access to courtrooms. This organization for news photographers across all media platforms holds yearly regional and national workshops. nppa.org

As online journalism grows, each of these organizations has modified its code to remain relevant for multimedia journalists (MMJs). These professional codes become critical ethical maps for news organizations, but without a strong, deeply personal code held by each individual journalist, they do not matter.

THE C-R-O-N-K-I-T-E CODE OF ETHICS

What codes of ethical conduct do journalists follow? Why? We begin our answers to these questions by thinking about a professional career as a life's journey—a voyage.

Walter Cronkite loved the ocean and spent every August sailing the New England coast. As captain of the ship, he knew how to navigate troubled waters. Armed with a compass, sextant and maps, Cronkite charted his course. Similarly, to guide him in the deadline decisions in the newsroom at CBS, he used his personal code of journalism ethics. Cronkite never wrote down his formal code, but he did offer keen insights on how to be an ethical journalist in his public speeches, his interviews and his autobiography, "A Reporter's Life."

Cronkite was a natural explorer and a journalism pioneer. He was a truly converged journalist, able to work in both print and broadcast—long before that attribute became the rule in the news business. Cronkite earned the respect of his U.S. audience and garnered a global reputation because he followed a personal code of professional ethics.

Cronkite used his own moral compass to chart a correct path in news coverage. His entire career is a model for ethical journalism practices. From studying his professional life, we've come up with eight key ethical points. We use a ship's wheel to illustrate these eight key points of what we call the Cronkite Code of Ethics.

Think of each point on the wheel as a letter standing for one principle of professional ethical conduct. Hold tight to these principles, and when an ethical dilemma strikes during a busy workday, you won't go spinning out of control but will stay rock steady—just like Uncle Walter.

Figure 12.1 **The Eight Key Points of the Cronkite Code of Ethics**

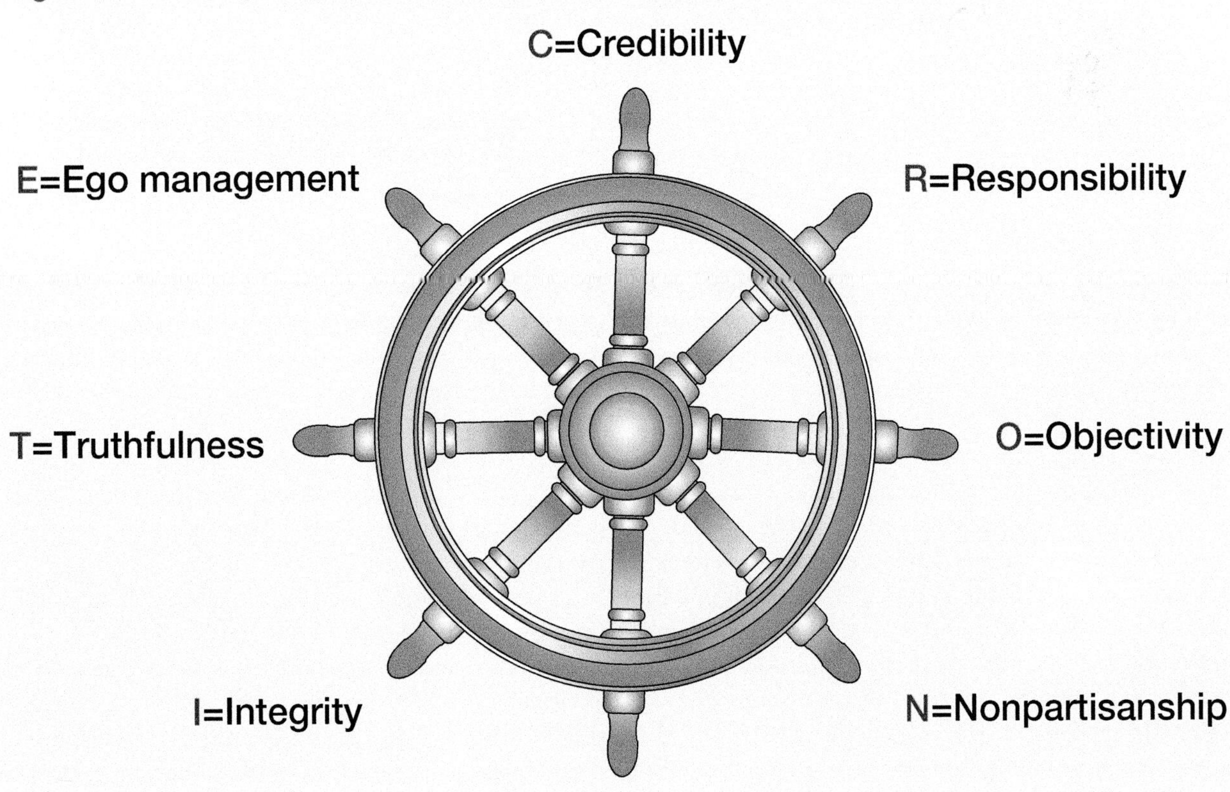

The Cronkite Code: Eight Core Concepts

Discussions of ethics codes usually stir up two types of thoughts: fascination and frustration. The fascination occurs when you discuss various examples and try to figure out if the choices made were correct. An example would be whether to name a 14-year-old charged with first-degree murder or how much bloody video to show from a terrorist attack. The frustration comes because often we want easy answers—right and wrong, clear-cut guidelines. The First Amendment provides for the open expression and practice of journalism not hindered by laws. As a journalist, you must learn how to navigate the sometimes tricky waters of professional life. We've tried to make ethics easy to recall through a code linked directly to each letter in Cronkite's name.

Credibility

In the context of journalism, **credibility** means being believable. A journalist's most priceless possession, credibility is the foundation of one's professional reputation and builds a relationship of trust between you and the audience. Guard it with your life.

Let's look at how journalists gain and maintain credibility, and explore the dire consequences—from being reprimanded to being fired—should they lose it.

How do you gain credibility? You begin to build a reputation the moment you take your first field assignment. In terms of your career, your credibility is on display each time you update a Facebook page or send out a tweet or check in on foursquare.

When your first story is uploaded onto the Web or to a radio Internet channel, the test of your credibility begins. Who's judging? First and always most important, the audience who watches, listens to and reads your stories. In college, your teachers and peers become judge and jury. Your mom will be your harshest but most honest critic. You earn your reputation for credibility one story at a time. As your stories meet with the approval of your audience, peers and professors or bosses, your reputation builds and your credibility grows. Tony Burman, former editor-in-chief of CBC (Canadian Broadcasting Corporation) News, says, "Every news organization has only its credibility and reputation to rely on."

The key to gaining credibility? Fact-based journalism!

Know your facts. Journalists John Maxwell Hamilton and George A. Krimsky urge you to "trade in facts, not emotions. Don't be a believer. Look dispassionately for proof."

Research, double-check and synthesize. Detailed fact collecting gives you the elements you need to craft credible sentences.

Elmer Lower, the ABC News president who hired anchors Peter Jennings, Ted Koppel and Sam Donaldson, wrote two words on the board every time he gave a college guest lecture: "Good Writing." Like Cronkite, Lower believed credible journalism was based on strong, fact-driven writing.

Fine-tune. To achieve credibility as a news writer requires a willingness to fine-tune copy over and over until the deadline forces you to release it. This is akin to the challenge of writing poetry. The poet Robert Frost wrote, "A poem is never finished, only abandoned."

Before you "abandon" your story, make sure it's filled with credible facts. Get used to the idea of a producer asking for more facts, more attribution.

View facts as the building blocks of a story. Brick-solid facts are the building blocks of which broadcast and all formats of news stories are constructed. Too often, journalists are tempted to brush them aside in the rush to create a fancy graphic or perfect audio sequence. As Bill Kovach and Tom Rosenstiel observed in their ethics book "The Elements of Journalism," "The discipline of verification is what separates journalism from entertainment, propaganda, fiction or art."

Fact-checking is critical to the journalist's routine. Unlike traditional newspaper or magazine offices, broadcast newsrooms—especially at local stations—typically do not employ people to verify the facts in each story. This is a reporter's responsibility. Learn to be your own disciplined fact-checker to gain and maintain your credibility.

Preserve your credibility

How do you maintain credibility?

1. **Correct factual mistakes quickly and carefully.** Some mistakes, like spelling errors, may seem minor in broadcast copy. But many an anchor has stumbled when reading copy on-air because of a misspelled word. Other facts, such as confusing Medicare with Medicaid, seriously affect the believability of your story and your media outlet. Your producers will let you know when a mistake is worth a formal correction. Corrections are far more rare on television than in newspapers.
2. **Develop a credible list of sources and mine them.** Sources establish your credibility in two ways: They can provide scoops that help you break a story, and they contribute to the building of your reputation. Because they're such an important part of credibility, it's critical to maintain solid professional relationships with sources. Never pay a source or offer or suggest any favors or compensation. You should, however, express gratitude. This could include occasionally writing a thank-you note or sending a card at holiday time.

How do you lose credibility?

1. **By making mistakes.** This can happen in various ways, sometimes by accident, such as a careless failure to double-check spelling.
2. **By burning a source** or revealing someone by name or supplying some other identifying references after agreeing not to do so. The consequence of burning a source is very serious. The RTDNA code offers this advice: "Confidential sources should be used only when it is clearly in the public interest to gather or convey important information or when a person providing information might be harmed. Journalists should keep all commitments to protect a confidential source."

Guard your credibility as carefully as you do your personal reputation, or run the risk of being reprimanded or fired. Sadly, recent journalism history is full of examples of reporters who lied about their sources and made up quotes and even people. We'll look at some of the more notorious ones, including Jayson Blair and Stephen Glass, in the "T" (for truthfulness) section of the Cronkite Code.

In addition to all its other values, credibility makes good business sense. In the marketplace of ideas where news lives and thrives, creating a credible news product builds reputation and raises ratings. As Scott Baradell and Anh Stack note: "Credibility is essential to mainstream news organizations from a business standpoint. If audiences don't believe they can trust what they're reading—and seeing—it's the equivalent of a broken product. And consumers don't buy broken products for very long."

CREDIBILITY: WHAT THE CODES SAY

RTDNA

Professional electronic journalists should understand that any commitment other than service to the public undermines trust and credibility.

SPJ

Professional integrity is the cornerstone of a journalist's credibility.

CREDIBILITY: WHAT YOUR PEERS SAY

We asked several student journalists at the Cronkite School about credibility. Here's what they had to say:

"Credibility is all a journalist has. Without it, he or she is a sprinter without legs."

—Brian Brennan

"Credibility comes from living your life so honestly and fearlessly that no failure can dishearten you or divert you from the path of integrity."

—Christopher Leone

"Credibility will be established with my readers by being honest, objective and approachable. If they feel they can trust me, they will find that I am a credible journalist."

— Joanne Ingram

"If you have credibility, people not only believe what you say but actually care about what you say."

—LaKeirdra Bronner

VOICES *from the* Newsroom

Missy Shelton-Belote, news director
KSMU–FM (NPR), Springfield, Mo.

Early in my journalism career, I learned the importance of credibility and how journalists build credibility with their sources. I had been covering the Missouri legislature for four or five years for Missouri's public radio stations. During this particular legislative session, the debates in the Missouri House of Representatives were especially partisan and bitter.

One day, I produced a feature story on an intense debate, making sure to include tape cuts of the debate from both Republicans and Democrats. Because the issue wasn't "Republicans on one side, Democrats on the other side," I made sure to report on the nuances of the different perspectives lawmakers brought out during the debate.

The day after my story aired, the House Speaker asked to see me. I was really concerned that I had made a mistake in my story or that I had unintentionally misrepresented someone's position in the way I told my story.

The House speaker, a Republican, and I sat down on one of the cushy benches in the side gallery. She said, "My husband heard your story on the radio this morning." My stomach turned as I waited for what was coming next. After all, when someone wants to talk to a reporter about a story, it's usually because that person is not happy with your coverage. She said, "My husband told me it was by far the best coverage of our debate, so I went online and listened to your story. You're the only one who got it right. You did an excellent job of getting at the complex nature of this issue and including all perspectives. I'm not complimenting you because I thought you favored Republicans in your story. I'm happy about your story because you were fair to everyone."

It was a good lesson to me about the importance of digging into a story and trusting my listeners to follow me as I explain complex issues. In the end, that kind of reporting earns you the respect of the people you cover and the public.

Responsibility

> "They (news people) should not try to write the stories, present the stories in print or in broadcast, on the basis of some preconceived notion of what that story should be or what angle should be played up or not played up on the basis of some political doctrine, economic doctrine, religious doctrine or any other doctrine."
>
> —WALTER CRONKITE

Let's begin with the bottom line. Responsibility is taking ownership of your actions. Journalists shoulder a responsibility *to do* and a responsibility *to be*. The responsibility of the reporter is to do news work—to interview, write, shoot, edit, produce and upload/broadcast—all within the framework of fairness. Doing so helps build a reputation of being a bias-free, responsible journalist. *To be* a responsible, unbiased reporter means developing the attitude of what we call a free agent.

Agency is a concept based on the idea of having the freedom to choose and to act—principles guaranteed by our First Amendment. Free agent journalists know where their loyalties belong—with the public.

While working as a free agent delivering on deadline, you're responsible for being loyal to those who write your paycheck—the station or website where you work.

One group you never have to be responsible to is advertisers. That's the sales department's job. Think of a literal firewall between your sphere of news reporting and that of the sales department.

For example, someone from the station's sales department might ask you as a reporter to shoot a feature story on a new bank that has a high-tech cash machine with extra security features. But this same bank also bought thousands of dollars in advertising from the station. It would not be ethically responsible to do this story because of the influence of the sales department—that is, the firewall would have been breached.

Your news director or manager will handle any conflicts that arise. As the SPJ code states, "Distinguish news from advertising and shun hybrids that blur the lines between the two." The RTNDA code echoes the commandment: "Recognize that sponsorship of the news will not be used in any way to determine, restrict, or manipulate content. Refuse to allow the interests of ownership or management to influence news judgment and content inappropriately." Pressure from advertisers might tempt you to compromise your personal ethics. Don't give in. Never change a story angle or drop a sound bite at the request of an advertiser.

WHAT WOULD YOU DO?

Reporters sometimes feel a churning internal conflict stirred up by competing loyalties—to the station, their audience and themselves. For example, you might be a news producer who has two young boys, ages 8 and 11. One of your reporters has an exclusive story that police have arrested a 12-year-old boy for brutally beating his uncle with a baseball bat after years of sexual abuse. Your reporter was given the name of the arrested boy in an interview with a detective.

You know your loyalty to the station is to be competitive, since this is an exclusive story. And in all likelihood, since the detective gave your reporter the name, it won't be long before other stations will have it too. For some, the ethically responsible thing to do is to report the full facts of the case, including the accused boy's name. But since you are a father with two boys of your own and know the permanent damage that could occur once the boy's name is made public, you feel some internal conflicts.

When loyalties conflict, an ethical issue is often at the root. To sort through loyalties, use a simple three-part formula developed by journalism educators Lee Wilkins and Philip Patterson for their textbook "Media Ethics: Issues and Cases." They adapted their formula from Harvard sociologist Sissela Bok.

Consult your conscience. For example, your conscience says, "A boy 12 years old is so young. What if the police are wrong? If we run this story, will it ruin this boy's reputation for life?"

Look for alternatives. For example, consider telling the viewers that you have the name but are choosing, for now, not to release it. Or you can decide to use only his first name. Or you might use only his initials. With the newsroom staff you can think of many other options as well.

Create a public dialogue about the decision. Share what you choose to do and *why* with the audience. After you broadcast the arrest story, follow it with a second story in the same newscast explaining the decision-making process. Ask viewers to offer comments and feedback on the station's website.

RESPONSIBILITY: WHAT THE CODES SAY

RTDNA

- Recognize that sponsorship of the news will not be used in any way to determine, restrict, or manipulate content.
- Refuse to allow the interests of ownership or management to influence news judgment and content inappropriately.

NPAA

As photojournalists, we have the responsibility to document society and preserve its history through images.

RESPONSIBILITY: WHAT YOUR PEERS SAY

We asked several student journalists at the Cronkite School about responsibility. Here's what they had to say:

> "*Responsibility is the act of informing citizens completely of all news regardless of personal bias, prejudice or subject unpopularity.*"
>
> —Brittny Goodsell

> "*Responsibility is to live so honestly and fearlessly that no outward force or personal failure can move you to act without anything but respect for yourself and your fellow man.*"
>
> —Christopher Leone

> "*Responsibility is to be willing to be held accountable for the news you report.*"
>
> —LaKeidra Bronner

VOICES from the Newsroom

David Louie, reporter
KGO-TV (ABC), San Francisco

Many of us who were among the first minorities to get hired in the newsrooms of the late 1960s and early 1970s struggled with an issue that continues today. Were we journalists who were minorities, or were we minority journalists?

Racially charged riots broke out in the Cleveland neighborhood of Glenville in 1968. Still in college, I was hired as a reporter trainee at the NBC News Bureau in Cleveland that summer. Mayor Carl Stokes had banned white police officers and white reporters from the area to defuse the tension. With few nonwhite reporters on staff, this Chinese-American was sent to help cover the story. At a police roadblock, the black news photographer and I were stopped. An officer took a look at me. He wasn't sure what to do. I wasn't white, but I wasn't black either. Was the mayor's intent to grant access only to blacks?

Should I argue that I'm not white? Or do I protest the mayor's order as discriminatory? I chose the first option on the basis that it was more important to cover the story than to be shut out. As a surrogate for the public, my ethical responsibility was to the audience. It was better for them to know what was happening than to be uninformed. Ultimately, a commanding officer let me through the barricade. This incident taught me that each of us must stand up as individuals for the principle of journalistic responsibility as the situation arises.

Anchorman Walter Cronkite conducts an interview during a reporting trip to South Vietnam in 1968. Notice the size of the large film camera. The cord is attached to the sound man, who is recording audio.

Objectivity

> "Objective journalism and an opinion column are about as similar as the Bible and Playboy magazine."
>
> —WALTER CRONKITE

Objectivity begins with accuracy—the careful collecting of facts by the reporter or the camera's chip. Subjectivity is opinion. Avoid it unless you clearly label your observations as commentary. You're not hired to be a commentator. Tuck your opinion in your pocket, and let your reporting of facts allow viewers to form their own opinions. Be the catalyst that helps them—through sound bites and visual images—to form their own ideas.

Walter Cronkite rarely offered commentary, but he once chose to do so as part of his Vietnam War coverage. In 1968 he took a documentary crew to the battlefields. During a later broadcast on the Tet Offensive, he offered a clearly labeled personal opinion, which some historians believe influenced Lyndon B. Johnson not to run for re-election as president:

> To say that we are closer to victory today is to believe, in the face of the evidence, the optimists who have been wrong in the past. . . . It is increasingly clear to this reporter that the only rational way out then will be to negotiate, not as victors, but as an honorable people who lived up to their pledge to defend democracy and did the best they could.[1]

Historian Irving Fang believes that when Cronkite returned from Vietnam "to report the United States was not winning the war, there was a turning point in national confidence." However, as noted, this was a very rare occurrence for Cronkite, who usually stuck to reportable facts.

[1]You can see Walter Cronkite's rare editorial criticizing the U.S. military's escalation in Vietnam on YouTube: youtube.com/watch?v=zDNJL0mTHWI

Today, cable news is full of a mixture of fact-driven news and loudly shouted opinions. So much so that the audience has a hard time discerning the difference. Can you offer your opinion and still be an objective journalist? Traditional journalists set personal opinion aside. Except for Vietnam, Cronkite did the same, adhering exactly to the "CBS Evening News" standards and his own code of ethics.

Objectivity relates not only to word choice but also to the images selected to match them. Visuals are a form of facts equal in power to written words and sound bites. Thus, the camera can deceive because of the way a photographer, editor or producer frames a shot. Simple photo-editing techniques found on most laptops can also be used to distort images.

Photojournalists who are true professionals belong to the National Press Photographers Association (NPPA). As their code cautions, "Editing should maintain the integrity of the photographic images' content and context. Do not manipulate images or add or alter sound in any way that can mislead viewers or misrepresent subjects."

Similarly, the SPJ code admonishes reporters and editors to "never distort the content of news photos or video."

Assuming you've accurately captured the visual facts of a story, the prime focus becomes the written word. What do you write? The truth, not opinion! As newspaper editor Lester Market wrote in 1946, "What you *see* is news, what you *know* is background and what you *feel* is opinion."

The truth of any story is built on the bedrock of objectivity. As Cronkite journalism student Christopher Hunt wrote, "Our perception and interpretation of a fact can dramatically affect what we think the 'truth' of a story truly is."

To be objective, you first need to be aware of your own potential for bias. Each reporter brings to every story experiences that can influence the interpretation of the facts and events. What are yours?

Let's say you grew up in a home with parents who were card-carrying members of the Sierra Club. Spending many family weekends in the woods hiking and bird-watching couldn't help but bias you toward environmental protection. This bias could in turn cloud your judgment against seeing the

A cartoonist pokes fun at the extreme viewpoints sometimes seen on cable TV news channels.

perspective of big business. Or you might have grown up in a family that opposed same-sex marriage on religious grounds. Being aware of your own background and current beliefs allows you to create an internal bias check on stories you cover. (Chapter 13, on diversity, looks further into this issue of personal bias.) Luckily, newsrooms have a set of checks and balances that help guard against bias. This is part of the editorial process. In a typical TV newsroom a producer or in some markets a news director will read your copy to make sure it's objective.

This does not mean that when you enter the newsroom, you leave at the door the fact that you're a human being with unique beliefs. The best newsroom will be composed of a multitude of voices with different backgrounds and perspectives on subjects from politics to religion, and these will most likely help create balanced coverage.

As author and journalist Elmer Davis notes, objectivity is not easy: The "good news broadcaster must walk a tightrope—on one side the false objectivity that takes everything at face value and lets the public be imposed on by the charlatan . . . on the other hand, the 'interpretive' reporting which fails to draw the line between objective and subjective, between a reasonably well-established fact and what the reporter or editor wishes were the facts. To say that is easy, to do it is hard."

RULE OF THUMB

Maintain Objectivity With the BAFT Test

To help maintain objectivity throughout the reporting and producing process, always be willing to use what we call the **BAFT Test.**

The acronym **BAFT** is formed from the first letters of these four key principles of objectivity:

Balanced
Accurate
Fair
True

As you strive for objectivity, ask yourself: Is what I'm writing balanced, accurate, fair and true? To the best of your ability, if you can answer "yes" to these key questions, then you can come as close as one can ever get to being objective.

SIDE BY SIDE

Objectivity

This image is what many Americans saw on live television during the early days of the Iraq War—shots of Iraqi citizens celebrating the collapse of the statue of Saddam Hussein in Firdos Square, pulled down with the help of U.S. Marines.

But in this picture, taken at the same time at a much wider angle, one can see that the crowd at the square was not really so large. An objective journalist would give the full picture of what happened that day—becoming the eyes and ears for the audience.

SIDE BY SIDE

OBJECTIVITY: WHAT THE CODES SAY

RTDNA

- Recognize that service in the public interest creates an obligation to reflect the diversity of the community and guard against oversimplification of issues or events.
- Provide a full range of information to enable the public to make enlightened decisions.

SPJ

Journalists should

- Be honest, fair and courageous in gathering, reporting and interpreting information.
- Tell the story of the diversity and magnitude of the human experience boldly, even when it is unpopular to do so.
- Examine their own cultural values and avoid imposing those values on others.
- Avoid stereotyping by race, gender, age, religion, ethnicity, geography, sexual orientation, disability, physical appearance or social status.
- Support the open exchange of views, even views they find repugnant.
- Give voice to the voiceless; official and unofficial sources of information can be equally valid.

OBJECTIVITY: WHAT YOUR PEERS SAY

"It requires maintaining a distance from the source outside of work in order to stay objective."

—Nick Kosmider

"Objectivity begins with the realization that nobody has a monopoly on the truth and that we all share pieces of the truth in some degree."

—Christopher Leone

"Objectivity allows us to view the world from an outside perspective without getting bogged down in our own thoughts and experiences."

—Kyle Legge

"Objectivity is my ability to see both sides of a situation and to provide a fair assessment of that situation without showing bias."

—Joanne Ingram

"Objectivity is being able to be direct by exhibiting impartial behavior during the entire reporting process. That is, not allowing your religion, race, gender, age or socioeconomic status and thus your personal experiences to influence your reporting."

—Natassja Stanton

Nonpartisanship

"A good deal of my acceptability has been that I have maintained this air of impartiality, which I feel is essential to do this job properly . . . but that doesn't mean I don't have deeply held feelings and thoughts about many major issues of the day. Some of them are conservative, some liberal, and some radical. But I've always held them back."

—WALTER CRONKITE

As a journalist, if you're covering politics or even working closely with those who do, you're bound to form opinions. Still, it is your responsibility to your employer and your audience to remain **nonpartisan,** or neutral. This could be one of the biggest challenges young journalists face, especially because you've grown up watching opinion blurred with news on some cable channels.

Here's what to do. Once you've determined your personal political beliefs and principles (write a list), you must keep your opinions to yourself. No bumper stickers or yard signs—not even a link to a political stand on your Facebook page.

VOICES *from the* Newsroom

Grett O'Connor, regional reporter
RTE-TV News, Cork, Republic of Ireland

When I was 26, I worked as a print journalist at a regional newspaper. The Roman Catholic Church in a particular parish was in poor repair, and a decision was about to be made on whether it was best to renovate it or demolish it and build a new one. I heard about this, thought it was scandalous to demolish such a beautiful building and decided to get a comment on the matter from the Irish conservation body An Taisce. They were strongly opposed to demolition, not surprisingly.

I published a piece to this effect, which I now realize must have revealed that this was my own view too. I went along to the well-attended public meeting, where local people were being told by the church committee that demolition was the best option for various reasons. Suddenly, the chairman said that there was somebody in the room who was not welcome there. He named me and asked me to leave. I was embarrassed; there were more than 200 people present. But I did leave.

I learned that there are two sides to every story. The parish needed a bigger church anyway, and it would have been very expensive to preserve the damp and rotting frame of the existing church. I should have put aside my own interest in history and old buildings or at least balanced it with a properly researched opinion from those in favor of demolition.

SIDE BY SIDE

NONPARTISANSHIP: WHAT THE CODES SAY

RTDNA

- Understand that any commitment other than service to the public undermines trust and credibility.
- Gather and report news without fear or favor, and vigorously resist undue influence from any outside forces, including advertisers, sources, story subjects, powerful individuals and special interest groups.
- Resist those who would seek to buy or politically influence news content or who would seek to intimidate those who gather and disseminate the news.
- Determine news content solely through editorial judgment and not as the result of outside influence.

SPJ

- Be vigilant and courageous about holding those with power accountable.
- Act independently. Journalists should be free of obligation to any interest other than the public's right to know.
- Avoid conflicts of interest, real or perceived.
- Remain free of associations and activities that may compromise integrity or damage credibility.

NONPARTISANSHIP: WHAT YOUR PEERS SAY

"Nonpartisanship is the ability to show balance in the political area when covering news regardless of one's political preferences."

—Carie Gladding

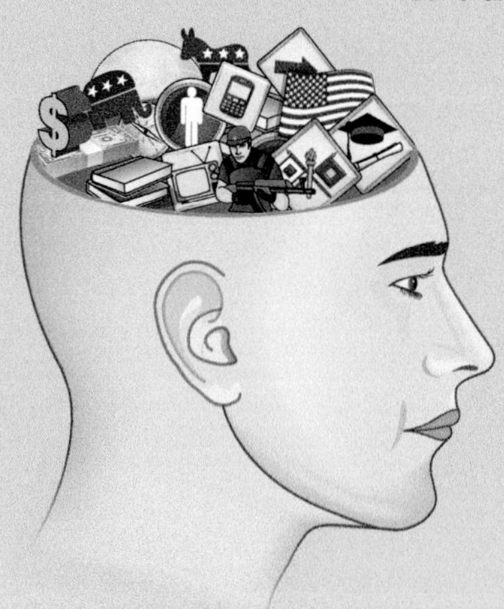

Our minds are full of personal opinions about politics. As a journalist, the challenge is not to let them lead to biased reporting.

Your voice is significant, but keep it silent when it comes to making public your partisan politics. Be discreet at parties. Some journalists don't even tell their spouse whom they're voting for. SPJ advises journalists to "refuse political involvement, public office and service in community organizations if they compromise journalistic integrity." The NPPA code urges you to "avoid political, civic and business involvements or other employment that compromise or give the appearance of compromising one's own journalistic independence."

In an era with so many platforms for ideas, you may be tempted to offer your opinion about a political issue or candidate on a personal Web page or Facebook. This would be a mistake. Your challenge is to remain a neutral conduit. In this spirit, SPJ urges you to "distinguish between advocacy and news reporting," while RTDNA reminds you that you work for the public.

Kindness

The Arizona Republic sent movie columnist Bill Goodykoontz to New York City to interview Walter Cronkite. Goodykoontz described the meeting:

> Sadly it was on Walter's first day back in the office after his wife died. We walked into his spacious office together, and Walter said to me, much to my surprise: "I hear you teach out there at that school they named after me."
>
> "Yes, sir," I said, because he's someone you need to say "Sir" to, I figured.
>
> "What's the name of your class?"
>
> "Media problems."
>
> He slapped me on the shoulder and said, "My God! Can one man handle it?"

Those who knew the man behind the term "most trusted man in America" were impressed with his kindness and sense of humor. Kindness, with a sense of humility, is an important trait to cultivate.

Many people affectionately referred to Walter Cronkite in the later part of his career as "Uncle Walter." As authors, we met him many times and found him to be what you would expect—an intelligent, thoughtful and approachable gentleman. Despite being surrounded by crowds wherever he traveled, he still managed to focus on the individual.

During one of Cronkite's visits to the Cronkite School, a faculty member interviewed him in front of a room of 300 students and members of the public. Later, after shaking more than a hundred hands, Cronkite sat down for a quiet conversation to compliment the teacher on the "great interview conducted." Imagine the satisfaction and thrill of being recognized by a great journalist for the quality of a journalistic skill.

In a professional world demanding snap judgments and straining nerves, kindness might seem an alien quality. But kindness is of great value, especially for clear thinking in breaking news situations.

Kindness is an attitude of professionalism. A good journalist has guts, tenacity and enough grit to tear into a story. Clark Kent hid his true identity underneath his shirt. Similarly, underneath that hard, tough journalistic suit you wear, have a big heart of kindness.

As theologian Albert Schweitzer said, "Ethics, too, are nothing but reverence for life."

Be kind to your audience. Kindness means remembering that the story is more important than you are. This attitude is tested when you meet people in public who might recognize you.

Be approachable. Don't hide behind sunglasses. A kind journalist returns compliments with a "thank you."

Be kind to your co-workers. Help create a newsroom culture of support and cooperation. Focus a competitive attitude on the station across town, not at the reporter who works alongside you. No matter how news is delivered—over the air, on the Web or on a cell phone—it's a team effort. Share credit for success widely. Far more people—as many as 30—work behind the scenes in the studio or the newsroom to make you look credible on-screen. A kind word to your floor director or camera operator on the live truck goes a long way toward building a sense of team unity.

Be kind to your sources. Kindness can talk a secretary into giving a phone number or a clerk into copying a file for you. Kindness shows you're credible, not irrational. Demanding, pushy behavior might work sometimes, but this is rare.

Walter Cronkite exudes kindness while meeting with students during his annual visit to the Walter Cronkite School of Journalism and Mass Communication.

VOICES *from the* Newsroom

Dave Price, weekend anchorman and political reporter
WHO–TV (NBC), Des Moines, Iowa

In 2002 I did a story about a Republican Iowa congressman named Greg Ganske, who challenged the incumbent senator Tom Harkin, a Democrat. Ganske faced an uphill battle to beat Harkin. My story included a standup where I said something like "The RNC (Republican National Committee) decided not to spend one single penny on Ganske's race." I received I don't remember how many nasty emails that accused me of being one of those members of the dreaded "liberal media."

Several years later, I did a story on the travels of Democratic governor Tom Vilsack. He had recently been dramatically upping his travel schedule at a growing cost to Iowa taxpayers. Critics say it was to beef up his national credentials as he prepared for his attempt to seek national office (he did later unsuccessfully run for president). In contrast, supporters say he was just increasing Iowa's presence in the world for business opportunities for the state. The story ended up a bit confrontational because Vilsack's staff refused to allow me to speak with him about the travel costs, which were four times the cost of his predecessor. After the story ran, his supporters harshly criticized my work as propaganda for the Republican Party. The story went statewide and dominated the news for three days until Vilsack had to address the costs.

I always fret over any appearance of bias in my political coverage. Working in Des Moines, I cover local and state politics extensively. Because of the first-in-the-nation Iowa caucuses, I also get to cover a lot of national politics. So, it's essential for me to show no signs of political leanings. I don't vote in primaries, just to be safe. And other than my wife, I don't really share political beliefs publicly with anyone. I don't pretend that I'm always 100 percent completely balanced. But I've been asked to run for office for both the Iowa Democratic Party and the Iowa Republican Party, so I must be doing something right.

Integrity

> "I see too many young journalists who are forgetting the principles of the craft in order to be on-air, to be a star. Stars don't belong in journalism."
>
> —WALTER CRONKITE

Integrity, which encompasses truth, credibility and responsibility, forms the bedrock of an individual's personal journalism ethics. Integrity is who you are when no one is watching. As journalists, you will face multiple challenges to your integrity. Let's look at two kinds: those that come from outside influences, such as PR practitioners hoping to influence you, and those that come from within.

Outside influences As ethics scholars Lee Wilkins and Philip Patterson observed, "The single biggest threat to continuing professional excellence is the increasing pressure to make a profit." News is a business. It's supposed to make money. Although the model might be changing in the digital age, advertising has traditionally powered the free press. The challenges advertisers pose to a journalist's integrity have been discussed earlier. "It is clear that advertising is the economic lifeblood of the media," wrote Anthony J. Cartese in "Provocateur: Images of Women and Minorities in Advertising."

Pressure from advertisers might tempt you to compromise your personal ethics. Don't give in. As the SPJ code states, "Distinguish news from advertising and shun hybrids that blur the lines between the two."

Never should a reporter change a story angle or drop a sound bite at the request of an advertiser. But a journalist's integrity can be tested in far more subtle ways. For example, a journalist should never accept anything given for free, no matter how small. Why? There could be an expectation of returning the favor and providing a longer story than warranted. Or a PR practitioner might expect favorable exposure for a client.

Examples of freebies:

- Food at a press conference, at a political event or in the sports skybox
- Media guest passes to major amusement parks from Disney World to Universal Studios
- Ski passes to winter resorts or nights at a hotel
- Tickets for movies, sports events and concerts
- CDs and books

The list above is not exhaustive. If you're a music critic or write film reviews, receiving advance promotional copies facilitates your work.

The professional codes are clear on how to handle freebies, but they differ in the stringency of their guidelines. For example, SPJ is the most direct: "Refuse gifts, favors, fees, free travel and special treatment." In other words, no gifts—period. In contrast, RTDNA admonishes journalists not to "accept gifts, favors, or compensation from those who might seek to influence coverage." The bottom line? Don't accept gifts if it threatens your ability to remain objective.

Some broadcast stations have written policies that forbid employees from accepting anything worth more than $25. At some stations, reporters are required to sign a document each year stating that they have not received anything over a certain amount.

Still, in some cases, you can use your own good judgment. If you're doing a feature story on a monastery that claims to make the best Christmas fruitcake in the world and a monk gives you one to take back to the station, you're probably not violating any ethical guidelines by accepting it and sharing it with the newsroom.

Many journalists believe that it's OK to eat whatever is offered and not feel one ounce of ethical remorse. Food is not mentioned specifically in any of the ethics codes. Still, one investigative reporter who worked at a large TV news station in the West for 25 years never accepted even one free lunch.

When it comes to the potential influence on your integrity from outside sources, follow your station and company policies. But also make sure you're true to yourself. Your own personal code might be a higher standard.

Inside influences You earn your reputation each day, which means you're only as good as your last story. In a world of professional jealousy crowded with colleagues trying to move to a larger market or get off the weekend shift, compromises occur. For TV reporters, this means not getting caught up in the glitz-and-glitter machine that can sometimes be part of local television news. Find a balance between maintaining your ethical standards, aggressively seeking opportunities and going the extra mile that will give you career breaks without smashing others down. It's tough to do.

INTEGRITY: WHAT THE CODES SAY

RTDNA

- Do not accept gifts, favors or compensation from those who might seek to influence coverage.
- Do not engage in activities that may compromise integrity or independence.

SPJ

Avoid conflicts of interest, real or perceived.

- Remain free of associations and activities that may compromise integrity or damage credibility.
- Refuse gifts, favors, fees, free travel and special treatment, and shun secondary employment, political involvement, public office and service in community organizations if they compromise journalistic integrity.
- Disclose unavoidable conflicts.
- Deny favored treatment to advertisers and special interests and resist their pressure to influence news coverage.
- Be wary of sources offering information for favors or money; avoid bidding for news.

SIDE **BY** SIDE

INTEGRITY: WHAT YOUR PEERS SAY

"If you don't have integrity, then you are missing an integral part of your moral code."

—Danny Darnell

"If you can't answer to yourself, then you shouldn't answer to anyone else. Be true to who you are and be the best version of you possible"

– Anna Consie

"Integrity is what makes each of our ethical codes different. Integrity is how strongly we adhere to what we believe and hold to be important. In our career, field competition is high, and the temptation to stray from our integrity is strong."

—Veronica Lumpkin

VOICES *from the* Newsroom

Zahid Arab, multimedia journalist
KLAS-TV (CBS), Las Vegas

Integrity in news—it's basically the difference between a journalist and a tabloid reporter. It's something easy to lose but almost impossible to earn back. When out on a story, the person you're interviewing puts trust in you to relay his point of view, opinion or emotion the way he intended it to be. A reporter's dream is to have someone speak eloquently in about seven to 10 seconds. It doesn't happen, so we have to chop off their lengthy explanation into something more concise. With that, a reporter runs the risk of losing the true meaning of what the source is saying. Integrity is essential in this process to make sure we deliver an honest product not only to that person but also to our viewers. Integrity is a matter of listening to that voice in your head. You know—the one who told you stealing that gum from the grocery store was wrong or as grown-ups telling us we really shouldn't make that fast food run after a night of unwinding at the bar with friends. Once you put on your professional hat, the voice is still there.

On one occasion as a reporter in Honolulu, I was sent out to cover this critical stabbing in a park. A homeless guy sleeping on the bench gets stabbed by another homeless guy—nothing too out of the ordinary, right? There was only one witness, and since witnesses tend to get camera shy, I walked up to him and had my photographer hold the camera down in his hand while still recording. I asked him what happened, what he saw, the normal stuff—and he gave some great sound. This was all on tape. But after a few minutes, a reporter from a competing station walked up and asked if he would go on-camera. The witness immediately shut down and made it known he didn't want to be interviewed.

I had him on tape; he talked and I got great stuff. But the question was—should I use it? While I knew I would scoop the competition, I decided not to use the footage before he said "no." He said he feared that someone would try to get revenge on him for talking. And while I technically could have used what he told me, I decided not to. The voice inside me told me it wasn't the right thing to do. I didn't want to bring harm upon this guy just for a win that night, which personally would have felt cheap anyway. You could write books about the word *integrity,* but sometimes understanding it is just a matter of shutting up and listening to that voice inside.

Truthfulness

> "In seeking truth, you have to get both sides of a story."
>
> —WALTER CRONKITE

The commandment not to lie crosses all religions and belief systems. But being truthful can be trickier than not lying. In an era of ethical violations in corporate America—and even in journalism—the basic concept of telling the truth is a critical part of the Cronkite Code.

As former NBC News executive Neal Shapiro put it, "There is something very honorable about finding the truth and doing the best you can do to eliminate your own prejudices and biases, and say, 'Wherever the story is going to take me is where I am going to go.'"

Journalism history is full of famous cases of journalists caught lying. A common trait among dishonest acts is the drive for success:

- **Janet Cooke,** a Washington Post staff reporter, wrote a story about an 8-year-old boy addicted to heroin. The piece, which ran in September 1981, won a Pulitzer Prize, but Cooke returned the award when she admitted the boy didn't exist. She had created him.
- **Jayson Blair,** a young journalist, quit The New York Times in May 2003 after he was caught making up sources, fabricating scenes and plagiarizing from other newspapers. In his autobiography "Burning Down My Masters' House: My Life at the New York Times," Blair blames his ethical mistakes on past drug abuse and bipolar disorder. After firing Blair, The New York Times published a detailed explanation of what had happened: "Every newspaper, like every bank and every police department, trusts its employees to uphold central principles, and the inquiry found that Mr. Blair repeatedly violated the cardinal tenet of journalism, which is simply truth."
- **Stephen Glass** was fired in 1998 for making up sources, quotes and even events while a reporter for The New Republic magazine. While at the magazine, he made up sources in 27 of 41 major stories. A popular film called "Shattered Glass" shows how Adam Penenberg, an online reporter for Forbes magazine, exposed Glass' lies.

Liars have also made headlines in news stories from the business world. In an era of corporate ethical crises at such companies as Enron and WorldCom, a business book became a global bestseller—"Absolute Honesty: Building a Corporate Culture That Values Straight Talk and Rewards Integrity" by Larry Johnson and Bob Phillips. From that book comes a list of "five tenets of ethical behavior" that have direct application for journalists who cover business or any beat. (Source: Copyright 2003. Reproduced with permission of AMACOM BOOKS in the format Other book via Copyright Clearance Center.)

1. Tell the truth.
2. Keep your word, always.
3. Respect the rights of others.
4. Avoid harming others.
5. Don't break the law.

SIDE BY SIDE

TRUTHFULNESS: WHAT THE CODES SAY

RTDNA

Professional electronic journalists should operate as trustees of the public, seek the truth, report it fairly and with integrity and independence, and stand accountable for their actions.

TRUTH: Professional electronic journalists should pursue truth aggressively and present the news accurately, in context, and as completely as possible.

SPJ

The duty of the journalist is to further those ends by seeking truth and providing a fair and comprehensive account of events and issues.

TRUTHFULNESS: WHAT YOUR PEERS SAY

"Truthfulness involves divulging facts accurately and not allowing your own personal agenda or external influences to affect the way you report."

–Nastassja Stanton

"Truthfulness is like a muscle you work out, so when you need it, it is there for you."

–Brandon Kamerman

"Truthfulness is to never put information in a story that you cannot verify with a source."

–Matthew B. Trotter

The 2003 film "Shattered Glass" depicts the true story of the rise and fall of a young journalist. Stephen Glass became a star reporter for The New Republic magazine, only to be fired for making up quotes and sources in several articles, including cover stories.

VOICES from the Newsroom

Samuel Burke, producer
CNN International, London

I often find that the gigantic ethics questions from journalism school come up in the seemingly smallest, most unpredictable situations working at CNN.

I was asked to create a digital word cloud looking at the number of times Hillary Clinton used the word "human rights" in a speech on Russia. The premise of our show was that the Obama administration was backing off from specifically tackling human rights. And sure enough, when I used the program that creates the word cloud on Clinton's speech, "human rights" didn't show up in the words used most. I told my producers the word cloud matched the theme, and they were excited to incorporate the word cloud graphic into the show.

As the day went by, I thought I'd better do a word search of the speech to see if Clinton had used the phrase "human rights" at all. I did a search, and sure enough she had used the phrase, but not much. I didn't know if we should keep the word cloud because she had indeed used the phrase, but still she had barely used it compared with the other keywords showing up in the word cloud. I was afraid that while accurate, it might be unethical to show the word cloud and make it appear as though Clinton hadn't mentioned human rights at all.

I decided it was unethical, and I told my producers. They quickly said, "Great you told us that. We can still use this great graphic, representing that Clinton didn't say it much, but the anchor can say she didn't completely neglect the phrase 'human rights.'"

In the end, we approached it in a fair and ethical way.

Ego management

> "There's a little more ego involved in these jobs than people might realize."
>
> –WALTER CRONKITE

The root cause of professional jealousy is a selfish ego. Managing your ego could prove the toughest part of your career. Tough because you have to be your own PR agent, which means you have to promote yourself, and that takes self-confidence and self-esteem—components of a healthy ego. No one will care as much about your career as you do, so a healthy ego is important for success. But if your need for success comes at the expense of colleagues, you're headed for trouble. A fine balance is needed. We call this ego management.

Controlling your ego begins with a clear vision of who you are personally and professionally. After setting your career goals, set up an internal checks-and-balances system to ensure that you remain true to who you are as a professional and as an individual. Case studies of journalists who've crashed and burned, such as Blair and Glass, reveal that when a reporter's ego-driven career collides with the wall of traditional journalism ethics, an internal implosion occurs.

One way to stay on course is to spend some time writing and reflecting on your professional life. What fundamentals will guide you? What core principles will you not compromise? Why? At what cost? What is the ethical bottom line that might lead you to walk away from a job? Answers to these questions and more will shape your personal code of professional ethics.

Visualizing Your Own Code of Professional Ethics

Each of us must ultimately come up with our own value system.

A journalist's code of ethics is composed of three codes: (1) your personal code, (2) a station code or company mission statement that you adhere to as part of your job and (3) a professional code upheld by a journalism organization such as RTDNA or SPJ.

Creating your own code can be a fun visual experience. Here's what to do:

1. Write a belief statement. This could be a paragraph that explains to a stranger your core values. Include items related to your personal life, such as family, religion, gender, ethnicity, nationality or whatever values *you* feel are important to *your identity*. Next, add items related to your professional life, such as the importance of truth telling or of being a watchdog for the people, a visual storyteller, an accurate reporter, a fresh and engaging writer.

   If you don't like the paragraph method, write 10 to 20 statements (you choose the number) that begin with the words "I am" and "I believe," and then fill in the blanks. Example: I am a proud African-American. I believe a journalist should bring the voice of the voiceless into the newsroom.
2. Copy and paste your belief statement into wordle.net
3. Follow the simple instructions on the website to create a word cloud. It will look something like this:

This word cloud is based on these 10 personal and professional statements:

I am Irish-American.
I speak Spanish.
I am of Catholic and Jewish ancestry.
I believe in freedom of the press.
I am a political reporter.
I am politically neutral.
I am the mother of two children.
I am a new media journalist.
I report for television, Web and radio.
I believe writers should be accurate, fair and balanced.

The website wordle.net allows you to choose font styles and colors. You might consider creating a word cloud that displays your personal code of professional ethics and posting it in your workspace in the newsroom. It becomes a constant reminder of who you are and what you believe.

Professional Codes of Ethics

RTDNA Code of Ethics and Professional Conduct

Preamble Professional electronic journalists should operate as trustees of the public, seek the truth, report it fairly and with integrity and independence, and stand accountable for their actions.

Public Trust Professional electronic journalists should recognize that their first obligation is to the public.

Professional electronic journalists should:

- Understand that any commitment other than service to the public undermines trust and credibility.
- Recognize that service in the public interest creates an obligation to reflect the diversity of the community and guard against oversimplification of issues or events.
- Provide a full range of information to enable the public to make enlightened decisions.
- Fight to ensure that the public's business is conducted in public.

Truth Professional electronic journalists should pursue truth aggressively and present the news accurately, in context, and as completely as possible.

Professional electronic journalists should:

- Continuously seek the truth.
- Resist distortions that obscure the importance of events.
- Clearly disclose the origin of information and label all material provided by outsiders.

Professional electronic journalists should not:

- Report anything known to be false.
- Manipulate images or sounds in any way that is misleading.
- Plagiarize.
- Present images or sounds that are reenacted without informing the public.

Fairness Professional electronic journalists should present the news fairly and impartially, placing primary value on significance and relevance.

Professional electronic journalists should:

- Treat all subjects of news coverage with respect and dignity, showing particular compassion to victims of crime or tragedy.
- Exercise special care when children are involved in a story and give children greater privacy protection than adults.
- Seek to understand the diversity of their community and inform the public without bias or stereotype.
- Present a diversity of expressions, opinions and ideas in context.
- Present analytical reporting based on professional perspective, not personal bias.
- Respect the right to a fair trial.

Integrity Professional electronic journalists should present the news with integrity and decency, avoiding real or perceived conflicts of interest, and respect the dignity and intelligence of the audience as well as the subjects of news.

Professional electronic journalists should:

- Identify sources whenever possible. Confidential sources should be used only when it is clearly in the public interest to gather or convey important information or when a person providing information might be harmed. Journalists should keep all commitments to protect a confidential source.
- Clearly label opinion and commentary.
- Guard against extended coverage of events or individuals that fails to significantly advance a story, place the event in context, or add to the public knowledge.
- Refrain from contacting participants in violent situations while the situation is in progress.
- Use technological tools with skill and thoughtfulness, avoiding techniques that skew facts, distort reality, or sensationalize events.
- Use surreptitious newsgathering techniques, including hidden cameras or microphones, only if there is no other way to obtain stories of significant public importance and only if the technique is explained to the audience.
- Disseminate the private transmissions of other news organizations only with permission.

Professional electronic journalists should not:

- Pay news sources who have a vested interest in a story.
- Accept gifts, favors, or compensation from those who might seek to influence coverage.
- Engage in activities that may compromise their integrity or independence.

Independence Professional electronic journalists should defend the independence of all journalists from those seeking influence or control over news content.

Professional electronic journalists should:

- Gather and report news without fear or favor, and vigorously resist undue influence from any outside forces, including advertisers, sources, story subjects, powerful individuals, and special interest groups.
- Resist those who would seek to buy or politically influence news content or who would seek to intimidate those who gather and disseminate the news.
- Determine news content solely through editorial judgment and not as the result of outside influence.
- Resist any self-interest or peer pressure that might erode journalistic duty and service to the public.
- Recognize that sponsorship of the news will not be used in any way to determine, restrict, or manipulate content.
- Refuse to allow the interests of ownership or management to influence news judgment and content inappropriately.
- Defend the rights of the free press for all journalists, recognizing that any professional or government licensing of journalists is a violation of that freedom.

Accountability Professional electronic journalists should recognize that they are accountable for their actions to the public, the profession, and themselves.

Professional electronic journalists should:

- Actively encourage adherence to these standards by all journalists and their employers.
- Respond to public concerns. Investigate complaints and correct errors promptly and with as much prominence as the original report.
- Explain journalistic processes to the public, especially when practices spark questions or controversy.
- Recognize that professional electronic journalists are duty-bound to conduct themselves ethically.
- Refrain from ordering or encouraging courses of action that would force employees to commit an unethical act.
- Carefully listen to employees who raise ethical objections and create environments in which such objections and discussions are encouraged.
- Seek support for and provide opportunities to train employees in ethical decision-making.

In meeting its responsibility to the profession of electronic journalism, RTNDA has created this code to identify important issues, to serve as a guide for its members, to facilitate self-scrutiny, and to shape future debate.

(Source: Radio Television Digital News Association, "Code of Ethics and Professional Conduct," adopted September 14, 2000)

SPJ Code of Ethics

Preamble Members of the Society of Professional Journalists believe that public enlightenment is the forerunner of justice and the foundation of democracy. The duty of the journalist is to further those ends by seeking truth and providing a fair and comprehensive account of events and issues. Conscientious journalists from all media and specialties strive to serve the public with thoroughness and honesty. Professional integrity is the cornerstone of a journalist's credibility. Members of the Society share a dedication to ethical behavior and adopt this code to declare the Society's principles and standards of practice.

Seek truth and report it Journalists should be honest, fair and courageous in gathering, reporting and interpreting information.

Journalists should:

- Test the accuracy of information from all sources and exercise care to avoid inadvertent error. Deliberate distortion is never permissible.
- Diligently seek out subjects of news stories to give them the opportunity to respond to allegations of wrongdoing.
- Identify sources whenever feasible. The public is entitled to as much information as possible on sources' reliability.
- Always question sources' motives before promising anonymity. Clarify conditions attached to any promise made in exchange for information. Keep promises.
- Make certain that headlines, news teases and promotional material, photos, video, audio, graphics, sound bites and quotations do not misrepresent. They should not oversimplify or highlight incidents out of context.
- Never distort the content of news photos or video Image enhancement for technical clarity is always permissible. Label montages and photo illustrations.

- Avoid misleading re-enactments or staged news events. If re-enactment is necessary to tell a story, label it.
- Avoid undercover or other surreptitious methods of gathering information except when traditional open methods will not yield information vital to the public. Use of such methods should be explained as part of the story.
- Never plagiarize.
- Tell the story of the diversity and magnitude of the human experience boldly, even when it is unpopular to do so.
- Examine their own cultural values and avoid imposing those values on others.
- Avoid stereotyping by race, gender, age, religion, ethnicity, geography, sexual orientation, disability, physical appearance or social status.
- Support the open exchange of views, even views they find repugnant.
- Give voice to the voiceless; official and unoffcial sources of information can be equally valid.
- Distinguish between advocacy and news reporting. Analysis and commentary should be labeled and not misrepresent fact or context.
- Distinguish news from advertising and shun hybrids that blur the lines between the two.
- Recognize a special obligation to ensure that the public's business is conducted in the open and that government records are open to inspection.

Minimize harm Ethical journalists treat sources, subjects and colleagues as human beings deserving of respect.

Journalists should:

- Show compassion for those who may be affected adversely by news coverage. Use special sensitivity when dealing with children and inexperienced sources or subjects.
- Be sensitive when seeking or using interviews or photographs of those affected by tragedy or grief:
- Recognize that gathering and reporting information may cause harm or discomfort. Pursuit of the news is not a license for arrogance.
- Recognize that private people have a greater right to control information about themselves than do public officials and others who seek power, influence or attention. Only an overriding public need can justify intrusion into anyone's privacy.
- Show good taste. Avoid pandering to lurid curiosity.
- Be cautious about identifying juvenile suspects or victims of sex crimes.
- Be judicious about naming criminal suspects before the formal filing of charges.
- Balance a criminal suspect's fair trial rights with the public's right to be informed.

Act independently Journalists should be free of obligation to any interest other than the public's right to know.

Journalists should:

- Avoid conflicts of interest, real or perceived.
- Remain free of associations and activities that may compromise integrity or damage credibility.
- Refuse gifts, favors, fees, free travel and special treatment, and shun secondary employment, political involvement, public office and service in community organizations if they compromise journalistic integrity.
- Disclose unavoidable conflicts.
- Be vigilant and courageous about holding those with power accountable.
- Deny favored treatment to advertisers and special interests and resist their pressure to influence news coverage.
- Be wary of sources offering information for favors or money; avoid bidding for news.

Be accountable Journalists are accountable to their readers, listeners, viewers and each other.

Journalists should:

- Clarify and explain news coverage and invite dialogue with the public over journalistic conduct.
- Encourage the public to voice grievances against the news media.
- Admit mistakes and correct them promptly.
- Expose unethical practices of journalists and the news media.
- Abide by the same high standards to which they hold others.

The SPJ Code of Ethics is voluntarily embraced by thousands of journalists, regardless of place or platform, and is widely used in newsrooms and classrooms as a guide for ethical behavior. The code is intended not as a set of "rules" but as a resource for ethical decision-making. It is not—nor can it be under the First Amendment—legally enforceable.

The present version of the code was adopted by the 1996 SPJ National Convention, after months of study and debate among the Society's members. Sigma Delta Chi's first Code of Ethics was borrowed from the American Society of Newspaper Editors in 1926. In 1973, Sigma Delta Chi wrote its own code, which was revised in 1984, 1987 and 1996.

(Source: Society of Professional Journalists Code of Ethics, 1996, found at: spj.org/ethicscode.asp)

NPPA Code of Ethics

Preamble The National Press Photographers Association, a professional society that promotes the highest standards in visual journalism, acknowledges concern for every person's need both to be fully informed about public events and to be recognized as part of the world in which we live.

Visual journalists operate as trustees of the public. Our primary role is to report visually on the significant events and varied viewpoints in our common world. Our primary goal is the faithful and comprehensive depiction of the subject at hand. As visual journalists, we have the responsibility to document society and to preserve its history through images.

Photographic and video images can reveal great truths, expose wrongdoing and neglect, inspire hope and understanding and connect people around the globe through the language of visual understanding. Photographs can also cause great harm if they are callously intrusive or are manipulated.

This code is intended to promote the highest quality in all forms of visual journalism and to strengthen public confidence in the profession. It is also meant to serve as an educational tool both for those who practice and for those who appreciate photojournalism. To that end, the National Press Photographers Association sets forth the following.

Code of Ethics Visual journalists and those who manage visual news productions are accountable for upholding the following standards in their daily work:

1. Be accurate and comprehensive in the representation of subjects.
2. Resist being manipulated by staged photo opportunities.
3. Be complete and provide context when photographing or recording subjects. Avoid stereotyping individuals and groups. Recognize and work to avoid presenting one's own biases in the work.
4. Treat all subjects with respect and dignity. Give special consideration to vulnerable subjects and compassion to victims of crime or tragedy. Intrude on private moments of grief only when the public has an overriding and justifiable need to see.
5. While photographing subjects do not intentionally contribute to, alter, or seek to alter or influence events.
6. Editing should maintain the integrity of the photographic images' content and context. Do not manipulate images or add or alter sound in any way that can mislead viewers or misrepresent subjects.
7. Do not pay sources or subjects or reward them materially for information or participation.
8. Do not accept gifts, favors, or compensation from those who might seek to influence coverage.
9. Do not intentionally sabotage the efforts of other journalists.

Ideally, visual journalists should:

1. Strive to ensure that the public's business is conducted in public. Defend the rights of access for all journalists.
2. Think proactively, as a student of psychology, sociology, politics and art to develop a unique vision and presentation. Work with a voracious appetite for current events and contemporary visual media.
3. Strive for total and unrestricted access to subjects, recommend alternatives to shallow or rushed opportunities, seek a diversity of viewpoints, and work to show unpopular or unnoticed points of view.
4. Avoid political, civic and business involvements or other employment that compromise or give the appearance of compromising one's own journalistic independence.
5. Strive to be unobtrusive and humble in dealing with subjects.
6. Respect the integrity of the photographic moment.
7. Strive by example and influence to maintain the spirit and high standards expressed in this code. When confronted with situations in which the proper action is not clear, seek the counsel of those who exhibit the highest standards of the profession. Visual journalists should continuously study their craft and the ethics that guide it.

(Source: © National Press Photographers Association/nppa.org 2011. All Rights Reserved.)

DIVERSITY

CHAPTER 13

> *Be kind to an old man.*
>
> —*WALTER CRONKITE*

CHAPTER OUTLINE

Covering Our Diverse Community

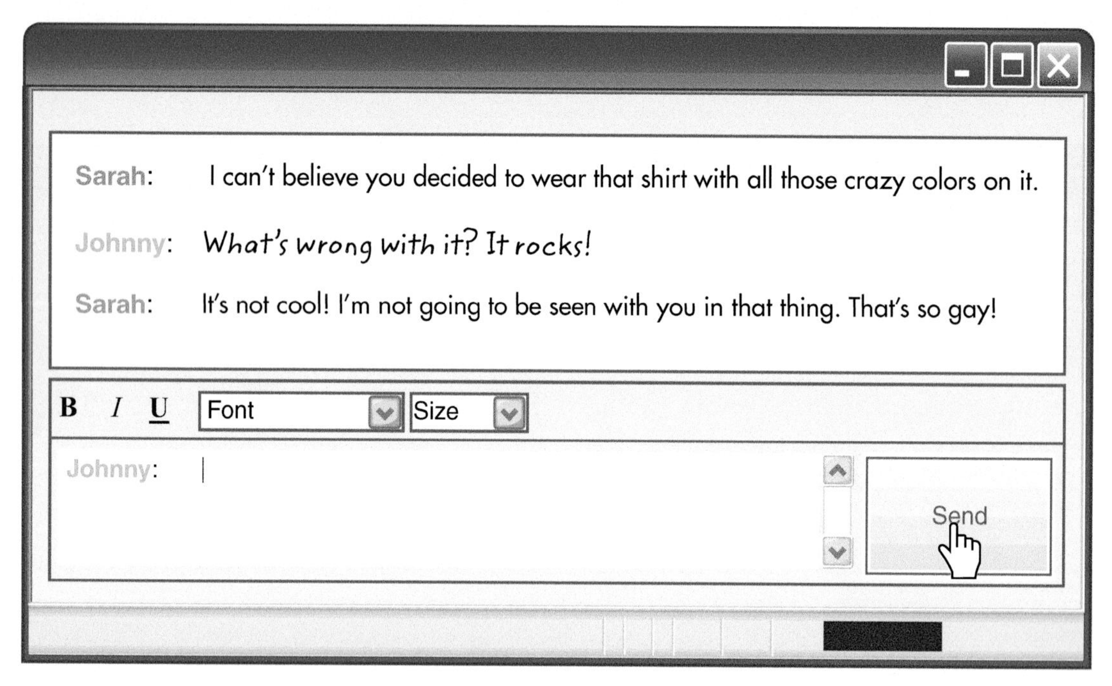

You might have texted something like this or even heard this type of conversation on campus any day of the week—two students chatting about going out, talking about what to wear and giving the thumbs down to a particular outfit. It might seem like harmless chatter, but the final three words carry an underlying message of disdain. As a matter of fact, in 2008 the Ad Council launched a series of public service announcements targeting the use of the phrase "That's so gay" to point out that the phrase can be inflammatory, hurtful and discriminatory.

An ad campaign launched by thinkb4youspeak.com targets anti-gay slurs.

That's what we're going to talk about in this chapter—the words, simple words, and pictures that affect every story you produce as a reporter, writer or photographer. We are going to talk about the power of words and why some members of a community might consider certain words inflammatory. This theme applies not only to words but also to pictures—the way you perceive images and the way others may perceive them. We are also going to talk about the effect that labels or stereotypes used in reporting can have on viewers or readers. And we will discuss how your own biases can influence your perceptions and the way you report them in your stories.

Most important, perhaps, we are going to talk about how becoming aware of your biases can help you produce fair and balanced stories because being fair and balanced is the job of all journalists. Being aware of the power of words and images will help you achieve those goals.

As journalists, it is our duty to recognize the power that words and pictures possess. And we must realize that our own experiences can have an impact on how we might view these pictures or words. We bring different perspectives to the table, and sometimes this can distort how we report a story.

Having different perspectives is not necessarily a bad thing. Diversity of voice in a newsroom, meaning different people with different viewpoints, means we will have diversity of coverage. The power here is when a newsroom can acknowledge differing viewpoints, listen to them and then include them in coverage. If you can just grab hold of the notion of diversity of voice and recognize that we are not always talking about race when we talk about diversity, then your reporting of issues will be even more powerful.

rac·ism

1: a belief that race is the primary determinant of human traits and capacities and that racial differences produce inherent superiority of a particular race

2: racial prejudice or discrimination

di-ver-si-ty

1: the condition of having or being composed of differing elements: variety; especially: the inclusion of different types of people (as people of different races or cultures) in a group or organization <programs intended to promote diversity in schools>

2: an instance of being composed of differing elements or qualities: an instance of being diverse <a diversity of opinion>

By permission. From Merriam-Webster's Collegiate® Dictionary, 11th Edition © 2011 by Merriam-Webster, Incorporated (www.merriam-webster.com).

We show respect for **diversity** by becoming part of the communities we cover before we need them as sources for stories. This has become even more important as newsrooms continue to shrink. Because we have fewer reporters on the streets, we must work even harder to reach out to underserved communities and make sure we can hear their challenges, report their stories and understand what makes them tick. We also need to immerse ourselves in these communities so we can learn why certain words or images might trigger anger.

For example, let's take a look at a city like Los Angeles, where in the past gangs have been a big problem. A reporter working in Los Angeles should spend some time in the south-central area or East Los Angeles or Compton in order to understand the impact that gangs have had there in the past.

By doing this, the reporter learns what gang signs look like and why some people get mad when a news story shows someone flashing a gang sign in the background of a live report or picture.

A group of young people flash gang signs.

As a reporter, if you spend time in that community, you know the signs, can anticipate the reaction and can decide whether the image you were really trying to focus on, not the gang sign, is important to the story. In other words, you can make an informed decision about what video to use in a package and what video to leave out. But you must also remember that gangs can exist in any community, so do not make the assumption that gang problems will only be in areas that have had gang challenges in the past. You can find gangs in some of the most exclusive areas of a city.

As journalists, you should be ready to challenge other journalists in your newsroom about words and images they use in stories. If you think there is something questionable or you are uncomfortable, don't be afraid to ask questions. During the O.J. Simpson trial in 1995 many newsrooms were having discussions about whether they could use the N word after the defense played a tape of a witness using the word dozens of times in a taped conversation. Many felt the word was just too inflammatory, no matter that many musicians or comedians or young people used it in everyday conversation. Others took the position that if the word was used in the trial, it should not be censored in the news. Some newsrooms bleeped it out of the newscast, while others used a graphic, **N*#*er,** displaying a few letters of the word so the viewer would know what it was without having it spelled out.

These conversations about the word and its usage are actually healthy and appropriate in newsrooms, as they should be safe environments for challenging and debating such topics.

The number of heated conversations this one word has caused in newsrooms is amazing, even today. On March 23, 2011, the CBS show "60 Minutes" aired a piece about how a publishing company had taken the word "nigger" out of Mark Twain's famous book "Huckleberry Finn." According to the report, the book

VOICES *from the* Newsroom

Martha Kang, Web journalist
KOMO News (ABC), Seattle

Most news outlets strive for diversity, both in the newsroom and in their coverage. But like anyone else, they're at risk of falling into comfortable patterns.

Whether it's using the same expert source over and over for a quick quote or habitually covering the same accessible neighborhoods, the patterns form gradually over time and often go undetected, especially as newsroom cutbacks push journalists to create more content with less time and resources. These shortcuts lead to a dead end. Journalists who are connected to just a fraction of their market cannot reach their coverage potential. Only diverse practices can yield a diverse set of stories and nurture robust, comprehensive news coverage.

This is especially important to remember as journalism's landscape evolves with the rise of online media. The Internet and blogs have given a voice to many who would have been unheard in a different time. Social networking tools have given journalists new platforms through which to gather sources and news tips. But as journalists embrace these new tools, the old tools of journalism should not be forgotten.

Some stories can only be found by shoe-leather reporting. Some sources have no plans to join Twitter or Facebook. Among them are the voiceless, the impoverished, the vulnerable. They are the ones who are often forgotten by the mainstream, the ones who pay the biggest price when public programs are slashed, the ones who struggle in silence.

With so much emphasis on online media, young journalists can easily fall into the trap of failing to distinguish the message from the medium. Doing so will surely lead them away from the stories unfolding on the street corners outside their windows. As new forms of journalism blossom, journalists must use all the tools in the toolbox, old and new. Only then could we hope to deliver balanced, comprehensive and well-rounded news coverage, in whatever medium.

used the word 219 times, and many schools had removed it from their reading lists because of this.

72 *THE ADVENTURES OF HUCKLEBERRY FINN.*

But I ain' gwyne to resk no mo' money in stock. De cow up 'n' died on my han's."

"So you lost the ten dollars."

"No, I didn' lose it all. I on'y los' 'bout nine of it. I sole de hide en taller for a dollar en ten cents."

"You had five dollars and ten cents left. Did you speculate any more?"

"Yes. You know dat one-laigged nigger dat b'longs to old Misto Bradish? well, he sot up a bank, en say anybody dat put in a dollar would git fo' dollars mo' at de en' er de year. Well, all de niggers went in, but dey didn' have much. I wuz de on'y one dat had much. So I stuck out for mo' dan fo' dollars, en I said 'f I didn' git it I'd start a bank mysef. Well o' course dat nigger want' to keep me out er de business, bekase he say dey warn't business 'nough for two banks, so he say I could put in my five dollars en he pay me thirty-five at de en' er de year.

MISTO BRADISH'S NIGGER.

"So I done it. Den I reck'n'd I'd inves' de thirty-five dollars right off en keep things a-movin'. Dey wuz a nigger name' Bob, dat had ketched a wood-flat, en his marster didn' know it; en I bought it off'n him en told him to take de thirty-five dollars when de en' er de year come; but somebody stole de wood-flat dat

The new version of "Huckleberry Finn" stirred up controversy because it deleted the N word.

The book was published in the U.S. in 1885, more than 125 years ago. But today it is still making history as the battle continues over the use of the N word. A "60 Minutes" report by Byron Pitts looked at whether it is OK for the publishing company to change the word from "nigger" to "slave."

The publishing company said it changed the word to something less offensive so schools could have the classic book returned to reading lists. But there are also some who believe we should not be changing classic writing. We should preserve it, their point being that the use of the word could actually be a good teaching moment.

Byron Pitts' story was about 12 minutes long, but the conversation about this piece continued long after in an online forum and in a personal interview with Pitts about the discussions that happened in the edit booth before the piece aired. Pitts said he expected there would be pushback about the decision to use the entire word, but there had been precedent at CBS in past stories concerning the use of the word and so he felt comfortable using it in his piece. But he did admit that the first version of the story that was screened did not use the actual word "nigger." It was after some research and discussion that "60 Minutes" decided to use the word.

This is how the process is supposed to work. Identify the potential issue, discuss it and then make a decision and stand behind it. As Byron Pitts was quoted in an interview on CBS News.com the day after the piece aired: "There is real value in truth. As my grandmother used to say, sometimes the truth is funny, sometimes the truth is painful, but the truth is always the truth."

Bias in the Media

The issue of diversity and the media was spotlighted during the 2008 presidential campaign. This election challenged norms because the face of politics, at least in past presidential elections in this country, had usually been white and male. But in 2008, we had diversity involving gender, with women running for president and vice president; race, with an African-American presidential candidate; and age, with one presidential candidate considerably younger than the other. Seeing this diversity of faces on TV, online and in newspapers every day has an impact on viewers as well as on the people reporting the news. Everyone was seeing and experiencing something new in politics, hearing different voices, seeing new faces, and it was playing out right in front of them.

During the year leading up to the election, the catchword was "change." Barack Obama ran on a platform for change. And his campaign used every form of communication, including traditional and social media, to reach out to voters of all ages and ethnicities. Hillary Clinton did the same, reaching out to audiences and challenging their views on whether this country was ready to accept a woman in the White House. Sarah Palin also challenged gender roles in politics. A mother of five, including a baby with Down syndrome, she was fighting to become the first female vice president of the country, hoping to win the position that Geraldine Ferraro first tried to grab in 1984.

This presence of new faces helped fuel talk of diversity. Not only did it challenge viewers, but it also challenged journalists to take a look at what and how they were reporting.

The campaign challenged journalists' abilities to deal with issues of race, gender, sexism and ageism, to name a few. For example, the media were accused of spending too much time talking about the clothes of the female candidates, the emotional displays of Hillary Clinton, Barack Obama's name and ethnic background and John McCain's age and ability to keep up.

FROM "A MORE PERFECT UNION"

Barack Obama

In March 2008, presidential candidate Barack Obama appeared on live television and delivered a speech about race in this country—now referred to as the "race speech" (see excerpt below). In this speech, Obama did not try to talk around race. Instead, he pointed out that in order to grow, the country needs to discuss this topic frankly. The same applies to newsrooms across the country. Journalists need to engage in these kinds of frank discussions if we want to make sure we are telling everyone's story and telling it correctly.

I chose to run for the presidency at this moment in history because I believe deeply that we cannot solve the challenges of our time unless we solve them together—unless we perfect our union by understanding that we may have different stories, but we hold common hopes; that we may not look the same and we may not have come from the same place, but we all want to move in the same direction—toward a better future for our children and our grandchildren.

This belief comes from my unyielding faith in the decency and generosity of the American people. But it also comes from my own American story.

I am the son of a black man from Kenya and a white woman from Kansas. I was raised with the help of a white grandfather who survived a Depression to serve in Patton's Army during World War II and a white grandmother who worked on a bomber assembly line at Fort Leavenworth while he was overseas. I've gone to some of the best schools in America and lived in one of the world's poorest nations. I am married to a black American who carries within her the blood of slaves and slave owners—an inheritance we pass on to our two precious daughters. I have brothers, sisters, nieces, nephews, uncles and cousins, of every race and every hue, scattered across three continents, and for as long as I live, I will never forget that in no other country on Earth is my story even possible.

It's a story that hasn't made me the most conventional candidate. But it is a story that has seared into my genetic makeup the idea that this nation is more than the sum of its parts—that out of many, we are truly one.

Source: Barack Obama, "A More Perfect Union," campaign speech, March 2008.

Some charged the so-called liberal media with falling in love with Barack Obama and his call for change. McCain supporters argued that their candidate also called for change, but, they claimed, his voice seemed to come in at a much lower decibel than Obama's—at least on the nightly newscasts and in the newspapers.

But were the media really biased, or were they just following the story? And if the Obama campaign did get more or better coverage, was it because his machine knew how to use modern technology to reach out and touch the media as well as the viewers and readers?

Well, the Pew Research Center's Project for Excellence in Journalism wanted to see what media coverage was like in 2008 and therefore conducted a study. The results revealed that just under a third of the stories about Barack Obama were negative. Slightly more than a third were positive, and the

FIGURE **13.1** **Tone of Coverage: MSNBC vs. FOX**

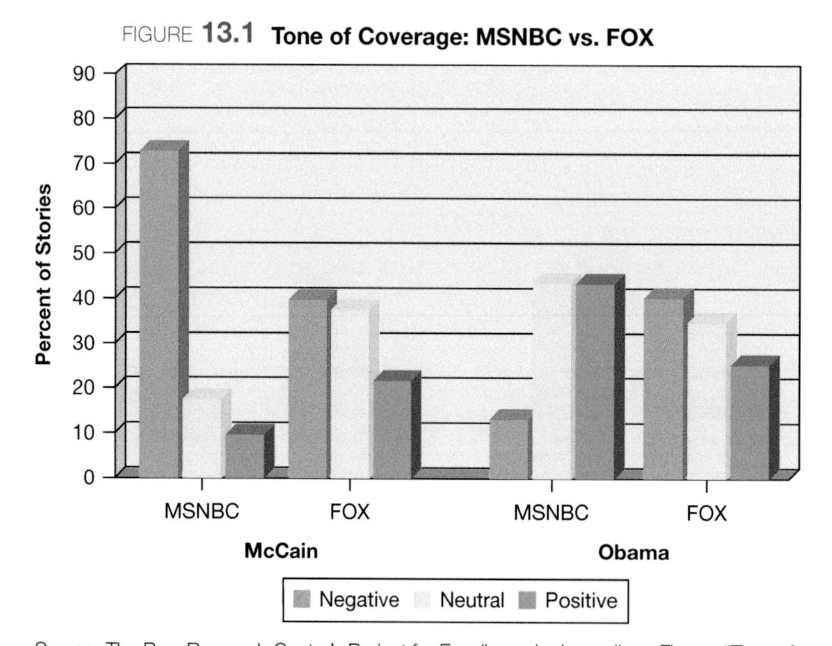

Source: The Pew Research Center's Project for Excellence in Journalism, Figure: "Tone of Coverage: MSNBC vs. Fox" in "The Color of News: How Different Media Have Covered the General Election," Oct. 29, 2008, accessed at http://www.journalism.org/node/13436

WHAT WOULD YOU DO?

You are out covering the protests at the state capitol in Arizona while everyone waits to see whether the governor will sign the new immigration bill into law. About 2,000 protesters are on the scene with signs, and they are chanting "Sí, se puede," which means "Yes, we can." Several students are arrested for chaining themselves to the door of the capitol to protest the bill. Across the street five supporters with signs are chanting in support of the bill. You have 1:15 to tell your story, and you want to make sure you tell both sides. How much time do you give to the supporters, and how much time do you give to the protesters? Should they get an equal amount of time when it comes to sound bites?

rest were primarily neutral. On the other hand, more than half the stories about John McCain cast the senator in a negative light, while only about 20 percent were positive.

The Project for Excellence conducted the study during the six weeks leading up to the final presidential debate by examining 857 stories from 43 news outlets, including major cable networks. According to the findings, MSNBC showed a huge negative slant toward McCain; by comparison, Fox News was more balanced in its coverage of both candidates (Figure 13.1).

The story is very different when it comes to the evening newscasts on the three traditional networks. ABC, CBS and NBC tended to be more neutral about both candidates and generally less negative about McCain than the cable networks.

If we take these numbers from the Pew Research Center study at face value, then, yes, we might conclude that some of the media displayed a bias for Obama and against McCain. But instead of pointing fingers, let's look at this as an opportunity for a learning moment. Do journalists have biases? Yes. They're human. Can they control these biases? Yes, as long as they acknowledge that biases exist and then make sure they're being true journalists by researching their stories and including voices from all sides.

For example, if you grew up poor, you might have a bias against rich people. Or if you grew up in a religious household, you might have a bias against those who support abortion issues. Likewise, if you were raised by strict grandparents, you might have a bias against the elderly. These are just a few examples. People have many other types of biases, whether based on gender, ethnicity or class, to name a few.

Your responsibility, no matter what story you're covering, is to make sure you're accurate and fair while never losing sight of the personal bias that might be driving your reporting process. How do you do that? First, acknowledge to yourself that you have a bias. And second, educate yourself so you can make sure your reporting does not reflect your bias. Education is the biggest advantage you have, the most powerful tool for overcoming biases. The more you educate yourself about an issue, the more accurate your story will be.

Having a bias usually means you are coming at the issue from one side only or with a preconceived notion. As a journalist, however, your job is to cover all sides of a story. Only then do you have a chance to tell it in a balanced and fair way.

Stereotypes: The Elephant in the Room

Let's talk stereotypes—you know, the idea that all Hispanics are illegal immigrants, or all black people are criminals or great athletes, or all Asians are highly educated, or all Jews are stingy, or all surfers are potheads, or all members of fraternities are hard-drinking party boys. We could go on and on. Stereotypes are generalizations about particular groups of people. Stereotypes work by applying some easily distinguishable set of characteristics to all members of a group. This is wrong.

A **stereotype** is basically an oversimplification where all members of a class or group are considered to be the same in particular ways. The term is often used with negative effect, as stereotypes can sometimes be used to deny individuals respect or even legitimacy because of the simple fact that they are members of a particular group.

Journalists who do not look beyond stereotypes, who do not see people as individuals, are not doing their job. Scholar Jean Gaddy Wilson wrapped it up brilliantly when she said, "Our goal should be to provide an inclusive, nonbiased and nonjudgmental language that reflects today's reality. By eliminating both blatant and subtle sexism, racism, ageism and other stereotypes from our writing and speech, we actually provide a more reliable, credible look at today's culture."

There is one simple strategy to use when trying to deal with the issues of stereotypes. If you don't understand something, ask. For example, if you don't understand why people take off their shoes when entering a mosque, ask. If you don't understand why the church plays such an important role in the African-American community, ask. If you

Let's say it's 2010, and you are working on a story about "Don't ask, don't tell," the controversial policy signed by President Clinton in 1993 that mandated the discharge of openly gay, lesbian or bisexual service members. You are talking to soldiers about whether they support the plan to do away with the policy and the impact that openly gay soldiers might have on the military. You talk to three soldiers to get their opinions. You later find out that one of the soldiers you spoke with is gay. Do you say that in your story? Why or why not? In what way is it relevant?

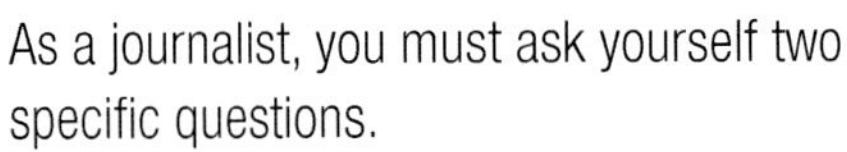

As a journalist, you must ask yourself two specific questions.

1. Is there anything in my writing or photos that could be considered a stereotype?
2. How can I do a better job of telling my story without giving in to these stereotypes?

don't understand why one of your fellow Jewish reporters cannot work after sundown on certain days of the week or year, ask. It's better to ask a question and get an accurate answer than to make incorrect assumptions and then look bad on the air or in print. The more questions journalists ask, the stronger their stories and the better they reflect the communities they cover.

The Poynter Institute, for example, a journalism think tank, sponsors workshops for journalists on subjects such as diversity and ethics. In Poynter seminars on diversity, journalists discuss the importance of having conversations about stereotypes in the newsroom before going to print, on-air or online. The Poynter Institute employs some of the country's most noted journalists. Keith Woods, now the vice president for Diversity in News and Operations for NPR, was a vocal voice as a recent member of the staff at Poynter. Woods suggests that journalists consider three key points when dealing with stories that test racial stereotypes.

Know the stereotype. There's no reason today, with information just a mouse click away, why anyone should tromp blindly into the briar patch of racial stigma. Anticipate the existence of stereotypes each time you delve into cultures different from your own. Read up on them.

Listen to trusted voices. Bring into the conversation those who know history and can articulate why something might be insulting. Then ask, "Who feels differently?" Listen to that point of view, too. Remember that you're not looking for someone to whom you'll cede decision-making power. Your independence, a cornerstone of ethical journalism, is heightened by knowledge, and that's what you're after.

Consider context. How central to the story or package is the stereotypical image? Is it really necessary to report a person's race in your story? Is it truly relevant? Same with gender or sexual orientation. If it is important to the story, then yes, bring it up, but if it has nothing to do with the story, then leave it out.

VOICES *from the* Newsroom

Luis Cruz, news director
KYMA-TV (NBC), Yuma, Ariz.

I'm a first-generation Mexican-American, so having a diverse staff is very important to me. I was born and raised in San Franoiooo, an oxtromoly divoroo oity. Yot whon I firot got into the business in 1993, I still did not see very many Latinos on television in the mainstream media. And that wasn't that long ago. It's actually one of the reasons I decided to go into broadcast journalism. I wanted to make sure our communities were being covered and covered fairly.

Now that I am news director, it's something I am very conscientious about. I take pride in having a diverse newsroom. People with different upbringings, different styles, different beliefs and different experiences have different idoao and wayo of ooing thingo. Thooo viowo aro thon brought to the table during our newsroom editorial meetings. I believe that helps us to achieve a more fair and balanced coverage of the communities we cover.

Five W's of Diversity

"Labels are supposed to help us organize the world. The trouble is most labels are too precise to fit something as imprecise as race."

—CLARENCE PAGE, CHICAGO TRIBUNE

RULE OF THUMB

References to ethnicity should only be used when they are pertinent to the story you are writing. If it is not germane to the story, don't use it.

The best way to approach inclusive storytelling is through the five W's of diversity—the who, what, when, where and why, as seen on the opposite page. Think about these five questions as you approach a story because they all have an impact on the eventual product. You can ask these questions of the sources you use, the areas of the city you visit to shoot, the people on the street you interview and even yourself.

An important question many people grapple with when dealing with particular ethnic groups is how to refer to someone. Terminology used to describe racial or ethnic groups has changed over the years. For example, the labels used to describe black Americans have gone through many changes. Most recently, the accepted labels used are blacks and African-Americans.

But no one term is right for everyone. A recent Gallup poll (below) asked more than 2,000 participants whether they preferred black or African-American or had no preference. While those who had an opinion showed a slight preference for the African-American label, most of those questioned in the poll actually had no preference.

Questions about labels can also apply to the Hispanic community, one of the fastest growing minority groups in the country, according to the U.S. Census Bureau. Some newsrooms refer to members of this community as Hispanic, while others use the term Latino. Which is correct? Both. Just as in the discussion over black versus African-American revealed, people differ in their position on the terms Hispanic and Latino. A study by the Pew Hispanic Center conducted in 2008 found that 36 percent of the respondents preferred the use of Hispanic, while 21 percent preferred Latino, and the rest didn't have a preference.

About now, you might be more confused than when we began. That's OK. The point we are trying to make is that these discussions need to happen in your newsroom. Some newsrooms will tell you what terminology they wish to use. Make sure you understand the reasons behind these decisions. If you think they should be challenged, then challenge them. Also, make sure you have a good reason to use such labels in your story. It is not usually necessary to state someone's ethnicity.

Blacks	African-American %	Black %	Doesn't matter %	No opinion %
2007 June 4–24	24	13	61	1
2003 June 12–18	23	15	59	3
2000 Dec. 15–18	19	13	66	2
1994 Aug. 23–24 †‡	18	17	60	5
1994 April 22–24 †‡	21	13	64	3
1992 May 7–10 †	23	22	56	—
1991 June 13–16 †	18	19	61	2

† = WORDING: *"Some people say the term 'African-American' should be used instead of the word 'black.' Which term do you prefer—'African-American' or 'black,' or does it not matter to you?"*

‡ = No opinion includes volunteered "other" responses.

SOURCE: http://www.gallup.com/poll/28816/black-african-american.aspx

FIGURE **13.2** **Gallup Poll on Use of Black or African-American**

Source: From Frank Newport, "Black or African American?" Gallup News Service, Sept. 28, 2007. Located at http://www.gallup.com/poll/28816/black-african-american.aspx

The Five W's of Diversity

Who

Who are you? Are you an undergraduate or a grad student? Do you come from a well-to-do family, or did you grow up in low-income housing? A big city or a small town? All these factors influence how you might begin to cover a story.

What

What's your ethnicity? Are you African-American, Latino, Asian, Indian, Native American, Irish, Cuban, Guatemalan, Haitian, Kenyan? Or do you come from a mixed household, whether it's a mix of ethnicities, ages, nationalities or religions? All this could influence how you view your story.

When

When did you grow up? Were you were brought up in a household with grandparents who suffered during the Great Depression? If so, their experiences may have an impact on how you tell your story, as well as how you feel about people who are rich and those who are poor. Their experiences (and, in turn, yours) could also influence the way you approach someone who lives on the so-called wrong (poor) side or on the right (rich) side of the tracks.

If you were brought up during the '60s and '70s and supported the protests and sit-ins of that era, you might consider yourself a liberal. But if you thought the demonstrations and sit-ins were wrong, you might consider yourself a conservative. If you grew up during the Gulf War or if your parents protested against the Vietnam War, these events can shape your response to covering issues related to the military or politics.

As journalists, we must recognize how our personal histories can affect our storytelling.

Where

Were you brought up in a town where racist attitudes are deeply ingrained? Or did you grow up in a big city where you encountered a greater diversity of people and opinions? Growing up in either place could have an effect on the way you view the world. If you grew up in a rural community, you might not have been as exposed to technology to the same extent as someone who lives in a city because it wasn't available. Or you might not have been exposed to as many people from different cultures. You may not have been exposed to as wide a range of art or music or theater as someone who grew up in a big city. But then again, if you grew up in a big city, you might not have been exposed to many of these diverse experiences either, perhaps because of economic challenges. All these experiences and influences will affect your comfort level in new situations.

Even if you grew up somewhere different from your story's subject, you can still empathize with that character and try to understand his or her feelings. But the only way to do that is by exposing yourself to communities and people who are different from you and asking them questions. Being inquisitive is one of the key tools for a journalist, one we should use every day.

Why

Why is it important to ask these questions? Because we are writing and reporting for a diverse audience and because awareness of diversity adds layers to our stories. If we report only on stories in our own neighborhoods and talk to the same experts or other sources we've spoken to for years, we'll get the same stories over and over. Bringing in voices that haven't been heard before will help you tell stories that might resonate with viewers and readers you haven't been able to reach before.

Our duty as journalists is to dig out the story. Find the why. Dig for those voices we don't usually hear. They have amazing stories to tell.

WHAT WOULD YOU DO?

Let's say you are covering a story about a synagogue that has been attacked by vandals. There is spray paint graffiti on the walls, and windows have been broken. The three people arrested in the case are juveniles. The police say they are connected to a series of attacks on several businesses in the area. The three teens also are African-American. Do you use the pictures of the teens charged in the case? If you don't use the pictures, do you say the teens are African-American?

A Story with two faces

As journalists, part of our job is to feel comfortable taking on any assignment, whether it's in a community we're familiar with or one we haven't had much interaction with. As journalists, we're trained to find good stories no matter where they are, but we must also recognize that at times, that can be challenging. Every member of your newsroom brings biases, background and beliefs to assignments every day. Thus, two reporters can look at the same event and yet tell the story in two completely different ways. And if they don't recognize and acknowledge their biases, those preconceptions could creep into the coverage.

The "Side by Side" box below shows how the same story can be covered from two different perspectives. Is one approach truer than the other? Not necessarily. As a journalist, you have to be able to identify the multiple effects of stories. Thus, for the 5 p.m. show, you might do the story on the raid and the cleanup of the community. Then, for the 6 p.m. show, you might air the story of the mother who now looks at her community as a safer place for her children to play. With the multiple newscasts we produce for TV, radio and the Web, we have many places to tell these stories. The first step is acknowledging that there are several stories, not just the story the police officers might be telling you about a violent community that is being cleaned up. When covering a story like this, take a minute and look at the impact beyond the flashing lights and handcuffs. That's what being a journalist is about: testing your skills at digging for stories. You have to take the time to look, but, more important, you have to want to look.

Let's say the police are called out to do a sweep in a neighborhood. One reporter might put together a story that shows a lot of police cars and police arresting people. The story might also show drugs or guns. The message: This is a dangerous place, so police are shutting it down.

But another reporter might produce a story showing how the neighborhood block watch worked together to make this a safe place for families to live and play. Told from a mother's point of view, the sweep is a good thing. Finally, her neighborhood is becoming safe enough for her kids to play outside.

Serving the Needs of Your Audience

> "Those who think talking about diversity is just another form of political correctness miss the point. Real diversity is not designed to be overly fair to one group by being unfair to another. It is not meant to stifle debate but to encourage dialogue and the lively exchange of ideas critical to a vibrant democracy like ours."
>
> —WILLIE CHRIESMAN, INTRODUCTION TO DIVERSITY TOOLKIT, RADIO TELEVISION DIGITAL NEWS ASSOCIATION, WWW.RTDNA.ORG; FOUND AT HTTP://WWW.RTDNA.ORG/PAGES/MEDIA_ITEMS/DIVERSITY-TOOLKIT540.PHP

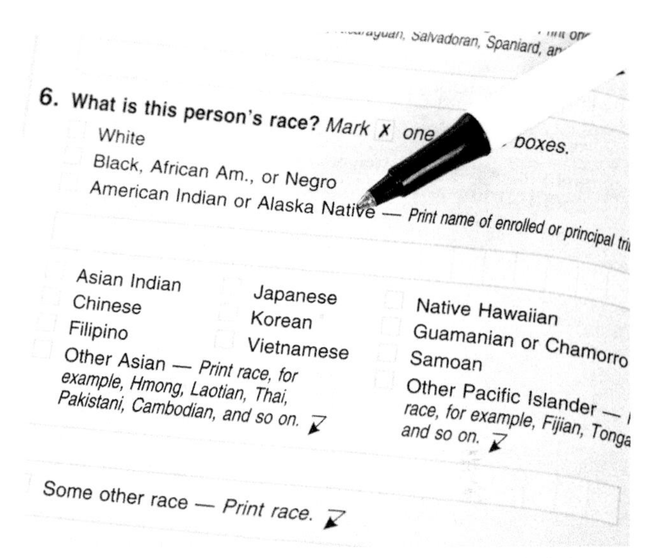
Salvadoran, Spaniard,
6. What is this person's race? Mark X one or more boxes.
White
Black, African Am., or Negro
American Indian or Alaska Native — Print name of enrolled or principal tri
Asian Indian
Chinese
Filipino
Other Asian — Print race, for example, Hmong, Laotian, Thai, Pakistani, Cambodian, and so on.
Japanese
Korean
Vietnamese
Native Hawaiian
Guamanian or Chamorro
Samoan
Other Pacific Islander — race, for example, Fijian, Tonga and so on.
Some other race — Print race.

The 2010 U.S. Census form asked respondents to identify their ethnicity.

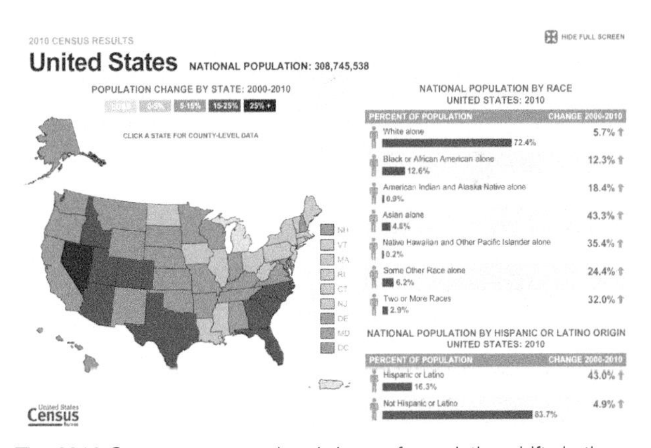

The 2010 Census gave us a breakdown of population shifts in the United States, which can help us determine areas of change and lead to story ideas.

Even though you might not be part of a particular community or have any obvious connection to the story in front of you, you still have the responsibility to do a thorough job. For example, a reporter who doesn't have children might not be attracted to doing stories about kids or families. Another reporter who has never spoken at length with a person who has a disability may feel uncomfortable covering stories that could interest this community.

Likewise, just because a reporter is black, she isn't the only one who can cover Martin Luther King Jr. Day. Similarly, the person who is gay is not necessarily the only reporter who can do the story on gay marriage. Just because someone is over 50 does not mean he should be the one to do the story about how the Internet generation is leaving older people behind. Good reporters know how to ask questions, good questions, so they can tell stories in the most interesting, compelling and accurate way possible—regardless of the group they belong to or the experiences that have shaped them. They must do their research and then tell the story as completely and accurately as they can.

Knowing who lives in the community you cover will help you make sure you report the stories that have a true impact on that community. Thus, understanding shifts in demographics is part of a journalist's job. The best place to get this information is through the U.S. Census Bureau.

The census is a treasure trove of information. It will tell you the average age of the population, who lives where, how many children are in a particular community. It can tell you how many people are single, married or just living together. All kinds of information is right at your fingertips, and remember that information is power!

Mining this information can help you understand what might interest people. For example, census data could reveal that a community that has been predominantly white for decades is changing, and the Hispanic population might have jumped by

20 percent. Awareness of this shifting demographic helps journalists focus on new issues that might be surfacing in this community. The impact might be visible in the schools, in new businesses that have opened to appeal to Hispanic customers, in conflicts between the longer-term and the newer residents or in new churches that may have sprung up.

The U.S. Census Bureau made a concerted effort in 2010 to reach out to some of these underserved communities, these sometimes "invisible" communities, to try and get more accurate numbers. There are always people who do not want to be counted, because they might have a bias against the government or maybe they are here illegally. The thing you must remember as a journalist is that while these people might not show up in the numbers, they are still living in communities and still having an impact. So they are still people you want to be aware of and make contact with because they can lead you to potential stories.

As a journalist, you have a responsibility to know and reach out to your audience, to all of your audience, no matter how small.

With the advent of new technology, it has become much easier to reach out to people. Social media such as Facebook or Twitter allow you to find people and gain access to groups you might not otherwise have access to. Still, many communities lack access to new technology, so nothing replaces good, old-fashioned, pavement-pounding journalism. Get out the door and talk to people face to face. The grapevine in a neighborhood can be just as effective, even more so, than a Facebook poke.

VOICES from the Newsroom

Brian Bull, assistant news director
Wisconsin Public Radio, Madison

I think new technologies, including the Internet in general, social networking sites and applications like Skype, will connect people in new and exciting ways. Virtual communities will be created where distance and time used to be barriers, and people who may not feel integrated in their "real world" neighborhood can reach out and connect to peers just a click of a mouse away.

What'll be important in making this happen will be reasonable access to computers. Inner-city schools, rural community centers and impoverished communities alike are often a few steps behind in the technological march ahead. Many people of color will find themselves either without access or perhaps stuck with older, obsolete technologies (think dial-up) that could make connections hard to establish and maintain. Hopefully our civic and city/state leaders can work to change this through increased funding and sharing of programs. And on a national level, hopefully initiatives like those to increase broadband in rural, isolated communities or for low-income areas can get under way to strengthen this virtual community.

Where media are concerned, computers and their technology are helping everyday people become citizen journalists. And people from underrepresented communities who aren't seeing their issues and stories shared on the local TV or radio news, tabloids, papers, etc. may well be compelled to do it themselves. Responsible and astute news managers should realize that your average PC user can do podcasts, blogs and mass emails with very little training and cash down anymore, so unless they really want to see their audiences (and ratings) depart for forums more to their liking (i.e., culturally attuned), they should make an honest and aggressive effort to recruit journalists of color and those from other groups in their market that may not be mainstream . . . yet.

Just looking through sites like YouTube, Twitter and several community blogs, you'll see that the issues of diversity and multiculturalism are gaining ground. Chat rooms and online forums are becoming the new barbershops or powwows, if you will. What'll be important for all members to keep in mind, though, is that while technology is helping connect and expand diverse communities in cyberspace, honest face-to-face communication is still essential.

It's up to both the professional journalist and the citizen journalist to be responsible and promote fair, accurate and truthful dialog as we all set out into this new virtual frontier. Exciting and challenging times are ahead.

Making Inclusive Reporting Your Standard

We've talked about your responsibility as a journalist to make sure your stories reflect a variety of voices. Now let's talk a little about how you do that.

The first thing you have to do is ask yourself these questions on every story: Am I getting the best subjects for my story? Do the people I choose to interview reflect as many different voices as possible for this story?

Britney Spears appears on the MTV Music Video Awards show in 2007.

Here's an example. A few years ago a student journalist was covering a story about Britney Spears, who had performed on the MTV awards show. People were talking about how fat Spears was. This interested the student journalist, who thought Spears actually looked very healthy. The student was going to head out to the Arizona State University campus to get students' reactions. She also planned to speak with a psychologist about the messages that body imaging issues send to young women and men.

The student shot her interviews, came back to the newsroom to write her story and then showed the edited story. She had done a nice job with the video. She got great sound from the psychologist and some good sound from the students, with the majority saying they felt Britney Spears was overweight and unattractive.

When the student was asked what was missing, she looked puzzled. Her supervisor then asked the student if she had spoken to anyone of color. The student said no; she hadn't even thought about it. On a campus of 60,000 students, the only people she spoke to for her piece were white, and they all felt the singer was overweight. This led to an interesting discussion of differing cultural views of what is attractive. In the black and Hispanic communities, for example, girls who are curvaceous are considered healthy and appealing. Having a diverse range of voices, then, would have made her piece stronger because she might have found that some people admired the way Spears looked, and the story would not have appeared one-sided.

Even more important, perhaps, was that the reporter realized she only approached people for comment who looked like her—primarily, she says, because she worried that others might reject her.

This young reporter learned a valuable lesson about her comfort zone, about making sure she expands the voices she brings to her pieces and about recognizing that her unconscious bias might have affected her story.

How do you make sure you're moving in the direction of more inclusive reporting? The first step is to do your homework before you are even assigned a story. And part of doing your homework is having a broad range of diverse sources to call. You'll find that it is far easier to call sources for help on a story when you know them than to call someone cold, introduce yourself and then ask for help. As a matter of fact, by getting to know a range of sources, you are just working your beat. Once you make those contacts and people come to trust you, great stories will come your way.

> **RULE OF THUMB**
>
> When you're told a name, repeat it to make sure you can say it correctly. If you're covering a community where the residents speak a different language than yours, learn to speak it. It's amazing how many stories you'll get when you speak the same language. It's a matter of trust and credibility. For some people, just the idea that you tried to learn their language will open doors.

Diversify Your Sources

We have discussed several strategies for building and working with a network of reliable sources. Here are additional strategies for making your pool of reliable sources more representative of your community. Using these strategies will give your stories a depth of perspective and context that will stand out.

Find sources before you need them. Drive a different way to work or school. It's amazing what you'll see on streets you've never traveled before. Go to street fairs in new communities. Strike up conversations with vendors or police officers on the corner. If you approach people in nonthreatening situations, they are more relaxed and usually more willing to talk. Later, when you need an interview or a comment, your contacts are more apt to return your call because they know you.

Eat lunch at a restaurant that has been around for years. It's amazing what regulars in the restaurant see and hear. Introduce yourself to the owners. Tell them you're trying to get to know their neighborhood better, and they'll probably call someone else over and introduce you.

Go to houses of worship in different communities. You'll meet people of all ages, people with money and people without. In many communities, churches can be segregated by socioeconomics and race, so you may find that they reflect some of the conflicts within a community.

Join chambers of commerce. Some communities have a black chamber of commerce, an Asian chamber of commerce and/or a gay and lesbian chamber of commerce. Attend their meetings, listen for trends, ask for business cards.

Have community newspapers delivered to your house, or visit their sites online. These papers report what's going on in the streets. They also run interviews with people you can contact and form relationships with. Such newspapers offer street-level or so-called mom and pop journalism, and thus they are rich sources for stories that connect with people on a human scale.

Visit online communities. Join Facebook groups to find out what people are talking about. Follow people on Twitter, which is a fast way to meet people and find out what they are thinking.

A Diversity Rolodex. One year The Arizona Republic offered a prize to the person in the newsroom who added the most names to the Diversity Rolodex, a collection of contacts the newsroom could use to bring fresh voices to stories. The newspaper ended up with hundreds of new names it might otherwise not have had. While it might seem a little crazy that we still have to collect sources in a Diversity Rolodex, sometimes it is needed. The goal is to get to the point where the people in your Rolodex are just sources and don't have to be categorized this way.

Take your assignment to a new neighborhood. Sometimes a story demands coverage in a specific city or neighborhood. But if not, avoid the path of least resistance. Report on a new town or neighborhood; give someone else a chance to weigh in.

VOICES from the Newsroom

Ian Lee, multimedia journalist
The Daily News Egypt, CNN

I think the most important thing about covering other cultures is learning about them first. Journalists make unnecessary mistakes by not understanding the people they are covering. After the hotel bombings in Jordan, I witnessed a lot of simple errors. One agency reported that al-Qaida targeted a wedding in one of the hotels because the bride wore white, a symbol of the West. When I heard this, I spat out my drink. Anybody who has spent time in the Middle East would know this is inaccurate. To prevent this in my reporting, I started studying Arabic and Middle Eastern cultures my sophomore year at Arizona State University. The following year I studied abroad in Jordan. Immersing myself in Jordan was the best way to learn about the culture. I also developed invaluable relationships with people in other Middle Eastern countries.

Another important thing to remember is that not every culture in a region is the same. When reporting in Jordan, tribalism is a factor, but it's not as big in Egypt.

But probably the biggest difference in reporting between the United States and the Arab world is government restrictions. I did a report on Christian and Muslim relations in Egypt. The story was interesting in itself, but during my report, I was stopped and questioned twice by the Egyptian secret police. Trying to get to the story sometimes is harder than actually reporting it.

Rule of Fours

> "Race/ethnicity pervades and invades, and as one of the most feared and least understood topics of journalists the world wide, it is potentially explosive each time it comes up.
> Covering such an issue requires awareness, skill, care, thoughtfulness and critical thinking. Doing it well means honoring the ethical principles of accuracy, fairness and contextual truth, along with the narrower journalistic goals of clarity and precision. Done well, reporting on race/ethnicity and race relations can illuminate, offer guidance, even help people heal."
>
> —KEITH WOODS, "HANDLING RACE/ETHNICITY IN DESCRIPTIONS," POYNTER.ORG, NOVEMBER 14, 2002. © COPYRIGHT 2002 THE POYNTER INSTITUTE. REPRINTED WITH PERMISSION.

When covering crime stories, reporters should attempt to have at least four pieces of information about a suspect before they go on the air (Table 13.1). Just saying the suspect is a white male in his 20s or a young woman who may be Hispanic isn't good enough. Those descriptions may fit thousands of people living in your town.

The lesson? Wait until you have at least four or more details—for example, a (1) white male (2) in his 20s (3) with brown hair who is (4) about 6 feet 2 inches tall and (5) has a scar on his right cheek. Or a (1) female teenager with (2) light brown skin who (3) weighs about 150 pounds and (4) has a tattoo of a knife on her left arm. Sometimes, to get this information, you have to ask questions of your sources. If the source says the suspect is Hispanic, ask if he knows what country the person is from. Naturally, not every Hispanic person is from Mexico. This extra information may help you track down others who have more insight connected to your story. You may also have to ask if a person's hair was curly or straight or whether the suspect spoke with an accent. Was it a Southern accent? A Boston accent? Did anyone notice the clothing? Was the suspect wearing the latest Air Jordans, which can go for hundreds of dollars and are tough to get? The lesson? Asking for details may jog your source's mind.

TABLE **13.1** **The Rule of Fours**

Inadequate Description	Good Descriptions
Hispanic male, 6 feet tall, 150 pounds	Hispanic male, close-shaved head, tattoo of skull on left arm, 6 feet tall, 150 pounds
Native American female, in her teens, with black hair and black clothes	Native American female, age 16 to 17, 150 pounds, black hair to her shoulders, wearing black jeans and black jacket with Harley-Davidson logo on the back
White male, small stature, about 115 pounds	White male, 5 feet tall, 115 pounds, multicolored Mohawk
Black male, braids, looks like a basketball player	African-American male, dreadlocks, 6 feet 8 inches tall, blue-and-purple hoodie, maroon knee-length shorts

Becoming an Inclusive Journalist

PITFALLS

It's easy to make mistakes when you're rushing to meet a deadline and are getting sketchy information from the police or witnesses. But lack of time is never an excuse for making statements that reflect badly on the community you are serving. This is especially relevant when it comes to descriptions of race and ethnicity.

A story on a local station in Phoenix dealt with a teenager killed late at night by an unknown shooter. Apparently the victim, Melissa Vigil, was coming home from a party when the truck she was riding in made a wrong turn. When the driver tried to make a U-turn, someone came out of a house and opened fire on the truck, which was carrying several young people. Vigil was shot in the head. The driver went to a nearby police station for help, and then police launched a search for several suspects.

The reporter went on the air, live from the scene. After describing what had happened, she came out of her story with this live tag, or ending: "Police say they have a very limited description of the shooters, just saying there were several black males."

So, you might ask, what's wrong with this? She was just repeating what the police told her. But that's not good enough. As journalists, we hold ourselves to a high standard.

Just because police tell us they're looking for "several black males" doesn't mean that's a good enough description to put on the air. When this statement is broadcast, it makes any black male in the city a potential suspect. The reporter should have said, "Police are still working on getting a full description of the suspects. As soon as we get that information, we'll pass it on to you." As journalists, even though you're in a so-called breaking news situation or because you think you need something to say, you can't be satisfied with what the police tell you.

Whether you become a photographer, a producer, a reporter, a manager or an editor, you must make a commitment to becoming a more inclusive journalist. This means you must become aware of your own biases and reach out to communities you might not have much experience with. This is a job requirement.

In concrete terms, being a good, well-rounded journalist means knowing that it is not only up to the Hispanic reporter to bring up issues for coverage in the Hispanic community, or the black reporter in the black community, or the gay reporter in the gay community, or the reporter with a disability in his community, or the Mormon reporter in her temple. By doing your research and reaching out to a diverse range of contacts, you can bring up any story. Become the best storyteller you can, and report the voices of diversity.

DIVERSITY QUESTIONS FOR YOUR NEWSROOM

1. Do you cover minority affairs all year long and not just during certain months?
2. Do minorities find themselves quoted in your stories, including stories that have nothing to do with minorities?
3. Do you always talk to the same so-called community leaders when you want quotes?
4. Do you concentrate on having diversity in the photos you use in your storytelling every day?
5. Do you absolutely have to say that a black, Hispanic, Asian or Native American is the first of his or her race to have attained the distinction in question? Is calling attention to someone's race relevant to the story?
6. In crime stories, is your mention that the criminals are black or Hispanic necessary?
7. Do you always assume that American means white? Do you assume that all Hispanics are from Latin America or that all people with Asian features were born abroad?
8. In covering politics, do you find that you usually make assumptions about the ethnicity of a person based on the party?
9. When working with surnames, do you make assumptions about a person's ethnicity because of his or her surname?

Producing Your CAREER

CHAPTER 14

> *I had a feeling that I had reached the pinnacle of journalistic success. I had a desk in the city room just like the big fellows, and I was dragging down $15 a week.*
>
> —WALTER CRONKITE

CHAPTER OUTLINE

Markets Large and Small

Now that you know what it takes to become a great visual storyteller, it's time to find a place to practice these skills. You've got to put it all together and get a job.Where do you begin?

As you'll see in this chapter, you begin while you're still in school—building your résumé and your reputation. Let's start by looking at markets for your work.

It used to be that finding a job in journalism entailed graduating from college, applying for a job in a small market and then working your way up to a large market. This system is set up like major league baseball: You have the minor leagues and then the majors. Of course, occasionally someone might luck out, get a job in a large market right away and then move around from there. A large market, according to the Nielsen Company, has at least 300,000 television-watching households; the largest markets, like New York, Los Angeles and Chicago, have millions of television-watching households.

The Nielsen Company tracks more than 200 markets in the country. (To consult the complete list, go to the Nielsen Company's website at en-us.nielsen.com and search for "DMAs.") A good way to begin your job search is to peruse Nielsen's list of markets, find the names and addresses of the **affiliates** and then send off your application to the news director. If you are looking for a production job, you would usually apply to the production manager at the station.

The same system applies to radio stations. You start with smaller markets. If you're looking for a newsroom job, you usually go through the news director for that station. If you want a position with a website, you usually apply to the managing editor. With websites, the size of the "station" is usually measured by the number of viewers, but websites usually are not broken down in the same manner as TV and radio station—meaning by large markets versus small markets.

Although many people starting out in the business still follow this traditional route, today's world has many more outlets for someone trained in journalism, which means many different kinds of jobs. You may break into a large market as a multimedia journalist or a production assistant and then move up within that large market station. Someone else might go work as a video journalist for a website or an on-camera reporter at a radio station website. A third person might find a job as a multimedia journalist for a public relations company or a government TV station.

More outlets mean more opportunities, and that's great news for journalists trying to break into the business! So, how do you start?

CLEAN UP YOUR ACT

You must remember that you are building your résumé throughout your college years. That means you have to start thinking and acting like a professional now. And that means you need to go into your Facebook or Twitter or other social-networking accounts and begin editing. Those pictures you took with your friends out at the neighborhood bar before the big football game don't need to be online. And yes, you might be a member of the Young Republicans, but you need to begin showing that you don't have biases. Some TV and radio stations require new employees to sign a form saying they are not a member of any group or organization that could have an impact on the way they perform on the job. Consider joining a range of political organizations to show that you have a broad range, and conduct research on all the major political organizations. Or, better yet, take charge of the privacy settings on your social media pages so that only your friends have access to your full profile information.

Another way to prepare for the job market is to clean up the comments you make online because these words can come back to haunt you. Saying that you hate the president's health care plan or have a problem with someone from PETA can get you in trouble. A news director only has to Google you to find an amazing amount of information. You don't want anything to stand between you and that job. So beware.

Internships: Grab One Now

First, make sure you have cleaned up your online footprint of questionable pictures or comments. Then start building your career by getting that internship. Begin to fill out your résumé with hands-on experience during your first year in college—or even before. Employers like to see that you were committed enough to give up your evenings and weekends to learn how to be a journalist.

You'll have an impressive résumé if you worked on your high school newspaper as an editor and also interned at the local TV station as an assignment desk assistant. It is also impressive when you can show that you interned almost every year in a journalism-related job. You may have worked with a photographer on a magazine or at a community paper as an assistant Web designer learning code, Flash or Photoshop. These are all skills that will impress an employer because they show you are well-rounded and committed.

CHECKLIST FOR FINDING INTERNSHIPS IN BROADCAST JOURNALISM

- Campus career center
- Campus journalism program's alumni outreach
- Websites for television and radio stations
- Professional organizations for journalists
- Human resources offices at television and radio stations
- Career fairs

VOICES from the Newsroom

Maxine Park, multimedia journalist
USA Today, Washington, D.C.

Internships. They're the building blocks of your journalism résumé. And as a broadcast journalism major at the Cronkite School, I knew I needed to get some experience under my belt in order to start building a strong résumé, so I started interning as a freshman. It's definitely challenging at times balancing an internship with school work, but you have to make the time. Internships are priceless, and it's important to get that real world experience in early. You have to get your feet wet.

During my years in college, I interned at several places, including KNXV-TV (ABC 15), KPHO-TV (CBS 5), KTVK-TV (3TV) and The Arizona Republic. I interned at several TV stations because I wanted to get the feel of a real newsroom and to immerse myself in the culture. I was able to go out in the field with reporters, learn how to edit packages and practice writing scripts. I learned how to do research, figured out whom to call and really became a part of the team. It was hands-on learning at its best.

At The Arizona Republic I worked as part of the breaking news team, covering stories for azcentral.com. I went out in the field by myself and covered numerous stories from murders to traffic accidents to officer-involved shootings. You can't get experience like this in a classroom. I felt it was important to do a print internship because the world of journalism is changing. You need to be well-rounded and able to transition between both styles of writing.

I applied for all the internships through the school and had to go through several interviews. The interview process was great because I was able to practice answering questions to learn the right technique.

I was the bureau chief for ABC News on Campus at school. It was a great opportunity. I worked with three other student reporters in producing content for ABC News. We produced everything from video packages to text articles to slideshows. I feel that all these internships helped prepare me for this position. I was able to assess the situation, know whom to call and work efficiently. Our bureau was like a real newsroom, and we produced the content.

In general, doing an internship while you're in school is important because it gives you a taste of the future and helps you build a professional résumé. Waiting until your senior year to try out your first internship is too late. Internships count as part of your journalism experience and help you grow as a student journalist. You learn from professional reporters and photographers who have been in the business for years. The knowledge and the experience are priceless.

Journalism internships are extraordinarily competitive. One way you can give yourself an edge is to begin building relationships with journalists (and journalism professors) whose work you admire. Begin building these relationships before you need them so that when you do apply for an internship, you'll already have a relationship inside the organization where you'd like to work. Another idea is to reach out to the people who produce websites you visit often and admire. Go to their contact information page online and write an email telling them what you like about their work.

People prefer working for a place that has a product they respect. This is far better than getting an internship anywhere because you need to fulfill a school requirement. Getting the internship is all about building your skill base. But in order to do that, you need to make contacts first. So start now, and you'll be able to make the internship work for you.

When in the newsroom, whether as an intern or an employee, you must dress like a professional, prepared to go on-air at any time.

The internship interview

An internship interview is like any other job interview. You want to present yourself as a professional journalist, one who will represent the company well if you are sent out on the streets to cover a story. So, dress like a professional.

For men, that means wearing a suit or sport jacket with color-coordinated pants. Wear a tie even if you will never be required to wear one on the job. No jeans. No holes or ragged edges. No baggy pants or shirts.

For women, professional dress means wearing a suit or a nice pair of slacks with a professional-looking top. No 4-inch heels. The employer wants to know that you can carry a camera and run if necessary, not topple over at the first breaking news opportunity. No revealing shirts or skirts. One news director sent an intern home because her belly button was showing, and he could not send her out on a story to the governor's office. A missed opportunity for that student!

Just remember: If you would wear it to the club, it's probably not something you would wear to work. Go easy on the perfume. You don't want an interviewer remembering your offensive perfume smell and not your work.

Prepare yourself for the interview by researching the company where you are applying, as well as the city, surrounding area and current events. Doing so will prepare you to ask the interviewer intelligent questions, and it will also prepare you to answer her questions. To see how well-informed you are, an interviewer might ask you a question about the governor or state budget issues. Your answers to such questions reveal what you know, but even more important, they reveal whether you are well-read and engaged in the community you will be covering. Be prepared to show them that you are.

TIMESAVER

Being on time for an interview is not good enough. Plan on being early, which means that you plan for the unexpected. You don't want to have the potential employer be ready to interview you and then have to wait because you had to work your way around a traffic accident that set you behind 15 minutes. The employer will not wait for you, so be there early.

I got the internship: Now what?

You need to follow a few rules if you want to have a positive experience. You don't want to hurt your career before you really get started.

1 Be on time. Yes, we already made this point about interviews, but we want to emphasize how important punctuality is. If you are late to work, you could miss out on an opportunity to be sent out on a major story. When there is breaking news, the station often looks for the first person in the door. Be that person! Establish a reputation as the committed worker who is there early and leaves late. In this way, you could become the "go to" intern in the office.

2 No drama. Do not be one of those people who spreads gossip or even listens to it. Not only is it a waste of your time, but it also wastes the time of your co-workers. Remember, you're there to *learn* and *contribute*—and to make a great impression. You can create positive workplace relationships (and have some wonderful, enriching conversations) if you ask your co-workers about their ongoing projects, their career paths, the most interesting stories they've covered or how they've seen journalism change.

3 This is not a popularity contest. Don't spend your time at work planning where you will be partying after work or trying to figure out who is dating whom. Don't take personal calls, and stay off IM and Facebook. Supervisors notice the difference between the interns who are working sources or going out in the field and the ones who are managing their popularity. In short, get to work.

4 Get busy. Do not sit in the workplace waiting for someone to hand you something to do. Stay busy. Talk to your supervisors; let them know you are ready to work and eager to do anything. Sometimes that might mean getting coffee. There is no job too small or too big. To succeed, we all must contribute to the team. Log tapes, answer phones, do research, comb through files when you're assigned an investigative piece. Establish a reputation as someone who is prepared, motivated and able to run down a story rather than waiting to be handed one.

5 Put in overtime. Be willing to stay until the job is done. If you are out working on a story, you have to finish it—even if you have plans to go out with your friends. You tell the news desk you will stay as long as you need to and reschedule with your friends. The people you work for in your internships are the ones you will be asking later to be your references. These are the people who you hope will sell you to your potential employers. Make sure the story they have to tell is a positive one.

6 Identify your mentor. Mentors are the people who can help you open doors in this business. A good mentor will take the time to read your writing, critique your standup or video, or have those tough conversations with you when you have stepped out of line.To find a good mentor, look for the hardest-working person in the newsroom, someone you respect and someone who is respected by senior professionals in the organization. Ask to go out on the streets with this person and pick her or his brain. Ask questions, but be sensitive about deadlines, and don't impose on anyone's time.

7 Mind your manners. Stay cheerful and positive, even under pressure. Never say "no" to a request. Acknowledge your assignments, and ask for further information and clarification if you're not sure of something. Remember to watch your language. Just because something might be acceptable around your friends or on the street does not mean it is acceptable in the newsroom. Even if other employees in the newsroom use inappropriate language, it does not mean it is OK for you to do so as well. You are in a professional environment, and you need to treat it that way.

8 Be gracious and express your gratitude. Finally, when your internship is over, send thank-you notes to your supervisor and anyone else in the newsroom with whom you worked, letting them know how much you appreciate all their time and guidance. And be sure to include your contact information in case an opportunity opens up at a later date.

Experience: Beyond Internships

Working freelance

Internships are not the only way to begin building your résumé. You can also find plenty of **freelance** opportunities. For example, you could work as a freelance operator shooting high school football games for the local television station. It might only pay 10 or 11 bucks an hour, but it is a paying job and not an internship, so on your résumé you can say that. If you hope to get a job working on a website, you might start out by working as a freelancer and designing websites for clients you find. Again, it's a paying job, and that shows potential employers that your work is good enough for others to pay for it.

You can also seek freelance work as a writer for websites. Some pay by the number of people who read the piece; others pay a flat fee for each piece you write. Although you may not earn much money, the payoff is that you have published work to show future employers during job interviews.

Some freelance opportunities have dried up in the past few years as businesses have tightened their budgets. Moreover, they may now pay less per project than they did in the past. Nevertheless, your goal is to build your reputation and résumé for the future, so those small paydays may pay off down the road.

When working as a freelancer, you still want to dress and act professionally because you never know whom you will meet.

Immersion programs

Another way to get experience is through immersion programs. Many universities now offer these programs as a training ground for students. An immersion program is one in which students produce their own newscasts, websites or newspapers. These programs help you understand the stresses of working under a deadline. Each day that you are in these newsrooms, you have deadlines. No longer should you be thinking that you have two weeks to shoot, write and edit a package for class because that's not reality. In the real world, if you need to write a piece for a website, you don't have three days. You're lucky if you have three hours. By your senior year, you should be pushing yourself to work under these types of strict deadlines.

When employers call references to check on students for their first job, the question they ask most often is, "Do they understand deadlines?" Employers want to know that you can get an assignment in the morning and have it finished for the evening newscast or the paper or a radio cut-in. The only way you can prepare for this kind of pressure is to experience it. When you are applying for a job, you should already know that you are up for the challenge. Because you will be feeding the news beast 24/7, you have to be nimble. You have to be able to multitask and do it fast. Challenging yourself and creating stress-filled opportunities will prepare you to handle anything.

During your senior year, set up your class schedule so that you have two whole days to work in a newsroom. If your school doesn't have a structured immersion program, then create one for yourself. On those days you set aside as your working news days, find a project and challenge yourself to get it done by the end of the day.

Create your own blog or website, and provide the content. Work on your writing and videography skills as you establish a professional footprint.

You can produce podcasts and video stories and upload them to your site. Post blog entries to demonstrate your writing skills. Showcase your photography skills on Flickr. This is an opportunity to display your skills to the person hiring you for an internship and, down the road, to an employer looking to see how comfortable you are working on multiple platforms.

Your site shows potential employers not only what you can do but also that you have a great work ethic. It shows that you don't need a teacher demanding that you complete a project for a grade before you turn something in. It also shows that you are motivated and passionate about wanting to succeed and will do whatever it takes to get the job done.

Because things move so fast in newsrooms, employers don't have time to be on top of a reporter or producer. They are looking for people who are used to challenging themselves and getting the job done. They are looking for responsible journalists. Show them you are the person they want in the newsroom.

As a student, Carolyn Carver spent one summer traveling, shooting stories and producing packages for a website. This experience helped her land a job as a multimedia journalist.

> "Being in an immersion program was probably the best decision of my college experience. Having to face some type of deadline several days a week helped me with my writing, my live shot performance and my speed with editing and shooting. It gave me much-needed confidence. As I begin my job search, I feel prepared to handle anything my first job might throw my way because I already feel as if I have been working in a newsroom."
>
> —Tia Castaneda, 2011 graduate, Cronkite School of Journalism and Mass Communication

Professional Programs

Another essential step in preparing yourself for the work world is to become involved in professional programs like the Radio Television Digital News Association (RTDNA), the Society of Professional Journalists (SPJ) or the Online News Association (ONA), just to name a few. Join any professional organization that has a connection to the job you want to do. In these organizations, you can find mentors, hear about job opportunities and learn about changes in the industry. Many of these organizations also offer scholarships, and some have student projects that allow you to get hands-on training with some of the best professionals in the industry.

These organizations charge students less to join than they do for working professionals, so it pays to join when you are still a student. If you can't afford the membership on your own, why not ask your parents to sign you up as a present? The investment you make in these organizations will pay off down the road, so get involved now.

VOICES *from the* Newsroom

Jim Willi, principal and senior vice president
AR&D, Fort Worth, Texas

Be competitive and energetic

The most important thing is to set yourself apart from the rest of your generation—the ones who grew up without keeping score in T-ball or with everyone getting a ribbon at a track meet or race to make sure no one felt bad or was left out.

That has created a generation that is too laid back and simply not competitive enough for the hard-charging news business, especially in this age of tireless multitaskers. It drives news directors nuts that their young reporters do not fight for the lead story or even bother to make contacts to come up with stories. News directors want to see a brash, competitive go-getter during the interview process.

Excel at multitasking

The TV news business is going through a huge transition from a generation where newsrooms grew and news employees became specialists. They produced one newscast—and that was the extent of their day. Reporters covered one story (without really much concern about whether they came in with a turnable story idea).

Those days have vanished. Now the most valued employees in a newsroom are the multitaskers—or, as we call them at AR&D, the multimedia journalists (MMJs). The valued TV news employees of the future (meaning right now) will generate story ideas; shoot and edit their own stories; send back a 15-second update from the field before the noon peak in Internet usage; post their story to the Web immediately, with updates throughout the day; take a quick picture from their Blackberry or iPhone when they get to the scene or a breaking story—or almost every story, for that matter—so it can be quickly posted to the Web; communicate with the producer about special graphic needs for their story; and so on.

If you want to get your foot in the door with any news director in the country, approach her or him with multitasking skills. These changes have altered the way news directors look at recent college graduates. They desperately need people with these multiple skills, and their veteran employees are either balking at the idea or simply can't do it.

Be curious and know your market

Back in the day, reporters were expected to know all about the market where they lived and worked, and they were expected to cultivate news sources. These days, there are some reporters who walk into the morning editorial meeting with no ideas and little knowledge of the issues where they live, and they expect to be handed a story from the assignment editor.

That is not the future reporter model. Stations have gone back to the future by having MMJs live in the county they cover, develop news sources in their area of the market and generate stories—multiple stories—every day. If you sell the news director on the idea that you are that kind of person, you will get a job.

Use social media

The TV newsroom of the future will do as much listening as it will reporting. Demonstrate skill in the use of social media (Facebook, Twitter, texts, emails) to create a network of sources for stories and to engage them in conversations about the big issues of the day and their takes on those issues.

Marketing Yourself

Now that you have built up that résumé, it's time to put it to good use. But to get your first paid job, you have to market yourself so that future employers know exactly what they are getting. You do so with your cover letter, your written résumé and your demo reel. All three of these elements show what you can do; they sell you to your employers.

Your cover letter

Let's start with the cover letter shown on the opposite page. Think of it as the handshake when you first meet someone. If you get a limp, wet handshake, you form an opinion of that person immediately—and it's probably not a good one. The same thing applies to a cover letter. It's your chance to offer your potential boss a good, firm handshake. Here's what you do.

First, address it properly. **1** Take the extra time to call the newsroom and get the correct spelling and gender of the news director, production manager or managing editor. A cover letter should not be addressed "To Whom it May Concern." Letters addressed that way can show the person on the receiving end that you are not the type of reporter or editor who takes the time to dig for information and, therefore, not the type of person she wants in her newsroom. As for gender, don't make assumptions. You need this information so you know whether to use Mr. or Ms., and some first names are ambiguous—for example, Andy or Chris.

Next, a cover letter should tell the person who you are and what you can do. **2** You want to sell yourself with a great attitude, as someone who understands the importance of teamwork and is willing to work hard and do whatever it takes to get the job done. This is the time to show that you can write, shoot and edit a story on deadline. If you have experience doing live shots, this is the time to say, "I have experience doing live shots and feel very comfortable covering breaking news." Let the prospective employer know what you can bring to the table. Show that you are a professional and not a student.

Also show that you know the market you are applying to. **3** Refer to an item of current news in the market. For example, let's say that you are applying to a station that is in a border town near Mexico. Mention in the cover letter that you understand the challenges of covering border issues and feel your Spanish language skills would help dig out stories that others might not be able to get. Show that you understand the challenges the station feels, as well as the challenges facing the viewers, listeners or readers.

About three or four paragraphs is the longest a cover letter should be. If it is too long, the person doing the hiring might not read it at all. These people are looking at dozens of cover letters and résumés for each job, so get to the point, intrigue them and then let them move on. Always spell-check before you send. A cover letter with typos and misspellings shows the work of a sloppy candidate, and no one wants a sloppy reporter on the payroll.

Joe Smith
9999 W. Van Buren St.
Phoenix, AZ 85007
Oct. 8, 2011

1 Kate Morris
Executive Producer
KGGG-TV
PO Box 7
Boise, ID 83707

Dear Ms. Morris:

2 When Arizona's controversial immigration legislation went into effect, I was covering the issue from the other side of the border in Mexico. I've walked through Phoenix neighborhoods with a young girl as she registered people to vote so their voices could be heard. And when it appeared Arizona would break a record for the number of migrant bodies found in the desert, I followed the coroner into the morgue where he examines migrants' remains every day to try to learn their identities. I want to tell important stories like these as a morning reporter for KGGG-TV.

3 I'd love to wake up Boise and send people off to work with the stories they need to make it through the day. I understand that your station prides itself on covering breaking news stories, and working quick and smart is something I can do. I'm a reporter and anchor for "Cronkite NewsWatch." I've done multiple live shots for the show, and every Thursday I anchor our live newscast, which airs on PBS World and reaches 1.2 million homes in Arizona. I am one of the few students selected nationwide to be a paid reporter for ABC News on Campus. I work out of the bureau at Arizona State University, producing pieces for the network on multiple platforms, including online and on-air. I'm also a multimedia journalist at Mesa Channel 11.

In December, I will graduate summa cum laude from the Walter Cronkite School of Journalism and Mass Communication at Arizona State University, and I want to bring the experience I've gained to KGGG-TV. This past summer, I was one of nine journalism students in the nation to receive the Roy W. Howard scholarship. As a morning reporter, I will bring my creative storytelling, outgoing personality and strong work ethic with me to the number one rated station in Idaho.

I have sent a résumé and résumé tape and will contact you in the coming weeks to see if you need any additional information.

Sincerely,

Joe Smith

Joe Smith
555-881-1391
JoeSmith@gmail.com

Your résumé

Now that you have your potential employer intrigued, it's time to lay out your job background and skills in a simple-to-read, one-page résumé. The résumé should be free of errors and misspellings, and it should be written in phrases rather than sentences. The person doing the hiring will probably be looking at or listening to a résumé tape at the same time he or she is reading, so the printed information must be concise.

The first items on the résumé are your name, phone number and email address. **1** You present this information first to make it as easy as possible for employers to find you if they are interested and want to set up an interview. Make sure this information is current and your email address is professional. Don't use the email you might have used in college, such as hotgirl88@gmail.com or baddude22@yahoo.com. While these might have been fun when you were a student, you are now a professional, and your email address needs to reflect that. You can have one email address for all your employee-related work and one for your friends. But again, be careful with this.

The next block on the résumé presents your experience, not your education. **2** Remember, you don't want to remind potential employers that you are a student. The image you want in their heads is of you working in their newsroom. That means showing the experience that will help you get the job—that is, the internships and work experience that directly relate to your being a journalist. A newsroom director is not interested in the job you had as a restaurant hostess or facilities manager for your school sorority.

The third section of the résumé focuses on your skills. **3** Here you feature your proficiency with Final Cut Pro or Avid, your experience shooting with a Sony XDCAM or using the Essential News Production System (ENPS) or iNEWS newsroom system. Here you can also note your fluency in other languages. If you are not fluent, though, don't say you are. Some employers will test your skills by bringing in someone to interview you in the language you claim to know. If you speak only some Spanish, note that you "speak some conversational Spanish." Be honest about your abilities. You want to market your strengths, but you don't want to oversell.

After the skills section of the résumé, you feature your education. **4** Do not include high school. Potential employers will know that because you are graduating from college, you obviously completed high school or got your GED. Students often wonder whether to include their grade point average. There are two schools of thought about this. Some employers say they only want to know if you graduated magna cum laude or summa cum laude because that shows you strive for excellence and can commit to a goal and achieve it. Others say that the GPA has no effect on whether you are hired. The bottom line? If your GPA is barely a 2.75, leave it off because it's not going to help you and could end up hurting you.

If you have room left, add the honors and awards you might have received that relate to journalism. **5** In other words, potential employers probably won't be interested in knowing you were the employee of the month at your local grocery store, but they will want to know if you were selected as a Hearst finalist for breaking news coverage.

As for references, do not say, "References available upon request." Remember that you want to make this process as easy as possible for the employer, so furnish the references on a separate page. List three or four references with names, titles, companies, phone numbers and email addresses. **6** Choose people who know you well because these are the people who will also be trying to sell you and your potential to your future boss. Never list people without their knowledge. If you do, they may not be prepared when the call comes, and as a result they might not have much positive to say. Finally, use a variety of people. For example, you might want to have one professor and two people from different internships you completed. This way, the potential employer can get a more complete idea of your work in a range of environments.

Use clean white paper or a muted beige. Select the standard Times New Roman font rather than a fancy font style. You want the résumé to be as clear and readable as possible. Finally, don't include an 8-by-10 glossy of yourself. Doing so can send a message to the employer that you are more interested in looking like a journalist than working as one.

1 **Joe Smith** 555-881-1391
JoeSmith@gmail.com

2 **Media Experience**

- KAET-TV (PBS) **NewsWatch**—Multimedia Journalist, Anchor Jan. 2010-Present
  - Reporter and anchor in an award-winning newsroom that produces multiple live newscasts each week that are broadcast to more than 1.2 million people throughout Arizona.
- Mesa Channel 11—Multimedia Journalist June 2009-Present
  - Film, edit and produce news packages and public service announcements for government television station. Run a Chyron graphic generator during live broadcasts of city council meetings and other civic events.
- Cronkite Village Television—Entertainment Show Anchor Sept. 2007-March 2008
- The Blaze Radio Station—News Reporter Sept. 2007-Dec. 2007

Internships

- KNXV-TV ABC 15, News Department Aug. 2008-Dec. 2008
  - Worked with crews to interview people, including Arizona Attorney General Terry Goddard, assisted on live shots, pitched and set up stories and wrote for ABC15.com and the 10 o'clock newscast.
- KNOW99 Television Jan. 2009-May 2009
  - Worked as a field reporter, shooting, editing, producing and writing 18 packages for air and posting them online for Phoenix's education channel.
- KNXV-TV ABC 15, Sonoran Living Jan. 2008-May 2008
  - Helped organize and book guests, set up props, wrote scripts, logged tapes and assisted on live shots.

3 **Skills**

- Proficient in Final Cut Pro, Avid, ENPS, Photoshop, WordPress, Dreamweaver, Sony XDCAM
- Fluent in Spanish

4 **Education**

Bachelor of Arts, Broadcast Journalism Class of 2011

Walter Cronkite School of Journalism and Mass Communication

Arizona State University

5 **Awards**

- Roy W. Howard National Collegiate Reporting Competition March 2010
  - One of nine winners nationwide selected to take a journalism study trip to Japan

6 **References**

Sue Brown	Steve Miller	Joe Grange
Executive Producer	News Director	Managing Editor
ABC News	KNXV-TV	NewsWatch
212-456-0000	602-502-4444	480-491-1111
SueBrown@gmail.com	Stevemiller@yahoo.com	joegrange@newswatch.com

Your résumé reel

Once you have captured attention with your résumé and cover letter, it's time to show your potential employer what you can do. And that's where your résumé reel—also called résumé tape, reel, DVD and link—comes into play. It's a means of delivering your work to an employer.

The reel is about eight minutes long and includes a slate, the montage and three or four packages.

Slate. The slate comes first and includes your name, email address and phone number. Make it look professional (no hot pink or other crazy background), and make it accurate. It might be the only way an employer can reach you if he misplaces your résumé, so double-check the information on the slate to make sure it's right. Keep the slate up for about five seconds.

Montage. The next part of the reel is about 45 seconds of some of your best standups sequenced together into one timeline. Forty-five seconds will allow for about six standups. Make sure to combine standups from the field with those from live locations, the newsroom or the set.

If you don't have a good montage, the news director or managing editor will never make it to the packages on your reel, so make sure the montage shows you at your best. Dress professionally, communicate great energy and move. None of the standups should be more than 10 seconds long. Settle on an image and stick with it. Otherwise, the person viewing the reel has no idea who you are. The quality must be as high as you can possibly make it. If you end up with a montage that is only 30 or 40 seconds long, that's OK—as long as it's the best 30 or 40 seconds you can put together.

Packages. Your packages should show that you are a great storyteller who understands the demands of a deadline and can cover anything you are sent out on. You want to show a variety—let's say a breaking news story, an issues story or investigative story and a feature piece. Place the best story first—one that showcases great writing, great videography, great standup, great energy and great originality. You want a story that prospective employers will remember. You do not need a slate between the packages, but you do need to apply the same rules of quality as you did for your montage. Don't give someone any reason to hit the "stop" button.

When you are finished with your reel, copy it to a tape, burn it to a DVD or upload it to a secure website to which you can provide a link. Most stations these days request DVDs. But before you send one in, be sure to put it into a player and watch it to make sure it has no audio or video problems. If your DVD doesn't play for the news director, you almost automatically land in the reject file. Your cover letter and résumé should include a link to your online video résumé. That way, if something is wrong with the DVD or tape, your potential employer can still watch it online.

You also might look into creating a website. There, you can include videos as well as links to your writing or to photos you have taken. A website can give employers the opportunity to look at more of your work and find it all in one place. You can find tools and tutorials online for building websites very cheaply, and some are even free. Having your own website also shows employers that you are comfortable working in digital media, especially if you can tell them you created the site yourself.

VOICES *from the* Newsroom

Joe Bartels, reporter
KOB-TV (NBC), Roswell, N.M.

My job-hunting experience was nerve-racking, to say the least. After looking at dozens of cover letter examples, I finally sat down and got to work. I think one of the biggest hurdles was sitting down and getting started. Besides putting together a great résumé tape, writing a coherent, well-rounded letter that makes you stand out is key. I agonized over each part of my résumé packet (résumé, cover letter, tape) for weeks—proofing, changing and rewriting until I thought it was perfect. I edited my résumé tape until my eyes crossed. In the end, I rewrote my cover letter twice from scratch and completely redid my résumé tape halfway through my job-hunting campaign.

While my classmates were getting callbacks and exciting offers, I sat and I waited, second-guessing myself. Was my cover letter too cheesy, my résumé tape too boring? I had spent more than $200 on DVDs, fancy paper, printing and postage, and the weeks turned into months—and still nothing.

In terms of a résumé tape, my first edition was boring, I'll admit. The pace was off and the rhythm was nonexistent, but I was blinded by my own cockiness and didn't see where it could be improved. I did have people look at it, and it was a decent tape. But it wasn't until I started to watch the people who were watching my tape that I knew I had to change it. They lost interest halfway through the montage because it was too boring and slow.

Finding Job Leads

Now that you have all the best experience and tools for promoting yourself, it's time to find the job. A good place to start is the Web—for example, exploring sites that specialize in listing jobs, such as JournalismJobs.com or TVJobs.com or indeed.com. You can also try the job banks on websites of professional organizations like Radio Television Digital News Association (RTNDA), National Association of Hispanic Journalists (NAHJ) or National Lesbian & Gay Journalists Association (NLGJA).

Another approach is to choose the city where you'd like to work and then survey the websites for each station in that city to check their job listings. At each of those station websites, take time to read the bio page for employees. If you find someone who went to your alma mater, reach out to that person. If she's willing, send her your résumé, and maybe she'll walk it into the boss' office. That will give you a huge advantage over other applicants.

Another way to find leads is to send your résumé to consulting companies like Broadcast Image Group, Talent Dynamics or Frank N. Magid Associates, which are clearinghouses for talent. News directors call them when they're looking for reporters or other personnel, and in response, these agencies put together several work samples and send them off to the station. These places don't charge you to be in their talent bank, so it's worth sending them your résumé and reel.

JournalismJobs.com is just one of several websites where you can find job listings.

VOICES from the Newsroom

Lindsey Reiser, reporter
KTSM-TV (NBC), El Paso, Texas

I've found that finding a job takes the same diligence as learning the skills to do that job. Just as a reporter must cultivate sources and form relationships in order to break stories, an applicant must meet with as many potential employers as possible—and stand out.

I completed my applications in rounds. First, over my spring break I took a road trip and visited nearby small markets. Before visiting, I had set up interviews with connections I had previously made from internships and simply sending out emails asking professionals to review my work.

I went prepared with story ideas for that market as well as a mental preparation of what questions the people who would interview me could possibly ask. I brought multiple copies of my cover letter, résumé and DVD demo reel so that I could drop those materials off at other stations within the market where I was unable to schedule a visit. I wanted to make the most of every opportunity.

Things to obsess over are not what kind of paper to use or which DVD label looks the most professional. I kept my materials simple and focused on perfecting the content—proofreading and double-checking every DVD, making sure I wouldn't ruin my own chances with a simple typo or scratched disc.

My hard work paid off, as I got multiple offers.

My best words of advice: Looking for a job takes time, research and tedious double-checking, but it is worth it. When you have your first paycheck, a new group of friends and a plethora of work to show for it, you will be satisfied that you jumped in, took a chance and never looked back.

Now What?

The next step is to follow up both informal conversations and formal interviews with a thank-you note to the person you spoke with. Also follow up after you send résumés. If a job listing says "no phone calls," then respect that. But you can follow with an email about a week after sending your résumé. Then you have to wait. Don't call or email every few days to ask if the news director or newsroom manager has received your stuff. If no one has called you back after several weeks, however, you can assume that the organization is not going to ask you in for an interview, and you should look elsewhere. You will send out dozens of reels and résumés. Because of the industry economics right now, some stations might post a job but won't fill it because it's been frozen until the next quarter. Be patient, and don't get down or give up. Getting a job is a lot of work!

If you do get called for an interview, be ready to travel. One news director called a job candidate and reached him on the golf course. The job candidate told the news director he was busy and asked him to call back later. This is the call you have been waiting for. Be prepared to take it. If a potential employer leaves you a voice mail message asking you to call back, do it.

This first exchange on the phone is the beginning of your job interview, so you want to impress. Thus, before that call comes in, you should have changed your voice mail greeting. No more "Yo dog, sorry I missed ya, but you know I am busy. So leave me your digits, and I'll get back at ya." While this might work with your buddies, it will not work with a potential employer. Keep it simple. "Hi, you have reached Carrie Clark. Sorry I am not here to take your call, but please leave your number, and I will get back to you."

At this point, you need to be flexible. If the potential employer wants to bring you in for an interview tomorrow, be prepared to jump on a plane even if you had plans. Again, this is one of the most important moment in your career, and you may have to make some sacrifices.

If you get the call, no matter what you're doing, even golfing on your favorite course, stop and answer the phone!

VOICES from the Newsroom

Ayana Harry, reporter/producer
ABC News

When I was a senior at Princeton, I met a contact at ABC. I bugged my contact every week, saying I wanted to be hired in New York as a desk assistant. Finally, in April of my senior year, I got a call asking if I wanted a job as a part-time vacation relief desk assistant. I said sure, I would love to. I didn't even hesitate. I was willing to move with no guarantee of a permanent full-time job, and it paid off. I went from working the desk to writing to shooting and moving into a position as a digital news associate. I think it's a great blend of everything I love. I see myself doing this for a long time.

My advice to someone wanting to succeed as a journalist is to be willing to stay late and meet with people whenever you can, even if it is hours after your shift has ended. You have to be willing to sacrifice to be successful. Meeting with people in the industry can help you get that next job, and they can teach you a lot. You have to be willing to sacrifice to be successful. I love my job, and I worked very hard to get it.

The Job Interview

When you finally land the interview, the really hard work of impressing the boss-to-be begins.

1 **Do your homework.** Research the government and politics of the area so you understand the big issues the community is facing. Come up with some stories you might pitch if you were working in the newsroom. Also look at the company's website so you understand the station's news identity. For example, some are breaking news stations. Others are more investigative. Still others pride themselves on having a consumer focus, and they cover many consumer stories. Whatever the station's identity, make sure you are prepared to talk about it. Be sure to look at the competitors' sites so you can talk about the differences between the two. Doing this kind of preparation shows the employer that you are driven, conscientious and thorough.

2 **If you are flying out of town, pack your clothing in your carry-on bag.** Don't take the chance of checking luggage and then losing it. For the interview, choose the same clothing you would wear if you were going to be on the air that day because you might be asked to be on-air as part of a test. Bring another hard copy of your résumé and a DVD of your reel. You always want to be overprepared for any possible situation.

3 **Make sure you arrive on time.** You've heard that repeatedly, but it's more crucial than ever now. Plan to be there a half hour early. This will allow time for traffic issues or delays. If you get there early, you can grab a coffee, relax and mentally prepare for the interview instead of panicking because you didn't give yourself extra time and might be late.

4 **Make a good impression on everyone.** At the station, you will probably begin by meeting the news director or managing editor—someone in a high supervisory position. Usually, you will spend the entire day at the station, and during this time you will meet with several people in the newsroom. You might be asked to meet with designers, editors, photographers, assignment managers or other reporters. They will pepper you with questions, and you need to ask questions in return. All these people are checking you out to see if you will fit into their newsroom, and at the end of the day they will report back to their supervisor. Make sure your passion for the job and the industry comes through.

5 **Be prepared to answer questions about your experience and to supplement your résumé.** Let the interviewers know that you shot everything on the résumé reel and that you edited your own stories and wrote them, too. Make sure they understand the extent of your experience. Sell yourself, but don't oversell. This can sometimes be difficult because you might not be comfortable talking about yourself and your accomplishments, but it is time to get comfortable. Just keep in mind that there is a fine line between confidence and cockiness.

POSSIBLE INTERVIEW QUESTIONS

- Tell me about your greatest success so far.
- Tell me about your worst failure. What was the lesson you learned?
- If I talked with the people you worked with, what would they tell me about you that I probably wouldn't know from this interview?
- What are your strengths/weaknesses? (Answering this isn't as easy as you think.)
- How will you continue growing?
- Tell me about somebody who has been a role model or inspiration. Whom have you learned the most from? Who has been your best critic?

6 **Be up on current events and ready for action.** Expect that you might be sent out with a crew to do a story. The potential employer wants to see you in action, so be prepared to turn a story quickly and demonstrate that you understand the pressures of working under a deadline.

7 **Be prepared to take a current events test.** Performing well on this test shows that you are well-read and understand history, so you need to read websites and newspapers and watch TV. Some managers won't hire a person who doesn't know how many justices sit on the U.S. Supreme Court or the name of the state's governor.

8 Be prepared to answer questions about your news philosophy. That is, why you are in news, what you believe and what you strive for as a journalist. WBOY-TV in Clarksburg, W.Va., posts its philosophy (right) on its website so viewers and readers have no question about it.

If all has gone well, you might be taken in to interview with the station manager or website manager. Although you may feel intimidated, this is usually a good sign. No one wants to take up the top manager's time if you're not a serious candidate. In this case, greet everyone with a firm handshake, look them straight in the eye and try to relax. The manager might ask you some of the same questions you have been asked throughout the day, but as you did before, answer truthfully. This final interview of the day typically lasts anywhere from 15 minutes to half an hour. If it goes longer, that's usually a good sign.

WBOY-TV'S NEWS PHILOSOPHY

WBOY-TV's vision is to be the No. 1 news resource for our viewers. Our mission is to report about our state and surrounding communities fairly, accurately and completely with the best informed and most professional news staff.

As professional journalists, we will:

- Assure fair and balanced coverage of all perspectives.
- Focus on meaningful stories that have an impact on our viewers' lives.
- Seek background information and conduct research to present the most accurate and in-depth stories possible.
- While examining the specific, offer a broader context.
- Treat interviewees with respect.
- Ask the tough, but fair question.
- Report on what's good about our community, as well as expose wrongs.
- Expect to be held accountable for producing fair and accurate reports.

In fulfilling our public trust to observe and report the news, WBOY-TV hopes to improve the quality of life for all those people who call this area home.

Source: WBOY–TV—WV MEDIA

Contracts

If you are offered a job, more than likely the news director will want you to sign a contract. The length varies from a year and a half to two or even three years. A three-year contract is usually for an anchor job. News directors feel that if they are going to invest in advertising and billboards for an anchor, they want the anchor to be in the market for an extended period of time. These days, producers are also being asked to sign job contracts.

But if you are being hired as a reporter, you will probably receive a two-year contract that will describe the job requirements, your pay, any potential raises and any moving expenses or clothing allowances. You will also receive information about when the contract will end and the limitations on outside work. The contract might also contain potential "outs." These are conditions that cover what employees are responsible for if they try to leave before the contract is over. Some stations are willing to add "outs" to a contract, but many will not negotiate in this area for first job contracts.

Keep in mind that contracts are weighted in favor of the station, not the employee. For most jobs, signing a contract is a condition of employment, so you have to decide whether you are comfortable with the conditions.

Many employers will ask you to take a drug test before you can officially be offered the job and can sign the contract. Most times, the employer will call you, tell you an address and give you a few hours to take the drug test. This is no big deal so long as you have not been using any drugs. Just remember that this test will pick up everything.

Now You Wait

If you're very lucky, you might get an offer the next day, or it might be a few days before you hear anything. Be patient. In the meantime, follow up your interview with an email thanking the people who met with you, telling them you are very interested in the job and letting them know you will wait to hear back from them.

Unfortunately, you are at their mercy unless you have another job offer come in. If this happens and the first station is the one you really want, call the news director, tell her or him that you really want to work at that station and explain about the other offer and your deadline for making a decision. The first station will either come back with an offer or tell you it can't make a move yet. Then the decision is yours.

The job offer usually comes via a phone call with the details. The manager will explain the position, the desired start date and your salary. She or he will also tell you about the benefits being offered, such as health insurance and vacation time. If the person who calls can't answer your questions, you can ask to speak to someone in the human resources department. You can also ask about other perks that might be connected to the position, such as a hair or clothing allowance or paid travel expenses. Most of these perks have disappeared because of budget cuts, but you might be surprised at what's offered.

Don't be surprised at the salary you are quoted. Your first job will likely pay $16,000 to $29,000 per year, depending on the position and the market you will be working in. Smaller markets, smaller salary. As you can see, you are not going to be rich, but if you are creative and get a roommate, you will be able to make it. You have to pay some dues, but if you love being a journalist, it's worth it.

Good luck!

A Brief History of Broadcast and Online Journalism

1900–1919

RADIO	**1901** Using a kite as an antenna, Italian inventor Guglielmo Marconi transmits the first radio signal across the Atlantic Ocean.	**1906** American Lee De Forest invents the vacuum tube that amplifies radio signals. **1906** Canadian Reginald Fessenden makes the first public broadcast of voice and music.	**1912** Russian-born radio operator David Sarnoff relays breaking news of the "Titanic" sinking.	**1920** KDKA, the first commercial radio station, goes on air in Pittsburgh to broadcast the election of President Warren Harding.
DIGITAL	**1900** Eastman Kodak introduces the Brownie camera. It's cheap and easy to use.	**1905** German inventor Alfred Korn sends the first photos by telegraph.	**1910** Thomas Alva Edison demos the first talking pictures.	**1914** Germany's Leica launches the first 35 mm camera.
LEGAL / BUSINESS		**1912** Radio Act requires that broadcasters need a license and that the U.S. government regulates the airwaves.		
WORLD NEWS	**1901** President William McKinley is assassinated. Theodore Roosevelt takes his place.	**1909** Adm. William Peary reaches the North Pole.	**1914** World War I erupts in Eastern Europe.	**1917** Lenin's Communist government crushes opponents during the Russian Revolution.
POP CULTURE	**1901** Actress Marlene Dietrich is born in Germany. **1903** Boston Americans beat Pittsburgh Pirates in first World Series. **1903** Orville and Wilbur Wright's airplane makes the first powered flight.	**1905** Columbia Phonograph Company makes the first two-sided disc. **1907** "Mutt and Jeff" is the first daily comic strip.	**1915** Albert Einstein postulates the general theory of relativity.	**1918** World flu epidemic kills 22 million people. **1919** Members of the Chicago White Sox throw the World Series to the Cincinnati Reds in the "Black Sox" Scandal.

1920–1929

RADIO	**1920** The world's first commercial radio station—KDKA-AM in Pittsburgh—presents the first news of the results of the 1920 Harding-Cox presidential race.	**1922** WEAF on Long Island, N.Y., broadcasts the first radio commercial about brownstone apartments. It lasts 10 minutes and costs $50.	**1922** BBC (British Broadcasting Company) is founded in London.	**1923** The World Series is carried by a linkup between stations in Newark, N.J., and Schenectady, N.Y.
TV	**1923** Investor Vladimir Zworykin begins experimenting with electronic camera tubes to transmit and receive TV signals.	**1926** Engineer J.L. Baird demonstrates the first practical TV system. It's based on a spinning mechanical disc.	**1928** WGY in Schenectady, N.Y., becomes the first experimental TV station.	**1927** Inventor Philo T. Farnsworth assembles a complete electronic TV system.
DIGITAL	**1926** Kodak produces the first 16mm movie film.	**1926** Warner Bros. releases "Don Juan," the first movie to use music and sound effects.	**1927** "The Jazz Singer" becomes the first film to feature spoken dialogue.	
LEGAL / BUSINESS		**1926** David Sarnoff launches NBC (National Broadcasting Company), the first radio network in the United States.	**1927** The Radio Act decrees that broadcasters must operate in the "public interest, convenience and necessity."	**1927** William Paley buys a group of 16 radio stations and creates CBS (Columbia Broadcasting System).
WORLD NEWS	**1920** The League of Nations is founded to preserve world peace.	**1924** While in prison, Adolf Hitler writes "Mein Kampf" and claims Aryan race will rule the world.	**1926** Adm. Richard Byrd and aviator Floyd Bennett first fly over the North Pole. **1928** Amelia Earhart is the first woman to fly across the Atlantic.	**1929** Stock market crash ushers in the Great Depression. Radio grows in popularity because it's free. Movies cost 10 cents.
POP CULTURE	**1923** George Gershwin performs "Rhapsody in Blue."	**1927** Grand Ole Opry debuts.	**1928** Mickey Mouse debuts in "Steamboat Willie."	**1930** First Academy Awards are broadcast on radio. 1929–1930 Outstanding Production goes to "All Quiet on the Western Front."

1930–1939

RADIO	**1930** NBC begins broadcasting hard news. Sarnoff leads the network.	**1933** CBS News Division begins under leadership of Paul White, a former United Press reporter. **1933** President Franklin Delano Roosevelt delivers first of 28 fireside chats.	**1934** WOR in New York and WGN in Chicago create MBS (Mutual Broadcasting System). **1936** CBS transmits first live battlefield report during Spanish Civil War.	**1938** Orson Welles' "War of the Worlds" documentary on CBS scares listeners. Panic follows. **1938** CBS World News Roundup first airs. **1938** Edward R. Murrow broadcasts live as Hitler invades Austria.
TV		**1935** Regular public TV broadcasts air in Germany.	**1936** BBC broadcasts are the first regularly scheduled TV shows in Britain.	**1939** Inventor Philo T. Farnsworth signs a TV patent with RCA. **1939** Television is displayed to the public at New York World's Fair.
DIGITAL		**1935** The first Associated Press wire photo shows a plane crash in New York's Adirondack Mountains.	**1937** John Atanasoff begins working on the first electronic digital computer.	**1939** "The Wizard of Oz" film shows the difference between black-and-white and color photography.
LEGAL / BUSINESS	**1933–35** Pressured by newspapers, the AP and UPI wire services refuse to sell stories to radio stations during the Radio Press War.	**1934** The Communications Act creates the FCC (Federal Communications Commission).	**1936** Vladimir Zworykin and Philo T. Farnsworth battle in court over TV patents.	
WORLD NEWS	**1931** Japan invades Manchuria.	**1932** The kidnapping of Charles Lindbergh's baby becomes a media circus.	**1935** The Social Security Act provides benefits for retirees and the unemployed.	**1939** World War II begins after Germany invades Poland.
POP CULTURE	**1931** At 1,250 feet, the Empire State Building reigns as the world's tallest building for 40 years.	**1933** The first car radio is introduced. **1933** "The Lone Ranger" debuts on radio, charged by Rossini's "William Tell Overture."	**1937** The founders of Alcoholics Anonymous develop the 12-step program. **1938** Superman flashes his cape in a comic book for the first time.	**1939** DuPont demos nylon products, including nylon stockings, at New York World's Fair.

1940–1949

RADIO	**1940-41** Edward R. Murrow reports live from rooftops in "This Is London" reports during the Nazi blitz.	**1941** The largest radio audience to date (62 million) listens to President Franklin Delano Roosevelt's "Day of Infamy" speech.	**1945** Edward R. Murrow's account of the Buchenwald concentration camp deeply affects Americans.	**1945** NBC's "Meet the Press" debuts on radio. The show moves to TV two years later.
TV	**1940** NBC covers the GOP convention—the first one televised. **1941** CBS and NBC launch commercial TV stations in New York but put them on hold until the end of World War II.	**1943** The FCC forces NBC to sell one of its two networks. NBC Blue stays NBC, while NBC Red eventually becomes ABC (American Broadcasting Company).	**1948** Douglas Edwards begins the first daily network evening newscast on CBS.	**1949** "Camel News Caravan" with John Cameron Swayze becomes the first NBC news program to use filmed news stories instead of newsreels.
DIGITAL/ TECHNICAL	**1940** Walt Disney's "Fantasia" is released, with eight-track stereophonic sound.	**1941** The first commercial FM broadcasting begins in the U.S.	**1947** The Polaroid instant camera debuts, thanks to Edwin Land. **1947** Ampex produces the first tape recorder.	**1948** Bell Labs invents the transistor.
LEGAL / BUSINESS	**1941** The FCC issues standards for TV, including 30 frames per second.	**1942** The U.S. government's OWI (Office of War Information) coordinates the release of war news at home.	**1948** The FCC appoints the first female commissioner—Frieda Hennock.	**1949** The FCC's Fairness Doctrine allows editorials on the air but requires equal time for the other side.
WORLD NEWS		**1945** The United Nations is founded to achieve world peace.	**1946** Winston Churchill coins the term "iron curtain."	**1948** After a lifetime of advocating nonviolence, Mahatma Gandhi is assassinated in India.
POP CULTURE	**1940s** Consumers snap up colorful plastic radios.	**1944** "Casablanca" wins three Oscars, including Best Picture.	**1947** Jackie Robinson breaks the color barrier when he plays second base with the Brooklyn Dodgers.	**1949** RCA Victor releases the first 45-rpm single record. Columbia counters with a $33\frac{1}{3}$ -LP (long-playing) album. **1949** The first DJs spin records.

1950–1959

RADIO	**1952** Comedian Bob Hope moves his popular radio show to TV.	**1954** Fans listen to the final episode of "The Shadow," on the air since 1931.	**1954** For the first time, radio makes less money than television.	**1959** Fibber McGee & Molly, a popular radio show, lasts only five months on NBC TV.
TV	**1951** CBS airs the first nationwide broadcast—"See It Now" with Edward R. Murrow. It shows live pictures of both the Brooklyn Bridge and the Golden Gate. Don Hewitt sits next to Murrow in the control room.	**1952** NBC develops the TV magazine format with the "Today" show, hosted by Dave Garroway. His sidekick is a chimp named J. Fred Muggs. Barbara Walters joins as a writer/researcher in 1961.	**1954** CBS creates the Sunday morning newsmaker interview format with "Face the Nation." **1954** NBC creates a late night twin of its morning show. Called "The Tonight Show," it's hosted by Steve Allen.	**1956** NBC begins dual anchors, with Chet Huntley in New York and David Brinkley in Washington, D.C.
DIGITAL/TECHNICAL	**1951** President Harry Truman addressing the Japanese Peace Treaty Conference in San Francisco marks the first coast-to-coast TV broadcast.	**1952** The first video recording on magnetic tape occurs in Los Angeles.	**1953** Color TV arrives in the U.S. when the FCC approves an RCA model. **1953** "Bwana Devil," the first 3-D film using a polarized lens, is released.	**1956** The Ampex Corporation introduces videotape, which replaces kinescope technology. Bell Labs tests the first Picturephone.
LEGAL / BUSINESS		**1954** The first color TV commercial—Castor Decorators—airs on local stations in New York.	**1958** Commercial ads on radio and TV top $2 billion.	
WORLD NEWS	**1950** President Truman approves production of the hydrogen bomb.	**1954** The U.S. Supreme Court bans school segregation.	**1957** The Soviet satellite Sputnik circles the Earth.	**1959** Fidel Castro comes to power in Cuba.
POP CULTURE	**1950** DJ Alan Freed gains national attention by playing rock and roll.	**1954** NBC broadcasts the first World Series in color.		**1957** Elvis Presley appears on CBS's "Ed Sullivan Show."

1960–1969

RADIO	**1960** Those who hear Vice President Richard Nixon debate Sen. John Kennedy think Nixon does better.	**1960** November 25 marks the last day of radio soap operas.	**1967** Britain makes pirate radio stations illegal. BBC starts its own pop music station.	
TV	**1960** Seventy million people watch the first televised presidential debate between Nixon and Kennedy. Many viewers believe Kennedy won, in part because Nixon sweated.	**1963** CBS doubles the length of the nightly news to 30 minutes and broadcast in color from the studio.	**1963** CBS anchorman Walter Cronkite confirms the first TV breaking news story: President Kennedy has been shot. Anchors cover the funeral. NBC viewers witness the first live TV murder when Jack Ruby shoots Lee Harvey Oswald.	**1968** Producer Don Hewitt creates the CBS news magazine format "60 Minutes." The show becomes the most financially successful and longest running primetime news magazine.
DIGITAL/TECHNICAL	**1962** Telstar launches the first communications satellites, making possible satellite telecast of part of a baseball game between the Cubs and the Phillies. **1962** The invention of the time code makes videotape editing possible.	**1963** The first instant replay in sports appears in a telecast of the Army-Navy game in color.	**1965** NBC is first to broadcast both news film and an anchor on a studio set in color. **1966** Xerox invents the tele-copier, which acts as the first fax machine.	**1969** The U.S. Department of Defense launches ARPANET, which eventually evolves into the Internet.
LEGAL / BUSINESS	**1961** FCC Chairman Newton Minow labels TV a "vast wasteland."	**1963** The Roper Poll shows Americans find TV more reliable (36%) than newspapers (24%).	**1967** Congress creates PBS (Public Broadcasting Service).	**1968** Spending for TV ads in the presidential campaign reaches $27 million, up from $10 million in 1960.
WORLD NEWS	**1963** Millions watch Dr. Martin Luther King Jr. deliver his "I Have a Dream" speech on TV.	**1963** The UPI wire is first to report Kennedy assassination four minutes after the shooting.	**1965** Former President Harry Truman is enrolled as the first Medicare beneficiary.	**1969** Neil Armstrong takes one "small step for man" on the moon.
POP CULTURE	**1962** Johnny Carson cracks jokes on "The Tonight Show" as the new host.	**1963** Julia Child stirs up gourmet meals as "The French Chef" on educational TV. **1964** The Beatles tour America.	**1965** Bill Cosby becomes the first African-American star in a primetime show—"I Spy."	**1967** The Monterey International Pop Festival becomes the first large rock music festival. **1969** Big Bird and his friends make their debut on "Sesame Street." **1969** Half a million music fans attend Woodstock.

1970–1979

RADIO	**1971** NPR (National Public Radio) is founded.	**1974** The CBS Radio Mystery Theater premieres.		
TV	**1976** Barbara Walters receives the first million-dollar anchor contract when she leaves NBC to join ABC.	**1978** ABC puts the news division under the control of Roone Arledge, head of the "Wide World of Sports."	**1979** "Nightline" begins on ABC as a 15-minute late night update on the hostage crisis in Iran. It later expands to 30 minutes and other topics.	**1979** CBS creates "Sunday Morning," showcasing American reporter Charles Kuralt and, later, Charles Osgood.
DIGITAL/ TECHNOLOGY	**1971** Computer engineer Ray Tomlinson sends the first email message. He designates @ as the locator symbol for electronic addresses.	**1974** A 2,121-foot Polish radio mast becomes the world's tallest structure—until it collapses in 1991.	**1974** ENG (electronic new gathering) begins replacing film. ENG is first used by networks covering President Richard Nixon's Moscow trip.	**1975** Bill Gates and Paul Allen found Microsoft. **1976** Steve Wozniak and Steve Jobs form Apple. A year later the Apple II is the first PC to use color graphics.
LEGAL / BUSINESS	**1970** Congress bans cigarette ads on radio and TV. **1970** The FCC's cross-ownership rule prohibits a broadcaster from owning a radio station and a TV station in the same market.	**1972** HBO invents pay-TV service for cable.	**1976** Owned by Ted Turner, WTBS in Atlanta becomes the first superstation, with local signals broadcast via satellite.	**1979** ESPN, a total sports network, becomes the largest and most successful cable channel, reaching more than 57 million households. **1979** Japan launches the first cell phone network.
POP CULTURE	**1972** Owned by Time Inc., HBO becomes the first pay-cable channel.	**1972** The "Magnavox Odyssey" debuts as the first home video game system. Atari produces "Pong," the first coin-operated video game.	**1975** "Saturday Night Live" premieres on NBC.	**1977** ABC's miniseries "Roots" attracts an audience of 130 million.
WORLD NEWS	**1970** The first Earth Day celebrates the environment.	**1973** The Watergate scandal breaks.	**1975** The death of Gen. Francisco Franco ends Fascist rule in Spain.	**1979** Mother Teresa wins the Nobel Peace Prize.

1980–1989

RADIO	**1980** Sony introduces the Walkman, a portable audio cassette player.	**1981** Nearly 150 local stations identify themselves as "all news."	**1984** During a radio mic level check, President Ronald Reagan quips, "We begin bombing in five minutes." The press covered it.	**1988** "Shock jock" Howard Stern begins broadcasting on WJFK in Washington, D.C.
TV	**1980** Ted Turner launches CNN (Cable News Network).	**1981** Dan Rather replaces Walter Cronkite, who had anchored the "CBS Evening News" for 19 years.	**1982** The Weather Channel begins.	**1983** ABC moves to a single anchor news format with Peter Jennings.
DIGITAL/TECHNICAL	**1980s** The age of video games begins. The most popular are "Pac-man" and "Space Invaders."	**1986** Colorization of black-and-white classics bothers some film fans.	**1987** Bill Gates becomes the computer industry's first billionaire.	**1988** After 38 years, the Soviet Union stops jamming foreign radio broadcasts.
LEGAL / BUSINESS	**1981** The Reagan administration's deregulation of broadcasting includes extending TV licenses from three to five years.	**1984** The Supreme Court rules that taping TV shows on home VCRs doesn't violate copyright.	**1985** Capital Cities pays $3.5 billion for ABC.	**1987** The FCC abolishes the fairness doctrine, so stations no longer have to air contrasting points of view.
WORLD NEWS	**1980** Soviets and mujahedeen guerrillas clash after the Soviet Union invades Afghanistan.	**1982** Argentina invades the Falkland Islands but is driven back and defeated by the British.	**1984** Medical researchers in France and the U.S. announce the discovery of the AIDS virus.	**1989** Chinese authorities use force to crush student protesters in Tiananmen Square.
POP CULTURE	**1981** MTV (Music Television) debuts on cable.	**1983** The last episode of "M*A*S*H" draws 125 million viewers.	**1984** Apple's Macintosh computer debuts during a Super Bowl commercial.	**1986** "The Oprah Winfrey Show" debuts in Chicago. **1986** Telemundo becomes the first Spanish-language network. It expands nationwide.

1989–1999

TV	**1991** TV networks and CNN broadcast extensive coverage of the Persian Gulf War.	**1992** Fox requires local affiliates to broadcast local news.	**1995** CNN International becomes a global, 24-hour news channel.	**1996** The News Corporation launches Fox News Channel. NBC and Microsoft create MSNBC.
DIGITAL TECHNICAL	**1991** Tim Berners-Lee, who invented the World Wide Web, introduces the world's first Web browser.	**1992** An experimental digital FM transmitter debuts in Paris.	**1996** Eighteen-inch digital satellite dishes become the biggest-selling electronic item after the VCR.	**1999** Sony releases a mini-digital videocassette called a mini-DV.
LEGAL / BUSINESS	**1991** Cablevision, NBC, Time Warner and American Lawyer Media launch the Courtroom Television Network.	**1993** Fox pays $1.58 billion over four years for the rights to broadcast the National Football League games. This leads to major shuffles in local station network affiliates.	**1996** President Bill Clinton signs legislation that significantly deregulates telecommunications and allows one company to own more than 40 radio stations.	**1997** TV ratings begin to appear in the upper left-hand corner of the screen.
WORLD NEWS	**1990** Iraq invades Kuwait. **1990** After 27 years in prison, South African activist Nelson Mandela is freed.	**1994** The Winter Olympics set ratings records on CBS as Tonya Harding is involved in an attack of fellow figure skater Nancy Kerrigan.	**1994** Some 95 million viewers watch live as football legend and actor O.J. Simpson leads police on a freeway chase in Los Angeles.	**1997** Princess Diana dies after a car crash in Paris. **1997** Great Britain cedes Hong Kong to China.
POP CULTURE	**1993** David Letterman begins to compete on CBS against Jay Leno on NBC after 11 years on the Peacock network.	**1994** NBC locks up Thursday night viewers with "Friends" and "ER."	**1997** Sixty percent of kids from ages 2 to 11 watch Nickelodeon.	**1998** An estimated 76 million viewers watch the last episode of "Seinfeld." **1999** Cheap-to-produce reality TV hits America with the British import "Who Wants to Be a Millionaire?"

2000–2010

RADIO				**2009** Paul Harvey, a folksy ABC radio news anchorman since the 1940s, dies on Feb. 28.
TV		**2005** Peter Jennings dies of lung cancer. America's youngest network news anchorman began his career in 1967 on ABC.	**2006** On Sept. 5 Katie Couric becomes the first solo anchorwoman at "CBS Evening News."	**2009** On Dec. 21 Diane Sawyer takes over as solo anchorwoman on "ABC World News."
DIGITAL/TECHNICAL	**2003** Release of the first DVD camcorder allows recording direct to disc. No tape!	**2005** HDTV becomes a best seller as almost all TVs sold are flat screen. **2005** YouTube shares its first video—a frank discussion about elephants.	**2006** Holding about 13 hours of standard video, Blu-ray Discs surpass the storage capacity of DVDs.	**2009** The FCC requires all local stations to broadcast in high-definition format. The U.S. government runs out of rebate coupons to help consumers convert analog sets to digital.
LEGAL / BUSINESS	**2000** AOL and Time Warner merge to become the largest media company of its kind in the world.	**2003** NBC purchases the entertainment arm of French conglomerate Vivendi Universal for $3.8 billion.		
WORLD NEWS	**2000** The Y2K bug fails to bite. No serious computer failures occur when clocks roll over to the year 2000.	**2002** Brazil wins the World Cup. **2003** U.S. invades Iraq.	**2005** London bombings on July 7 kill 52.	**2008** Barack Obama beats John McCain in the U.S. presidential election.
POP CULTURE		**2001** DVDs become common as most movie studios now release films on both DVD and VHS.	**2009** "Avatar" film with 3-D glasses becomes highest-grossing film of all time.	**2010** J.D. Salinger, author of "Catcher in the Rye," dies.

Glossary

5 W's Who, what, when, where and why.

Accuracy Facts gathered and shared in a clear, concise manner. Often includes saying what you don't know as well as what you do.

Actuality A portion of an audio interview. The radio broadcast equivalent of a direct quote in print.

Ad-libbing Communicating in clear and concise sentences what you are thinking when there is no written script.

Affiliate A station that has an agreement with a network to run its programming and usually produces local news.

Agency Free choice.

Arbitron Generally correspond to the Metropolitan Statistical Areas (MSAs) defined by the U.S. Government's Office of Management and Budget.

Aspect ratio The dimensions in which video is shot and displayed. For example, high-definition wide screen is usually 16:9 or 16 inches horizontally by 9 inches vertically. A standard definition aspect ratio is 4:3.

Assignment editor The person in charge of story coverage, including coming up with story ideas, organizing field crews to cover stories and making sure the correct information gets from crews in the field to producers in the newsroom.

Audio Sound. Video cameras capture both video and audio, which can be separated during editing. Quality audio is important for a strong interview.

Audio input Where a microphone is connected to the camera directly or with an audio extension cable. Most video cameras have at least two audio inputs.

Average Quarter Hour Persons (AQH) The average number of persons listening to a particular station for at least five minutes during a 15-minute period.

Average Quarter Hour Ratings The AQH Persons estimate expressed as a percentage of the population being measured.

Background information Information that helps you or your audience understand the story but not necessarily something you'd want to use for a direct quote or sound bite.

Backtime A producing formula for estimating the start time of individual stories by subtracting the length of each from the total or end time of a newscast.

Beat See focus area.

Bias Slanting a story. Giving unequal representation to different sides. A prejudice or leaning of the mind, shall we say, about something or someone that can have an influence on how we perceive people or situations.

Blocks of a newscast The content-filled segments of the show divided by the commercial breaks. A newscast with three commercial breaks will have four blocks. The blocks are usually referred to by letter, with the first called the A-block, the second called the B-block and so on.

Body language Body movements or posture. Can indicate how someone feels about a particular situation or question.

Breaking/spot news A fast-developing story.

Bridge A standup that links one part of a story to another.

b-roll (cover video) Known from the days of film, b-roll refers to sequences of shots that illustrate a story. B-roll is not the source being interviewed on camera, the reporter's standup or graphics. Everything else in a television news story is b-roll.

Bureau A small satellite newsroom used to give a news organization a presence in another city within its market.

Central compelling character (CCC) The most important person in a story.

Chemistry How the audience perceives the interpersonal relationship among the anchors on a set.

Circulation The number of newspapers distributed by a news organization on a daily, weekly or monthly basis.

Cliché An expression that has been used so much it loses its punch.

Climax The peak of the action or conflict in a story, usually occurring toward the end. Always comes before the resolution because the issue or problem has to arise before it can be resolved.

Copyright A right granted by federal statute to authors of certain types of literary and artistic works. This right grants the owner, for a limited period of time, the sole privilege of copying, publishing and selling the copyrighted work.

Credibility A reputation for truthfulness.

Cume The total number of different persons who tune to a radio station during the course of a daypart (the time segments that divide a radio or

TV day for ad scheduling purposes) for at least five minutes.

Cutaway shot Any shot that is not part of the main action but still contributes to visually explaining the scene to the viewer.

Daybook A tool used by the assignment desk to keep track of dates, times and information about stories.

Diversity Understanding that each person is unique, and recognizing and celebrating our individual differences. These differences can deal with issues of race, socioeconomic factors, gender, age or religious beliefs, to name a few.

Executive producer Newsroom manager who is in charge of producers and reporters involved in one or more newscasts or who leads a news division, such as an investigative team or a special projects unit.

External conflict Conflict from an outside source.

Fairness Balance achieved in a story through careful control of facts presented and interviews shared.

Fair use When certain material can be used without infringing on the copyright. Examples of fair use of a copyrighted work often occur in criticism, comment, news reporting, teaching, scholarship and research.

Feed To transmit a story from one location to another, often via microwave signal, satellite or Internet.

Focus area A topical or geographical area of interest. Also called a beat.

Frame rate The number of frames captured per second. Most television news is shot at 30 frames per second.

Freedom of Information Act A law requiring federal agencies to disclose records requested in writing by any person. States also have public records laws.

Freelance Working for an employer on a project-by-project basis rather than as a full-time employee.

General assignment A reporter who is qualified and expected to cover a range of assignments from hard news to features.

IFB The intercom system a producer uses to talk with anchors on the set or reporters in the field.

Infringement When a protected work is reproduced, adopted, distributed, publicly performed or publicly displayed without the permission of the copyright owner.

Iris Controls the amount of light coming through the camera lens. The more it's open, the more light comes in, and the brighter the shot will be. The more it's closed, the less light comes in, and the darker the shot will be.

Jump cuts Shots that when edited together are jarring or visually do not work together.

Kicker A memorable line or sentence at the end of a story.

Lead The beginning of a story. A lead grabs the audience's attention and instantly telegraphs what's ahead.

Libel A false, defamatory written statement of fact that concerns a particular person and injures that person's reputation.

Live Happening in real time, not prerecorded.

Made for hire A work created by an employee within the scope of his or her employment, or a work specially ordered or commissioned in certain specified circumstances. When a work qualifies as a work made for hire, the employer or commissioning party is considered to be the author.

Market The city where the television station is located and the surrounding community that is within reach of the broadcast signal.

Media literacy Knowing that some pieces of information or sources are more valuable and reliable than others.

Medium shot Provides visual focus and eliminates distractions.

Mini-softbox A filter mounted on a light that softens the effect.

MMJ Mutimedia journalist. Someone who is adept at reporting, capturing video and editing a news story. Also known as a backpack journalist or a one-person band.

Mult box A multiple input box. An electronic piece of equipment that is made to handle multiple microphone connections at one time. Often provided at press conferences.

Nat pop A brief burst of natural sound at full audio level. Gives viewers a sense of what is being heard on location and improves the pacing of a package or newscast.

Natural sound The audio that already exists at a given location. Capturing these sounds and editing them into a piece gives the viewer a sense of what it was like to be at the scene.

Natural sound package Video and audio presented together as a package without a reporter's track.

Network tie-in Special report or information that can be used to tease other programming on a given network, such as a behind-the-scenes feature on "CSI" to air in a local newscast immediately before or after the season premiere.

News director Manager in charge of the newsroom. Oversees content, promotion, personnel and budgets.

News judgment Deciding what is important, timely, interesting and relevant.

Newscast director Manager who makes sure that technically the newscast goes on the air without a problem. In charge of the production crew. Works hand in hand with the producer.

Nielsen ratings Demographic information about viewers—age, ethnicity, location, socioeconomic level—gathered in an attempt to figure out what type of programming appeals to certain segments of the population.

Nonpartisan Neutral when it comes to political choice. Not disclosing publicly your preferences for a special cause, candidate, political party or ballot issue.

Objective Neutral, factual information that has been observed, described or measured.

Objectivity Objectivity in the journalistic sense means that the reporting seeks to give fair treatment to all important and viable arguments surrounding a particular issue.

Open meeting law (OML) All meetings in which lawmakers propose, discuss or take legal action must be open to the public.

Pacing The tempo and rhythm of a story.

Package A prerecorded television story that includes a reporter's narration, video and often sound bites, natural sound and a standup.

Parody A funny or satirical imitation of a serious work of literature, art or music. Parody, by its nature, makes use of another's work.

Pivot table A tool used to summarize data in visualization programs like spreadsheets. Pivot tables can automatically count, sort or average the data.

POS Person on the street.

Producer The person responsible for the editorial content of the newscast, including deciding the lead, writing stories, communicating the vision with the team, deciding who is live on location and getting the show on and off on time.

Production crew Employees who typically work in the control room and studio to help produce news and other programming.

Promotions department A unit within a television station or other media outlet responsible for promoting content, including news.

Public figures Individuals who have assumed roles of special prominence in society or who occupy positions of power and influence.

Public information officer (PIO) A department or agency official assigned to work with the media.

Public officials All elected officials or government employees who have, or appear to have, substantial responsibility for the conduct of government affairs.

Pull quote A sentence or quote that's pulled out of the story and set in larger type. Also known as a callout.

Racism The belief that race accounts for differences in human character or ability and that a particular race is superior to others. Discrimination or prejudice based on race.

Ratings The number of people or households that watch a single broadcast or showing of a particular program.

Reader A TV news story presented by an anchor, generally less than 30 seconds long, with no video to support it. Also called a copy story.

Real people (RP) Ordinary people (as opposed to PR practitioners, officials and experts) who provide emotional context by describing their experiences.

Recorded An interview or video captured on some sort of device (memory card, videotape and so forth) that can be edited and/or played back at a later time.

Resolution Conclusion at the end of a story. It resolves the conflict, solves the mystery or ties up the loose ends.

Satellite An interview or video that is transmitted via a satellite in space. Proximity to the location isn't a concern because satellites can reach worldwide. Satellite feeds are more expensive than other methods, such as microwave, phone or Internet.

Search engine optimization (SEO) Techniques for writing online headlines, content and code so stories, blogs, pictures, videos and social media messages have a better chance of being served up to users of Google, Bing, Yahoo and other search engines.

Semantic/relational Web technology Applications that create and organize content on your behalf based on your previously known activity and preferences.

Sequence A series of matched action shots used as the visual building blocks for a story.

Sequencing A series of shots that, when edited together, flow seamlessly.

Setup shot Video of the interview subject beyond the basic interview shot.

Share The percentage of those listening to a particular radio station in a Metropolitan Statistical Area (MSA) as defined by the U.S. Government's Office of Management and Budget.

Sidebar A short companion piece related to another story.

Silence A lack of sound used as an interview or editing technique.

Slander A false, defamatory verbal statement of fact that concerns a particular person and injures that person's reputation.

Sound bite A portion of a video interview. The visual equivalent of a direct quote in print.

Standup A reporter's appearance on camera.

Stereotype When someone has a fixed notion of a person or group based on an observed or imagined trait of behavior or appearance.

Stinger A graphic element, usually a full page, that helps transition from one element to the next, such as from an anchor in the studio to a reporter at a live shot.

Story slug The short title for a story that appears on the rundown.

Subhead A short title that breaks up long text stories and summarizes what follows.

Subjective Information that has been colored by someone's opinion, belief, perspective or emotion. It can't be verified with facts and figures.

Super time Exact time within a VO, SOT or package in which the text identifying the video or person talking in the video should be inserted during the live broadcast.

Talker story A story that people are talking about that day. Even if there's no video, it should be included in the newscast as a reader or with a graphic.

Tight shot Shows lots of detail by zeroing in on a certain feature of a person or object. Also called a close-up.

Tolerance A fair, open and permissive attitude toward those whose religion, race or attitudes differ from our own.

Torts A wrongful act for which an injured person may bring a lawsuit to recover monetary damages.

Traffic The number of times a Web page is viewed in a period of time (page views) or the number of individual visitors to a Web page or website in a period of time (unique visitors).

Transparency Disclosure of personal bias.

Tripod A three-legged, adjustable stand for a camera. Its main purpose is to help provide steady, level video.

Values/ethics Values are standards by which we act and principles in which we believe. Ethics are a set of guidelines or rules based on principles we value.

Vlogs Video logs that incorporate video footage, audio, still images and a little text.

VO Voice-over. A short television story with an anchor or reporter reading while video or a graphic appears on screen.

VO/SOT Voice-over/sound on tape. A television story with an anchor or reporter reading while video or a graphic appears on screen, followed by a sound bite.

Voicer A traditional radio story with a reporter's narration but no quotes from sources.

Wallpaper video Disconnected shots that don't match the words viewers are hearing.

Weasel word A vague word used to fudge the facts or make unsubstantiated claims.

Web 1.0 Early version of the Internet, which consisted of simple graphics and text.

Web 2.0 Upgrades in Web-based applications and services made multiway communication easy and allowed people without a high level of technical knowledge to publish and share content, including audio and video.

Web 3.0 Technologies and services available on the Internet in the future.

Wide shot Establishes the relationship of the people in the frame to the location or setting.

Wrap A radio version of the television package, including a narration track and sound bite(s).

Zoom A camera function that allows the lens to vary the shot (focal length) from wide to tight.

Bibliography

Baradell, Scott, and Anh D. Stack. *Photojournalism, Technology and Ethics*. New York: Black Star Publishing Co., 2008.

Source: Joann Byrd, "A Guide for Evaluating Sources," Poynter.org, Aug. 13, 2002. © Copyright 2002 The Poynter Institute.

Briggs, Mark. *Journalism Next: A Practical Guide to Digital Reporting and Publishing*. Washington, D.C.: CQ Press, 2010.

Cartese, Anthony J. *Provocateur: Images of Women and Minorities in Advertising*. New York: Rowman & Littlefield Publishers, 1999.

Cronkite, Walter. *A Reporter's Life*. New York: Alfred A. Knopf, 1996.

Fang, Irving E. *Television News, Radio News*. St. Paul, Minn.: Rada Press, 1985.

Gillmor, Dan. *We the Media: Grassroots Journalism by the People, for the People*. Sebastopol, Calif.: O'Reilly, 2006.

__________. *Mediactive*. Raleigh, N.C.: Lulu.com, 2010.

Hamilton, John Maxwell, and George A. Krimsky. *Hold The Press: The Inside Story on Newspapers*. Baton Rouge: Louisiana State University Press, 1996.

Hawes, William. *Television Performing: News and Information*. Waltham, Mass.: Focal Press, 1991.

Johnson, Larry, and Bob Phillips. *Absolute Honesty: Building a Corporate Culture That Values Straight Talk and Rewards Integrity*. New York: MAMCOM, 2003.

Kalbfeld, Brad. *Associated Press Broadcast News Handbook*. 3rd ed. New York: McGraw-Hill, 2000.

Keeble, Richard. *Ethics for Journalists*. London: Routledge, 2001.

Libin, Scott. "Leading Beyond 'Both Sides.'" Poynter Institute for Media Studies, January 24, 2005. Updated March 2, 2011. Retrieved from http://www.poynter.org/how-tos/leadership-management/what-great-bosses-know/30467/leading-beyond-both-sides/

McAdams, Mindy. "RGMP: Tell a Good Story With Images and Sound." Teaching Online Journalism, March 18, 2009. Updated March 19, 2009. Retrieved from http://mindymcadams.com/tojou/2009/rgmp-11-tell-a-good-story-with-images-and-sound/

Seymour, Ruth Ann. "Eight Steps Toward Cultural Competence." Poynter Report, Poynter Institute for Media Studies, Special Issue, November 2002. Updated March 2, 2011. Retrieved from http://www.poynter.org/uncategorized/3331/eight-steps-toward-cultural-competence/

Silcock, B. William, Don Heider, and Mary T. Rogus. *Managing Television News: A Handbook for Ethical and Effective Producing*. Mahwah, N.J.: Lawrence Erlbaum Associates, 2006.

Strunk, William, and E.B. White. *The Elements of Style*. Any edition. Also available online at http://www.bartleby.com/141/

Tompkins, Al. "Guidelines for Interviewing Juveniles." Poynter Institute for Media Studies, August 14, 2002. Retrieved from http://www.poynter.org/uncategorized/1819/guidelines-for-interviewing-juveniles/

Wilkins, Lee, and Philip Patterson. *Media Ethics: Issues and Cases*. 7th ed. New York: McGraw-Hill, 2010.

Credits

Chapter 1

Page 1: Pearson Education, Inc., **Page 4 (top):** Susan Van Etten/PhotoEdit, **Page 4 (bottom left):** Iain Masterton / Alamy, **Page 4 (bottom right):** Pearson Education, Inc., **Page 6:** Mary Altaffer, File/AP Photo, **Page 7 (top):** NetPhotos/Alamy, **Page 7 (middle):** © amer ghazzal / Alamy, **Page 7 (bottom):** Moodboard/Alamy, **Page 8:** Rigucci/Shutterstock.com, **Page 9:** Photo by Chevaan Daniel, Hubert H. Humphrey Fellow, Walter Cronkite School, **Page 12 (top left):** Craig Ruttle/Alamy, **Page 12 (top right):** Creatas Images/Thinkstock, **Page 12 (bottom left):** Salim October/Shutterstock.com, **Page 12 (bottom right):** © MareISO/iStock PhotoLibrary, **Page 13 (top):** Cameron Cross/Shutterstock.com, **Page 13 (second):** Digital Vision/Photodisc/Thinkstock, **Page 13 (third):** Jeff Greenberg/PhotoEdit, **Page 13 (bottom):** Norbert Michalke/Imagebroker.net/Photolibrary, **Page 14:** Pearson Education, Inc., **Page 15 (left):** Wavebreakmedia ltd/Shutterstock.com, **Page 15 (right):** The Nielsen Company, **Page 18 (top):** Pearson Education, Inc., **Page 18 (bottom):** ©GlobalStock/iStock, **Page 20 (top):** ©withgod / iStock, **Page 20 (bottom):** Pearson Education, Inc.

Chapter 2

Page 21: Courtesy of Carol Schwalbe, **Page 22:** Jeff Greenberg/PhotoEdit, **Page 23 (top):** s70/ZUMA Press/Newscom, **Page 23 (bottom):** Ariel Skelley/lend Images/Alamy, **Page 24 (top):** CenLu/Alamy, **Page 24 (middle):** © Artfoliophoto/iStock, **Page 24 (bottom):** © ulimi / iStock, **Page 25:** Paul McKinnon/Shutterstock.com, **Page 26 (all):** Courtesy of Cronkite NewsWatch at Arizona State University, **Page 27 (top):** Courtesy of Cronkite NewsWatch at Arizona State University, **Page 27 (middle):** Courtesy of Cronkite NewsWatch at Arizona State University, **Page 27 (bottom):** Courtesy of Cronkite NewsWatch at Arizona State University, **Page 28 (top):** Courtesy of Life in a Jar Foundation (irenasendler.org), **Page 28 (bottom):** Photo by Kenny Felt, courtesy of Life in a Jar Foundation (irenasendler.org), **Page 29:** © NBC NEWSWIRE/Getty, **Page 30:** Photo by Brandon Quester, **Page 33 (all):** Photo by Brandon Quester, **Page 34 (top left):** Tsian/Shutterstock.com, **Page 34 (bottom left):** Courtesy of Cronkite NewsWatch at Arizona State University, **Page 34 (right):** Mark Baker/AP Photo, **Page 35 (all):** Courtesy of Cronkite NewsWatch at Arizona State University, **Page 37 (top):** Courtesy of Cronkite NewsWatch at Arizona State University, **Page 37 (bottom):** Courtesy of Susan Green, **Page 38 (all):** Courtesy of Cronkite NewsWatch at Arizona State University.

Chapter 3

Page 39: Wiskerke/Alamy, **Page 42 (left):** DBURKE/Alamy, **Page 42 (right):**©US Department of Agriculture, **Page 43 (top left):** Courtesy of Mark Lodato, **Page 43 (top center):** The Image Works, **Page 43 (top right):** ©Vocus Inc., **Page 43 (bottom):** Bob Daemmrich/PhotoEdit, **Page 47 (left):** Mangostock/Shutterstock.com, **Page 47 (right):** Courtesy of B. William Silcock, **Page 48:** Pearson Education, Inc., **Page 52:** Courtesy of Leslie Jean Thornton, **Page 55:** Credit is AP Photo/Mike Adaskaveg, **Page 56:** Courtesy of Diana Alvear, **Page 59 (left):** Courtesy of Janie Porter, **Page 59 (right):** Morry Gash/AP Photo, **Page 61:** Courtesy of Anne McCloy, **Page 62:** Courtesy of Gina Silva.

Chapter 4

Page 63: Photo by Brandon Quester, **Pages 64–65 (all):** Courtesy of Mark Lodato, **Page 67:** Mark Ralston/AFP/Getty Images, **Page 70 (all):** Photo by Brandon Quester, **Page 71:** Eddie Gerald/Alamy, **Page 74:** Peter Steiner/Alamy, **Page 75:** © EdStock / iStock, **Page 77:** © totalpics / iStock com, **Page 78 (top):** Age fotostock/SuperStock, **Page 78 (middle):** Michael Craig/Alamy, **Page 78 (bottom):** iPhoto.ca/Newscom, **Page 79:** Chris Smith/PhotoEdit, Inc.

Chapter 5

Page 81: Courtesy of B. William Silcock, **Pages 84–85:** Guy Croft/Alamy, **Page 88:** © ZUMA Press, Inc./Alamy Stock Photo, **Page 92:** Cappi Thompson/Shutterstock.com, **Page 93 (left):** Qaphotos.com/Alamy, **Page 93 (right):** Mike Margol/PhotoEdit, **Page 94:** ©Chris Cooper-Smith/Alamy, **Page 96:** Photo by Brandon Quester, **Page 97:** Courtesy of B. William Silcock, **Page 98:** Scott J. Ferrell/Congressional Quarterly/Newscom, **Page 99:** Steven Day/AP Photo, **Page 100:** Anthony Correia, 2010/Used under license from Shutterstock.com, **Page 101:** Stefanovi/Shutterstock.com, **Page 102 (all):** Courtesy of Cronkite NewsWatch at Arizona State University.

Chapter 6

Page 106: Courtesy of Mark Lodato, **Page 107:** Trinity Mirror/Mirrorpix/Alamy, **Page 108 (all):** Courtesy of Jim Manley, **Page 110 (top left):** Kike Calvo/VWPICS/Visual&Written SL/Alamy, **Page 110 (top center):** Bobby Bank/WireImage/Getty Images, **Page 110 (top right):** Timothy A. Clary/AFP/Getty Images, **Page 110 (bottom):** Bobby Bank/WireImage/Getty Images, **Page 111:** AP Photo/Paul Connors, **Page 112:** Courtesy of Jim Manley, **Page 113:** Courtesy of Janie Porter, **Page 114 (all):** Courtesy of Jim Manley, **Page 115 (all):** Courtesy of Jim Manley, **Page 116:** Jeff Thrower/Shutterstock.com, **Page 119 (top):** Courtesy of Jim Manley, **Page 119 (bottom):** Courtesy of Jim Manley, **Page 120:** Courtesy of Jim Manley, **Page 121 (all):** Courtesy of Jim Manley.

Chapter 7

Page 123: Photo by Brandon Quester, **Page 124:** Courtesy of Mark Lodato, **Page 125:** Photo by Brandon Quester, **Page 126:** © Aristan/iStock, **Page 128:** Dwayne Newton/PhotoEdit, **Page 129:** Photo by Brandon Quester, **Page 134:** Cal Vornberger/Alamy, **Page 142:** Photo by Brandon Quester.

Chapter 8

Page 145: Pearson Education, Inc., **Page 146:** Visions of America/SuperStock, **Page 150:** Courtesy of Mark Lodato, **Page 151:** Photo by Courtney Sargent, **Page 154:** Courtesy of Susan Green, **Page 157 (top):** Courtesy of Cronkite NewsWatch at Arizona State University, **Page 157 (second):** Courtesy of Susan Green, **Page 157 (third):** Courtesy of Susan Green, **Page 157 (bottom):** Courtesy of Cronkite NewsWatch at Arizona State University, **Page 159:** Courtesy of Melanie Asp Alvarez, **Page 161:** Courtesy of Melanie Asp Alvarez, **Page 164:** Courtesy of Melanie Asp Alvarez, **Page 165 (all):** Courtesy of the Walter Cronkite School of Journalism and Mass Communication at Arizona State University.

Chapter 9

Page 166: Photo by Brandon Quester, **Page 167:** Photo by Brandon Quester, **Page 168:** ©Francis Miller/Getty, **Page 170:** Courtesy of Erisa Nakano, **Page 171 (top):** ©Everett Collection Historical/Alamy, **Page 171 (Cronkite):** Courtesy of the Walter Cronkite School of Journalism and Mass Communication, **Page 171 (Walters):** United Archives GmbH/Alamy **Page 171 (Jennings):** AF archive/Alamy, **Page 171 (Stewart):** k03/k03/ZUMA Press/Newscom, **Page 171 (Williams):** Helga Esteb/Shutterstock.com, **Page 171 (Curry):** Alamy/Alamy, Page 173: AP Photo, **Page 174:** Bill Greenblatt/UPI/Newscom, **Page 175:** Photo by Brandon Quester, **Page 176:** Courtesy of Aleksandar Miladinovic, **Page 177:** Courtesy of Christi Schreiber, president/CEO Colour Basis, Forth Worth, Texas, **Pages 182–183 (background):** Photo by Brandon Quester, **Page 182 (top):** Courtesy of Lena Sadiwskyj, **Page 182 (bottom left):** Courtesy of Brian Curtis, **Page 182: (bottom right):** Courtesy of Erin Christiansen, **Page 183 (top):** Courtesy of Jan Tennant, **Page 183 (bottom):** Courtesy of David Klugh, **Pages 184–185 (background):** Photo by Brandon Quester, **Page 184 (left):** Courtesy of Eric Chaloux, **Page 184 (right):** Courtesy of Chris Wright, **Page 185 (top):** Courtesy of Justin McHeffey, **Page 185 (bottom):** Courtesy of Emily Schmidt.

Chapter 10

Page 186: Pearson Education, Inc., **Page 189:** AP Photo/Damian Dovarganes, **Page 195:** Image Source/Alamy, **Page 196:** Pearson Education, Inc., **Page 199:** MediaStorm.com, **Page 200 (top left):** Courtesy of CBS5/Facebook, **Page 200 (top right):** ©NetPhotos/Alamy, **Page 200 (bottom left):** Courtesy of CBS5, **Page 200 (bottom right):** ©PjrStudio/Alamy, **Page 201:** ABC15.com.

Chapter 11

Page 202: Photo by Brandon Quester, **Page 203 (left):** Linda Roberts/Shutterstock.com, **Page 203 (right):** © Alija / iStock, **Page 204:** © Wavebreakmedia / iStock, **Page 206 (top left):** Aspen rock/Shutterstock.com, **Page 206 (top right):** Barry Brown/Splash News/Newscom, **Page 206 (bottom):** Prisma/SuperStock, **Page 208:** David R. Frazier Photolibrary, Inc./Alamy, **Page 210:** Ho New/REUTERS, **Page 211:** PMB/ZOJ/Newscom, **Page 213:** Steve Skjold/Alamy, **Page 214 (left):** BananaStock/Thinkstock, **Page 214 (second):** Amy Walters/Shutterstock.com, **Page 214 (third):** Richard Heyes/Alamy, **Page 214 (right):** ©sx70/iStock, **Page 215 (top left):** Dave Ellison/Alamy, **Page 215 (top right):** ©Mari/iStock, **Page 215 (bottom left):** Mikael Karlsson/Alamy, **Page 215 (center right):** Dennis Hallinan/Alamy, **Page 215 (bottom right):** imagebroker.net/SuperStock.

Chapter 12

Page 216: Photo by Brandon Quester, **Page 217 (left):** © Martinan/iStock, **Page 217 (right):** Courtesy of the Walter Cronkite School of Journalism at Arizona State University, **Page 219:** ©leonardo255/iStock, **Page 223:** Mark Hamilton/Alamy, **Page 224:** National Archives, **Page 225:** Nate Beeler/Cagle Cartoons, Inc., **Page 226 (left):** Trinity Mirror/Mirrorpix/Alamy, **Page 226 (right):** Kyodo News/Newscom, **Page 229:** Courtesy of the Walter Cronkite School of Journalism and Mass Communication at Arizona State University, **Page 233:** AF archive/Alamy.

Chapter 13

Page 239: Photo by Brandon Quester, **Page 240:** ©Image obtained from GELSEN and "Think Before You Speak," a GELSEN and Ad Council program, **Page 241:** ©Axel Koester / Corbis, **Page 242:** Adventures of Huckleberry Finn (Tom Sawyer's comrade). Scene: The Mississippi Valley. Time: Forty to fifty years ago. (PS1305 .A1 1885). Clifton Waller Barrett Library of American Literature, Special Collections, University of Virginia Library, **Page 243 (top left):** Paolo Vairo, 2009/Used under license from Shutterstock.com, **Page 243 (top right):** Kristin Callahan/Everett Collection/Everett Collection Inc./Alamy, **Page 243 (bottom left):** © EdStock / iStock, **Page 243 (bottom right):** R. Gino Santa Maria/Shutterstock.com, **Page 245 (left):** CREATISTA/Shutterstock.com, **Page 245 (right):** Tomas Abad/Alamy, **Page 246:** Douglas Healey/AP Photo, **Page 249 (top):** Golden Pixels LLC/Alamy, **Page 249 (middle):** Folio/Alamy, **Page 249 (bottom):** Tina Manley/Alamy, **Page 250 (top):** Uriel Sinai/Getty Images, **Page 250 (bottom left):** Photo by Susan Green, **Page 250 (bottom right):** Photo by Susan Green, **Page 251 (top):** blackwaterimages/istockphoto.com, **Page 251 (bottom):** Courtesy of United States Census Bureau, **Page 253:** Mark J. Terrill/AP Photo.

Chapter 14

Page 257: Photo by B. William Silcock, **Page 258:** Digitallife/Alamy, **Page 260:** Pearson Education, Inc., **Page 263:** © RoBeDeRo/iStock **Page 264:** Courtesy of Carol Schwalbe, **Pages 270–271 (all):** Courtesy of Natalie Podgorski, **Page 272:** Journalismjobs.com.

Other

Web clock icon: John T. Takai/Shutterstock.com, **Thumbs up icon:** Shutterstock.com, **Warning sign icon:** WonderfulPixel/Shutterstock.com, **Volume icon:** cg-art/Shutterstock.com, **Communications icon:** Kathy Konkle/istockphoto.com, **Computers icon:** Kathy Konkle/istockphoto.com.

Subject Index

Note: t refers to tables.

Name Index